THE PRINCIPALSHIP
A Reflective Practice Perspective
Second Edition

Thomas J. Sergiovanni
Trinity University
San Antonio, Texas

Allyn and Bacon
Boston London Toronto Sydney Tokyo Singapore

Thomas J. Sergiovanni is Lillian Radford Professor of Education and Educational Administration at Trinity University in San Antonio, Texas. Prior to joining the faculty at Trinity, he spent 18 years as Professor of Educational Administration at the University of Illinois at Urbana-Champaign. His long-term research interests have been in the areas of leadership and motivation to work. Most recently he has focused on the nature and characteristics of effective schools from a leadership perspective. He is the author of several books including *Leadership and Organizational Culture* (1984), *Supervision Human Perspectives*, Fourth Edition (1988), and *Value-Added Leadership* (1990). Professor Sergiovanni is consulting editor to the *Journal of Curriculum and Supervision*, the *Journal of Educational Research, Teaching Education*, and the *Journal of Personnel Evaluation in Education* and has served on the editorial boards of the *Journal of Research and Development in Education, Educational Administration Quarterly*, and the *Journal of Educational Equity and Leadership*.

Copyright © 1991, 1987 by Allyn and Bacon
A Division of Simon & Schuster, Inc.
160 Gould Street
Needham Heights, Massachusetts 02194

Library of Congress Cataloging-in-Publication Data

Sergiovanni, Thomas J.
    The principalship: a reflective practice perspective / Thomas J.
Sergiovanni. – 2nd ed.
        p.   cm.
    Includes bibliographical references and index.
    ISBN 0-205-12697-9
    1. School principals–United States.   2. School management and organization–United States.   3. School supervision–United States.
4. School improvement programs–United States.   I. Title.
LB2831.92.S47   1991
371.2'012'0973–dc20   90-44691
                                                                        CIP

Printed in the United States of America

10 9 8 7 6 5 4 3 2 1 94 93 92 91 90

Contents

Foreword

On the day I finished reading the manuscript of the second edition of Tom Sergiovanni's *The Principalship* I had a very exciting interview with a principal of an elementary school that had been nominated to receive an "excellence of program" award in New York State. I sat in the principal's office for about an hour and a half, chatting with her about her work, about how she learned to do what she did, and how she put the things she learned into practice.

The theme that ran through this principal's discussion with me was that every school day presented itself to her as a new opportunity to learn something about her work and about herself. As I thought about it, it became clear to me that this principal was more or less a model of what Sergiovanni had in mind when he subtitled his book "A Reflective Practice Perspective." That is, it seemed clear, as I listened to her and walked around the school and observed her interaction with teachers, pupils, and staff, that a day at school for her was a never-ending opportunity to act and then think about and reflect on her action. What I take to be the results of her expending her energy this way was evident in the character of the school as well as its nomination for excellence. Though this principal may not have been the one to write this book, she obviously believed what it is all about.

Well, what is it all about? I read the book from the point of view of a professor, which was easy for me, and from what I thought might be the point of view of a school principal. This was a bit more difficult.

The "me" that is the professor found a number of ideas to mull over. In particular I liked some of the metaphors that were used. The idea of the central metaphor of mindscapes of practice with a subset of mindscapes that includes Mystics, Scruffies, and Neats, for example, was one that tickled my conceptual funny-bone. And the further thought that we need a "scruffy" theory in order to account for a scruffy world was one that—well, it made sense and set me to thinking of the scruffiness of my own organization. I was led further to think that a major error we may make in graduate programs in school administration is to create "neat" programs that emphasize orderliness—programs that are essentially dysfunctional for what practitioners will tell you is a disorderly world.

Other thoughts also interested the me who is the professor. The whole idea within the discussion of school goals, for example, of what Sergiovanni calls the covenant of a school. Maybe this gets at the root of things—the concept of covenant, that is. It is a much more powerful idea than mission, implying, as the dictionary tells us, "a binding and solemn agreement." And so the professor me is intrigued and asks, "How can I find out about and understand this covenant idea better?"

The point I make here is that though *The Principalship* is about practice, it is also about problems of practice that should whet the curiosity-appetite of professors who want to follow up on any one of a number of good research questions even though they may not be so stated.

Reading the book from the point of view of a school principal was, of course, not easy for me. I have never been one of those brave souls whom I so much admire, but I've observed and talked with many of them. I think that the extent to which a school principal will find this book useful will be somewhat related to the imagination of the principal-reader. What I mean by that is that, as I noted in the foreword to the first edition, one way to understand this book is to see it as a continuous extending of invitations to a school principal to join a large number of "parties," so to speak. "Come join the party," says Tom Sergiovanni. "Here's one about the differences between 'effective' and 'successful' schools. Would you like to sample the buffet table? And another party about school climate. Test it out."

I don't want to make light of all this. Sergiovanni is not really dealing with a real party, of course, but rather, as I noted above, the work-oriented imagination of school principals. At least, that is the way I see it, and it may be that the distance that a principal can move from "what is" to a realistic but also imaginative "what might be" may well be related to the character of the school under consideration. This book indeed, if it is to be useful to a principal, asks him or her to exercise his or her imagination of what the work of school principals might be.

It is suggested by Sergiovanni that the reader go first to the final chapter so that she or he can get a sense of the goal that is being worked on in the preceding chapters. I agree. But the reader should also make sure to read the last chapter, "Administering as a Moral Craft," a second time. It is well worth it.

Finally, one might ask what there is that is new about this second edition of *The Principalship*. Quite a bit, it seems to me. As one indication there are a hundred references that were not in the first edition. (That is the me that is the professor reacting again.)

Arthur Blumberg
Professor of Education
Syracuse University

Preface

Everywhere one looks there is someone with an easy solution for improving schools. "Research says" if you put these correlates in place; if you teach, manage, or supervise using this list of behaviors all will be well. Careers are built, journals are filled, and, for some with entrepreneurial bents, fortunes are amassed as the "solutions" are proposed.

The engine that drives this grand solutions machine is our search for simple answers. This searching, I fear, drives us to think in the rationalistic tradition about our work, to make unwarranted assumptions about the linearity and predictability that exist in the world, and to overestimate the tightness of links between research and practice. The result is the adoption of management theories and leadership practices that look great on paper, sound compelling when heard, and maybe even make us feel good, but which don't fit the actual world of schooling very well.

The word *rationalistic* is chosen over *rational* or *irrational* deliberately, for what is often thought to be irrational is actually rational, and vice versa. Winograd and Flores (1986) sort the differences as follows:

> In calling it [traditional theory] "rationalistic" we are not equating it with "rational." We are not interested in a defense of irrationality or a mystic appeal to nonrational intuition. The rationalistic tradition is distinguished by its narrow focus on certain aspects of rationality which often lead to attitudes and activities that are not rational when viewed in a broader perspective. Our commitment is to develop a new ground for rationality—one that is as rigorous as the rationalistic tradition in its aspirations but that does not share the presuppositions behind it. (8)

In a similar vein, Alex Kozlov (1988) uses the categories "Neats" and "Scruffies" to sort researchers in the field of artificial intelligence as follows: "For a Neat, if an idea about thinking can't be represented in terms of mathematical logic, it isn't worth thinking about. For a Scruffy, on the other hand, ideas that can't be proved are the most interesting ones" (77–78).

It isn't easy for anyone to be a Scruffy. After all, it's very comfortable to be a Neat. You have all the answers and you fit nicely into our bureaucratic, technical, and rational culture. Fitting nicely reaps many career rewards. But still, many of us feel uncomfortable with the position of the Neats. A frequent first response to this uncomfortableness is to try to change the world to fit our theories and to damn those aspects of the world that will not cooperate. A better alternative, I propose, is for us to change our theories to fit the world. A scruffy world needs scruffy theories. Reflective practice, as I will argue in Chapter 1, is key to making scruffy theories work. John Stuart Mill wrote, "No great improvements in the lot of mankind are possible, until a great change takes place in the fundamental constitution of their modes of thought." His prophetic statement describes the situations we face today. If we want better schools, we are going to have to learn how to manage and lead differently. This book doesn't provide the answers, but it can help you find them.

I owe a debt of gratitude to far too many people to acknowledge adequately. The list of colleagues from the University of Illinois, Urbana-Champaign, who taught me so much for 19 very special years, is indeed long. A warm acknowledgment goes to Trinity University for providing the environment, support, and stimulation that one often dreams about in academic life but rarely finds. My colleague John H. Moore, Trinity Education Department Chairperson, deserves special mention. The combination of passion and support that characterizes his leadership practice is a constant source of inspiration. Most important is the debt I owe to hundreds of school leaders in the United States, Canada, and Australia who generously shared their wisdom with me formally through my ongoing research on leadership and informally through many fruitful conversations.

Throughout the book, readers will find a number of inventories and questionnaires. Their purpose is to help raise and clarify issues, stimulate thought, encourage reflection, and provide a basis for discussion of concepts and ideas. They are not presented as fine-tuned measurement devices suitable for "research purposes," though faculties and groups may benefit from collecting school data and using results as a basis for discussion and reflection.

Phillip Schlechty is fond of saying, "We are flying the airplane as we build it" whenever he describes the various programs comprised in his school reform initiatives. This was certainly the case with the first edition of *The Principalship: A Reflective Practice Perspective*. The book promised more than it could deliver in building a reflective practice perspective. The idea of reflective practice is further developed at this writing, but we are still learning about what reflective practice is, what it means, and how it can be enhanced. I hope this edition comes a bit closer to the mark, although Schlechty's description still holds.

Readers are encouraged to read the last chapter (Chapter 15, "Administering as a Moral Craft") before examining the book's contents more systematically. Enhancing the principalship is the road on which this book journeys, and Chapter 15 lets readers know how the journey ends. Knowing the book's ending first may be helpful in providing an integrating perspective for the concepts, ideas, values, principles, and practices discussed in other chapters.

Thomas J. Sergiovanni

REFLECTIVE PRACTICE IN THE PRINCIPALSHIP

CHAPTER 1

The Nature of
Reflective Practice
in the Principalship

Principals and other school leaders are faced with an important choice. On the one hand they can base their practice on the assumption that predetermined solutions exist for most of the problems they face in the form of research-based theories and techniques. On the other hand they can base their practice on the assumption that few of the problems they face lend themselves to predetermined solutions and resign themselves to the difficult task of having to create knowledge in use as they practice. Principals who make the second choice acknowledge that despite the attractiveness of the first, predetermined solutions can only be trusted to work for problems that are fixed and that are located in stable situations and environments. They believe that the majority of problems and situations that principals face are characterized by ambiguity and confusion that defy clear-cut technical solutions. These problems are located in a turbulent environment where practice is largely indeterminate. They would argue, as does Donald Schön, that the most important problems principals face comprise zones of practice that are beyond the reach of technical, rational solutions. In Schön's words: "The practitioner must choose. Shall he remain on the high ground where he can solve relatively unimportant problems according to prevailing standards of rigor, or shall he descend to the swamp of important problems and nonrigorous inquiry?" (Schön, 1987:3).

The choice that one makes is largely dependent on her or his theory or "mindscape" of practice. Do you remember, for example, the picture in your introductory psych textbook chapter on perception of the vase formed by the two profiles? If that picture were shown to a novice, she or he would probably see only one of the two images. A conversation with someone who saw the other image would be difficult. The image each sees functions as a mindscape that creates a different reality. Similarly, our mindscapes of leadership, how schools work, and the nature of human rationality shape the way we think about theoretical knowledge and the link between this knowledge and how we practice.

Mindscapes of Practice

In many respects, mindscapes are our intellectual security blankets and road maps through an uncertain world. As road maps they provide the rules, assumptions, images, and principles that define what the principalship is and how its practice should unfold. These road maps make us feel safe, certain, and secure. Mindscapes are so dominant that their assumptions and related practices are not thought about much. They are just assumed to be true. Thus, when a mindscape does not fit the world of practice, the problem is thought to lie with that world. Rarely is the world accepted for what it is and the prevailing mindscape changed.

An important question is: To what extent do mindscapes of the principalship fit the actual landscapes of teaching, administering, and schooling? Unfortunately, they often don't fit very well.

Though many scholars might take exception to the way I categorize mindscapes, three distinct views of schooling and administering can be identified, are worth describing and understanding, and can be evaluated for good fit with the real landscape of professional practice. The three are the mindscapes of the "Mystics," "Neats," and "Scruffies." Principals and researchers who are Mystics, Neats, or Scruffies have widely different conceptions of the nature of practice and of the relationships between this practice and theoretical knowledge. For Mystics no relationship whatsoever exists; for Neats theoretical knowledge is superordinate to practice; and for Scruffies theoretical knowledge is subordinate to practice. Their respective views can be summarized as follows.

- *Mystics* hold the view that educational administration resembles a nonscience and thus scientific principles gleaned from theory and research have little relevance to professional practice. Scientific principles and professional practice are disconnected. Instead, professional practice is driven by the principal's tacit knowledge, intuitive feel for situations, sixth sense, and other more transcendental factors.

- *Neats* hold the view that educational administration resembles an applied science within which theory and research are directly and linearly linked to professional practice. The former always determine the latter, and thus knowledge is superordinate to the principal and designed to prescribe practice.

- *Scruffies* hold the view that educational administration resembles a craftlike science within which professional practice is characterized by interacting reflection and action episodes. Theory and research are only one source of knowledge, which is subordinate to the principal and is designed to inform but not to prescribe practice.

There are intuitive aspects of administrative and teaching practice that must be appreciated and accounted for, but the mystical end of the continuum is characterized by the belief that no formal knowledge is of use, that the world is hopelessly phenomenological, that everything is relative, that only personal knowledge counts, that all knowing is tacit, that teaching and administrative skills are gifts, and that in the end it is one's intuition or other manifestation of some mysterious sixth sense that counts. The principal functions as a clairvoyant. The view of the Mystics is the least tenable of the three and is not at the center of the debate regarding knowledge development and use in the principalship. Therefore, only the positions of the Neats and the Scruffies will be examined for their ability to fit the real world of practice.

Though its popularity is waning, the Neats' view of applied science remains the dominant metaphor for the study and practice of educational administration. In applied science, knowledge is created through theorizing and research. This knowledge is then used to build and fieldtest models of practice from which universal prescriptions and treatments are generated. These, in return, are communicated to professionals for their use in practice. Applied scientists talk a great deal about knowledge development and utilization chains within which scientific knowledge is used to build practice models and standard practice treatments. Within applied science it is thought that professionals bring to their practice a set of standardized skills linked to a series of scientifically verified standard practice treatments. The professional then searches the context in which she or he works, carefully diagnosing and characterizing contingencies and situations according to predetermined and standardized protocols. Depending on the diagnosis the appropriate treatment is then applied.

The Neats seek to apply scientific knowledge directly to problems of professional practice. A basic assumption is that a one-to-one correspondence exists between knowledge and practice. Therefore, the Neats seek to establish the one best solution to a problem and the one best way to practice. The truth of analysis and of methods based on true facts is supreme. For example, the Neats accept the research on effective teaching without question. They believe that a generic set of teaching effectiveness behaviors exists that can be applied by all teachers in all situations to all students. The research on effective schools, leadership styles, and conflict-management strategies are viewed similarly as truths to be accepted and applied. Further, principalship practice is considered to be a research-based technology that can be directly learned and routinely applied. The principal is presumed to function as a highly trained technician.

How do these conceptions of educational administration fit the real world of practice? Not very well. Patterns of school practice are actually characterized by a great deal of uncertainty, instability, complexity, and variety. Value conflicts and uniquenesses are accepted aspects of educational settings. According to Schön (1983) these characteristics are perceived as central to the world of professional practice in all the major professions, including medicine, engineering, management, and education. He concludes: "Professional knowledge is mismatched to the changing characteristics of the situation of practice" (14). Though one may be comfortable in viewing the principalship as a logical process of problem solving with the application of standard techniques to predictable problems, a more accurate view may be a process of "managing messes" (Schön, 1983:16).

In the actual world of schooling the task of the principal is to make sense of messy situations by increasing understanding and discovering and communicating meanings. Situations of practice are typically characterized by unique events; therefore, uniform answers to problems are not likely to be helpful. Teachers, supervisors, and students bring to their classrooms beliefs, assumptions, values, opinions, preferences, and predispositions. Thus, objective and value-free administrative strategies are not likely to address issues of importance. Uncertainty and complexity are normal aspects in the process of schooling. Intuition becomes necessary to fill in the gaps of what can be specified as known and what cannot. But ordinary intuition will not do. Intuition must be *informed* by theoretical knowledge on one hand and adept understandings of the situation on the other.

Reflective Practice: The Paradigm of the Scruffies

What kind of science is needed that will enable principals to practice successfully in a messy world? One that resembles a craftlike science, within which professional practice is characterized by interacting reflection and action, and episodes. Webster defines *science* tightly as "knowledge covering general truths or the operation of general laws esp. as obtained and tested through scientific method" and loosely as "knowledge attained through study and practice." I use the term loosely. Theory and research are only one source of knowledge, and this knowledge is always subordinate to the principal, teacher, or other professional, serving to inform but not to prescribe practice. Indeed, professional knowledge is *created in use* as principals and teachers think, reflect, decide, and do.

The mindscape of the Neats, by contrast, places principals and teachers in positions subordinate to scientific knowledge. Principals and teachers are well-trained technicians. Their job is to follow the script as written. Since it is the script that counts, the paradigm of the Neats provides that professional knowledge must be identified and set prior to occasions of actual practice. But, unfortunately, in schooling the occasions are typically unpredictable and always changing. Further, under conditions in which individual differences count, the matching of predetermined remedies for teaching, managing, or leading to situations of practice is impossible.

The Scruffies' view of the principalship is that of a science of the practical – a science that stems from theories of practice and which provides principals with practical as well as theoretical mindscapes from which to work. The concept *reflective practice* is critical to this new science.

Reflective practice is based on the reality that professional knowledge is different from scientific knowledge. Professional knowledge is created in use as professionals who face ill-defined, unique, and changing problems decide on courses of action. Ralph Tyler maintains that researchers don't have a full understanding of the nature of professional knowledge in education. He states:

> Researchers and many academics also misunderstand educational practices. The practice of every profession evolves informally, and professional procedures are not generally derived from systematic design based on research findings. Professional practice has largely developed through trial and error and intuitive efforts. Practitioners, over the years, discover procedures that appear to work and others that fail. The professional practice of teaching, as well as that of law, medicine, and theology, is largely a product of the experience of practitioners, particularly

those who are more creative, inventive, and observant than the average (cited in Hosford, 1984:9).

Scientific studies in the various professions are important. But science, according to Tyler, "explains phenomenon, it does not produce practices" (cited in Hosford, 1984:10). Professionals rely heavily on informed intuition as they create knowledge in use. Intuition is informed by theoretical knowledge on the one hand and by interacting with the context of practice on the other. When teachers use informed intuition, they are engaging in reflective practice. When principals use informed intuition, they too are engaging in reflective practice. Knowing is in the action itself, and reflective professionals become students of their practice. They research the context and experiment with different courses of action. Schön (1983) suggests:

> They may ask themselves, for example, "what features do I notice when I recognize this thing? What are the criteria by which I make this judgment? What procedures am I enacting when I perform this skill? How am I framing the problem that I'm trying to solve?" Usually, reflection on knowing-in-action goes together with reflection on the stuff at hand. There is some puzzling, or troubling or interesting phenomenon with which the individual is trying to deal. As he tries to make sense of it, he also reflects on the understandings which have been implicit in his action, understandings which he surfaces, criticizes, re-structures and embodies in further action.
>   It is this entire process of reflection-in-action which is central to the "art" by which practitioners sometimes deal with situations of uncertainty, instability, uniqueness, and value conflicts (50).

To Schön (1984), reflection-in-action involves "on-the-spot surfacing, criticizing, re-structuring and testing of intuitive understandings of experienced phenomenon; often, it takes the form of a reflective conversation with the situation" (42). Reflection-in-action captures the principal at work as she or he makes judgments in trying to manage a very messy work context.

The Importance of Craft Knowledge

In his groundbreaking book *School Administration as Craft*, Arthur Blumberg (1989) uses the metaphor *craft* to provide a refreshing and compelling view of the nature of administrative work that can provide the long-missing bridge between what is known in the mind and experience of successful principals and teachers and the practice situations that they face.

To some, *craft* communicates an endeavor that is low-level, perhaps even pedestrian. But Blumberg has in mind the accomplished and prized work of *artisans* that stands out from the work of the amateur hobbyist. This distinction between amateurism and artisanship strengthens the use of the craft metaphor, for though principals and other school administrators do not hold a monopoly on exercising management and leadership, their practice should be qualitatively different.

Blumberg explores the craft concept by describing how the mind, heart, and head of the artisan "potter" working with the "clay" together produce something useful. Similarly, the craft of administration "is the exercise in individual fashion of practical wisdom toward the end of making things in a school or a school system 'look' like one wants them to look" (46). Recognizing that there are certain skills involved in any craft, Blumberg focuses on the kinds of know-how that go beyond just being able to employ these skills. It is this know-how that differentiates the artisan from the more pedestrian amateur, the treasured craft item from the run-of-the-mill trinket.

Attributes associated with artisanship are dedication, experience, personal knowledge of the material, mastery of detail, sense of harmony, integration, intimate understanding, and wisdom (Mintzberg, 1987). Artisans, according to Blumberg (1989), develop a special kind of know-how that is characterized as having a refined "nose" for things, a sense of what constitutes an acceptable result in any particular problematic situation, an understanding of the nature of the materials they work with, a mastery of the basic technology undergirding the craft, skill to employ this technology effectively, and, most important, knowing what to do and when to do it. They make pragmatic (and in the case of educational administration, *moral*) decisions and are able to diagnose and interpret what is occurring as they work in any situation.

In sum, reflective principals practice as artisans by bringing together deep knowledge of relevant techniques and competent application of tried-and-true "rules of thumb" with a feel for their practice and a penchant for reflecting on this practice as they create something of practical utility. Craft knowledge represents an anchor equal to and sometimes superior to theoretical knowledge in making up one's theories of practice and informing one's professional practice. The hallmark of the artisan is ability to reflect on practice.

The Importance of Theoretical Knowledge

To many readers the foregoing critique of applied science and particularly the emphasis on the mismatch between theoretical knowledge viewed as singular truth and its subsequent ill-fitting application to practice may seem to suggest that research-based theoretical knowledge is useless. Reaching this conclusion would be a mistake. The issue is not the usefulness of theoretical knowledge but its presumed truthfulness given the idiosyncratic and dynamic nature of administrative problems and situations. In applied science, for example, theoretical knowledge is used to establish a body of "artificial" professional intelligence. Principals would merely have to diagnose problems they face and draw standard treatments to apply from this intelligence. By contrast, reflective practice seeks to establish "augmented" professional intelligence. The principals themselves would be key aspects of this intelligence. Augmented professional intelligence serves to inform, not replace, the intuitions of administrators as they practice.

Mary Kennedy (1984) speaks of two important ways in which theoretical knowledge can be used in practice: *instrumentally* and *conceptually*. When used instrumentally, theoretical knowledge is presumed to be instructive and the decision as to what to do is relatively straightforward. As Kennedy explains, "Whereas the central feature of the instrumental model is the *decision*, the central feature of the conceptual model is the *human information processor* (principal)," and, further, "Whereas a decision may follow automatically from the instructions contained in the evidence, information processors (principals) 'interact' with the evidence, interpret its meaning, decide its relevance, and hence determine when and how they will permit the evidence to influence them" (207–208). Her latter point is key. Scruffies believe that since the principal, not the theoretician or the researcher, is in command of the idiosyncratic nature of the situation she or he must be in control of the available scientific knowledge.

For Scruffies, managing and leading resemble a game of golf in which the distance to the hole is always changing. You know the hole is straight ahead, but you can never be sure just how far away it is. You have a pretty good understanding of the distances that you can get from each club (club payoff), but you cannot choose a club based on where the hole is at the moment. You must guess where the hole will be after you swing. Knowledge of club payoff remains important in this context, but it cannot be used directly. Instead, this knowledge becomes part of one's conceptual framework for making an educated guess in choosing the right club for an assumed distance. In this game, laws exist that determine where the hole will be next, but they cannot be fully understood.

The better golfers are those who develop an intuitive feel for past, current, and likely patterns of appearance of the hole as the game is played. Their play is neither whimsical nor random. Instead, they make mature, educated guesses (in the case of principals, informed professional judgments). These guesses combined with knowledge of club payoff helps them to win. Being familiar with the topographical features of each of the holes to be played, the play of the greens, the texture of the grass and rough, and the idiosyncracies of each of the sandtraps yields other pieces of information that might or might not come in handy should a hole pop up here rather than there. Having a firm fix on topography and club payoff is not enough if one cannot develop a feel for the patterns that are likely to emerge. On the other hand, and equally as important, being pretty good at predicting the patterns but having little understanding of course topography or club payoff will not be of much help.

The key to reflective practice can be found in William James's 1892 message to the teachers of Cambridge, Massachusetts. He pointed out the importance of "an intermediary inventive mind" in making practical application of scientific knowledge. In his words:

> The science of logic never made a man reason rightly, and the science of ethics . . . never made a man behave rightly. The most such sciences can do is to help us catch ourselves up and check ourselves, if we start to reason or behave wrongly; and to criticize ourselves more articulately after we have made mistakes. A science only laws down lines within which the rules of the art must fall, laws which the follower of the art must not transgress; but what particular thing he shall positively do within those lines is left exclusively to his own genius.

The idea of reflective practice is relatively new, and much more thinking needs to be given to its development and use in educational administration. It seems clear, nonetheless, that reflective principals are in charge of their professional practice. They do not passively accept solutions and mechanically apply them. They do not assume that the norm is a one best way to practice, and they are suspicious of easy answers to complex questions. They are painfully aware of how context and situations vary, how teachers and students differ in many ways, and how complex school goals and objectives actually are; they recognize that, despite difficulties, tailored treatments to problems must be the norm. As the same time reflective professional practice requires that principals have a healthy respect for, be well informed about, and use the best available theory and research and accumulated practice wisdom. All these sources of information help increase understanding and inform practice.

Informing Practice

The major issue in practice is deciding what to do. What purposes should be pursued? What strategies should be used? What should be emphasized and when? In what ways should resources be deployed? How will we know we are on track, and so on? In sum, and for better or worse, how is practice *informed?* The informing process can be understood and enhanced by examining three interrelated components of administrative practice: practice episodes, theories of practice, and antecedents. The three are illustrated in Figure 1–1 and discussed in the remainder of this chapter.

Administrative work takes the form of a seemingly endless series of *practice episodes* made up of intentions, actions, and realities. The substance of intentions are the priorities, preferences, strategies, and decisions of the principal. These lead to actions in the form of her or his leadership and management tactics and behaviors. Actions lead to situational feedback in the form of results and consequences. The interplay among the three is dynamic, with realities changing actions and actions subsequently changing as a result of new realities, and so on. The interplay of actions and realities shapes intentions in much the same way. One episode affects the next, and so on. Throughout this interplay the principal thinks and acts, formulates and implements. Doing leads to ideas, and one idea leads to another. New patterns or strategies emerge. These strategies lead to new thinking. There is an interaction between the two. Strategies emerge in response to evolving situations. The principal doesn't think on one occasion and act on the other. Mind and hand are constantly moving in tandem. Strategies are neither deliberate nor emergent but are both. Rarely does the principal wind up where intended, but she or he always begins with some idea as to where to go.

The interactive cycles of intentions, actions, and realities are influenced by the administrator's known and unknown *theories of practice*. Theories of practice can be thought of as bundles of beliefs and assumptions about how schools and school systems work, authority, leadership, the purposes of schooling, the role of competition, the nature of human nature, and other issues and concerns. These beliefs and assumptions function as mindscapes. Mindscapes program thinking and

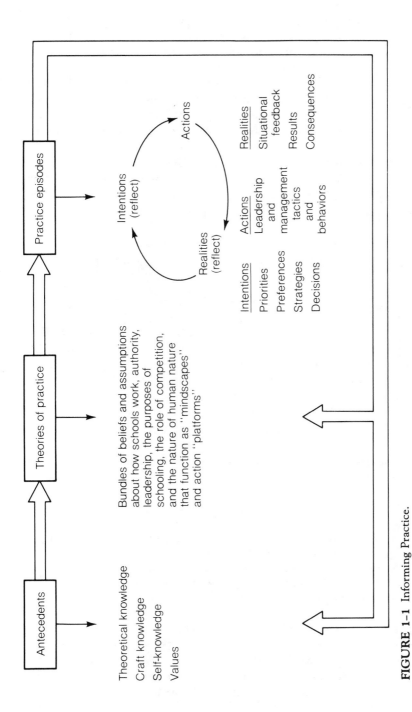

FIGURE 1–1 Informing Practice.

From: Sergiovanni, Thomas J., 1989. "Informing Professional Practice in Educational Administration." *Journal of Educational Administration.* Vol. 27 No. 2 p. 186.

11

belief structures about administrative study and practice. Though not thought about formally very much, they ultimately become the powerful forces that drive one's practice.

Take, for example, the issue of how schools and school systems work. The "Clockworks I" mindscape provides an image of school operation that is characterized by managerial tightness and cultural looseness. "Clockworks II," on the other hand, provides the opposite image, a world of schooling that is managerially loose and culturally tight (Sergiovanni, 1987). Depending on which image is fixed as dominant in one's theory of practice, different intentions, actions, and realities will result. Other bundles of beliefs and assumptions (i.e., theory X or Y; one's view of human rationality) work similarly in contributing to different professional practice episodes. These examples will be discussed further in Chapter 3.

Theories of practice do not just emerge but are formed and shaped by a number of *antecedents*. Important antecedents include one's theoretical knowledge, self-knowledge, craft knowledge, and one's values.

It is useful to think of four levels of reflective practice:

1. Technical (cognitive-rational, theoretical knowledge)
2. Interpretive (craft knowledge, tacit knowledge, feeling for practice)
3. Personal (self-understanding and self-management)
4. Critical (moral consciousness, moral agency, moral development)

Technical reflection can be enhanced by the body of theoretical knowledge and values of rational thought that are now in place. But they must be considered in a context that allows for their metaphorical use as supplements and complements to interpretive, personal, and critical reflection.

Interpretive and personal reflection can be enhanced by principals learning more about their theories of practice; by critiquing them; by broadening their content, substance, and structure; and by linking them more deliberately to practice episodes. Learning more about one's theories of practice is not easy because they exist at two levels, as espoused theories and as theories in use. Argyris and Schön (1974) elaborate:

> When someone is asked how he would behave under certain circumstances, the answer he usually gives is his espoused theory of action for that situation. This is the theory of action to which he gives allegiance, and which, upon request, he communicates to others. However, the theory that actually governs his actions is his theory in use. This theory may or may not be compatible with his espoused theory; furthermore, the individual may or may not be aware of the incompatibility of the two theories. (6–7)

It is important to bring to the forefront theories in use and to help principals in preparation and in service to contrast them with espoused theories in an effort to bring the two closer together. The more manifest one's theories of practice becomes the more deliberately can antecedents be developed and the more rational will be one's intentions, actions, and realities on the job.

The definition of a professional practice episode illustrated in Figure 1-1 is deliberately "intents, *actions*, and realities" as opposed to the more common "objectives, behavior, and evaluation" for good reason. Administrative behavior and administrative actions are not the same thing. Actions are always governed by intents, preferences, and values. Behavior, by contrast, is more neutral if not responsive in a stimulus-response sense. The work of principals is more accurately characterized by actions, not behaviors, and moral actions at that; ". . . educational administration is an ethical science concerned with good or better processes, good or better means, good or better ends and as such is thoroughly immersed in values, preferences, ideas, aspirations, hopes . . ." (Sergiovanni and Carver, 1973:5).

Every action of an administrator requires choices among several alternatives and is thus an expression of preferences based on a hierarchy of values. For this reason, according to Starratt, administrative actions are moral actions—moral actions that are expressed

> in a context of limits, limits of understanding, limits of maturity, limits of virtue, limits of power. In a sense morality is never a given; it is always something to be negotiated, it is always something only partially achieved. The values we seek are always, in a sense, beyond us. Our actions become moral only as we reach out for what lies beyond those limits and the definitions of human possibility which those limits tend to impose. (Sergiovanni and Starratt, 1988:219)

To Starratt, administration as moral action must be understood as a struggle to do the right thing according to some sense of values, to some sense of what it means to be and become a human being. Reflective practice within the principalship needs to be concerned with what is good as well as what is effective.

Life would be simpler if accepting the paradigm of the Scruffies meant that the position of the Neats was false. The reality is that both are true. For simple problems that exist in stable environments under determinate conditions, thinking like a Neat will serve principals well. But for complex problems that exist in turbulent environments under indeterminate conditions, thinking like a Scruffy makes more sense.

Granted that tactically each of the views might fit if appropriately matched to practice situations, which of the two views should make up one's strategic mindscape? To help answer this question, Chapter 2 examines the work of the principalship and compares what experts say the proper roles and tasks should be with those that emerge from practice. This analysis will not only introduce us to the job of being a principal but can also help us decide which of the two positions makes the most sense most of the time. A new theory of management is then proposed in Chapter 3 to help guide practice when the world of schooling is more scruffy than neat.

References

Argyris, Chris, and Donald A. Schön. 1974. *Theory in Practice: Increasing Professional Effectiveness.* San Francisco: Jossey-Bass.

Blumberg, Arthur. 1989. *School Administration as Craft*. Boston: Allyn & Bacon.

Hosford, Philip L. 1984. "The Problem, Its Difficulties and Our Approaches," in Philip L. Hosford, Ed., *Using What We Know About Teaching*. Alexandria, VA: Association for Supervision and Curriculum Development.

James, William. 1892. *Talks to Teachers on Psychology: And to Students on Some of Life's Ideals*. New York: Holt.

Kennedy, Mary M. 1984. "How Evidence Alters Understanding and Decisions," *Educational Evaluation and Policy Analysis* 6(3), 207–226.

Mintzberg, Henry. 1987. "Crafting Strategy," *Harvard Business Review* July–August 1987, 66–75.

Sergiovanni, Thomas J. 1987. "The Theoretical Basis for Cultural Leadership," in Linda T. Sheive and Marion B. Schoenheit, eds., *Leadership: Examining the Elusive*, 116–129. Alexandria, VA: Association for Supervision and Curriculum Development.

Sergiovanni, Thomas J., and Fred D. Carver. 1973. *The New School Executive: A Theory of Administration*. New York: Dodd Mead.

Sergiovanni, Thomas J., and Robert J. Starratt. 1988. *Supervision Human Perspectives*, 4th ed. New York: McGraw-Hill.

Schön, Donald A. 1983. *The Reflective Practitioner: How Professionals Think in Action*. New York: Basic Books.

Schön, Donald A. 1984. "Leadership as Reflection in Action," in Thomas J. Sergiovanni and John E. Corbally, Eds., *Leadership and Organizational Culture*, 64–72. Urbana-Champaign, IL: University of Illinois Press.

Schön, Donald A. 1987. *Educating the Reflective Practitioner*. San Francisco: Jossey-Bass.

CHAPTER2

Actual and Ideal Views of the Principal's Job

In this chapter we continue our study of the principalship by examining the job itself and the expectations commonly held for the work of principals. An important theme is that in order to succeed, principals must master the art of managing complexity. Key to this mastery is knowing the differences between effective, efficient, and good practice and the differences that exist between ideal views of administrative work as proposed by theorists and actual descriptions of work that evolve from the world of practice. The terms *administration, management,* and *leadership* are often used interchangeably in the literature and in conversations about the principalship, but for clarity important differences in meaning and practice need to be highlighted.

Administration

Administration can be broadly defined as a process of working with and through others to accomplish school goals efficiently. The essential elements of this definition are action, goals, limited resources, and working with other people. When principals are successful in matching their actions to goals with goals subsequently advanced, they are considered to be *effective*. Principals typically work in an environment characterized by limited resources, and this too becomes an important consideration. Time is limited. There seems never to be enough money. Additional staff are often required. Space too is often limited. Thus, principals have to decide how to best use limited resources to obtain maximum benefits for the school. When they are able to accomplish this feat, they are considered *efficient*. Effectiveness and efficiency are two universal concerns of administration.

Neither effectiveness nor efficiency, however, is the same as *good*. A school can be effective and efficient in achieving its goals but not be very good if the goals themselves are defined too narrowly or are otherwise suspect. A management procedure might effectively and efficiently get results but not be very good if it compromises democratic values or raises moral questions. A teaching strategy may be effective and efficient in getting students to learn something but not very good if they come to dislike learning as a result. If goodness is important, then it becomes clear that administrative practices cannot be based simply on research and theory.

15

Goodness is not something one discovers but something one decides. As Paul W. Taylor (1961) explains, when it comes to goodness "we must decide what ought to be the case. We cannot *discover* what ought to be the case by investigating what is the case" (248).

Management and Leadership

Most administrative theorists consider management and leadership to be two distinctive expressions of administrative practice. They point out that the principal is responsible for teachers and others who have specifically designed tasks. The principal's job—to coordinate, direct, and support the work of others—is accomplished by defining objectives, evaluating performance, providing the necessary resources, building a supportive climate, running interference with parents, planning, scheduling, bookkeeping, resolving teaching conflicts, handling student problems, dealing with the school district central office, and otherwise helping to keep the school running day by day. When done well, these practices help the school achieve its goals.

James Lipham (1964) considered the preceding activities to be associated with management rather than leadership. Management, according to him, refers to the routine behaviors associated with one's jobs. He believed that the differences between management and leadership are revealed in the latter by the initiation of new structures, procedures, and goals. Leadership suggests an emphasis on newness and change. Similarly, Abraham Zaleznick (1977) describes leaders as follows:

> They are active instead of reactive, shaping ideas instead of responding to them. Leaders adopt a personal and active attitude toward goals. The influence a leader exerts in alerting moods, evoking images and expectations, and in establishing specific desires and objectives determines the direction a business takes. The net result of this influence is to change the way people think about what is desirable, possible, and necessary.

Distinctions between management and leadership are useful for theorists and help to clarify and sort various activities and behaviors of principals. For practical purposes, however, both emphases should be considered as necessary and important aspects of a principal's administrative style. The choice is not whether a principal is leader or manager but whether the two emphases are in balance and, indeed, whether they complement each other.

Successful leadership and management within the principalship are directed toward the improvement of teaching and learning for students. Though assuming an active role in this improvement, the principal needs to give equal attention to *enabling others* to function more effectively on behalf of the school. One rarely finds a successful school without an effective principal. By the same token, rarely does the principal accomplish much without empowering others to act.

Your View of the Principal's Job

Let's begin our examination of the principal's job with your perceptions of the tasks and functions that should make up this role and of their relative importance.

Imagine yourself as a candidate for the principalship of an 800-student junior high school in a community close to Philadelphia. You have taught for several years in a school and community much like this one; but, beyond temporary administrative assignments (such as chairing committees and project teams), you have had no full-time administrative experience. Your overall credentials and your background as a teacher are, nonetheless, sufficiently impressive that the search committee considers you one of its top three candidates. You have been invited to visit the school and to be interviewed by the committee and the superintendent for this job. To help you prepare for your visit, the committee informs you of a number of areas that they wish to explore and a number of issues that they wish to discuss. Among these are:

What do you consider to be the major tasks of a principal?

Which of these tasks do you believe to be most important?

As you plan your daily and weekly schedule, what proportion of time would you allocate to each of these tasks?

You want to be as prepared as possible for your visit and interview. Therefore, consider these questions and write down some of your ideas. Start by writing a brief general description of your perception of the role of the principal and her or his prime reasons for existing as part of the structure of schooling. Follow this general description with a listing of roles and task areas that you believe should define the principal's responsibilities. Curriculum and program development, supervision and evaluation, and student discipline are examples of task areas that might come to mind. As you examine your list, rank the tasks in order of their importance to you. Then, using 100 percent of the time available to you in an average work week, allocate percentages of time that you would try to spend in each area if you were to obtain this principalship.

In your deliberations about principalship responsibilities, roles, and tasks, you have probably been thinking in terms of the school in the ideal. You have been describing your perceptions of what is important and what you think the principal *ought* to do. The next section examines what the experts say principals ought to do. This discussion will allow you to compare your views with those of the experts. Later we shall examine how your views and those of the experts compare with the roles and tasks that emerge from actual practice.

Ideal Conceptions of the Principalship

Administrative theorists have spent much time over the years coming to grips with what they consider to be the essential roles and tasks of administrators. Planning, organizing, leading, and controlling are four functions that theorists often mention. *Planning* means the setting of goals and objectives for the school and the developing of blueprints and strategies for implementing them. *Organizing* means the bringing together of the necessary human, financial, and physical resources to accomplish goals efficiently. *Leading* has to do with guiding and supervising subordinates. *Controlling* refers to the principal's evaluation responsibilities and includes reviewing and regulating performance, providing feedback, and otherwise tending to standards of goal attainment.

The acronym POSDCoRB is another example of how administrative processes have been defined. Proposed in 1937 by Luther Gulick, POSDCoRB stands for planning, organizing, staffing, directing, coordinating, reporting, and budgeting. Lists such as these are continuously being revised. In 1955, for example, the American Association of School Administrators added such processes as stimulating staff and evaluating staff to the POSDCoRB list.

Exhibit 2–1 provides a summary of principalship tasks and functions that encompasses common themes from many available lists (Miklos, 1980). The summary combines a list of administrative processes proposed by Russell Gregg (1957) and a list of principalship task areas proposed by Roald Campbell (1971), both noted theorists in educational administration.

Gradually, lists of tasks and roles have given way to lists of competencies and proficiencies as the favored way to map out the territory of educational administration. For example, in 1986 the National Association of Elementary School Principals issued the document "Elementary and Middle School Proficiencies for Principals," which contained a list of 74 proficiencies grouped into 10 categories that define *expertness* in the principalship. The categories and the first three proficiencies listed for each category follow.

Leadership Behavior

Inspire all concerned to join in accomplishing the school's mission . . .

Apply effective human relations skills . . .

Encourage the leadership of others . . .

Communication Skills

Persuasively articulate their beliefs and effectively defend their decisions . . .

Write clearly and concisely so that the message is understood by the intended audience . . .

Apply facts and data to determine priorities . . .

Group Processes

Involve others in setting short- and long-term goals . . .

Apply validated principles of group dynamics and facilitation skills . . .

Understand how to resolve difficult situations by use of conflict-resolution methods . . .

Curriculum

Understand the community's values and goals and what it wants the curriculum to achieve . . .

EXHIBIT 2-1 Ideal Administrative Processes, Task Areas, and Activities for School Principals

Task Areas for School Principals

Components of Process	School Program	Pupil Personnel	Staff Personnel	Community Relations	Physical Facilities	Management
1. Planning	Identify specific objectives and devise means	Inventory of numbers and special needs	Staff needs and staff development	Program of school, community contact	Design of buildings, facilities	School management systems
2. Decision making	Select objectives and means; decide content of program	Space and services required	Recruitment and selection of staff	Form and frequency of contact	Best use of available space, changes	School needs, requisites
3. Organizing	Schedule courses and individual programs	Grouping pupils, accounting procedures	Assign teaching duties	Schedule contacts for year	Use of space and equipment	Procedure, delegation of duties
4. Coordinating	Maintain balance in program	Special services, movement of groups	Related work of teachers	School and community activities	Relate need to availability	Management with other activities
5. Communicating	Among staff members on program involvement	Needs to higher levels	Provide and receive information	Exchange information	Needs to higher levels	On needs with staff
6. Influencing	Availability of resources and work on program improvement	Pupil control, provision of services	Motivate teacher improvement	Attitudes toward school	Extent of use of facilities	Allocation of resources
7. Evaluation	Assess outcomes and adequacy of program	Pupil progress, adequacy of services	Assist with self-evaluation, formal evaluation	Effectiveness of relations	Use of present facilities	Efficiency of procedures

Adapted from Erwin Miklos, 1980, "Approaches to School Administration," in John Smyth and Richard Bates, Eds., *Educational Leadership in Schools: Reader I*, Geelong, Australia: Deakin University, 23.

19

Set forth, as a continuum, the skills and concepts the curriculum is designed to provide . . .

Monitor the curriculum to ensure that the appropriate content and sequence are followed . . .

Instruction

Understand and apply the principles of growth and development . . .

Regularly assess the teaching methods and strategies being used at the school to ensure that they are appropriate and varied . . .

Understand and apply validated principles of teaching and learning . . .

Performance

Set high expectations for students, staff, parents, and self . . .

Appropriately match particular learning styles with particular teaching styles . . .

Enhance student and staff strengths and remediate weaknesses . . .

Evaluation

Use a variety of techniques and strategies to assess—
Student performance
Individual teacher and staff performance
The achievement of curriculum goals
The effectiveness of the total instructional program . . .

Assess progress toward achieving goals established for students, teachers, the principalship, and the involvement of parents and the community at large . . .

Seek and encourage input from a variety of sources to improve the school's program . . .

Organization

Comprehend and employ validated principles of effective time management . . .

Capitalize on the findings of research and making program decisions . . .

Develop and implement equitable and effective schedules . . .

Fiscal

Understand the school district budget and its specific implications for the school . . .

Plan, prepare, justify, and defend the school budget . . .

Manage the school within the allocated resources . . .

Political

Understand the dynamics of local, state, and national politics . . .

Develop plans and strategies for helping to achieve appropriate financial support of education . . .

Involve the community's movers and shakers in the development and support
of the school's program . . .

(National Association of Elementary School Principals, 1986)

Modern lists of proficiencies provide a rendering of tasks and roles that are
much more descriptive than the generic lists of the past and that emphasize much
more the specific context of schooling, teaching, and learning.

The Complex Nature of Managerial Work

What is the world of work for principals actually like, and how does this world
shape the actual roles and tasks of principals? Further, how does this world stack
up with the views of the experts and your own listing and ranking of principalship
roles and tasks?

Comparing actual and ideal conceptions of tasks and roles is comparing *descriptive* and *normative* views of the principalship. Normative is the ideal view. Descriptive encompasses actual choices made by principals to accommodate the constraints
they face (for example, conflicting expectations, ambiguous goals, political realities,
declining enrollment, labor unions, financial shortfalls, de facto autonomy of
teachers), sometimes at the expense of their intentions and preferences.

The 1973 publication of Henry Mintzberg's book *The Nature of Managerial Work*
sparked a great deal of interest in descriptive studies of administration in education. Mintzberg studied five executives, including a school superintendent. He relied
on continued, detailed, and systematic observations of what these administrators
actually did, almost moment by moment, over an extended period of time. His
research has become a model for others who have studied the specific context of
educational administration. In one such study, Sproul (1976) found that such words
as *local, verbal, choppy,* and *varied* were most often used to describe the typical admin-
instrative work day. Choppiness, for example, was evidenced by the presence of
many activities of brief duration. A composite administrator in Sproul's study engaged in 56 activities daily, each averaging about nine minutes; and participated
in 65 events, each averaging six minutes. Events were described as periods of time
one minute or longer during which administrators used one medium of communication such as the phone, a conversation, or a memo.

Similarly, Mintzberg found that the work of administrators was characterized
by brevity, variety, and fragmentation and that the majority of administrative activities were of brief duration, often taking only minutes. Activities were not only
varied but also patternless, disconnected, and interspersed with trivia; as a result,
the administrator often shifted moods and intellectual frames. These findings suggest a high level of *superficiality* in the work of administration. Mintzberg noted
further that, because of the open-ended nature of administrative work, the ad-

ministrator is compelled to perform a great number of tasks at an unrelenting pace. This contributes further to superficiality. Free time is only rarely available, and job responsibilities seem inescapable.

The administrators in Mintzberg's study demonstrated a preference for live action and for oral means of handling this action. They favored the job's current and active elements over abstract, technical, and routine elements. They preferred to visit with others personally, to talk on the telephone, and to conduct formal and informal conferences, rather than to rely on written means of communication. Because of this propensity for oral action, most of the business of the organization remained unrecorded and was stored in the administrator's memory. This, in turn, made delegation and shared decision making difficult. Mintzberg found that administrators are overloaded with *exclusive* knowledge about the organization and overburdened, as well, with incursions on their time as others seek this information. He observed further that administrators had difficulty in keeping on top of events and that no mechanisms existed to relieve them of minor responsibilities. Faced with the apparent requirement that one be involved in almost everything, the recourse was to treat work activities in a distinctly superficial manner.

School principals, too, often must deal with aspects of work superficially. The reasons for this can be understood as one examines the full range of responsibilities that principals have. Roland Barth (1980) describes the extent of such responsibilities as follows:

> The principal is ultimately responsible for almost everything that happens in school and out. We are responsible for personnel — making sure that employees are physically present and working to the best of their ability. We are in charge of program — making sure that teachers are teaching what they are supposed to and that children are learning it. We are accountable to parents — making sure that each is given an opportunity to express problems and that those problems are addressed and resolved. We are expected to protect the physical safety of children — making sure that the several hundred lively organisms who leave each morning return, equally lively, in the afternoon.
>
> Over the years principals have assumed one small additional responsibility after another — responsibility for the safe passage of children from school to home, responsibility for the safe passage of children from home to school, responsibility for making sure the sidewalks are plowed of snow in winter, responsibility for health education, sex education, moral education, responsibility for teaching children to evacuate school buses and to ride their bikes safely. We have taken on lunch programs, then breakfast programs; responsibility for the physical condition of the furnace, the wiring, the playground equipment. We are now accountable for children's achievement of minimum standards at each grade level, for the growth of children with special needs, of the gifted, and of those who are neither. The principal has become a provider of social services, food services, health care, recreation programs and transportation — with a solid skills education worked in somehow. (4–6)

How is the challenge of superficiality in administrative work met by those who prescribe how administrators should behave? The well-known management consultant and theorist Peter Drucker recommended that principals set and stick to priorities. This is good advice, when it can be followed. Another well-known theorist, Chester Barnard (1938), suggested that administrators be more selective in the questions they address. In his words: "The fine art of executive decision-making consists of not deciding questions that are not pertinent, in not deciding prematurely, in not making decisions that cannot be made effectively, and in not making decisions that others should make" (194). How realistic are these prescriptions? When is it not possible to follow them, and what gets in the way of following them? How might practicing principals react to them? Let us look further at the job of the principal as revealed by actual practices.

Following the Mintzberg research approach, Van Cleve Morris and his colleagues (1984) studied elementary and secondary school principals in Chicago. They concluded:

> The principalship is a moving, dynamic occupation in almost a literal sense; the rhythm of the job, from arrival at the parking lot to the close of the business day, is typified by pace and movement, by frequent and abrupt shifts from one concern to another, and by the excitement pervading any institution dealing with young people . . . , the principal's job is different from other managerial positions because it is essentially an oral occupation, a job of talking. The principal governs the school mostly by talking with other people, usually one at a time, throughout the day.(209)

They noted that principals spend about 50 percent of their time outside the main office and in face-to-face contact with teachers and students. In their words:

> A busy principal covers a great deal of ground. In making these rounds, from office to corridor to classroom to gymnasium to boilerroom to playground and back, the principal is managing the school. But it is management in a form unusual for most organizations because it is, in large part, administration at the work stations of other persons. This means that the principal carries the office around with him or her through at least 50% of the work day. . . . It is the principal who gets around, who visits teachers in *their* offices, who investigates areas of potential trouble, who smooths the flow of messages from one area of the building to another, who is on call and easily summoned by those needing assistance. (211)

Morris and his colleagues noted that the job of building principal is open-ended; that is, the job becomes largely what each principal wishes to make of it. Despite a tightly structured paper hierarchy, principals have a great deal of autonomy that allows their own values and preferences to influence the job (220). This open-endedness is not to suggest that principals are free to do whatever they wish, for they still must cope with constraints they face. It does suggest, however, that options do exist, that principals are not necessarily hopeless victims, and that principals do have some control over their priorities and the extent to which they pursue priorities.

Studies of principals at work indicate that the real world of school administration is often quite different from the world described in the theoretical literature and in principals' preferences. At the end of this chapter two appendices appear. Appendix 1-1 is a detailed portrait, in the form of a time log, of a day in the life of a high school principal. The 98 entries begin at 7:35 A.M. with arrival at the school and end at 3:50 P.M. with the principal leaving school for a personal appointment. Appendix 1-2 is a portrait, in the form of a case study, of one day in the life of an urban elementary school principal. How do these descriptions of actual administrative work contrast with normative descriptions provided earlier by Gulick and by Miklos? Which of these views best corresponds to your knowledge of the principalship?

Demands, Constraints, and Choices

Rosemary Stewart (1982) describes managerial jobs "as consisting of an inner core of *demands*, an outer boundary of *constraints*, an in-between area of *choices*" (14). Demands are the things that principals must do. If they fail to do these things, sanctions are invoked, and often these sanctions are serious enough to endanger one's job. Demands are determined by school outcome specifications, legal requirements, bureaucratic rules and regulations, and the array of role expectations of important others such as superintendents, school board members, teachers and parents. Constraints are determined by norms and values that exist in the community or school, availability of human and material resources, union contracts, space limitations, and the capability limitations of teachers and others with whom the principal must work. As with demands, principals who ignore constraints face the likelihood of threatened job security.

Though two principals may be subjected to the same demands and constraints, their leadership practices nonetheless typically vary. Within any demand-and-constraint set there are always choices in the form of opportunities to do the same things differently and to do other things that are not required or prohibited. It is in this area of choices that the opportunities for excellence exist. Whether these opportunities flourish or not depends on the latitude that principals are able to make for themselves. One hallmark of a successful principal is her or his ability to expand the area of choices and thus reduce demands and constraints. This extra margin of latitude makes an important difference in enhancing the overall effectiveness of the school.

A 1978 study conducted under the auspices of the National Association of Secondary School Principals (NASSP), for example, found that successful school principals use time differently than do their more ordinary counterparts. Two of the NASSP researchers, Richard A. Gorton and Kenneth McIntyre (1978), studied time use by successful high school principals and found that real and ideal allocations of time corresponded fairly well. In a parallel study conducted by Lloyd E. McCleary and Scott D. Thomson (1979) the actual and ideal time allocations of a random sample of principals were surveyed. Table 2–1 summarizes the data from these studies, showing that though "successful" and "random" principals agree on how time should be spent, successful principals came closer to this ideal. The sum

TABLE 2-1 Comparing Rankings of Ideal and Actual Allocation of Time for Successful and Randomly Selected High School Principals

Task Areas	SUCCESSFUL PRINCIPALS*			RANDOM PRINCIPALS**		
	Ideal Time Planned (Ranked biweekly)	Actual Time Spent (Ranked biweekly)	Difference	Ideal Time Planned (Ranked biweekly)	Actual Time Spent (Ranked biweekly)	Difference
Program development (curriculum, instructional leadership)	1	3	2	1	5	4
Personnel (evaluation, advising, conferencing, recruiting)	2	1	1	2	2	0
School management (weekly calendar, office, budget, correspondence, memos, etc.)	3	2	1	3	1	2
Student activities (meetings, supervision, planning)	4	4	0	4	3	1
District office (meetings, task forces, reports, etc.)	5	5	0	9	6	3
Community (PTA, advisory groups, parent conferences)	6	6	0	8	8	0
Planning (annual, long-range)	7	9	2	5	7	2
Professional development (reading, conferences, etc.)	8	8	0	6	9	3
Student behavior (discipline, attendance, meetings)	9	7	2	7	4	3
			Sum = 8			Sum = 18

*Data are from Richard A. Gorton and Kenneth McIntyre, *The Senior High School Principalship. Vol. II: The Effective Principal*, Reston, VA: National Association of Secondary School Principals, 1978.

**Data are from Lloyd E. McCleary and Scott D. Thomson, *The Senior High School Principalship. Vol. III: The Summary Report*, Reston, VA: National Association of Secondary School Principals, 1979.

of differences between actual and ideal rankings for successful principals was 8, while that for randomly selected principals was 18.

The randomly selected principals, according to McCleary and Thomson (1979:16), appear to fall short of devoting the time they would like in two areas of responsibility: (1) program development and (2) professional development. They report spending considerably more time than they would like dealing with problems of student behavior. According to these researchers, principals who are able to spend time as they intend credit this fact to their ability to delegate, to having capable assistant principals, to having faith in the competence of others, and to concentrating on priority goals. It appears that successful principals are able to devote more time and effort to a few critical areas; perhaps, as a result, they neglect other areas of comparatively less importance. Further, they bring to their practice a high regard for those with whom they work and a commitment to the concept of empowerment.

In a more recent study contrasting problem-solving strategies of moderately and highly effective principals, Leithwood and Stager (1986) concluded that highly effective principals are more task-focused and reflective. They bring to their leadership practice a concern for substance that overrides management processes and human relationships. When concerned with people, highly effective principals view them as human resources that are key to the work of the school. Some of their findings are summarized in Exhibit 2–2.

In their monumental study of how principals make a difference in promoting quality schooling, Wilma F. Smith and Richard L. Andrews (1989) concluded that strong principals functioned as forceful and dynamic leaders who brought to their practice high energy, initiative, tolerance for ambiguity, a sense of humor, analytical ability and a practical stance toward life (8). They identified four broad areas of strategic role interaction between principal and teachers: (1) the principal as resource provider, (2) instructional resource, (3) communicator, and (4) visible presence. Their research reveals important differences in the ways teachers viewed strong, average, and weak principals across these four role dimensions. In every case strong principals received more positive ratings than average and weak, and average principals more positive ratings than weak. Their findings are summarized in Exhibit 2–3. The Smith and Andrews research demonstrates the importance of principals giving prime attention to the schools' *core technology*, teaching and learning: a finding now well established in the literature (Teddlie, Kirby, and Stringfield, 1989).

Other studies of successful principals will be examined in chapters 4, 5 and 6. These studies suggest that the ability to rely on symbolic and cultural leadership as enhancements of the more traditional technical, human, and educational leadership may provide an additional margin of latitude that expands choices in a world of demands and constraints. Further, as will be discussed in Chapter 3, successful principals are able to expand their practice beyond the limits of traditional management theory, and this too may help account for their success in expanding choices.

Certain personal qualities of principals seem also to make a difference. For example, a pioneering study of the characteristics of principals of successful elementary schools, conducted by Keith Goldhammer, Gerald Becker, and their colleagues

EXHIBIT 2-2 Principals' Problem Classification and Management, Problem-Solving Strategies, and Influences

	Highly Effective Principals	Moderately Effective Principals
Specific Strategies	Use a more deliberate model for problem solving	Tend to use more imprecise "rules of thumb"
	Agree that any strategy must include certain elements (i.e., communications, participation by stakeholders, extensive information collection)	
	Clarify many facets of problem-solving situation (e.g., type of problem, own position, own and others' roles)	May use strategies (e.g., not delaying) that prevent much clarification
	Have organizational structures in place for group problem solving	
	Have, as reasons for involving others, those cited by moderately effective principals and, in addition: to help with school-wide problem management; to produce better solutions; to help other staff develop as problem solvers	Have, as reasons for involving others: to gather information; to increase ownership; to (less often) "bounce solutions"
Knowledge	List more crucial knowledges (e.g., of resources outside school, of self) and skills (of problem solving, of communication, of leadership)	Regard, as crucial, knowledge of staff and their strengths and weaknesses, and "people skills"
	List more specific sources of knowledge (especially other principals' experiences and networks outside of school and system)	Rely on smaller number of sources, often only staff in own school
Experience as an Administrator	Report, as main change, more reflection on problem solving and a more refined, considered process	Report, as main changes, more involvement of others in problem solving and more skill in accomplishing this
Personal Values and Beliefs	Are better able to articulate values	Are less able to articulate visions
	Focus more on their own staff and "responsibilities"	Do not appear to be aware of making decisions with reference to principles or values
Determination of Priorities	Give emphasis to programs, overall school directions, building staff morale, and excitement about programs	Give emphasis to building or maintaining interpersonal relationships
	Provide arguments in support of priorities	Provide little rationale for priorities
	Work harder to manage their time to free themselves for their "proper" work (i.e., program development, planning, initiating change)	Are marginally more satisfied with how they spend their time, but express desire to spend more time in classrooms, with students and staff
	Mention more specific strategies to control paperwork	

27

EXHIBIT 2-2 (Continued)

	Highly Effective Principals	Moderately Effective Principals
Problem Difficulty	Tend to label as easy problems those encountered before, for which they have clear procedures	Find hardest problems are those involving teacher firings or other less critical personnel problems
	Find hardest problems are those outside their control, those impacting widely, and those concerned with staff morale	Tend to view most problems as familiar or "old," and display a greater tendency to be bored by them
	Insist that there are some entirely new problems facing principals, and see clearly the ways in which problems are related to former similar ones	
Overall Style	Refer more often to solving problems with others (e.g., "collaborative" or "shared")	
	Are "front-end" risk-takers, but careful information collectors	Are "tail-end" risk-takers, and less careful to collect comprehensive information
	Are more reflective about their own style and process	
Attitude Toward Problem Solving	Are definitely aware of problem solving as an activity	Little sense of problem solving as an activity, and may even reject idea of "designed" problem-solving strategies
	Enjoy new problems and see problems as opportunities	
	Are confident, but realistic about inevitability of making some mistakes	

Excerpted from K. J. Leithwood and M. Stager, "Differences in Problem-Solving Processes Used by Moderately and Highly Effective Principals," paper presented to the annual meeting of the American Educational Research Association, San Francisco, 1986.

EXHIBIT 2-3 How Teachers Rate Their Principals: A Comparison of Strong, Average, and Weak Leaders

	Percentage of Positive Ratings		
Principal as Resource Provider	Strong Leader ($n = 800$)	Average Leader ($n = 2,146$)	Weak Leader ($n = 300$)
1. My principal promotes staff development activities for teachers.	95	68	41
2. My principal is knowledgeable about instructional resources.	90	54	33
3. My principal mobilizes resources and district support to help achieve academic achievement goals.	90	52	33
4. My principal is considered an important instructional resource person in this school.	79	35	8
Principal as Instructional Resource			
1. My principal encourages the use of different instructional strategies.	89	78	75
2. My principal is sought out by teachers who have instructional concerns or problems.	72	47	25
3. My principal's evaluation of my performance helps improve my teaching.	78	46	17
4. My principal helps faculty interpret test results.	54	35	9
Principal as Communicator			
1. Improved instructional practice results from interactions with my principal.	80	49	25
2. My principal leads formal discussions concerning instruction and student achievement.	85	41	17
3. My principal uses clearly communicated criteria for judging staff performance.	90	63	17
4. My principal provides a clear vision of what our school is all about.	90	49	17
5. My principal communicates clearly to the staff regarding instructional matters.	92	50	17
6. My principal provides frequent feedback to teachers regarding classroom performance.	68	29	18
Principal as Visible Presence			
1. My principal makes frequent classroom observations.	72	31	17
2. My principal is accessible to discuss matters dealing with instruction.	94	68	66
3. My principal is a "visible presence" in the building to both staff and students.	93	75	46
4. My principal is an active participant in staff development activities.	97	64	50

Source: Wilma F. Smith and Richard L. Andrews, *Instructional Leadership: How Principals Make a Difference*, Alexandria, VA: Association for Supervision and Curriculum Development, 1989. This exhibit combines data from figures 2.4, 2.5, 2.6 and 2.7 in the original, pp. 32–37.

in 1971, found that successful principals frequently tested the limits of bureaucracy and were driven by a commitment to schooling that resembled missionary zeal.

As we shall see in Chapter 4 a 1984 study by Joan Lipsitz confirms many of the characteristics found by Goldhammer, Becker, and their colleagues. Less successful schools in the 1971 study were characterized by weak leadership, poor teacher and student morale, control by fear, traditional and ritualistic instructional programs, a general lack of enthusiasm, and principals who were "serving out their time." More successful schools, by contrast, were characterized by high morale, enthusiasm, and adaptability. They were uplifting places to visit and inhabit. The principals of those schools were able not only to recognize problems but also to face up to them with inspiring leadership and hard work. They displayed leadership supported by a belief system that included an overriding commitment to children, teaching, and teachers. They seemed to follow Peter Drucker's (1967) advice to concentrate "efforts and energies in a few major areas where superior performance produces outstanding results" (24). They established priorities and stayed with priority decisions. They seemed to feel that they had no alternative but to do first things first. The characteristics shared by these principals of successful schools are described in Exhibit 2–4.

EXHIBIT 2–4 Characteristics of Successful Principals

1. Most did not intend to become principals. Most indicated that they had intended to teach, but were encouraged to become principals by their superiors.

2. Most expressed a sincere faith in children. Children were not criticized for failing to learn or for having behavioral difficulties. The principals felt that these were problems that the school was established to correct; thus the administrators emphasized their responsibilities toward the solution of children's problems.

3. They had an ability to work effectively with people and to secure their cooperation. They were proud of their teachers and accepted them as professionally dedicated and competent people. They inspired confidence and developed enthusiasm. The principals used group processes effectively; listened well to parents, teachers, and pupils; and appeared to have intuitive skill and empathy for their associates.

4. They were aggressive in securing recognition of the needs of their schools. They frequently were critical of the restraints imposed by the central office and of the inadequate resources. They found it difficult to live within the constraints of the bureaucracy; they frequently violated the chain of command, seeking relief for their problems from whatever sources that were potentially useful.

5. They were enthusiastic as principals and accepted their responsibilities as a mission rather than as a job. They recognized their role in current social problems. The ambiguities that surrounded them and their work were of less significance than the goals they felt were important to achieve. As a result, they found it possible to live with the ambiguities of their position.

6. They were committed to education and could distinguish between long-term and short-term educational goals. Consequently, they fairly well had established philosophies of the role of education and their relationship within it.

7. They were adaptable. If they discovered something was not working, they could make the necessary shifts and embark with some security on new paths.

8. They were able strategists. They could identify their objectives and plan means to achieve them. They expressed concern for the identification of the most appropriate procedures through which change could be secured.

Source: Keith Goldhammer et al., *Elementary School Principals and Their Schools,* Eugene, OR: Center for the Advanced Study of Educational Administration, 2–3.

Early studies of principals of successful schools conducted in the 1970s and more recent studies conducted in the 1980s reveal a hopeful portrait. The work of successful principals corresponds more closely to what principals themselves say they should emphasize. Further, in the face of the same demands and constraints successful principals are able to find the necessary latitude that provides them with expanded choices and thus the extra margin needed for better performance. They do this, in part, because their view of how schools as organizations work and their conceptions of management theory and leadership practice are able to expand the concepts and practices of traditional management theory, and this is the theme of the next chapter.

References

American Association of School Administration. 1955. *Staff Relations in School Administration.* Washington, DC: American Association of School Administration.

Barnard, Chester. 1938. *The Functions of an Executive.* Cambridge, MA: Harvard University Press.

Barth, Roland S. 1980. "Reflections on the Principalship," *Thrust for Educational Leadership* 9(5).

Campbell, Roald, Edwin M. Bridges, John E. Corbally, and Raphael O. Hystrand. 1971. *Introduction to Educational Administration,* 4th ed. Boston: Allyn and Bacon.

Drucker, Peter. 1967. *The Effective Executive.* New York: Harper & Row.

Elementary and Middle School Proficiencies for Principals. 1986. Alexandria, VA: National Association of Elementary School Principals.

Goldhammer, Keith, Gerald Becker, Richard Withycombe, Frank Doyel, Edgar Miller, Claude Morgan, Louis DeLoretto, and Bill Aldridge. 1971. *Elementary School Principals and Their Schools.* Eugene, OR: University of Oregon, Center for the Advanced Study of Educational Administration.

Gorton, Richard A., and Kenneth E. McIntyre. 1978. *The Senior High School Principalship. Vol. II: The Effective Principal.* Reston, VA: National Association of Secondary School Principals.

Gregg, Russell T. 1957. "The Administration Process," in Roald F. Campbell and R. T. Gregg, Eds., *Administrative Behavior in Education.* New York: Harper & Row.

Gulick, Luther, and L. Urwick, Eds. 1937. *Papers on the Science of Administration.* New York: Institute for Public Administration.

Leithwood, K. J., and M. Stager. 1986. "Differences in Problem-Solving Processes Used by Moderately and HIghly Effective Principals." American Educational Research Association, San Francisco.

Lipham, James. 1964. "Leadership and Administration," in Daniel Griffith (ed.), *Behavioral Science and Educational Administration.* Sixty-third Yearbook of the National Society for the Study of Education. Chicago: University of Chicago Press, 119–141.

McCleary, Lloyd E., and Scott D. Thomson. 1979. *The Senior High School Principalship. Vol. III: The Summary Report.* Reston, VA: National Association of Secondary School Principals.

Miklos, Erwin. 1980. "Approaches to School Administration," in John Smyth and Richard Bates, Eds., *Educational Leadership in Schools: Reader 1.* Geelong, Australia: Deakin University.

Mintzberg, Henry. 1973. *The Nature of Managerial Work.* New York: Harper & Row.

Morris, Van Cleve, Robert L. Crowson, Cynthia Porter-Gehrie, and Emmanuel Hurwitz, Jr. 1984. *Principals in Action: The Reality of Managing Schools.* Columbus, OH: Merrill.

Smith, Wilma A., and Richard L. Andrews. 1989. *Instructional Leadership: How Principals Make a Difference.* Alexandria, VA: Association for Supervision and Curriculum Development.

Sproul, Lee S. 1976. "Managerial Attention in New Educational Systems." Seminar on Organizations as Loosely Couple Systems, University of Illinois, Urbana, Nov. 13–14.

Stewart, Rosemary, 1982. "The Relevance of Some Studies of Managerial Work and Behavior to Leadership Research," in James G. Hunt, Uma Sekaran, and Chester A. Schriesheim, Eds., *Leadership Beyond Establishment Views.* Carbondale, IL: Southern Illinois University.

Taylor, Paul W. 1961. *Normative Discourse.* Englewood Cliffs, NJ: Prentice-Hall.

Teddlie, Charles, Peggy D. Kirby, and Sam Stringfield. 1989. "Effective Versus Ineffective Schools: Observable Differences in the Classroom," *American Journal of Education* 97(3).

Zeleznik, Abraham. 1977. "Managers and Leaders: Are They Different?" *Harvard Business Review* 55(3).

APPENDIX 2-1 Time Log of a High School Principal

7:35 a.m.	Arrived at school. Picked up mail and communications. Unlocked desk.
7:36 a.m.	Looked for dean who wasn't in yet. Left word for him to see me.
7:38 a.m.	Looked at mail—Heart Association wanting to promote a "Heart Day." Worked at desk, proofread two teacher evaluations.
7:47 a.m.	Secretary came in. Gave her evaluations of teachers for retyping.
7:49 a.m.	Checked with substitute clerk for absentees and late-comers (exceptionally foggy morning).
7:50 a.m.	Spoke briefly with arriving English teacher about his spelling bee and award certificates I had signed.
7:52 a.m.	Called five administrative offices, suggesting they check classrooms for possible late teachers.
7:54 a.m.	Gave secretary instructions on duplicating and distribution of material on change in graduation requirement.
7:55 a.m.	Saw dean about student who had called after school yesterday—threatened and beaten up by other students getting off bus.
7:58 a.m.	On way to staffing, stopped at attendance office to visit with parent who was in about son not doing well in school.
8:00 a.m.	Joined staffing with social worker, psychologist, counselor, therapist, parent, and student who had been removed from all classes for truancy.
9:10 a.m.	Left staffing to look for student who had been told to wait in outer office but had wandered off.
9:15 a.m.	Found student in hall, returned to staffing.
9:30 a.m.	Left staffing to keep appointment with candidate for maintenance job.
9:31 a.m.	While waiting for building and grounds director to arrive, gave secretary instructions for cover and illustrations for the open house printed program.
9:33 a.m.	While waiting read: Note from student needing early release. Bulletin from National Federation of Athletic Associations on college recruiting of high school athletes. Note from teacher upset over misbehavior in previous day's home room program. Staff absentee report for the day.
9:36 a.m.	Went to outer office to greet candidate and explain why we were waiting.
9:37 a.m.	Called building and grounds director and learned he wasn't coming over.
9:39 a.m.	Interviewed maintenance supervisor candidate.
10:00 a.m.	Took call from registrar—to be returned.
10:07 a.m.	Completed interview.
10:08 a.m.	Saw teacher who had pictures from German exchange program.
10:09 a.m.	Called for building and grounds director—busy.
10:10 a.m.	Returned call to registrar about purging of records of a dropout.
10:11 a.m.	Called building and grounds director to discuss maintenance candidate.
10:14 a.m.	Returned call to personnel director about administrator's inservice program next week. Agreed to make a presentation.
10:22 a.m.	Read: Two suspension notices. Plans of special programs coming up.
10:25 a.m.	Saw special programs coordinator in outer office. Approved her plans and discussed possible appearance of Navy Band in February.
10:27 a.m.	Saw dean to learn what he had done about yesterday's incident.
10:30 a.m.	Left for cafeteria—talked with counselor in hall about Guidance Information Service (computer service for college selection).

From Gilbert R. Weldy, *Principals: What They Do and Who They Are,* Reston, VA: National Association of Secondary School Principals, 1979, 65–71.

APPENDIX 2–1 *(Continued)*

10:31 a.m.	Stopped by to see psychologist to hear outcome of staffing meeting.
10:36 a.m.	Stopped by health center to give nurses information from Heart Association about "Heart Day."
	Talked with nurse about her program at a PTSA meeting the previous day.
10:37 a.m.	Stopped in Audiovisual Center to ask director to prepare transparencies I had given him for inservice program.
10:40 a.m.	Stopped by athletic director's office to relate comments by parents about physical education that had come up at the PTSA meeting.
10:45 a.m.	Checked on the room where I was to have lunch with two students. Visited with a student congress representative who was there.
10:46 a.m.	Looked in on yearbook photographer who was waiting for students to come in for underclass pictures.
	Visited with student who had performed with choir previous day when students had misbehaved.
10:49 a.m.	Walked down to maintenance office to tell men about holes broken in wall of the student council office.
10:52 a.m.	Stayed around student cafeteria. Spoke with teacher who was in school exchange.
10:54 a.m.	Stopped in faculty lounge to visit with three soccer coaches who were concerned about new play-off rules that eliminated our team.
10:57 a.m.	Picked up lunch and went to council office to meet students.
11:00 a.m.	Lunched with two students.
11:30 a.m.	Stopped and visited with a few students in the cafeteria.
11:35 a.m.	Returned to the office. On the way, stopped to visit with CVE teacher about cosmetology program and a student in the program.
11:38 a.m.	Visited with workmen installing new air conditioning units in office area.
11:40 a.m.	Made four telephone calls. No answer on two of them.
11:47 a.m.	Returned call from fellow principal, discussed graduation requirement proposal.
11:48 a.m.	Answered note from teacher.
11:50 a.m.	Reviewed minutes of previous day's principal's advisory committee meeting (principal is chairman and secretary).
11:51 a.m.	Read note from teacher about a student's early release.
11:52 a.m.	Looked up material needed for next day's athletic conference meeting.
11:58 a.m.	Read communications:
	Memo regarding special education student.
	Note from teacher about conduct in homeroom.
	Memo from special program coordinator about upcoming program.
	Board of Education summary.
	November homeroom calendar.
12:07 p.m.	Called in building manager to discuss his problems that students had brought up in advisory meeting.
12:22 p.m.	Saw student who was upset with dean's handling of his absence.
12:28 p.m.	Took call from a mother who didn't want her daughter to drop out of school.
12:30 p.m.	Met with two teachers to make plans for disseminating information to faculty, parent, and student groups on graduation requirement change.
1:08 p.m.	Completed conference.
	Instructed secretary to prepare materials.
1:09 p.m.	The day's mail—read, routed, and filed.
1:12 p.m.	Made two calls. No answer for either.
1:13 p.m.	Called PTSA president. No answer.
1:15 p.m.	Wrote note to superintendent to accompany graduation requirement proposals.
1:20 p.m.	Saw student council representative about floor hockey marathon project.
1:23 p.m.	Gave dictation to secretary:
	Memo to administrators and faculty inservice committee about faculty meeting date.

APPENDIX 2–1   *(Continued)*

	Petition form for faculty for graduation requirement proposal.

Petition form for faculty for graduation requirement proposal.
Letter to parents for principal's coffee next month.
Welcome letter to parents for the open house program.
Faculty bulletin for next day.

1:46 p.m.	Took call from district administrator's secretary.
1:48 p.m.	Received note from teacher on a student's early release.
	Gave secretary several instructions
1:54 p.m.	Called PTSA president. No answer.
1:55 p.m.	Called assistant administrator about our school hosting a student congress (forensic event).
1:56 p.m.	Went to student services office to review memo to teachers responsible for the previous day's homeroom.
2:02 p.m.	Walked out to smoking area. Admonished a student athlete for being there.
2:11 p.m.	Called both fellow principals, neither in, left word to call.
2:14 p.m.	Called administrator at sister school who was on graduation requirements committee.
2:15 p.m.	Conferred with secretary about dictation.
2:15 p.m.	Called personnel office about tuition scholarships from college whose student teachers we help train.
2:18 p.m.	Read more communications:
	Five suspension notices.
	Note from teacher on the early release of student.
	Daily bulletin.
2:20 p.m.	Wrote note to student services director about homeroom programs for November.
2:21 p.m.	Read bulletin from National Federation of Activities Associations.
2:27 p.m.	Studied six-week grade distributions—computer printout.
2:33 p.m.	Answered question for student reporter about early dismissal on open house day.
2:34 p.m.	Continued study of grade distributions. Made summary table of withdraw-passing and withdraw-failing grades.
2:42 p.m.	Read confirmation of an order to change telephone service.
2:44 p.m.	Read principals' association newsletter.
2:48 p.m.	Took return call from fellow principal. Discussed institute day program.
	Arrangements for next day's league meeting.
	Graduation requirements proposal strategy.
2:50 p.m.	Received material from superintendent to be distributed to faculty—read material and gave secretary instructions for distribution.
3:00 p.m.	Saw newspaper adviser about a story on graduation requirement proposal.
3:02 p.m.	Returned to reading principals' newsletter.
3:05 p.m.	Called fellow principal about ride to league meeting next day.
3:07 p.m.	Called PTSA president. No answer.
3:08 p.m.	Reviewed agenda for league meeting—got material together.
3:10 p.m.	Took call from athletic director about cuts in capital equipment budget.
3:12 p.m.	Read a teacher evaluation.
3:15 p.m.	School is out.
3:18 p.m.	Went into hall—watched students and teachers leave.
3:22 p.m.	Helped a student look for a lost jacket.
3:25 p.m.	Back in office, went over open house program with secretary.
3:30 p.m.	Called assistant administrator. No answer.
	Left word to call.
3:33 p.m.	Called PTSA president. Busy this time.
3:37 p.m.	Studied curriculum council's grade weighting system.
3:45 p.m.	Called PTSA president—discussed agenda for next week's board meeting.
3:50 p.m.	Left school for a personal appointment.

APPENDIX 2–2 A Day in the Life of an Urban Elementary Principal

When Mary Stewart arrived at Blaire Elementary School at 8:15 a.m., the teachers were stopping by the office to sign in on their way to their classrooms. Stewart removed her coat and boots, hanging them in the closet outside her office. She put on a pair of medium heeled shoes, explaining to the researcher, " . . . the children like to see the principal a little dressed up." Joining her clerk in the outer office, the two of them reviewed the list of teachers who would be absent and the steps to be taken to secure substitutes. One substitute, sent by the central office "Sub Center," had already arrived, and Stewart asked the clerk to give her the regular teacher's file containing a class seating chart and lesson plans.

Returning to her desk, Stewart's eyes drifted to the Continuous Progress Program packet and accompanying memorandum from district offices which had arrived the previous afternoon. It was a reminder that the next reporting period was imminent and that all forms must be filed this coming Friday before the close of business. This meant that Stewart would be spending part of each of the next three days buttonholing the teachers to get their reports to her on each child, and then summarizing these figures in an all-school report. Stewart anticipated that she would have to divert some time from other managerial duties to get this paperwork finished on time.

As she reviewed her calendar, Stewart mentally prepared for a meeting with faculty representatives of the Professional Problems Committee. The Union contract provided that this group, elected by the teachers, must meet regularly with the principal. At 8:30, Stewart left her office for the short walk to the school library, where the committee members were gathering. Stewart called the meeting to order about 8:35. High on her list of items was the matter of selecting textbooks for next year. But before this discussion got underway, the teachers wanted to relay questions to Stewart that individual teachers had raised with them: a problem in supervising the third floor washrooms, a question about how next year's faculty advisor to the eighth grade graduating class was to be selected, and a problem in getting supplies during a particular free period when the office clerk was often not available. After promising to work on these problems, Stewart spent most of the remaining time discussing plans with the teachers to host upcoming meetings with publisher representatives. Together they also reviewed plans to form faculty textbook review committees, and procedures for selecting a common textbook for each grade level.

After the meeting, Stewart was approached by two teachers with individual questions. Miss La Pointe wanted to know whether Stewart would be available during eighth period. Stewart nodded and invited her to stop by the office at that time. Mr. Fields, the gym teacher, informed her that the basketball team did well at yesterday's game. They came close to beating Doyle, which is one of the best teams in the district. Stewart congratulated him, and took the opportunity to ask how Marvin Goth was behaving in class lately. Fields said that Marvin still got "edgy," but in general was "doing a lot better."

As Stewart walked through the hallway back to her office, Mrs. Noyes motioned to her from inside the classroom. The students were already in their classrooms or moving quickly through the halls in the last moments before the class bell rang. Noyes told Stewart that she was scheduled to take the students on a field trip this morning, but that one of the parents had called at the last moment to say that she would not be able to come. This left Noyes one parent volunteer short. Should she cancel the trip? Stewart remembered that Mrs. Case would be volunteering in the reading center this morning. She offered to ask her if she would fill in.

On the way to the reading center, Stewart peeked into several classrooms. As she passed the student washrooms she quickly looked into each, checking to see that no students were present and that the rooms were in order. As one student hurried past her, she asked him why he was not in class. He said that he had arrived late. She checked to see that he had a late admittance slip, and then urged him to get to school on time in the future.

When she entered the reading center, she nodded in the direction of the reading teacher and motioned that she wanted to speak with Mrs. Case. Mrs. Case quickly joined her and agreed to

From Van Cleve Morris, Robert L. Crowson, Emanuel Hurwitz, Jr., and Cynthia Porter-Gehrie. "The Urban Principal: Discretionary Decision-Making in a Large Educational Organization," Washington, D.C. National Institute for Education, NIE-G-79-0019, 1981, 40–47.

APPENDIX 2–2   *(Continued)*

help with the field trip. On her way out the door, Stewart complimented the reading teacher on a bulletin board entitled "Read for Experience."

Instead of returning to her office, Stewart continued to walk the halls on the second and third floors. On the third floor, she spent a few minutes studying the washroom situation. Then, stopping briefly at each classroom, she asked the teachers to be sure that only one student at a time was excused to use them. On her way back down the stairs, she detoured for a moment on the second floor to swing by a classroom with a substitute teacher, "just to see how he's doing." Finding the students somewhat unruly, she stopped into the classroom, fixing the well-known principal's stare on the children. As expected, her presence quieted the room. She greeted the substitute and inquired whether the regular teacher's substitute file was in order. He said that everything seemed fine, "they're just testing a little bit."

When Stewart returned to the office, she spoke briefly with the clerk, reviewing the arrival and assignment of substitute teachers. Stewart asked the clerk to inform the librarian that she would have to cover one of the classes during second period, if the substitute teacher did not arrive by then. Then Stewart picked up the mail that had arrived via the school system's delivery service. She asked the clerk to inform Mrs. Noyes that Mrs. Case would come on the field trip. She also asked the clerk to be sure that a teacher aide was available during seventh period to give out teaching supplies. As they talked, the clerk handed her two telephone messages.

Stewart entered her office, leaving the door to the outer office open. (A second door connecting directly to the hallway was kept closed. In this way, anyone who wanted to see Stewart had to go through the clerk. Stewart, herself, usually passed through the outer office in order to exchange information with the clerk on the way in or out of her own private office.) She quickly wrote a note to Mrs. Reynolds, on the second floor, informing her that the teacher aide would be available during seventh period to give out supplies. She also wrote a bulletin to all teachers in longhand: "Teachers: It appears that students from different classes are meeting at pre-arranged times in the third floor washrooms again. When excusing students to the washrooms, please be sure they use the nearest washroom, only. Thank you." She got up, walked to the outer office and taped the bulletin on the counter by the sign-in book. She also placed the note to Mrs. Reynolds in her mailbox.

Stewart returned to her office and placed a call to another principal who had left a message. The principal told her that he was calling a meeting of the district's science fair committee and would appreciate knowing when a convenient time would be for Stewart. They agreed to meet at 10:00 a.m. the following day at Blaire School. After the phone conversation, Stewart wrote a note to the cafeteria director, asking that coffee and some rolls be available the next morning in the conference room adjoining her office. She consulted the teachers' schedule and then also wrote a note to Mrs. St. Antoine, asking her to come to her office during seventh period. She got up, walked to the outer office and placed the notes in St. Antoine's and the cafeteria director's mailboxes.

Returning to her office, Stewart once again picked up the telephone and dialed the number of a representative from a photography company that took students' yearly pictures. No answer, so Stewart left a message that she called. She set the phone message at the corner of her desk, so that she "would remember his name when he calls again."

She then began to look at the morning mail and some items the clerk had placed in her "in" box:

- a personnel bulletin listing several openings in the system for teachers and administrators.
- an announcement of a conference for reading teachers.
- a set of rating cards to be completed for each teacher. These teacher rating cards were filled out each year by the principal and placed in the teachers' personal files.

Stewart placed the rating cards to one side on her desk, then got up, taking the other items to the outer office with her. She placed the conference announcement in the reading teacher's mailbox and tacked the personnel bulletin to the teacher's bulletin board. As she did so, the clerk informed her of an incoming telephone call.

Returning to her desk, she picked up the phone and heard the voice of the photographer's representative, glancing in recognition at the name on the earlier phone message. After some preliminary pleasantries, this: "Mr. Haskins, every year we make a selection from among several school photographers to take school pictures. You say you'd like to be considered this year? Fine, I'll be glad to include you in the group. Could you send me some materials – a list of the size and kind of photo to be included in each student's packet . . . maybe a sample packet, O.K.? Also the cost to the student, and the amount the school keeps for each packet sold. Also any other items that you make available, such as class pictures and teacher photographs."

Stewart went on to explain to the photographer that the eighth grade faculty sponsor participated in the selection. However, the sponsor for the following year had not yet been picked out. "I'll make sure that you get the information on the selection process and the date and time of the meeting when we ask all photographers to come to the school to demonstrate their work. However, I'd appreciate it if you would not meet directly with the faculty sponsor, except of course at the demonstration session. I look forward to seeing your materials, and thanks for your interest in the school."

Stewart put down the phone and turned to the researcher: "You know, it's a pleasure dealing with these photographers. They really enjoy coming to the school, and I must say, the kids get a kick out of these sessions too." Then, turning to another subject, Stewart explained to the researcher that she had gotten a hurry-up phone call from downtown headquarters a day or so ago calling her to a special meeting on the Access to Excellence program. "It's scheduled for Friday at eleven, and that's just when I'll be putting the finishing touches on the Continuous Progress materials. I hope I can get them done in time. But, you know, these meetings . . . they're having more and more of them. They want to turn this school into an "academy," whatever that is. And we've got to go downtown and sit around for a couple hours to be told what it is. Then, no doubt, there'll be more meetings at district (headquarters) setting it up. Seems as if I spend more and more of my time away from here, going to meetings, meetings. Hard to keep on top of things here when I'm not around."

The researcher listened intently, and the two of them discussed the possibility of "academy" status and what that would mean for the school and for the community.

After a discussion of fifteen minutes, Stewart looked at her watch and saw that it was nearly time for the primary grades recess. Breaking off the conversation with the researcher, she got up, walked through the outer office, and went to stand by the exit doors to the primary play area. When the bell sounded, the children were escorted through the building toward the exit. In the ensuing commotion, Stewart spoke sharply to a few boisterous children, telling them to "walk, don't run," and to "move slowly down the stairs."

She explained in an aside to the researcher that her customary practice was to accompany the youngsters out onto the playground where she and the teachers could supervise their play. However, today, she had to get back to the office to prepare a schedule for teacher rating conferences with each teacher. Returning to her desk, she assembled the teacher evaluation materials and got from her drawer the teachers' daily schedules. Allowing 20 minutes for each teacher, she began making up a conference schedule. In the middle of this activity, she was interrupted by three boys entering the outer office, with a teacher aide following close behind. One of the boys was crying and holding the back of his head. The aide explained that the injured boy had fallen and hit his head on a patch of ice near the rim of the play area. The other two boys, she reported, had been chasing the injured boy.

Stewart moved to the outer office and told the two chasers to sit down at a bench inside the hallway door. She inspected the head injury and found that it was beginning to swell at the point of impact. Sending a student helper to the cafeteria to fetch some ice, she asked the injured boy for his name, his home telephone number, and his mother's name. She then dialed the number and spoke with the mother. After hearing what had happened, the mother said that she would come pick him up as soon as she could get a neighbor to drive her to the school. The helper soon arrived back with the ice, and Stewart wrapped it in a paper towel and gave it to the boy to place on the bump. She told him to sit down on the bench and wait for his mother, whereupon she invited the two chasers into the inner office, and closed the door. "Now look, you know you're not supposed to run where there is ice . . . it's too dangerous. Now that someone's hurt, the matter is serious. I want your parents to know about this." She filled out a form that requested a parent to come to school with the boys the following morning. With the boys still at her desk, she telephoned their homes and orally requested that a parent come to see her the next morning. She explained to the boys' mothers "there's been an injury and your son was involved. Something must be done about their wild behavior during recess." She then sent the boys back to their classrooms, explaining that she would see them again in the morning.

As she gave them their hall passes, the injured boy's mother arrived. Stewart explained to her that two other boys had been involved and that she would be meeting with their parents in the morning. The mother asked her son, "Who did it?" and he replied it was "Jeff and Michael." "Those boys," the mother said, "why do they pick on him so much? Last week they pushed him in the bushes on the way home from school. Now they've gone too far." Stewart asked the mother to "let me see if I can't work something out." She promised to call her back in the morning, after she met with the other parents.

As the boy and his mother left, Stewart looked up and saw that it was beginning to snow heavily. She went to the public address system and announced that students eating lunch at school would remain inside the building during the lunchtime recess.

Stewart returned to her desk and worked on the conference schedule, but was shortly interrupted by two phone calls. One concerned the placement of a student teacher in the school. The other was from her husband, asking if she would like to meet him downtown for dinner. As Stewart was finishing the schedule, the clerk brought in a master copy of the parents' bulletin for her to approve before it was duplicated. She set aside the schedule and read through the bulletin as the clerk waited to one side. She pointed out two typos and then placed her signature on the copy master. The clerk took it and left. A moment later she returned with the U.S. mail. Stewart took a quick glance at the envelopes before setting them to one side and continuing to finish the schedule. Stewart neatly copied the final schedule by hand and then asked the clerk to place a copy of the schedule in each teacher's mailbox.

Stewart then headed toward the cafeteria, speaking with students in the hall on the way, telling them to "slow down" and "go to your recess areas." She took a tray and moved through the lunch line. Instead of going to the faculty room, she returned to her office to eat. There, she was available for teachers who might want to stop by. As she ate, she looked through the U.S. mail: promotional material for textbooks, school administration booklets, and instructional supplies. Also an announcement of a tea at a local Catholic High School for the eighth graders. Stewart set this aside and threw out the rest.

A student asked to see Stewart. As student council president, she wanted to know when the next student council meeting would be (the last meeting had been cancelled because of snow). They picked a date and the student said that she would inform the council members. Stewart chatted for a few minutes with the girl about her plans for high school.

Getting up from her desk, Stewart carried her tray and the tea announcement to the outer office. She left the announcement in the eighth grade class sponsor's mailbox and returned her tray to the cafeteria. Then she began her tour of the hallways, inspecting the building as the students returned to their classes to settle down for the afternoon's course work.

When she returned to her office, the clerk handed her a phone message. Stewart dialed the phone for an in-house call and reached the building engineer. He told her that a small window at the back of the building had been broken during the lunch hour by some loitering high school students. He said he had covered it with some heavy cardboard, "but I thought you should know about it. Also, you know the art room . . . the shades in there have been damaged. The (art) teacher just lets the kids go wild in there during seventh and eighth periods. I think you should talk to him." Stewart agreed to check on it.

Miss La Pointe arrived. She had agreed to start a dramatic program in the school and wanted to report to Stewart the plans she was making for a Spring production. They discussed use of the auditorium, rehearsal schedules, the play La Pointe had selected, and the tryout announcement

APPENDIX 2–2 *(Continued)*

La Pointe had prepared. Toward the end of the seventh period, the conference was concluded and La Pointe left to return to her classroom. Stewart got up and, checking to make sure that the teacher's aide was on station in the outer office to give out supplies, headed for the art room to see the damaged shades and to make sure the students were under control.

When she returned to the office, Stewart found Mrs. St. Antoine waiting for her in the outer office. Stewart invited her into her own office and asked for an update about the plans for the eighth grade tea, dinner and other graduation festivities. St. Antoine discussed with her the results of faculty and student committee meetings to that point. Then Stewart asked St. Antoine whether she was thinking about remaining eighth grade sponsor next year. St. Antoine seemed a bit embarrassed. She said that she enjoyed working with the students very much, but that there was some jealousy from some of the other eighth grade teachers who felt excluded. They discussed how some of the other eighth grade teachers might be brought more closely into the planning, and St. Antoine left agreeing that she would try to mend some of the fences that had been neglected.

Seeing that it was near the end of the day, Stewart checked her desk to see what remained to be done. Noting the stack of material in the "in" box, she looked through it. It contained several forms that required signing; they pertained to the ordering of supplies, teacher absences, and a field trip permission. Stewart signed all of the forms but one. It was a request to order a film. Stewart was unfamiliar with the film and wanted to discuss its nature and use with the teacher before signing.

Stewart put on her hat and coat and walked to the main exit doors just as the students were beginning to leave. Stationed just outside the exit, she called to the students inside the hallway and out on the playground to "slow down," and "watch out, it's slippery." When the students were gone she returned to her office to find a tiny kindergartner sitting with tear-filled eyes next to the teacher aide. The aide explained that the girl's father was supposed to pick her up from school, but had not arrived. They tried to make some phone calls to find out who was coming for the girl, but could not get an answer. The girl suggested that they call her aunt, which they did. The aunt agreed to take the girl, but said no one could come and get her right now. Stewart agreed to bring the girl by the aunt's house. "There now," the aide told the girl, "the principal will take you to your aunt's house." Stewart placed a few items in a small brief case and was ready to leave. She waited as the aide and clerk prepared to leave also. As they put on their coats, she checked the teachers' sign-in sheets to be sure that they were all out of the building. Then she locked the office as they left together. Stewart reached for the small girl's hand and helped her down the slippery steps. Before going to her car, she muttered to the researcher, "I suppose I shouldn't be doing this . . . liability and all. But someone has to."

CHAPTER 3

Toward a New Theory of Management for the Principalship

In Chapter 1 it was pointed out that principals have different practical theories about the nature of human rationality, how schools work, and what really matters to people. The mindscapes of Mystics, Neats and Scruffies were discussed as examples. These mindscapes determine what principals believe about management and leadership and how they practice as a result. Different mindscapes mean different theories. Different theories mean different approaches to management and leadership and different school improvement strategies.

Not all management and leadership mindscapes, however, are equal. Some fit the world of practice better than do others. The better the fit the more successful will be the practice. This chapter compares the assumptions and principles of traditional management theory, the theory of the Neats, with the scruffy context and problems of school practice that principals and teachers face every day, noting where the theory fits and where it doesn't. The framework for a new theory of management is then proposed as a viable candidate for those instances in which traditional management does not fit. *Both traditional and new theories have important roles to play in bringing about quality schooling providing they are appropriately matched to situations of practice.* Deciding when to use each of the theories requires a level of sophistication and skill that is not as widespread as it should be in the principalship.

Changing Mindscapes

Traditional management enjoys official sanction in many state capitols and in many university preparation programs for school administrators. It is also the mindscape that dominates much of the literature on school improvement. It's no surprise, therefore, that this mindscape is entrenched in the thinking of many school principals and is difficult to change.

Consider, for example, the case of elementary school principal Jane. Jane now spends from one-third to one-half of her time trying to be an "instructional leader" as prescribed by a recent state law. This law requires that she evaluate every teacher in her building three times a year, using a state assessment instrument composed of a generic list of 50 teaching behaviors gleaned from dozens of independent research reports on "effective teaching." The instrument is several pages long and involves a good deal of paperwork in addition to one hour of classroom observation for each evaluation. Jane takes her responsibilities seriously and estimates that a conscientious job takes about three hours for each evaluation.

Teachers are required to develop "growth plans," which Jane must monitor as well. The growth plans indicate how each teacher intends to improve her or his teaching and thus earn higher evaluation scores. Jane estimates that she spends 270 hours or 33 days a year just conducting the required evaluations. She dreads the many hours it takes to collect, study, and comment on the growth plans and then figure out sensible, albeit efficient, ways to follow up what teachers claim they will do. She notices that the growth plans are often perfunctory in tone, and this bothers her.

Among Jane's other instructional leadership responsibilities are daily monitoring of teachers to ensure that they follow the district-mandated objectives for each of the subjects or courses taught and that they adhere to the proper time allocations as provided by the mandated schedule. Jane can keep tabs on this process by practicing "management by walking around" but is not able by relying on this process alone to demonstrate concretely to her superiors that her school is in compliance. Seeking to avoid a poor evaluation from her supervisors, Jane requires that teachers indicate the objectives they intend to teach on their daily lesson plans, as well as the amount of time they spend teaching to each of these objectives. She dutifully collects these lesson plans each Friday and examines them to be sure that teachers are in compliance. As time permits, Jane tries to write comments on the plans that might result in teachers thinking about their lessons more effectively and teaching better.

In Jane's school district heavy reliance is placed on the use of criteria-referenced tests that are closely linked to the required objectives. These tests are given periodically, and the results must be submitted to the school district's central office and by that office to the state department of education. The results are then published in the newspaper, with statewide comparisons made district by district and within districts, comparisons made school by school. There is enormous pressure for schools to do well on the test comparisons. If the test scores in her school are not high enough, she hears about it from the superintendent's office.

Sometimes Jane gets the impression that the superintendent wants the scores up at any cost and that all that counts is the bottom line. In turn she puts enormous pressure on her teachers to be sure that the students do well on the tests. All teachers, for example, have been "inserviced" so that their day-by-day teaching should now be based on a popular teaching model made up of a series of specific steps thought to result in better student achievement. In addition to the evaluation system that is now in place and the monitoring of lesson plans and test scores, Jane spends much of her time coaching and monitoring the teachers to be sure that they are using the required teaching techniques.

In her school, Jane supervises a tightly connected "instructional management system" that seeks to link together measurable objectives, a highly specific curriculum, and required, detailed time schedules with a monitoring system of controls to ensure that teachers are doing what they are supposed to be doing and at the right time. Despite this management system the results have been frustrating. Though there have been modest gains in test scores, particularly with respect to lower-level skills, a number of problems have emerged. The curriculum is becoming increasingly narrow, absentee rates are up, and Jane worries that teachers are using fewer and fewer of their talents and skills. She shudders at the harshness of the term "deskilled" but is haunted by its imagery nonetheless.

A number of other "unanticipated consequences" from using this particular instructional management system are emerging. Teachers seem to be teaching more and more to the test. Further, Jane is convinced that they are "showboating" the indicators that appear on the required teacher evaluation instrument when she is present and observing but not at other times. She suspects that she is often observing staged lessons that allow for easy display of the indicators in the teachers' efforts to get higher evaluation scores. Higher scores increase their eligibility for merit-pay-ladder advancement and thus Jane does not begrudge them.

Jane wonders what is wrong. Could Murphy's Law be true? Though from a traditional management perspective Jane can provide evidence that she is doing what she is supposed to, that the required instructional management system is in place, and that (at least overtly) teachers are doing what they are supposed to, Jane feels that appearances do not match reality and that things are just not working well. After much painful soul searching she reaches the conclusion that something different must be done.

This conclusion is very disconcerting for Jane. She feels that she is on the verge of experiencing a professional career crisis that resembles the proverbial "midlife crisis." After all, Jane was an outstanding student during her years of graduate study in educational administration. She took the required workshops offered by the state-sponsored Leadership Development Academy and did so well that last summer she was an academy trainer. She knows how important such management ideas as POSDCoRB are to providing the kind of rational and efficient management needed for schools to work well. She knows how to demonstrate the leadership behaviors learned in a recent workshop and last summer developed workshops of her own on conflict management and on how to conduct a successful conference. She has earned a reputation for knowing how to handle people.

On the walls of Jane's office are displayed several plaques containing sayings of widely accepted management principles. Each of the plaques was given to her as an award for completing one of the Leadership Development Academy's workshops. One says, "If you can't measure it, you can't manage it." Another says, "What gets rewarded gets done." Others remind Jane of the importance of having clear objectives, letting people know exactly what is expected of them, and of being a rational and objective manager.

Jane is surrounded by the dimensions, principles, and expressions of traditional management theory, the theory of the neats. Further, this theory matches well her own mindscape of what management is, how schools are to operate if they are to function well, and the kind of leadership she should provide as a school principal. Finally, this mindscape is nurtured by the system of rewards in place in her school district. The more her practice reflects traditional management theory the more successful she is assumed to be. It is no wonder Jane experiences dissonance and anxiety from the realization that it doesn't work very well. Changing one's mindscape is a little like changing one's religion.

In recent months, Jane has come to realize that for traditional management to work, schools need to be more tightly structured and predictable than is typically the case and people need to be more passive and uniform than is typical. At first she responded to this awareness by continuing to do the same things, only doing them better. But gradually she accepted the reality that *when the world cannot be changed to fit your theory, you had better change your theory to fit the world*. This thought made more sense when she read somewhere about the differences between management and leadership. Management is concerned with doing things right, she remembered. Leadership is concerned with doing right things.

Jane realizes that successful principals are both effective managers and effective leaders. But if one has to choose between the two, the only sensible choice is to do right things, even if it means that you are not doing them in the way specified by the system. Arriving at this decision was an important and courageous milestone for Jane. Though anxious at first, she now feels comfortable with the idea that when bureaucratic and moral authority are in conflict, moral authority must always take precedence.

Jane was not known as a reckless person. Indeed, if anything she was considered to be quite conventional and conservative in the way she did things. Thus, she began to respond to the looseness she found in the structure of schooling by bending rules and interpreting issues in a fashion that always reflected the spirit of the rule but not the letter. When Jane encountered the system tightening up because her supervisors practiced close supervision, or when she was forced by the system to ignore individual differences in people and situations, she would follow the opposite tack by emphasizing the letter of the rule but not the spirit. Perfunctory execution became part of her management repertoire—a skill she realized that teachers often used to advantage when locked into the same predicament.

During the evaluation of teachers using the standardized system, for example, Jane took liberties with the required procedures by not insisting that all the listed teaching behaviors be displayed by teachers, but only the ones that made sense. She would talk to teachers about what they wanted to accomplish in their lessons and how. She was sensitive to and respectful of the differences in personality that determined their teaching styles. She realized, for example, that reticent teachers had a harder time providing the kind of bubbling reinforcement and feedback that "win points" than did their more outgoing counterparts. Together, Jane and the teachers would look over the four-page list of required teaching behaviors, deciding on the 8 or 10 behaviors that seemed to make the most sense for the particular teaching episode to be evaluated and in light of particular teaching problems identified. The evaluation was then based on this shorter but more meaningful version.

Whenever Jane's supervisors got wind of what was going on and cracked down on her to comply more specifically with the system, Jane shifted her strategem by routinely evaluating people with dispatch to save as much time as possible for other things. Once the evaluations were complete and the paperwork filed, Jane and her teachers were able to work more meaningfully and in better ways on the improvement of teaching. Jane is learning fast how to provide leadership in the complex, messy, and nonlinear scruffy world. Her mindscapes of management and leadership theory are changing to match the actual landscapes she encounters in practice.

The Limits of Traditional Management Theory

It would be a mistake for Jane to believe that traditional management theory is useless. She should not abandon it but should, rather, learn how to use it to her best advantage. Traditional management theory has its merits and limitations, and it is important for principals to know the difference.

- Traditional management theory is suited to situations of practice that are characterized by linear conditions. But the usefulness of this theory ends where *nonlinear conditions* begin.
- Traditional management theory is suited to situations of practice that can be tightly structured and connected without causing unanticipated harmful effects. But the usefulness of this theory ends where *loosely structured* conditions begin.
- Traditional management theory is suited to situations in which the need exists to bring about a routine level of competence and performance. But the usefulness of this theory ends when the goal is to bring about *extraordinary commitment and performance.*

Linear and Nonlinear Conditions

When deciding on management and leadership strategies, it is important to take into account the extent to which conditions are or are not *linear.* Linear conditions are characterized by:

Stable, predictable environments

Tight management connections

Loose cultural connections

Discrete goals

Structured tasks

Single solutions

Easily measured outcomes

Sure operating procedures

Determinate consequences of action

Clear lines of authority

Under linear conditions, simplicity, clarity, order, and predictability are present. Examples of administrative tasks that typically fit linear conditions include the routing of bus schedules, purchasing books, planning conference times, and other events and activities in which human interactions are simple, incidental, or non-existent. But even these tasks can quickly become nonlinear. An eight-inch snow-storm can create havoc with a bus schedule.

By contrast, nonlinear conditions are characterized by:

Dynamic environments

Loose management connections

Tight cultural connections

Multiple and competing goals

Unstructured tasks

Competing solutions

Difficult-to-measure outcomes

Unsure operating procedures

Indeterminate consequences of action

Unclear and competing lines of authority

The vast majority of human interactions that take place in schools can be described as nonlinear. James Gleick writes in *Chaos Making a New Science*: "Nonlinearity means that the act of playing the game has a way of changing the rules" (1987:24). In nonlinear situations every decision that is made in response to conditions at the base (time 1) time changes these conditions in such a way that successive decisions also made at time 1 no longer fit. It is difficult, therefore, for a principal to plan a series of steps, commit to a set of stepwise procedures, or other-wise make progressive management and leadership decisions based on the initial assumptions. When the context changes, the original sequence no longer makes sense. One cannot predict the conditions of time 2 until they are experienced.

Under nonlinear conditions, management resembles the following of a com-pass when the position of north changes with each step you take. As Cziko (1989) phrases it: "A process demonstrating chaos is one in which strict deterministic causality holds at each *individual* step in an unfolding process, and yet it is im-possible to predict the outcome over any *sequence* of steps in the process." In sum, nonlinear relationships between two events lead to consequences that are unpredic-table. Further, if the context for action changes, as is often the case in managing, leading, and teaching, the original sequence no longer makes sense.

Take, for example, application of motivation theories in an effort to increase teacher performance. Providing rewards to a teacher might result in a certain amount of motivation at time 1. This relationship may actually be linear, with the amount of motivation increasing proportionally as rewards are provided at times 2 and 3. But more rewards can result in less motivation if they are no longer valued, if they are viewed as manipulative, or if they are taken for granted. Moreover, individual differences come to play, so that what person A values differs from person B. Person B may tire more quickly of the same rewards than does person A. While person A might feel manipulated as a result of receiving rewards and respond negatively, person B feels attended to and responds positively.

Though the typical textbook version of traditional management theory would have us believe otherwise, the consequences of using the same motivational strategies for different people and under different conditions typically are indeterminate and unpredictable. Their link to people and consequences is nonlinear. This is the case as well for leadership, conflict resolution, and other categories of management behavior. They are all linked to people and events in nonlinear ways. *The fact is that in management and leadership identical situations and strategies give rise to different outcomes and consequences.*

Peter Vaill (1989) aptly describes the nonlinear context for management as "permanent white water." White water is the frothy, turbulent water found in waterfalls, breakers, and rapids. This metaphor was suggested to Vaill by a manager who observed:

> Most managers are taught to think of themselves as paddling their canoes on calm, still lakes. They are led to believe that they should be pretty much able to go where they want, when they want, using means that are under their control. . . . But it has been my experience that you never get out of the rapids! . . . there are lots of changes going on at once. The feeling is one of continuous upset and chaos (2).

Vaill points out that in management "things are only partially under control, yet the effective navigator of the rapids is not behaving randomly or aimlessly" (2). In sum, it is the dynamic nature of unfolding events resembling "permanent white water" that differentiates linear from nonlinear situations. Successful practice in the latter requires the kind of reflection that enables principals and teachers to constantly test what they know against what is happening.

Tight and Loose Structure

Karl Weick (1976) has argued compellingly for viewing schools as loosely coupled organizations. His point is that while aspects of schools are connected to each other in such a way that one influences the other, these connections are often confounded by other connections and are rarely characterized by strong and direct influence. As March and Simon (1958:176) point out, loose coupling does not mean that decisions and actions and programs in effect are unrelated but that they are only loosely related to each other.

The issue of school goals and purposes provides a good example. It is generally assumed that there is a tight connection between stated goals and the policies, decisions, and actions that take place in an organization. But the problem is that schools have multiple goals and are expected to achieve them. Sometimes the goals conflict with each other such that making progress toward one means losing progress toward another. Always thinking in terms of discrete goals or even discrete multiple goals with each attended to sequentially, therefore, does not fit the special character of the schools' unique value system. Under nonlinear and loosely structured conditions, schools don't achieve goals as much as they respond to certain values and tend to certain imperatives that ensure their survival over time (Parsons, 1951).

Jean Hills (1982) points out that, rather than discrete goal attainment, school administrators bring to their practice what he calls "pattern rationality." Principals, by his way of thinking, respond in response to "a conception of a pattern development on a number of mutually limiting dimensions with respective gains in a given area having implications for other areas" (1982:7). Successful principals become surfers, skilled at riding the wave of the pattern as it unfolds. They respond to value patterns when discrete goals are in conflict with each other. Important to this concept of pattern rationality is the principal's concern with the costs and benefits of her or his actions.

Teachers respond similarly. Though the literature overwhelmingly portrays teaching as a rational and linear act whereby teaching behaviors and decisions about instructional materials and time are made in response to objectives and intended outcomes, a glimpse into the real world reveals that these connections are much looser and confounding. Goals and outcomes, for example, are selected as often as a result of materials available as are materials selected as a result of goals. Teaching styles and preferences determine objectives as often as objectives determine teaching styles and preferences. Outcomes become goals as often as goals determine outcomes. Teaching, like management, is largely nonlinear and indeterminate. Stated goals and objectives are constantly shifting and changing and are often displaced by others once the teaching begins and as it continues. Indeed, teachers are just as likely to discover their goals during and after their teaching than they are to state them beforehand (a theme explored further in chapters 14 and 15).

Perhaps the most noticeable example of looseness in schools is the connection of teachers to rules. Principal Jane became aware of this reality the hard way as she tried to implement the required teaching evaluation system. When she was in class observing lessons using the instrument she saw what she was supposed to because the teachers did what they were supposed to. But when she left the classroom, teachers taught in ways that made sense to them and to their colleagues. They were more tightly connected to values, beliefs, and norms than they were to the imposed management system.

Ordinary and Extraordinary Commitment and Performance

The management and leadership needed to bring about "a fair day's work for a fair day's pay" and for transcending this minimum contract to achieve inspired and extraordinary commitment and performance in schools are different (see, for example, Burns, 1978; Bass, 1985; Hertzberg, 1966; Kelley, 1988; Sergiovanni, 1990). Traditional management theory and practice can provide the former but not the latter. Principal Jane noted, for example, that by practicing traditional management she was able to get teachers to do what they were supposed to but could not get *sustained* and *extraordinary* results.

There are two reasons why traditional management theory and practice are limited to achieving minimums, not maximums. First, the theory is based on authority. It is assumed that most teachers and students respond to authority—which they do. But authority has the tendency to cause people to respond as *subordinates*. Good subordinates always do what they are supposed to but little else. Transcending ordinary competence for extraordinary commitment and performance requires that people be transformed from subordinates to *followers*, which requires a different kind of theory and practice. Subordinates, for example, respond to authority, but followers respond to ideas, values, beliefs, and purposes. Traditional theory encompasses the former but not the latter.

Second, traditional management theory, with its bureaucratic roots, is heavily biased toward standardization and routinization. Though many aspects of schooling should be routinized, traditional theory seeks to routinize that which should be varied as well. For schools to excel, teachers and administrators need to be concerned with uniqueness and specialness in their interactions with each other and with students. The test of their effectiveness is their ability to ensure that every student is successful in achieving high academic, social, and personal goals—a task that cannot be accomplished by applying a standard recipe for organizing, presenting the curriculum, and engaging in teaching and learning. Standardization and routinization may be the formula for simple work that takes place in a stable environment where modest results are acceptable. But it is not the formula for extraordinary commitment and performance.

Toward a New Theory

To overcome the limits of traditional management and leadership a new theory for the principalship must be developed—a theory more responsive to nonlinear conditions and loose structuring and that can inspire extraordinary commitment and performance. This theory should not replace but subsume the old. The role of traditional management must change, for example, from being the *strategic model* for developing school policies and practices to being a valued, albeit limited, *tactical option* within a new, more broadly based and powerful management theory. In constructing this new theory many time-honored principles of traditional management will need to be rethought, expanded, and sometimes even inverted *whenever nonlinear and loosely structured conditions or extraordinary performance requirements are present.* The following subsections discuss examples of such principles.

The Issue of How Schools Are Structured

The Traditional Rule. *Schools are managerially tight but culturally loose.*

The Problem. This traditional rule assumes that schools are structured and function much like the mechanical workings of a clock made of cogs and gears, wheels, drives, and pins all tightly connected in an orderly and predictable manner (Sergiovanni, 1987). The task of management is to gain control of and regulate the master wheel and pin. The principal, for example, might put into place a well-oiled instructional delivery system composed of the "right" teacher evaluation system or the "right" alignment system or some other "right" control mechanism that defines in detail what teachers teach, when, and how. Once the master wheel and pin are under control, all the other wheels and pins will move responsively and the principal's intents will be accomplished.

As Jane came to realize, though many aspects of the school are indeed tightly connected in this clockworks fashion, other aspects are not. Further, teachers and students are more tightly connected to values and beliefs than they are to management systems and rules (see, for example, March, 1984; Deal and Kennedy, 1982; Weick, 1982; Shils, 1961). The more typical view of how schools operate is that of a clockworks gone awry—cogs, gears, and pins all spinning independently of each other (Sergiovanni, 1987). Though practices based on managerial tightness and cultural looseness can often get people to do what they are supposed to, the rule casts them in roles as subordinates and thus cannot inspire sustained and extraordinary commitment and performance. Further, it is unable to provide the connections needed among loosely connected parts to get the job done well.

The Alternative: Schools are Managerially Loose but Culturally Tight. Karl Weick (1986) pointed out "that indeterminancy can be organized not just by rules, job descriptions, and a priori specifications, but also by such things as shared premises, culture, persistence, clan control, improvisation, memory and imitation." Weick continues:

> In a loosely coupled system you don't influence less, you influence differently. The administrator . . . has the difficult tasks of affecting perceptions, and monitoring and reinforcing the language people use to create and coordinate what they are doing. . . . Administrators model the kind of behavior they desire . . . identify key issues so they can centralize control over a few (not all) issues and help people see them similarly. Leaders in loosely coupled systems have to move around, meet people face-to-face, and to do their influencing by interaction rather than by rules and regulations. . . . Personnel selection is more crucial than in other systems, because the common premises that are selected into that system will guide how the dispersed activities are executed. (10)

The Issue of Strategic Planning

The Traditional Rule. Clarity, control, and consensus are important to effective management and are achieved by detailed planning. Therefore:

1. *State measurable outcomes* (indicate specifically what is to be accomplished).

2. *Provide behavioral expectations* (decide and communicate who will do what and how it will be done).

3. *Practice monitoring* (compare expected behavior with observed and correct when necessary).

4. *Measure outcomes* (compare observed outcomes with stated and correct when necessary).

The Problem.   There are many paradoxes in management, and planning is one of them. By planning in a linear-stepwise way one assumes that it is possible to control the future, but often one actually loses control. Detailed plans and surefire objectives take over from people, becoming scripts on the one hand that program future actions and self-fulfilling prophecies on the other that determine our destiny *even when we are no longer interested in either the journey or the destiny.* For linear conditions with tight structures, planning as traditionally conceived is a useful management *tactic* that can achieve the anticipated results. But as a *strategy* traditional planning locks us into a course of action that often does not make sense at times 2 through *n*.

Further planning, as described above, has the tendency to result in the "escalation of commitment" to a course of action that sustains itself irrationally long after the original course of action should have been abandoned (Staw, 1984). Sinking huge sums of money into facilities for the high school's interscholastic sports program makes it difficult to de-emphasize sports even when doing so may be a good idea. Commitment to the teacher evaluation system that took so many hours of planning time to develop is likely to remain firm even in light of evidence that the teaching effectiveness research upon which it is based is faulty and teacher morale is suffering as a result.

And, finally, the measurement aspects of traditional planning place severe limits on developing powerful strategies that encourage innovation and excellence. By establishing worth as the consistency that exists between stated and observed outcomes, too many worthwhile outcomes not stated or unanticipated don't count. New priorities and new courses of action are missed and innovation is discouraged – hardly conditions for excellence. Citing a study of planning in 75 corporations that appeared in the *Economist*, Peters (1989a) notes that firms without central planners tended to produce better results. A better strategy, Peters suggests, is that of General Bill Creech of the Tactical Air Command: "Organize as we fight . . . organize in accordance with the human spirit" as a way to best use talents of people, to respond to the idiosyncratic nature of situations, and to build esprit and small-group cohesiveness deep into the enterprise (Peters, 1989a). It appears that planning, the sacred cow of traditional management, needs to be understood differently.

The Alternative.   *Clarity, control, and consensus are important to effective management and are achieved by planning strategically. Therefore:*

1. *Be clear about basic directions* (set the tone and charter the mission).

2. *Provide purpose and build a shared covenant* (what are our shared goals, values, and operating principles?).

3. *Practice tight and loose management* (hold people accountable to shared values but provide them with empowerment and enablement to decide what to do when and how).

4. *Evaluate processes and outcomes* (be sure that decisions and events embody shared values).

The principles that support this alternative rule will be examined in some detail in subsequent chapters. Suffice to say here that in a nonlinear and loosely structured world it makes managerial sense to allow people to decide in ways that make sense to them providing that the decisions they make embody shared values and commitments.

The Issue of Where to Fit People into the Improvement Planning Process

The Traditional Rule. When it comes to fitting people in,

1. *First emphasize ends* (determine objectives first).
2. *Then ways* (figure out how you will reach your objectives).
3. *Then means* (identify, train, place and supervise people).

The Problem. Deciding where to fit people into the planning process influences the outcome in important ways (Hayes, 1985). Should one start with people first or fit them in after work requirements are identified? The traditional ends, ways, and means rule is compatible with a "cannonball" theory of management suitable for stable environments where targets don't move. Unfortunately, as Harry Quadracci (Peters, 1989b) points out, we live in a "cruise missile" world. Cannons are excellent weapons for hitting fixed targets under stable conditions. One need only identify the target (ends), take careful aim calculating distance and wind (ways), and give the order to fire to a well-trained crew (means). A hit is virtually guaranteed. But hitting moving targets is another matter. Moreover, changing one's mind to enable hitting a better target than the initial one after the cannon has been fired is impossible. Yet in the world of schooling most of our targets are moving and different and more desirable targets are frequently discovered during the course of our actions. Cannons won't do here. Cruise missiles, to continue Quadracci's admittedly surly metaphor, have built into them the capacity to chase shifting targets and indeed to change targets after they are launched.

The Alternative. When it comes to school improvement

1. *First emphasize means* (concentrate on people first, build them up, increase their commitment, link them to purposes, help them to be self-managed).

2. *Then ways* (let them figure out what to do and how).
3. *Then ends* (they will decide on and achieve objectives that are consistent with shared purposes).

Robert H. Hayes (1985), who proposed this alternative rule, believes that it provides the basis for developing strategies that are more responsive to today's complex world. Key in concentrating on means first is to build up the capacity for people to be self-managers and to connect them to shared values and commonly held purposes. Robert E. Kelly (1988) believes that self-management is an essential ingredient in being a good follower. Followers, he maintains, share a number of essential qualities:

- They manage themselves well.
- They are committed to the organization and to a purpose, principle, or person outside themselves.
- They build up their competence and focus their efforts for maximum impact.
- They are courageous, honest, and credible. (144)

Once followership is built up, the other steps in the alternative rule's chain unfold in a manner that inspires performance and brings about extraordinary results. The traditional rule, by contrast, is based on authority and determinism. The likely result is the establishment of subordination rather than followership in the school, with mediocre rather than extraordinary results.

The Issue of Getting and Maintaining Compliance

The Traditional Rule. To manage compliance:

1. *Identify and announce your goals* (what are your major objectives?).
2. *Use goals to develop work requirements* (decide how the work will be done).
3. *Use work requirements to develop your compliance strategy* (given above, figure out how you will get people to do what they are supposed to do).
4. *Observe involvement and commitment consequences and correct as necessary* (are people properly motivated? If not, figure ways to motivate them).

The Problem. The organizational theorist Amitai Etzioni (1961) noted that one universal requirement of management is the need to obtain and maintain compliance. By compliance he means how schools get teachers and students involved in their work in the first place and how this involvement is maintained over time. A key point in his compliance theory is that the compliance strategy the manager uses to obtain and maintain involvement has a powerful influence on forming the kind of identification and attachment people have for their work and for the school itself, on shaping the goals of the school, and on the kind and character of work that takes place within the school as goals are pursued. *This is so even when goals and work requirements are set first.* Goals and work requirements are ultimately shaped to fit the means that schools use to get and keep teachers involved in their teaching and to get and keep students involved in their learning. These means then influence the kind and degree of involvement with work and school.

Given this influence it is too chancy to let the compliance strategy evolve naturally as a result of stated goals and work requirements. Some compliance strategies, whether evolved deliberately or accidentally, can result in the emergence of dysfunctional school goals and work processes regardless of what is intended, with negative effects on involvement. Consider, for example, a prison that has as its goal order among the inmates. To achieve this goal it relies on the establishment of closely monitored daily routines and a system of compliance based on punishment for infractions. As a result, prisoners became alienated and would not choose freely to stay in prison. Alienated involvement reinforces the use of rules and punishment to maintain compliance. Changing the goal for this prison from order to rehabilitation will not likely be accomplished without changing what prisoners do and the means for ensuring compliance with the new system. Prisoners will have to come to see the value of rehabilitation, and the activities they engage in will have to be more meaningful to them.

Etzioni (1961) suggests that the strategies an organization or manager uses to get and keep people involved can be grouped into three broad categories:

1. *Coercive* (people, students, and teachers, for example, are forced by the threat of penalties)

2. *Remunerative* (people are attracted by the promise of tangible rewards such as money, career advancement, grades, working conditions, political advantage, enhanced social standing)

3. *Normative* (people are compelled because they believe what they are doing is right and good and/or because they find involvement intrinsically satisfying)

Each of the three compliance strategies results in a particular kind of involvement, which in turn shapes the nature and character of school work and school goals. These relationships are illustrated as follows:

	School A	School B	School C
The School's Dominant Compliance Strategy	*Coercion:* Force people by using bureaucratic controls and penalties for infractions	*Remunerative:* Provide people with material rewards in exchange for involvement	*Normative:* Bond people to shared values, beliefs, and norms
Resulting Involvement of Teachers and Students	*Indifferent,* often alienated (they won't be involved unless they have to)	*Calculated* (they will be involved as long as they get something of value back in exchange)	*Moral* (they will be involved because they believe it is the right thing to do)

How the Work of Teaching and Learning Gets Done	Routinely (the hand works only)	Instrumentally (the mind drives the hand)	Intrinsically (Mind, hand, and heart work together)
The Resultant Dominant Goal of Management	Maintain order by getting and keeping control	Barter by making the best deal and monitoring the deal, patching cracks that appear	Develop and maintain a strong culture

Given the powerful chain of events that results from choice of compliance, the traditional rule needs to be inverted so that principal and school begin first with the compliance strategy.

The Alternative Rule. To manage compliance:

1. *First establish your compliance strategy* (how do we want to involve people in work and keep them involved? Use the strategy that reflects desired involvement).

2. *Develop complementary work requirements* (what kind of connections will people need to make for them to be properly involved?).

3. *Decide on work strategy* (given the connections desired, what kind of work designs and settings do we need?).

4. *Evaluate* (what kind of commitment and involvement is observed? Make adjustment in compliance strategy if necessary).

Moral involvement has the best chance of ensuring and maintaining inspired commitment and performance from students, teachers, and parents. Strategic commitment to moral involvement does not preclude the tactical use of coercive and remunerative compliance, but it does suggest that the overarching framework for compliance must be normative.

The Issue of Monitoring and Controlling People and Events

The Traditional Rule. *Hands-on management gets results* (the principal should be on top of things by supervising firsthand and monitoring closely what people do).

The Problem. There is a great deal of emphasis on the importance of management by walking around (MBWA), and for good reason. This tactic provides an opportunity for principals to engage in conversations with teachers and others about their work, to communicate ideas, to exchange perceptions, and to highlight important aspects of school life. Further, MBWA can be viewed as a symbolic act that gives evidence of the principal's interest in the work of the school. But management by walking around should not be confused with close supervision or a system of monitoring that is designed to ensure that people are doing what they are supposed to.

Perhaps the Hanson Corporation best exemplifies the shortcomings of the "hands-on management gets result" rule. In describing its corporate philosophy, Hanson, owner of 13 companies including Jacuzzi, Kaiser, British Ever Ready, and SCM Chemicals, stated: "The problem with hands on management is what happens when you take the hands off" (*New York Times*, 1989). Not only do close supervision and tight monitoring have a tendency to put a cap on performance and discourage entrepreneurship; they create dependency. In tomorrow's world, self-management will be increasingly important to success. Dependency will need to be exchanged for interdependency and bureaucratic authority for moral. Peters (1989b) points out that one of the paradoxes of control is "less is more." In his words, "Less paper-driven central control and more genuinely seated self control for those closest to the action translate into tight controls overall."

The Alternative. When it comes to control, practice tight-loose management, but get it right. Emphasize developing self-management in others and building commitment to ideas.

Tight-loose management, an idea proposed by Peters and Waterman (1982), seeks to tightly connect people to values, commitments, and purposes but to free them up so that they are able to choose the ways and means by which these values and purposes might be embodied. The leadership needed to practice this role is one of the themes of chapters 5 and 6.

The Issue of Developing a Motivational Strategy

The Traditional Rule. What gets rewarded gets done.

The Problem. This rule cannot be disputed. What gets rewarded does get done. But what happens when rewards are not available to principals, teachers, students, or parents? Unfortunately, the rule's flip side is true, too. What does not get rewarded does not get done.

Relying on rewards to obtain compliance leads to calculated involvement (Etzioni, 1961). Further, this rule has a tendency to change other kinds of work involvement to calculated. A student, for example, might be engaged in a learning activity because of its intrinsic interest. No gold stars, grades, or other external rewards are provided for her or his involvement. Once such rewards are introduced, the student's connection to the learning activity has a tendency to change from intrinsic to extrinsic. Take the rewards away and the student is not likely to engage further in the activity (Deci and Ryan, 1985; Greene and Lepper, 1974). By the same token, teachers who are engaged in certain kinds of activities for moral reasons—that is, because they feel a sense of obligation or believe that something is right or important to do—forsake moral involvement for calculated once rewards (or punishments) are introduced.

The Alternative. What is rewarding gets done, gets done well, and gets done without close supervision or other controls. What we believe in and feel obligated to do because of moral commitments gets done, gets done well, and gets done without close supervision or other controls.

Calculated involvement may be able to get people to do what they are supposed to as long as rewards are forthcoming, but it is not a potent enough strategy to inspire extraordinary performance. A new theory of management for the principalship needs to subsume such ideas as what-gets-rewarded-gets-done into a broader motivational strategy that recognizes the importance of morality, emotions, and social bonds (Etzioni, 1988:xii). Though often underplayed and sometimes overlooked in traditional motivation theories, what counts most to people are what they believe, how they feel, and the shared norms and cultural messages that emerge from the small groups and communities with which they identify. Some principals, for example, refuse promotion or transfer because they feel a sense of obligation to see projects they initiated through to conclusion and thus give up such extrinsic gains as higher salaries, career advancement, and more prestige.

Following Etzioni (1988) a new theory of management must provide for the development of motivation strategies that are based on psychological and moral authority as well as bureaucratic authority. Some key dimensions of such a strategy appear below.

Authority Type	The Rules	Why People Behave	Motivational Type	Involvement
Bureaucratic authority	What gets rewarded gets done	Extrinsic gain	Instrumental	Calculated
Psychological authority	What is rewarding gets done	Intrinsic gain	Expressive	Intrinsic
Moral authority	What is good gets done	Duty/ obligation	Moral	Moral

Controlling Events or Probabilities?

Both traditional and new management and leadership theories are theories about control. Without some minimum level of control no organization can survive; thus, control is a managerial imperative. Control is intended to reduce ambiguity and indeterminancy, thus increasing reliability and predictability. For example, both clockworks and clockworks-gone-awry theories want the same thing—to get the cogs and gears moving in reliable and predictable ways. But how this control is sought differs depending on the theory one has in mind. The traditional theory seeks to increase control over events and people, which is a *power over* approach to leadership and management. The new theory, by contrast, seeks to control probabilities—the probability that shared goals and purposes are embodied and reached. This is a *power to* approach to management and leadership. Often, increasing probabilities means giving up control over events and people.

One important key to seeking and maintaining control is to solve the *coordination paradox*. As Mintzberg (1979) points out:

> Every organized human activity . . . gives rise to two fundamental and opposing requirements: the *division of labor* into various tasks to be performed and the *coordination* of these tasks to accomplish the activity. The structure of an organization can be captured simply as the sum total of ways in which it divides its labor into distinct tasks and then achieves coordination among them. (2)

Every school faces the same problem: How should the work of teaching and learning be divided, and, once divided, how should it be coordinated so that control is maintained and things make sense as a whole? Each person has something important to do, but it must be done in coordination with what others are doing if schools are to work well. As is the case with most problems of control, tackling the coordination paradox would be much easier if schooling was largely the linear and tightly structured world of the neats and if the goal was to achieve a routine level of competence. All one would need to do would be to practice traditional management leadership. But in a largely nonlinear, loosely structured Scruffy world when the goal is inspired levels of commitment and extraordinary performance, solving the paradox is more complex.

Solving the Coordination Paradox

It is useful to think of six fundamental control strategies that can be used to help solve the coordination paradox: direct supervision, standardizing the work processes, standardizing outcomes, emphasizing professional socialization, emphasizing purposes, and structuring for collegiality and natural interdependence.* Though all six of the strategies should be used tactically at one time or another, it makes a difference which of the six or which combination is the school's basic strategy for achieving control.

The matching of strategy to the amount and kind of complexity found in the work to be done and in the work environment is key. *This matching is critical, for if the strategy used does not fit, the level of complexity will be changed to match the strategy.* This is a variation of the ominous organizational rule "Form should follow function or function will be shaped to fit the form." Accordingly, a simple control strategy applied to the normally complex work of teaching will simplify this work, with negative effects on what is learned and how it is learned. The six control strategies are summarized in the following paragraphs.

Direct Supervision

The simplest way to control the work of people who have different responsibilities is by having one of those persons take responsibility for the work of others by providing directions, close supervision, inspection, and otherwise executing the

---

*This discussion of control strategies is based largely on the typology proposed by Mintzberg (1979). His typology reflects the conclusions of Simon (1957) and March and Simon (1958). Important to the discussion as presented here is the work of Weick (1982) and Peters and Waterman (1982). See also Sergiovanni (1987b; 1990).

well-known planning, organizing, controlling, directing, motivating, and evaluating linear chain of management functions. In effect, as Mintzberg (1979) points out, one brain coordinates several hands. This simple approach to control works best for simple work that is done in a routine fashion. Direct supervision is a highly appropriate control strategy for a fast-food restaurant, but not for a school.

Standardizing Work Processes

Mintzberg (1979) refers to standardizing work processes as coordination achieved on the drawing board before the work is actually undertaken. This strategy works best in an environment that is highly determinant and predictable. Work processes are standardized when what needs to be done is specified in great detail and when how one does it is programmed. Very detailed and tightly connected curriculum and teaching and evaluating alignment strategies that make up "instructional delivery systems" are examples of standardizing work processes.

Standardizing Outputs

Standardizing outputs is accomplished by requiring everyone to produce similar products or to reach the same level of performance. In schools we do this by relying heavily on standardized test scores, measurable objectives, and generic teaching behaviors as a way to get people to do what they are supposed to when they are supposed to. But standardizing outputs is potentially different from standardizing work processes in that once the output requirements are set, people are essentially free to decide how they are going to accomplish them.

Providing discretion over means is a strength of this strategy. The question, however, is whether output requirements can be standardized and specified in sufficient detail and at the same time not result in undue narrowing of the curriculum and undue neglect of individual differences. Further, does standardizing the outputs ultimately compromise the degrees of freedom people have with respect to work processes? For example, defining quality schooling as levels of gains on standardized tests may dictate how principals and students will spend time, what they will learn, and how they will learn it to the exclusion of other more suitable or better choices.

Professional Socialization

By relying on professional socialization one need not standardize either work processes or outputs and can still solve the coordination paradox (Mintzberg, 1979). *Professional socialization* refers to the upgrading and standardizing of the knowledge base for teaching and emphasizing one's professional obligations as a teacher. Once a professional level of training and socialization has been accomplished, teachers and other educational workers will presumably know what to do, when they ought to do it, and how to do it. Professional socialization is the way in which more advanced professions such as medicine solve the coordination paradox. As Mintzberg points out, "When an anesthesiologist and a surgeon meet in the operating room to remove an appendix, they need hardly communicate; by virtue of their respective training, they know exactly what to expect of each other" (7). Though professional socialization has much merit, it is less a strategy available to principals for solving the coordination paradox and more a long-term strategy to upgrade the teaching profession itself. As this upgrading occurs, issues of control will become less difficult to resolve.

Purposing and Shared Values

Karl Weick (1982) noted that in schools

> [A]dministrators must be attentive to the "glue" that holds loosely coupled systems together because such forms are just barely systems. In fact, this borderline condition is their strength, in the sense that it allows local adjustment and storage of novel remedies. It is also their point of vulnerability, because such systems can quickly dissolve into anarchy. . . . The effective administrator . . . makes full use of symbol management to tie the system together. People need to be part of sensible projects. Their action becomes richer, more confident, and more satisfying when it is linked with important underlying themes, values, and movements.

Purposing and shared values provide the substance for symbol management and are the "glue" that bonds people together in a loosely connected world. Traditional management theory provides that teachers and others respond to superordinates and to the requirements of the management system. In the new theory a new kind of hierarchy needs to be envisioned—one that places purposing and shared values at the apex and teachers, students, parents, as well as principals below. Once common purposes and shared values are in place, they become compass points and mileposts for guiding what is to be done and how. As Selznick (1957) observed, "The need for centralization declines as the homogeneity of personnel increases. . . . [W]hen the premises of official policy are understood and widely accepted, centralization is more readily dispensable." (113). Purposing and shared values are key themes in the discussion of leadership that appears in Part II.

Collegiality and Natural Interdependence

Collegiality refers to the extent common work values are shared and teachers work together and help each other as a result of these values. *Natural interdependence* has to do with the extent to which teachers must work together and cooperate in order to get the job done properly. In both cases the coordination paradox is solved by the process of informal communications and the need for people to cooperate with each other in order for each to be successful.

The New Theory and Control

Professional socialization, purposing and shared values, and collegiality and natural interdependence are unique in that they are able to solve the coordination paradox under nonlinear and loosely structured conditions by providing the kind of normative power needed to get people to meet their commitments. A new theory of management for the principalship must give primary attention to these methods of control, not only because they match the complexity of schooling but because of the negative consequences of work simplification inherent in using the first three. As Mintzberg (1971) notes, direct supervision is effective for simple work. But as work becomes more complex, the emphasis needs to shift from direct supervision to standardizing the work, to standardizing the outputs, and, finally, to emphasizing professional socialization, purposing, colleagueship, and natural interdependence. He points out that if the coordination strategy does not match the work to be done, then the work changes to match the coordinating strategy. Simplifying the work of the school has regressive effects on the quality of teaching and learning.

Theory and School Organization

Good organization provides the administrative structures, arrangements, and coordinating mechanisms needed to facilitate teaching and learning. What are the implications of the new management theory for how we organize schools?

Some Basic Principles of Organizing

Whatever decisions are made about organizing, the new theory suggests that they should reflect the following basic principles:

1. The principle of *cooperation*. Cooperative teaching arrangements facilitate teaching and enhance learning. Further, they help overcome the debilitating effects of the isolation that presently characterizes teaching. In successful schools organizational structures enhance cooperation among teachers.

2. The principle of *empowerment*. Feelings of empowerment among teachers contribute to ownership and increase commitment and motivation to work. When teachers feel like pawns rather than originators of their own behavior, they respond with reduced commitment, mechanical behavior, indifference, and, in extreme cases, dissatisfaction and alienation. In successful schools organizational structures enhance empowerment among teachers.

3. The principle of *responsibility*. Most teachers and other school professionals want responsibility. Responsibility upgrades the importance and significance of their work and provides a basis for recognition of their success. In successful schools organizational structures encourage teacher responsibility.

4. The principle of *accountability*. Accountability is related to empowerment and responsibility. It provides the healthy measure of excitement, challenge, and importance that raises the stakes just enough so that achievement means something. In successful schools organizational structures allow teachers to be accountable for their decisions and achievements.

5. The principle of *meaningfulness*. When teachers find their jobs to be meaningful, jobs not only take on a special significance but also provide teachers with feelings of intrinsic satisfaction. In successful schools organizational structures provide for meaningful work.

6. The principle of *ability-authority*. The noted organizational theorist Victor Thompson (1965) stated that the major problem facing modern organizations is the growing gap existing between those who have authority to act but not ability and those who have ability to act but not authority. This principle seeks to place those who have ability to act in the forefront of decision making. In successful schools organizational structures promote authority based on ability. In schools and school districts where it is necessary for authority to be formally linked to one's position in the organizational hierarchy, day-by-day practice is characterized by formal and informal delegation of this authority to those with ability.

As these principles are manifested in the ways in which schools are organized, schools increase their capacity to respond to their problems, principals are able to lead more effectively, teaching is enhanced, and learning increases.

Organizational Intelligence

The six basic principles described above help schools to become "smarter" as they pursue teaching and learning objectives. Smarter schools are better able to efficiently and effectively use existing human resources than are "average" schools. Smarter schools are more intelligent organizationally. Gerald Skibbens (1974) defines *organizational intelligence* as the sum of the organization's ability to perceive, process information, reason, be imaginative, and be motivated. He maintains that as different dimensions and features of organization are emphasized, these intelligence indicators can be increased or decreased. His ideas are illustrated in Table 3-1. Across the top of the table are standard organizational variables such as span of control, degree of centralized decision making, emphasis on ability-authority, emphasis on formalization, and so on. The left-hand margin contains the indicators of organizational intelligence. The links between the two are provided within the table.

Consider, for example, the organizational variable "Specificity of Job Goals." Skibbens asserts that low specification or avoiding the specification of detailed objectives leads to increased organizational *perception* since individuals are required to focus attention on overall goals and aims; enhances *meaning* by widening the data base for decision making as individuals use their own resources, talents, and interests rather than highly structured and programmed objectives; enhances *reason* by linking decisions, activities, and behaviors to broader purposes rather than to fragmented and smaller objectives that often become ends in themselves; and enhances *motivation* by providing discretion to individuals and groups and by building commitment.

As you review the links between intelligence and organization, to what extent do you recognize the six basic principles of administration? The principle of empowerment, for example, is embedded in each of the organizational variables. As organizations take on configurations that encourage empowerment, each aspect of organizational intelligence increases. To what extent are the principles of cooperation, responsibility, accountability, meaningfulness, and ability-authority embodied in the organizational features contributing to intelligence?

Skibbens's conception of organizational intelligence and its link to how the organization structures itself may be more metaphorical than real; nonetheless, the idea is sufficiently powerful and intriguing to be worth further consideration. He asserts that as organizations are structured in ways that enhance their "smartness," human intelligence increases. In your view, is there a relationship between the development and growth of a school organization's perception, memory, reasoning, imagination, and motivation and similar characteristics in the organizational functioning of that school's classrooms? Further, are these classroom organizational features contributors to enhanced student perception, memory, reasoning, imagination, and motivation—the building blocks of human intellectual development? If these assertions are plausible, then organizational and structural features of schooling may be more important to improving teaching and learning than is now commonly thought.

The Language of Theory

The heart of any theory is the language used to describe and implement it. The words we use program our thinking about management and leadership by highlighting certain aspects of reality and covering up other parts. For example, when schooling is described as an "instructional delivery system," our mind automatically thinks about such management issues as delivery, targets and goals; steps, procedures, and schedules that promise the best delivery routes and timetables; the need to provide clear instructions to the deliverers of instruction; monitoring the delivery process; and evaluating to be sure that what is supposed to be delivered is, and on time.

Getting the Words Right

But what seems sensible and true can change when the language system being used changes. Try thinking about schooling as a "learning community." What issues now come to mind, and how are they different?

Communities, for example, can be thought of as having "centers" that are repositories of shared values that give direction, order, and meaning to community life. The center is the cultural heart of any community. Edward Shils (1961) explains:

> The center . . . is a phenomenon of the realm of values and beliefs . . . which govern the society. . . . In a sense, society has an official "religion." . . . The center is also a phenomenon of the realm of action. It is a structure of activities, of roles and persons, within the network of institutions. It is in these that the values and beliefs which are central are embodied and propounded. (119)

TABLE 3-1 Dimensions of Organizational Intelligence

	ORGANIZATIONAL VARIABLES			
Indicators of Organizational Intelligence	Span of Control	Leadership Density*	Time Span over Which Employees Can Commit Resources and Meet Goal Deadlines**	Degree of Centralization in Decision Making
Perception	A large span of control enlarges a supervisor's breadth of view and thereby increases his perception.	High density increases the number of personnel responsible for overseeing the work of others and thereby augments perception.		Decentralized decision making causes personnel throughout the organization to involve themselves in decision problems and thereby encourages perception among these personnel.
Memory	A wide span of control enlarges a supervisor's scope of concern and thereby involves him in a larger body of data and increases his memory.	High density increases the number of personnel entrusted with broad data and thereby enlarges memory.		Decentralized decision making forces personnel throughout organization to store data for future decision problems and thereby enlarges memory.
Reason		High density increases the number of personnel concerned with decision making and thereby augments reason.		Decentralized decision making brings more minds into decision-making processes and thereby augments reasoning capacity in the organization.
Imagination		High density increases the number of personnel employed to generate new ideas and thereby enlarges imagination.	A long time span allows employees to ponder problems and purposes at length, which permits imaginative ideas to arise in the mind.	Decentralized decision making causes more minds to be engaged in problem solving and thereby increases the use of imagination among personnel.
Motivation		High density increases the number of personnel with a career interest in the organization and thereby augments motivation.	A long time span enables the employee to accomplish major tasks of great importance and thereby furthers motivation.	Decentralized decision making accords greater responsibilities for important work to more personnel and thereby increases motivation.

Leadership density is substituted for *Ratio of Administrative to Production Personnel* in the original.

**With respect to Time Span the phrase *and Meet Goal Deadlines* is added.

†*Emphasizes Values over Directions* is substituted for *Versus Orders* in the original.

Source: Adapted from Gerald Skibbens, *Organizational Evolution*, New York: AMACOM, a division of the American Management Association, 1974, pp. 248–249. © Change Systems Corporation. All rights reserved.

TABLE 3–1 *(Continued)*

ORGANIZATIONAL VARIABLES

Proportion of Persons in One Unit Having Opportunity to Interact with Persons in Other Units	Quantity of Formal Rules	Specificity of Job Goals (Local vs. Global)	Advisory Content of Communications (Emphasizes Values over Directions†	Knowledge-Based Authority (vs. Position-Based)
A high proportion enlarges the exposure of personnel to activities throughout the organization and thereby increases perception.	A small quantity of rules makes personnel receptive to innovative ideas and thereby encourages perception.	A low specificity of goals causes personnel to relate to overall aims of the organization and thereby promotes a greater breadth of perception among personnel.	A high advisory content leaves more personnel with the responsibility of managing their own activities and thereby encourages greater perception.	A high knowledge orientation places a premium on awareness among personnel and thereby promotes perception in the organization.
	A small quantity of rules broadens the scope of potentially relevant data and thereby enlarges the memory in the organization.	A low specificity of goals widens the base of data relevant to individual personnel and thereby increases memory.		A high knowledge orientation forces personnel to amass data in order to advance and thereby enlarges memory.
A high proportion encourages the pooling of minds in response to problems to be solved and thereby augments reason.	A small quantity of rules exposes more procedures and practices to critical evaluation and thereby increases reason.	A low specificity of goals causes personnel to concentrate their thoughts on the ultimate objectives of the organization and thereby augments effective reason.	A high advisory content leaves more personnel with problem-solving responsibilities of their own and thereby enlarges the exercise of reason.	A high knowledge orientation furthers logical thought activity among personnel in their effort to expand their knowledge and thereby increases reason.
A high proportion tends to draw many minds into problem-solving processes and thereby enlarges the exercise of imagination.	A small quantity of rules frees the minds of personnel for creative thinking and thereby encourages imagination.		A high advisory content allows greater freedom of action among personnel and thereby encourages the use of imagination.	A high knowledge orientation encourages growth in the data base as a stimulant to new ideas and thereby promotes imagination.
A high proportion makes personnel aware of their own places in the overall functions of the organization and thereby increases motivation.	A small quantity of rules permits personnel to exercise individual preferences and thereby increases motivation.	A low specificity of goals involves personnel in the ultimate, major aims of the organization and thereby encourages higher identification and motivation.	A high advisory content promotes participatory management in the organization and thereby increases motivation.	

Different management issues emerge from the metaphor of school as learning community. How will this learning community be defined? What relationships among parents, students, teachers, and administrators are needed for us to be a community? What are our shared values, purposes, and commitments? How shall we work together to embody these? What kinds of obligations to the community should members have? How will obligations be enforced? What "wild cultures" exist (e.g., perhaps a student subculture excessively themed to football, beer, music, and sex; or devoted to mediocre academic performance or to stealing hubcaps; or a faculty subculture more concerned with its own welfare than that of the school) that provide competing and work-restricting norms? How can these wild cultures be "domesticated" and thus subsumed under the overall culture that defines our learning community?

The fact that different management issues emerge from different metaphors for schooling suggests that validity in management and leadership is both subjective and objective. The management concepts, rules, and practices that are valid for schools as learning communities are not valid for schools as instructional delivery systems, and vice versa. Validity is subjective between conceptual systems and objective within (Lakoff and Johnson, 1980). The presence of both subjective and objective validity in management is one reason why it's so hard to have a successful argument with someone who uses a language system different from yours. Further, it is hard for you to think differently about leadership, management, and schooling unless you are willing to change your own language system—the metaphors and ultimately the mindscapes that create your reality.

The Power of Language

Another important aspect of the language we use is that it can become a source of power that forces others to think in our terms. This is particularly true in instances in which one person has more hierarchical authority than another. As Greenfield (1982) explains: "Language is power. It literally makes reality appear and disappear. Those who control language control thought—and thereby themselves and others" (8). He maintains that language can be used to dominate others by building categories of thinking and logic that they must use whether they want to or not. Getting others to think in your terms is a powerful form of domination. For example, superintendents who use the language of instructional delivery systems in their protocols for evaluating principals force principals to have to defend themselves in those terms no matter how effective they might be otherwise. A similar fate awaits teachers who are evaluated by principals who control the language of evaluation.

Domination is virtually total when one person not only controls the categories that another has to use but also controls the criteria for defining effectiveness. Imagine, for example, two youngsters about to open their lunchboxes at school. One says to the other, "I bet you a soda that the fruit in my box is better than yours." The youngster then sets the criteria for *better* as follows: The redder the fruit and the rounder the fruit, the better. Unfortunately, the other youngster's lunchpail contains a banana. Had the second youngster been the one in control of the language criteria, we would have a different winner.

Winning and losing are functions of the language used (Sergiovanni, 1989a). Lakoff and Johnson (1981) summarize the subjective nature of validity as follows:

> Truth is relative to understanding, which means that there is no absolute standpoint from which to obtain absolute objective truths about the world. This does not mean that there are no truths; it means that truth is relative to our conceptual system, which is grounded in, and constantly tested by, our experiences and those of other members of our culture in our daily interactions with other people and with our physical and cultural environments (193).

Though the power of language is very real, it has not received much attention in the management literature.

Changing Our Metaphors

Since traditional management theory does not work well in nonlinear and loosely structured situations or under conditions that require extraordinary commitment and performance, a great deal is at stake in developing a new and better-fitting theory. But for this to happen, our metaphors for management, leadership, and schooling must change. Subsuming "instructional delivery system" as a tactical option under the more encompassing and strategic "learning community" is an important beginning. Two other candidates for change are the popular view of management as "running a railroad" and of problem solving as "puzzle." Though the metaphors are typically unstated, they are firmly grounded in the traditional mindscape of school management. As these and alternative metaphors are discussed, think of others that are worthy candidates for change.

In nonlinear and loosely structured situations it makes more sense to think *amoeba* instead of *railroad* (Sergiovanni, 1989b). Thinking amoeba is a rational approach to understanding the nature of administrative work. Running a school is like trying to get a giant amoeba to move from one side of the street to another. As the glob slips off the curb onto the street and begins its meandering journey, the job of the principal is to figure out how to keep it together while trying to keep it moving in the general direction of the other side. This involves pulling here, pushing there, patching holes, supporting thin parts, and breaking up logjams. The pace is fast and furious as the principal moves first here then there. Throughout, the principal is never quite sure where the glob will wind up but never loses sight of the overall goal of getting it to the other side. Mind, heart, and hand become one as the principal "plays" the glob, relying on her or his feeling for globbiness and ability to discern and anticipate patterns of movement that emerge.

How different is this view from the railroad metaphor offered in the literature—a view that would have us attempt crossing the street by first specifying our destination as a highly specific outcome and then implementing an explicit, linear, and managerial chain of planning, directing, doing, and evaluating as if context were fixed and people inanimate. This simplistic pattern might be rational for running a railroad, but it is *rationalistic* when applied to running a school. As will be discussed in Part II, leadership in an amoebalike world is very different from that needed for running the school as a railroad.

Under traditional management, solving problems resembles the solving of a *puzzle* (Lakeoff and Johnson, 1980). Puzzles represent problems for which there is only one solution, and the idea is to find that solution. When that solution is found, the puzzle is presumed to be solved once and for all. If for some reason the puzzle is scrambled, all one need do is reassemble the parts according to the original formula. One puzzle equals one solution. The problems-as-puzzles metaphor may be hopeful, but it is misleading.

A more realistic view of problem solving is one in which no single solution exists, at least for long. As soon as one begins to apply any solution to a problem, all the characteristics of the problem change, calling for a subsequent change in the originally proposed solution. To handle this indeterminancy, Lakeoff and Johnson suggest the *chemical* metaphor as a replacement for the puzzle. When using this metaphor, the solution of one's problems isn't an answer to a puzzle but metaphorically

> a large volume of liquid . . . containing all of your problems, either dissolved or in the form of precipitates, with catalysts constantly dissolving some problems (for the time being) and precipitating out others. . . . The best you can hope for is to find a catalyst that will make one problem dissolve without making another one precipitate out. And since you do not have complete control over what goes into the solution, you are constantly finding old and new problems precipitating out and present problems dissolving, partly because of your efforts and partly despite anything you do. (Lakeoff and Johnson, 1988:143–144)

Within the chemical metaphor one accepts the reality that problems cannot be made to completely disappear. The reoccurrence of problems is natural rather than negative. Temporary solutions are considered to be accomplishments rather than failures. Further, as Lakeoff and Johnson point out, principals would need to accept the fact that since no problem disappears forever, it is best to direct one's energies "toward finding out what catalysts will dissolve your most pressing problems for the longest time without precipitating out worse ones" (144).

The railroad metaphor and the puzzle metaphor are useful and make sense for determinate and tightly structured situations. The issue is which metaphor should dominate one's strategic mindscape and thus subsume the other? Learning community, amoeba, and chemical solutions can subsume their counterparts (instructional delivery system, railroad, and puzzle) but cannot be subsumed by them. For example, sometimes it's perfectly natural for an amoeba to follow the straight and narrow path of a railroad, but railroads should never meander willy nilly. Changing our metaphors is an important prerequisite for developing a new theory of management and a new leadership practice that is more responsive to the nonlinear and loosely structured world of schooling and to conditions that require extraordinary commitment and performance.

One test of a good metaphor is whether it is beautiful or not, as reflected by the language used to describe it. The language of traditional management theory lacks "aesthetic qualities." Such qualities are one important criterion that Kaplan proposes in his *Conduct of Inquiry* (1961) for validating theories. More pointedly, Mintzberg (1982) describes the language of traditional management theory as being *ugly*. In his words: "If a theory is not beautiful then the odds are good that it is not very useful" (250). Apply this rule, for example, to determine the "usefulness" of such concepts and ideas as instructional delivery system and learning community, instruction and teaching, training and educating, POSDCoRB and purposing, objectives and goals, measuring and valuing, monitoring and coaching, bureaucratic and moral, quality control and obligation, and motivate and inspire.

A Practical Theory of Educational Administration

In sum, a practical theory of educational administration should fit the complex, nonlinear, and loosely connected but real world of practice. This standard will require that we give much more attention to putting practice into theory than theory into practice. A practical theory should inform rather than prescribe practice. This standard will require that we view research and theory as more metaphorical than true. A practical theory should be concerned with what is good as well as effective. This standard will require that moral authority replace bureaucratic authority as the cornerstone for developing policies and practices. And, finally, a practical theory should be beautiful. This standard will require that an aesthetic ruler be used to evaluate the acceptability of concepts and ideas and the language used to explain them. Developing such a theory will not be easy, for the standards proposed go against the grain of customary thinking about management and leadership. As Alfred North Whitehead stated: "To know the truth partially is to distort the Universe. . . . An unflinching determination to take the whole evidence into account is the only method of preservation against the fluctuating extremes of fashionable opinion."

References

Bass, Bernard M. 1985. *Leadership and Performance Beyond Expectations*. New York: The Free Press.

Burns, James MacGregor. 1978. *Leadership*. New York: Harper & Row.

Campbell, P. J. 1974. "Evolutionary Epistemology," in P. A. Schlipp, Ed., *The Philosophy of Karl Popper*, 413–463. La Salle, IL: Open Court Press.

Cziko, Gary A. 1989. "Unpredictability and Indeterminism in Human Behavior: Arguments and Implications for Educational Research," *Educational Researcher* 18(3), 17–25.

Deal, Terrence E., and Allen A. Kennedy. 1982. *Corporate Cultures*. Reading, MA: Addison-Wesley.

Deci, Edward L., and Richard M. Ryan. 1985. *Intrinsic Motivation and Self Determinism in Human Behavior*. New York: Plenum Press.

Etzioni, Amitai. 1961. *A Comparative Analysis of Complex Organizations*. New York: The Free Press.

Etzioni, Amitai. 1988. *The Moral Dimension Toward a New Economics*. New York: The Free Press.

Friedson, Elliot. 1972. *Professional Medicine: A Study of the Sociology of Applied Knowledge*. New York: Dodd Mead.

Gleick, James. 1987. *Chaos Making a New Science*. New York: Viking Penguin.

Greene, David, and Mark R. Lepper. 1974. "How to Turn Play Into Work," *Psychology Today* 8(4).

Greenfield, Thomas B. 1982. "Against Group Mind: An Anarchistic Theory of Education," *McGill Journal of Education* 17(Winter).

Hanson Corporation, *New York Times*. 1989. Jan. 29.

Hayes, Robert H. 1985. "Strategic Planning—Forward in Reverse?" *Harvard Business Review* Nov.–Dec.

Hertzberg, Frederick. 1966. *Work and the Nature of Man*. New York: World.

Hills, Jean. 1982. "The Preparation of Educational Leaders: What's Needed and What's Next." UCEA Occasional Paper No. 8303. Columbus, OH: University Council for Educational Administration.

Hogben, Donald. 1981. "The Clinical Mind: Some Implications of Educational Research and Teacher Training," *South Pacific Journal of Teacher Education* 10(1).

James, William. (1984). *Talk to Teachers on Psychology: And to Students on Some of Life's Ideals*. New York: Henry Holt.

Kaplan, Abraham. 1961. *Conduct of Inquiry Methodology for Behavioral Sciences*. San Francisco: Chandler.

Kelly, Robert E. 1988. "In Praise of Followers," *Harvard Business Review* Nov.–Dec.

Kennedy, Mary. 1984. "How Evidence Alters Understandings and Decisions," *Education Evaluation and Policy Analysis*. 6(1).

Lakoff, George, and Mark Johnson. 1980. *The Metaphors We Live By*. Chicago: University of Chicago Press.

March, James G. 1984. "How We Talk and How We Act: Administrative Theory and Administrative Life," in T. J. Sergiovanni and J. E. Corbally, Eds., *Leadership and Organizational Culture*, 18–36. Urbana, IL: University of Illinois Press.

March, James G., and Herbert A. Simon. 1958. *Organizations*. New York: Wiley.

Mintzberg, Henry. 1979. *The Structuring of Organizations*. Englewood Cliffs, NJ: Prentice-Hall.

Mintzberg, Henry. 1982. "If You're Not Serving Bill and Barbara, Then You're Not Serving Leadership," in James G. Hunt, Una Sekaran, and Chester Schrlesheim, Eds., *Leadership Beyond Establishment Views*, 239–259. Carbondale, IL: Southern Illinois University.

Noblit, George W. 1984. "The Prospects of an Applied Ethnography for Education: A Sociology of Knowledge Interpretation," *Educational Evaluation and Policy Analysis* 97(2).

Parsons, Talcott. 1951. *Toward a General Theory of Social Action*. Cambridge, MA: Harvard University Press.

Peters, Tom. 1989a. "Structure vs. Spirit Battle Lines are Drawn," *San Antonio Light*, July 25.

Peters, Tom. 1989b. "Business Can Learn From Military Strategy," *San Antonio Light*, Jan. 24.

Peters, Tom. 1989c. "Control Paradox: Less Is More," *San Antonio Light*, July 15.

Peters, Thomas J., and Robert H. Waterman. 1982. *In Search of Excellence*. New York: Harper & Row.

Selznick, Phillip. 1957. *Leadership in Administration*. New York: Harper & Row.

Sergiovanni, Thomas J. 1987a. "The Metaphorical Use of Theories and Models in Supervision: Building a Science," *Journal of Curriculum and Supervision* 2(2), 221–233.

Sergiovanni, Thomas J. 1987. *The Principalship: A Reflective Practice Perspective.* Boston: Allyn and Bacon.

Sergiovanni, Thomas J. 1989a. "Science and Scientism in Teaching and Supervision," *Journal of Curriculum and Supervision* 4(2), 93–106.

Sergiovanni, Thomas J. 1989b. "Value-Driven Schools: The Amoeba Theory," in Herbert J. Walberg and John J. Lane, Eds., *Organizing for Learning: Toward the 21st Century,* 31–41. Reston, VA: National Association of Secondary School Principals.

Sergiovanni, Thomas J. 1990. *Value-Added Leadership: How to Get Extraordinary Performance in Schools.* New York: Harcourt Brace Jovanovich.

Shils, Edward A. 1961. "Centre and Periphery," in *The Logic of Personal Knowledge: Essays Presented to Michael Polanyi.* London: Routledge and Kegan Paul.

Simon, Herbert A. 1957. *Administrative Behavior,* 2nd ed. New York: The Free Press.

Skibbens, Gerald. 1974. *Organizational Evolution.* New York: American Management Association.

Staw, Barry. 1984. "Leadership and Persistence," in T. J. Sergiovanni and J. E. Corbally, Eds., *Leadership and Organizational Culture.* Urbana, IL: University of Illinois Press.

Taylor, Paul W. 1961. *Normative Discourse.* Englewood Cliffs, NJ: Prentice-Hall.

Thompson, Victor A. 1965. *Modern Organizations.* New York: Knopf.

Vaill, Peter B. 1969. *Managing as a Performing Art.* San Francisco: Jossey-Bass.

Weick, Karl E. 1976. "Educational Organizations as Loosely Coupled Schools," *Phi Delta Kappan* 27.

Weick, Karl E. 1986. "The Concept of Loose Coupling: An Assessment," *Organizational Theory Dialogue,* Dec.

PART II

PRINCIPAL LEADERSHIP AND SCHOOL SUCCESS

CHAPTER 4

Characteristics of
Successful Schools

Since the beginning of schooling in America the relationship between quality of schools and quality of learning for students has been accepted as an article of faith. But with the 1964 publication of Benjamin Bloom's *Stability and Change in Human Characteristics* and the 1966 publication of James Coleman's *Equality of Educational Opportunity*, this faith was broken. Many teachers and principals joined the general public in a widespread acceptance of the belief that schools were not very important.

Coleman's study suggested that social inequality, poverty, and segregated schooling were key elements in determining inadequate levels of learning for many students and that improving learning would require the correction of these social factors. Regardless of one's race or region, it was the home environment (social class and income of parents, exposure to books, need for achievement, and modeling differentials) that was far more important in explaining differences in student-learning outcomes than were school facilities, teacher salaries, or even the curriculum itself.

Bloom's classic work on the development of educational capacity reinforced the primacy of nonschool over school factors in determining the amount and extent of student learning. He noted, for example:

. . . by about 4, 50% of the variation in intelligence at age 17 is accounted for . . . in terms of intelligence measured at age 17; from conception to age 4, the individual develops 50% of his mature intelligence; from ages 4 to 8 he develops another 30%, and from ages 8 to 17, the remaining 20%. . . . We would expect the variations in the environments to have relatively little effect on the I.Q. after age 8, but would expect such a variation to have marked effect on the I.Q. before that age, with the greatest effect likely to take place between the ages of about 1 to 5. (Bloom, 1964:68)

As these ideas became accepted, principals and teachers came to believe that the home or basic educational capacity, not the school, accounted for major differences in student achievement. Some principals and teachers welcomed this news, seeing within it a legitimate excuse for their own results. After all, they reasoned, the research shows clearly that poor student performance is linked to conditions beyond control of the school.

The 1980s provided quite a different picture as to the relationship between schooling and quality of learning for students. The belief that schooling does make a difference became once more the accepted stand. Quality schooling indeed leads to quality learning, and an important key to quality schooling is the amount and kind of leadership that school principals provide directly and promote among teachers and supporting staff.

These assertions are supported by hundreds of studies on school effectiveness and success. For example, a classic study conducted in 1978 by Gilbert Austin and his colleagues compared 18 high-achieving and 12 low-achieving schools carefully selected from among all schools in Maryland, using that state's accountability data. Schools selected were considered "outliers" for scoring outside the average statistical band of test scores for all Maryland schools. This research indicated that one difference between high- and low-achieving schools was the impact of the principal. In higher-achieving schools, principals exerted strong leadership, participated directly and frequently in instructional matters, had higher expectations for success, and were oriented toward academic goals. It seems clear from this study, and many others like it, that quality of schooling is greatly influenced by direct leadership from the principal.

Direct principal leadership, however, is only part of the answer to establishing successful schools. Many experts and many supporting studies point out that equally significant—perhaps even most significant—is the amount and quality of leadership density that exists in schools. *Leadership density* refers to the total leadership available from teachers, support staff, parents, and others on behalf of the school's work. Of course, the principal plays a key role in building and maintaining leadership density. In this sense, principal leadership can be understood as an enabling process. Principals practice enabling leadership when they help teachers, students, and staff to function better on behalf of the school and its purposes, to engage more effectively in the work and play of the school, and to promote the achievement of the school's objectives. It is crucial to build up the leadership capacity of others, and in this sense the principal is a leader of leaders.

Effectiveness and School Success

Are *effective* and *successful* schools the same? The terms are often used interchangeably to describe the same school or to communicate the same level of accomplishment, but this can cause confusion. *Effectiveness* has both common and technical meanings. It is commonly understood to mean the ability to produce a desired effect. Thus, in a sense any school that produces effects desired by some group would be considered effective by that group. But, technically speaking, within educational circles, school effectiveness has taken on a specific and special meaning. An effective school is understood to be a school whose students achieve well in basic skills as measured by achievement tests. The dimensions of management, teaching, and leadership that are included in the school effectiveness model have been convincingly linked to this limited view of effectiveness, but not to broader, higher-order, and more qualitative intellectual and academic views of effectiveness.

To avoid confusion this book emphasizes the image of "successful" rather than "effective" schooling. *Successful* is meant to communicate a new and broader definition of effectiveness. The differences between the two "models" of schooling are compared across several dimensions in Appendix 4–1. The successful school image is more comprehensive and expansive and seems more consistent with the high-quality schooling that most Americans, rich and poor, urban and rural, new and old, want for their children (Goodlad, 1983).

With these distintions in mind, let's address the question What is a good school? How does one know such a school when it is seen? Can "goodness" be defined? Just how does one determine if a school is doing a good job or not?

Such questions usually receive quick answers: For example, graduates of good high schools get jobs or are admitted to college in larger numbers. Test scores of students are at or above average for similar groups of students. High school teachers remark that incoming students from the junior high are well prepared. Students spend approximately two hours each evening on homework. A survey of the number of books checked out of the school library during the last year reveals that students in that school check out more books than students in other area schools. The average salary of former students 10 years after graduation is high. Attendance at school is up. Teachers agree as to what the purposes of schooling are. Discipline problems are on the decline. Students select tougher courses. Teachers report that students are working harder. Students report that teachers are working harder. Surveys indicate that students are satisfied with their school. Parents indicate that if they had to choose between sending their children to this or another school, they would choose this one. Faculty members carefully plan lessons. Tax referenda are passed. The North Central Association Accrediting Team praises the school. Faculty members are available to students. The Christmas play, the Chanukkah program, and other seasonal pageantry are well attended year after year, and parents report being pleased with the results. The school has a winning football team. Faculty members work together, share ideas, and help one another. The number of Merit Scholars is increasing. Teacher turnover is low. The number of students referred to mental health services is low when compared with similar schools. More students study foreign languages. More students study art. More students study physics. Morale of faculty is high. . . .

This list of responses could easily be extended. Clearly, the problem of defining what is a good school is more complex than it seems at first appearances. Indeed, educators and parents alike often have difficulty in coming to grips with an adequate description, definition, or list of criteria.

Still, intuitively "goodness" is a known quality no matter how difficult it is to precisely articulate its essence. Joan Lipsitz (1984), for example, found that the principals of the successful schools she studied had difficulty in articulating what it was that made their schools special or what the dimensions of successfulness were. "You will have to come and see my school" was the typical and predictable response.

Similarly, we know successful schools when we experience them, though we cannot always specify their precise components. In successful schools things "hang together"; a sense of purpose exists, rallying people to a common cause; work has meaning, and life is significant; teachers and students work together and with spirit; and accomplishments are readily recognized. To say that successful schools have high morale or achieve higher test scores or send more students to college—and to leave it at that—is to miss the point. Success is all of these and more.

Should we expect more from our schools than the satisfaction of knowing that they are performing "up to the standard" and that students are competent performers as measured by such typical indicators as test scores? The situation is sufficiently poor in some schools that, if they were indeed to achieve such a modest standard, it would be cause for celebration. Most surveys indicate that basic skill learning and developing fundamental academic competence (the indicators of effectiveness common to the school effectiveness literature) are paramount school goals in the minds of parents and teachers. But the question of success does not end with this emphasis. Pushed a bit further, most parents and teachers provide a more expansive view of school success. Educational goals typically espoused by parents include developing a love of learning, critical-thinking and problem-solving skills, aesthetic appreciation, curiosity and creativity, and interpersonal competence. Parents want a complete education for their children (see, for example, Goodlad, 1983). Indeed, our society requires a complete education for its youth if it is to survive and flourish. What is needed is that our young become cultured and educated citizens, able to participate fully in our economic and social society, not just trained workers with limited potential for such participation. These aspirations include all of America's youth including urban and rural poor and minority students, for whom more limited definitions of school effectiveness are often applied.

Important differences exist among incompetent, competent, and successful schools and the leadership that characterizes these schools. Schools managed by incompetent leaders simply don't get the job done. Typically, such schools are characterized by confusion and inefficiency in operation and malaise in human climate. Student achievement is lower in such schools. Students may not be giving a fair day's work for a fair day's pay. Student absenteeism, discipline, and violence may be problems. Conflict may characterize interpersonal relationships among faculty or between faculty and supervisors, and parents may feel isolated from the school. Competent schools, by contrast, measure up to these and other measures of effectiveness. They get the job done in a satisfactory matter. In this sense they are considered to be effective; successful schools, on the other hand, exceed the ordinary expectations necessary to be considered satisfactory. In such schools, students accomplish far more, and teachers work much harder, than can ordinarily be expected.

How Researchers Identify Effective Schools

Researchers investigating the characteristics of effective schools typically rely on such important student outcome data as test scores. The outlier concept, as used in the Austin (1974) study cited earlier, is an example. Schools having students who perform significantly higher than the statistical average are compared with schools having students whose scores are within or below this average range. The now famous Edmonds (1979) and Brookover and Lezotte (1979) studies of more and less effective elementary schools serving primarily urban, poor, and minority students are examples of this approach. Effectiveness in these schools was determined by pupil performance on standardized tests of reading and math skills.

Student achievement in basic skills is undoubtedly the most popular criterion for determining an effective school. One reason for its popularity is the ease with which one is able to define and measure school effectiveness. But the reliance on test scores to identify effective schools is not without its critics. Rowan, Dwyer, and Bossert (1982), for example, feel that effectiveness is too often narrowly defined:

> The use of achievement scores as the sole criteria for judging school effectiveness is common. For example, virtually all the studies in the effective schools tradition employ this unidimensional criterion. Yet as Steers (1975) pointed out in his general discussion of measures of organizational effectiveness, most theorists and participants in organizations view effectiveness as a multidimensional construct. By viewing school effectiveness as a unidimensional phenomenon, current research neglects a number of interesting and important issues. For example, numerous constituencies view the purpose of schooling as broader than simple academic training. Citizenship training, development of self-esteem, independence training, and the development of self-discipline exist as important alternative goals. By focusing exclusively on academic achievement, much of the literature on school effectiveness has ignored the relationship between achieving effectiveness in academic outcomes and achieving effectiveness among these other dimensions. We urge more attention to the relationship between these various criteria, a process that would require the development of a multidimensional view of school effectivensss. (8)

Some researchers provide a more expansive definition of school effectiveness. Joan Lipsitz (1984) used the following six general criteria in identifying the successful middle schools she studied:

1. These schools contain safe and orderly environments where student achievement is up to or exceeds expectations. More specifically, scores on standardized achievement tests are above or approach the county mean or the mean of some other comparative reference group; low absenteeism and turnover rates among students and staff exist; vandalism and victimization are not frequent occurrences or indeed are nonexistent; there is lack of destructive graffiti; and low suspension rates for students exist.

2. These schools respond appropriately to the developmental levels of students. Basic skills and other intellectual objectives are considered important, but are best pursued in a healthy psychological environment for students.

3. Teachers and students in these schools pursue competency in learning.

4. These schools are accepted within the context of the local community and its expectations.

5. These schools enjoy a reputation for excellence in the community.

6. These schools function well in response to or despite national issues such as desegregation, busing, and other problems. (11)

It is clear that measurement and evaluation experts and organizational sociologists who specialize in studying effectiveness in all kinds of organizations feel that many dimensions of effectiveness need to be accounted for. Some of these dimensions are illustrated in Exhibit 4-1 in the form of criteria and measurements. It is possible, nonetheless, to group various dimensions into a handful of primary approaches based on theme similarities. Three such approaches come to mind: the goal-attainment approach, the environmental response approach and the process approach (Robbins, 1983:24-33). These approaches will be examined in the sections that follow.

EXHIBIT 4-1 Dimensions and Measures of School Effectiveness

School measurement and evaluation experts, along with organizational sociologists who specialize in studying effectiveness of other organizations, concentrate on many dimensions as they conduct their studies and make their calculations. School effectiveness researchers typically take a more limited view. But most experts agree that effectiveness is a multidimensional concept. The following list illustrates some criteria and measurements often used.

1. *Productivity*—the extent to which students, teachers, groups, and schools accomplish outcomes or services intended.

2. *Efficiency*—the ratio of individual and school performance to the costs involved for that performance. Costs are calculated not only in terms of time and dollars but also in objectives or outcomes neglected so that other objectives or outcomes might be emphasized or accomplished.

3. *Quality*—the level and quality of accomplishments, outcomes, performance, and services of individuals and the school.

4. *Growth*—improvements in quality of offerings, responsiveness and innovativeness, talent, and general competence when a school's present status is compared with its own past state.

5. *Absenteeism*—number of times not present and frequency of nonattendance by teachers, students, and other school workers.

6. *Turnover*—the number of voluntary transfers and terminations on the part of students, faculty, and other workers.

7. *Teacher job satisfaction*—the extent to which teachers are pleased with the various job outcomes they are receiving.

8. *Student satisfaction*—the extent to which students are pleased with the various schooling outcomes they are receiving.

9. *Motivation*—the willingness and drive strength of teachers, students, and other school workers as they engage in the work of the school.

10. *Morale*—the general good feeling that teachers, parents, students, and others have for the school, its traditions, and its goals, and the extent to which they are happy to be a part of the school.

11. *Cohesion*—the extent to which students and teachers like one another, work well together, communicate fully and openly, and coordinate their efforts.

12. *Flexibility-adaptation*—the ability of the school to change its procedures and ways of operating in response to community and other environmental changes.

13. *Planning and goal setting*—the degree to which the members plan future steps and engage in goal-setting behavior.

14. *Goal consensus*—the extent to which community members, parents, and students agree that the same goals exist for the school.

15. *Internalization of organizational goals*—the acceptance of the school's goals, and belief by parents, teachers, and students that the school's goals are right and proper.

EXHIBIT 4–1 *(Continued)*

16. *Leadership-management skills*—the overall level of ability of principals, supervisors, and other leaders as they perform school-centered tasks.

17. *Information management and communications*—the completeness, efficiency of dissemination and accuracy of information considered critical to the school's effectiveness by all interested parties including teachers, parents, and the community at large.

18. *Readiness*—the probability that the school could successfully perform some specified task or accomplish some specified goal if asked to do so.

19. *Utilization of the environment*—the extent to which the school interacts successfully with its community and other arenas of its environment and acquires the necessary support and resources to function effectively.

20. *Evaluation by external entities*—favorable assessments of the school by individuals, organizations, and groups in the community and in the general environment within which it interacts.

21. *Stability*—the ability of the school to maintain certain structures, functions, and resources over time and particularly during periods of stress.

22. *Shared influence*—the degree to which individuals in the school participate in making decisions that affect them directly.

23. *Training and development emphasis*—the amount of effort and resources that the school devotes to developing the talents of teachers and other school workers.

24. *Achievement emphasis*—the extent to which the school places a high value on achieving existing and new goals.

Adapted from John P. Campbell, "On the Nature of Organizational Effectiveness," in P. S Goodman, J. M. Pennings, and Associates, Eds., *New Perspectives on Organizational Effectiveness*, 36–41, San Francisco: Jossey-Bass, 1977.

The Goal-Attainment Approach to School Effectiveness

Common sense tells us that a good school is one that achieves its goals and purposes. This truism provides the basis for popular definitions of effectiveness articulated by well-known experts. Etzioni (1964:8), for example, defines effectiveness simply as the degree to which an organization achieves its goals; Steers (1975:555) urges that in measuring effectiveness, one should give attention to the operational goals that an organization is pursuing; and Torbert (undated:10) would define effectiveness as the congruence between organizational purposes and organizational outcomes. In his view a school would be increasingly effective as its outcomes become increasingly congruent with its purposes and, by contrast, increasingly ineffective as incongruence increases.

Goal-Oriented Research. Despite the obvious fact that student and school outcomes are varied, and despite the widely stated belief that a multidimensional approach is needed to determine what a good school is, effectiveness *in practice* is viewed as largely a unidimensional phenomenon. Most of the research on school effectiveness relies solely on student achievement, as measured by standardized tests, as the sole criterion of effectiveness. Advocates of this unidimensional approach readily admit that schools have other purposes and goals, but they argue nonetheless that schools unsuccessful in teaching most students the basic skills will not be considered successful by students, parents, and other audiences to which they must respond. Squires, Huitt, and Segars (1981), for example, state:

> To be sure, testing doesn't tell the whole story, nor is it the only valued result of education. Indeed, some skills—such as writing, oral language skills, and group problem solving—are difficult to assess with traditional standardized instruments, but that does not mean they should be ignored as important outcomes or significant parts of the curriculum. We use standardized tests as benchmarks for a school's success because they are more reliable, valid and accepted than other outcome measures. (7)

It is clear that student achievement does and should play a significant role in determining effectiveness in schooling. After all, the schools are institutions designed to promote the intellectual development and basic skill competence of its students. Though successful schools are concerned with more than student achievement, such measured achievement remains critical.

Successful schooling should be measured and determined on the basis of standardized content and national norms as well as on content and learning objectives considered important by local school authorities and parents. The first is an example of norm-referenced measurement; the second, of criterion-referenced measurement. Relying only on norm-referenced measurements provides a biased and limited view of school success. Even if norm-referenced testing is balanced with criterion-referenced testing, the result is still a limited definition that represents more testimony to a school's basic competence than it does to its success. This is a point made by Ronald Edmonds (Brandt, 1982), a pioneering school effectiveness researcher:

> I acknowledge that available standardized tests do not adequately measure the appropriate ends of education. However, I also urge that it is important for students to learn minimum academic skills as a prerequisite to successful access to the next level of schooling. The reality is that poor children especially are sometimes portrayed as having made satisfactory progress when they're actually not even close to mastery. I find that unacceptable. I think it enormously important that students and their parents know how they are doing in relation to what they are required to do. And despite all the limitations of standardized tests, I would argue as forcefully as I can that they are—at this moment—the most realistic, accurate, and equitable basis for portraying individual pupil progress. (14)

In response to the problem of using such test scores as the sole criterion, Edmonds replies:

> Excellent means that students become independent, creative thinkers, learn to work cooperatively, and so on, which is also enormously important. I see no reason why making the school instructionally effective ought to preclude educational excellence. In fact, it is hard for me to conceive of an educator who can obtain

excellence but who is incapable of managing these rather more modest chores. I would take the position that you have to earn the right to experiment with something as precious as excellence. The way you earn it is by just teaching the kids to read and write. (14)

Thus, it is clear that many researchers who use test scores as the sole criterion recognize that they are concerned more with basic competence in schooling than with broader indicators of success. Still, critics of this unidimensional approach cannot be ignored. As Rowan, Dwyer, and Bossert (1982) point out in their criticisms of shortcomings in the school effectiveness research:

> By viewing school effectiveness as a unidimensional phenomenon, current research neglects a number of interesting and important issues. For example, numerous constituencies view the purpose of schooling as broader than simple academic training. Citizenship training, development of self esteem, independence training, and the development of self discipline exists as important alternative goals. By focusing exclusively on academic achievement, much of the literature on school effectiveness has ignored the relationship between achieving effectiveness in academic outcomes and achieving effectiveness along these other dimensions. We urge more attention to the relationship between these various criteria, a process that would require the development of a *multidimensional* view of school effectiveness. (8)

Shortcomings of the Goal-Attainment Approach. The goal-attainment approach is concerned more with student outcomes than with means or processes. Despite the logic and importance of this approach in determining and measuring school success, its viability is threatened unless it meets the following conditions: Schools must indeed have goals; these goals must be identified and defined with enough precision so that they are readily understood by teachers and others; these goals must be few enough to be manageable; a reasonable amount of agreement as to goals must exist among supervisors, principals, and teachers; and it must be possible to measure progress toward these goals (Robbins, 1983:24). Very often these conditions are not found in schools. Reaching consensus on goals is a difficult process. The question of goal ownership is important. Are stated goals those of the principal, school board, teachers, students, community or state? Official goals often differ from actual goals. Which goals, official or actual, should guide the goal-attainment approach? Goals that meet specificity and measurability criteria are likely to get more attention than those that do not, even if the easily measured ones are less important. Short-term goals often differ from long-term goals and indeed sometimes conflict with them. In fact, most schools have multiple goals, and often they are in competition with each other.

Although the goal-attainment approach is not likely to be implemented in the ideal, schools have no choice but to struggle with the approach. With shortcomings in mind, useful information can be obtained and the decision-making process can be informed by this approach. Further, the facts of the world are that schools are expected to have goals, and the rationality of this approach (no matter how frail this rationality may be in actual practice) legitimizes the school's existence as a competent organization in the eyes of important groups, such as school boards, state education agencies, the local press, federal funders, the community, and indeed school members themselves. Principals should view the goal-attainment approach as an ideal mechanism that, with understanding of its shortcomings and deceptive features, needs to be translated into workable programs for assessing school success. Further, this approach should be combined with process and environmental response approaches, each of which is described in the following sections.

A multidimensional goal attainment approach to determining school success requires that equal attention be given as well to social, affective, and psychomotor goals, purposes, and objectives. Further, more advanced indicators of cognitive achievement than those that measure basic skills need to be used if higher-level learnings are considered important. The goal-attainment approach weighs heavily in this book as various leadership processes are linked to school outcomes, but throughout, the plea is for use of a multidimensional perspective that includes not only student achievement test scores but also higher-cognitive-level learning indicators, affective indicators, and other indicators of successful schooling.

The Process Approach

It might be useful, for purposes of analysis, to distinguish between student outcomes and school characteristics, though such a distinction may be weak in actual practice. The term *student outcomes* refers to cognitive, affective, and psychomotor gains that students make as a result of schooling. *School characteristics* is a more encompassing designation for such school features as high morale, improved school-community relationships, efficient teaching, improved supervisory and evaluation systems, increased loyalty and commitment of teachers to the work of the school, improved school discipline, better leadership, and improved decision making.

It is generally assumed that a link exists between many of these school characteristics and student outcomes. For example, few would refute the generalization that schools characterized by a high concern for student welfare and students' academic success and by instruction given by highly committed teachers are likely to be more successful in achieving student outcomes than are similar schools without these characteristics. In this sense, school characteristics define the *processes and means* that principals and teachers use to enhance student outcomes.

Process-Oriented Research.   Austin's research (1979), cited earlier, found that schools characterized by such principal leadership processes as being involved in classroom instructional programs and teaching; providing a strong emphasis on goals and purposes; and taking a more active, indeed controlling, role in the functioning of the school, especially in areas of curriculum and teaching, had student achievement records superior to those in schools lacking such characteristics. As a result of his study of secondary schools in London, Rutter (1979) concludes that a "climate" of success is an important means to improve student outcomes. The climates he discovered in these schools were composed of norms and values that defined appropriate behavior for teachers and students. These schools were characterized by consistency of belief, commitment, and acceptance of these norms. Leadership and climate in these schools become processes and means that enhanced student outcomes.

The process approach has a long-standing tradition in administrative theory and enjoys wide acceptance among researchers in educational administration and elsewhere (Likert, 1961, 1968; Sergiovanni and Starratt, 1983; Silver, 1983). It assumes that principals can work directly to affect student outcomes but should give attention, as well, to improving processes and conditions that set the stage for, nurture, enhance, and evoke these outcomes. These processes and means are defined by school characteristics such as climate, decision-making patterns, and teacher morale.

Shortcomings of the Process Approach. Many authorities feel that by concentrating on school means and processes the issue of pupil gain is avoided. Indeed, during the so-called "theory movement" in educational administration during the 1960s and early 1970s, so much attention was given to concerns such as school climate, leadership characteristics and styles, decision-making practices, and conflict resolution strategies as separate and self-standing issues that topics of student learning and concern for student outcomes were neglected. *The process approach makes sense only when school characteristics are in turn linked to student outcomes.* Principals, theorists, and researchers should not choose between school characteristics and student outcomes approaches. It is not necessary, for example, for them to subscribe to the adage "It is not how you play the game that counts but whether you win or lose." Indeed, how one plays the game is a very important concern. Further, by viewing the process approach as addressing school characteristics linked to student outcomes, one is viewing this approach as also being goal-oriented. At play here are two sets of important goals—*means* goals and *ends* goals—both of which should receive attention. In sum, the process approach, when combined with the goal-attainment approach, provides a fuller and more comprehensive understanding of the nature of school success and of the link between the principalship and improved schooling.

The Environmental-Response Approach to School Effectiveness

One of the realities that principals face is that school success may be more a matter of perception than reality. No sleight of hand is intended here, nor is it being suggested that all that really matters are impressions of success. Successful schooling can be defined, its dimensions can be established concretely, and consensus can be established. Still, principals face the problem of legitimizing what they do and how their school functions in the eyes of important publics. Let's face it—if the school board does not *believe* that a school is successful, problems will arise regardless of the facts attesting its success. The same can be said for perceptions by parents and other interest groups. It is important for schools to be perceived as legitimate, and much of what a principal does is to seek this environmental legitimacy. This is especially true, as Meyer (1984) suggests, when it is difficult for a school to show that it is being successful by more objective means.

At the very least, schools must have stated purposes, appear thoughtful and rational, give the impression of order and control, have sensible structures and procedures, provide for accountability, and appear certain in their actions. Teacher evaluation systems, for example, often exist as devices enabling schools to gain the legitimacy they require in order to survive, rather than as ways to improve instruction, though this latter purpose is obtainable and important. Such evaluation systems are, in reality, means by which the school advertises its competency. They are (or, at least, they appear) purposeful, rational, orderly, and controlling, and they testify to the importance of accountability and certainty. These are the characteristics of the school demanded by external parties and often by teachers and others within the school.

In sum, an effective school is one that convincingly communicates its viability and effectiveness to its school community and other important groups. Other evidence notwithstanding, if the school does not obtain such legitimacy, it cannot be considered effective. The environmental-response approach adds still another dimension to building school effectiveness and requires unique considerations and leadership emphases from principals.

Characteristics of Successful Schools

It is fashionable to talk about the correlates of effective schools, and it is common practice for school districts and even states to settle on a particular list of such correlates (for example, strong instructional leadership from the principal, academic focus on the basic skills, safe and orderly environment, high expectations for students, close monitoring of instruction by supervision and testing) to apply uniformly to all schools. But recent research and reasoned thought suggest that *correlates* may be too strong a designation and uniform application of any particular list may be hazardous for the long-term health of the school. The research and thought, however, do provide us with a number of insights in the form of general characteristics that can help us decide what counts in our own unique situation.

Research Revelations

The work of Edmonds (1979), of Brookover and Lezotte (1979), and of Brookover and colleagues (1979) consistently reveals that effective schools are characterized by high agreement among staff as to goals and purposes, a clear sense of mission, and the active presence of purposing. Studies by Bossert and his colleagues (1982) and by Greenfield (1982) reveal that goal orientation and the articulation and modeling of school purposes by principals are also common characteristics.

Blumberg and Greenfield's (1980) research reveals that successful principals are pro-active and direct behaviors at building and articulating a vision of what the school is and can become. This notion of vision is supported, as well, by the case study research of Prunty and Hively (1982) and of Newberg and Glatthorn (undated). Nearly all these studies, as well as that of Rutter and his colleagues (1979), identify the concept of ethos (shared goals and expectations and associated approved modes of behavior) or strong school culture as being an important characteristic. Important to this culture are norms and values that provide for cohesion and identity and that create a unifying moral order or ideology from which teachers and students derive direction, meaning, and significance.

Of particular significance in understanding the depth of detail that characterizes life in successful schools is the research of Joan Lipsitz (1984). In summarizing her case studies of four successful middle schools, she reaches the following conclusions about principal leadership and school characteristics.

- The four schools achieved unusual clarity about the purposes of intermediate schooling and the students they teach.
- The schools made powerful statements, both in word and in practice, about their purposes. There is little disagreement within them and little discrepancy between what they say they are doing and what they are actually doing. As a result, everyone can articulate what the school stands for.
- These are confident schools. Each one stands for something special, whether it is being the best in the country, desegregation, diversity, or the arts. Each has a mission and knows what it is and in each case it is both academic and social.
- In every case, a principal . . . took hold of the possible for definition and proclaimed it within the school and throughout the community. Each school became special.
- Made to feel like chosen people, staff and students have banded together in their specialness and achieved accordingly. The sense of definition that comes from the exclusivity felt by each school is important in keeping staff morale high and retaining parent support. More important, though, is the sense of purpose it gives the young adolescents. It helps bind them to the school.
- Each of the four schools has or has had a principal with a driving vision who imbues decisions and practices with meaning, placing powerful emphasis on why things are done as well as how. Decisions are not made just because they are practical but for reasons of principle.
- Through their vision and practicality they articulate for their schools . . . a collective ideology that defines an organization's identity and purposes. The principals make these schools coherent, binding philosophy to goals, goals to programs, and programs to practices.
- The principals see their major function to be instructional leadership. It is their job to sustain their faculty's commitment. They set standards for performance and establish the norms and taboos for adult–child relationships.
- The major contribution of the principal is to make the schools larger than one person. They institutionalize their vision in program and organizational structure.
- The principals are good enough to leave a legacy behind: their staff, a powerfully defined school, an educated community and a tradition of excitement, sensitivity, and striving for excellence.
- Most striking is the level of caring in these schools.
- Most striking is the lack of adult isolation in these schools. . . . Common planning and lunch periods, team teaching encourage constant communication and allow for high levels of companionship.

- . . . teachers have high expectations for *themselves* and . . . they believe that they are capable of making a difference in their students' learning.
- Each school's principal has been a driven, energetic worker, committed to establishing the best possible school environment for the age group.
- The principals' authority is derived from their acknowledged competence. They are authoritative, not authoritarian leaders, although one often senses that a strain of authoritarianism is being kept carefully in tow.
- While the particulars of school governance differ from school to school, the schools have in common highly autonomous teachers. They understand how the whole school works, and in most cases they know why.
- These driven, possessive, and sometimes defiant principals are critical to the continued excellence and support of their schools; but they are not alone responsible for their schools' success, nor are they indispensable.*

Duttweiler's (1988; 1990) review of the more recent literature (Purkey and Smith, 1982; Rouche and Baker, 1986; Stedman, 1987; Wayson and Associates, 1988; and Wimpelberg, Teddlie, and Stringfield, 1989) reveals a much more comprehensive picture of what constitutes an effective school than that provided by earlier studies. Though Duttweiler continues to use the word effective to describe these schools she has redefined the term. The folowing characteristics emerge from her synthesis.

Effective Schools Are Student-Centered.   Effective schools make an effort to serve all students, create support networks to assist students, involve students in school affairs, respect and celebrate the ethnic and linguistic differences among students, and have student welfare as a first priority. They use community volunteers, parents, teacher aides, and peer tutors to provide close, personal attention to students. They involve students in many of the activities of running a school. Student needs are given priority over other concerns. An atmosphere of cooperation and trust is created through a high level of interaction between students and teachers.

Effective Schools Offer Academically Rich Programs.   Student development and the provision of a well-rounded academic program are the primary goals. Effective schools address higher- as well as lower-order cognitive objectives; provide an enriched environment through a variety of options; have an active co-curricular program, provide in-depth coverage of content; and appropriately monitor student progress and provide feedback.

Effective Schools Provide Instruction That Promotes Student Learning.   Effective schools have a distinctive normative structure that supports instruction. They design their programs to ensure academic success and to head off academic problems. Teachers and administrators believe that all students can learn and feel responsible for seeing that they do. Teachers and administrators believe in their own

*The conclusions from Joan Lipsitz's work are verbatim statements drawn from chapter 7, "The Challenge of the Schools" (Lipsitz, 1984): 267–323. Published by permission of Transaction, Inc. from *Successful Schools for Young Adolescents,* copyright © 1984 by Transaction, Inc.

ability to influence students' learning. Teachers communicate expectations to students, provide focused and organized instructional sessions, adapt instruction to student needs, anticipate and correct student misconceptions, and use a variety of teaching strategies. In general, effective schools set high standards, closely and regularly monitor performance, and recognize and reward effort and success.

Effective Schools Have a Positive School Climate.   Effective schools have a clear organizational personality, characterized by stated missions, goals, values, and standards of performance. They have a sense of order, purpose, and direction fostered by consistency among teachers; an atmosphere of encouragement in which students are praised and rewarded; a work-centered environment; and high optimism and expectations for student learning. Teachers and principals commit themselves to breaking down institutional and community barriers to equality. They create a learning environment that is open, friendly, and culturally inviting. Using community resources, they acknowledge the ethnic and racial identity of their students. They provide encouragement and take a positive approach to discipline. Administrators model the behaviors that they say are important.

Effective Schools Foster Collegial Interaction.   Effective schools strive to create professional environments for teachers that facilitate the accomplishment of their work. Teachers participate in decisions affecting their work, have reasonable control or autonomy to carry out work, share a sense of purpose and community, receive recognition for contributions to the organization, and are treated with respect and dignity by others in the workplace. Teachers work together as colleagues to carry out instruction, to plan curriculum, and to refine teaching practices.

Effective Schools Have Extensive Staff Development.   The teacher evaluation system is used to help teachers improve their skills. Inservice is practical, on-the-job training tailored to meet the specific needs of staff members. The emphasis is on the exchange of practical teaching techniques and on making training an integral part of a collaborative educational environment. Teachers and administrators conduct inservice programs and are provided with ample staff-development opportunities to help them develop further. Administrators and teachers are encouraged to reflect on their practices.

Effective Schools Practice Shared Leadership.   Instructional leadership does not depend solely on the principal. School administrators understand and use a leadership style appropriate for professionals; solve problems through collaboration, team, or group decision making; know their staff members and delegate authority; communicate and build cohesiveness; and use their positions to recognize and reward accomplishments of both staff and students. While no single leadership style dominates, common leadership features include setting and maintaining direction for the school and facilitating the work of teachers by adopting a wide range of supportive behaviors. Involvement in decision making is a critical element. Involvement begins with members of the school community developing the goals, mission, and values of the school. Decisions are made with input from those to be affected by the decision.

Effective Schools Foster Creative Problem Solving. Staff members in effective schools are unwilling to accept defeat or settle for mediocrity. They turn their problems into challenges, design solutions, and implement them. They go about their tasks with commitment, creativity, persistence, and professionalism. Resources such as time, facilities, staff expertise, and volunteers are used to maximum advantage to facilitate the process of teaching and learning.

Effective Schools Involve Parents and the Community. There is a partnership linkage between the school and the community. Effective schools establish a variety of methods for communicating as well as working with parents and the community. They involve parents and community members in the teaching and learning activities of the school, include them in the decision-making process, have them serve as resources to extend the efforts of the school, and depend on them to be advocates as well as to provide good public relations for the school. They make sure that parents are involved in all aspects of their children's learning. Effective schools are contributory partners to the community they serve. They teach young people that they have a responsible part to play in society and that their contributions are valued and needed. (Duttweiler, 1990: 72-74)

To this list Stedman (1987) would add ethnic and racial pluralism, student responsibility for school affairs, and shared governance with parents and teachers. Stedman's conclusions are interesting because they rely on studies of successful schools conducted in the 1960s and early 1970s as well as more recent studies and thus provide a more "longitudinal" view.

Though lists of general characteristics are helpful, they are not readily translated into specific prescriptions for management and leadership practice. What needs to be done to increase effectiveness and how one does it are situationally specific. As will be discussed in Chapter 6, what worked for a failing school will not necessarily work for a competent school. What works for low socio-economic status schools will not necessarily work for middle socio-economic status schools (Hallinger and Murphy, 1986; Evans, 1988). The early school-effectiveness studies, for example, pointed out the importance of strong instructional leadership by the principal. Following this script, the Minnesota Department of Education (1989) believes that the principal of an effective school is one who

> establishes specific procedures and criteria for evaluating classroom instructors . . . is knowledgeable about the process of schooling . . . is trained to evaluate instruction . . . observes classroom regularly and meets with teachers to discuss and improve classroom practices . . . offers ongoing, constructive feedback to the teaching staff on their effectiveness . . . rewards teachers for excellence in teaching. . . . (20).

Clearly, such principalship behaviors make sense in many situations but not in others. Being a strong instructional leader may be a good idea in schools where teachers are poorly trained or lacking in commitment, but it is not a good idea in schools where competence and commitment are not issues. In some schools, for example, teachers know more than the principal about matters of teaching and learning. To persist in providing strong instructional leadership in such a situation locks in teachers as instructional followers or subordinates and puts a cap on the total amount of leadership available in the school to promote better teaching and learning.

A number of researchers (e.g., Gersten, Carnine, and Green, 1982; Pajak and Glickman, 1989) have found that the leadership provided by lead teachers, assistant principals, grade-level heads, central office supervisors, department chairpersons, and teams of teachers are often the most critical factors in improving teaching and learning. What seems crucial to school improvement is not so much who provides the leadership but how much leadership there is. To that end the principal as leader of leaders may well be a more appropriate role where competence and commitment are not issues than would the role of instructional leader, a theme further developed in Chapter 6.

In sum, indiscriminate application of school-effectiveness research findings and, in particular, the development of generic lists of correlates or indicators that are subsequently applied uniformly to schools pose serious questions about the proper use of research and can result in negative, unanticipated consequences for teaching and learning. Wimpelburg, Teddlie, and Stringfield (1989) put it more bluntly: "It is patently foolish to attempt 'effective schools' changes in schools that are wholly different from the settings in which the 'effective schools' correlates were isolated" (103). Lists of effectiveness characteristics as proposed by knowledgeable researchers remain useful if viewed as general indicators. They are not so much truths to be applied uniformly, but understandings that can help principals and others make more informed decisions about what to do and how in improving schools.

References

Austin, Gilbert. 1979. "Process Evaluation: A Comprehensive Study of Outlines." Baltimore, Maryland State Department of Education. ERIC: ED 160 644.

Bloom, Benjamin S. 1964. *Stability and Change in Human Characteristics*. New York: Wiley.

Blumberg, Arthur, and William Greenfield. 1980. *The Effective Principal: Perspective on School Leadership*. Boston: Allyn and Bacon.

Bossert, Steven T., D. D. Dwyer, B. Rowan, and G. V. Lee. 1982. "The Instructional Management Role of the Principal," *Educational Administration Quarterly* 18(3), 34–64.

Boyer, Ernest. 1983. *High School: A Report on Secondary Education in America*. New York: Harper & Row.

Brandt, Ronald. 1982. "On School Improvement: A Conversation with Ronald Edmonds," *Educational Leadership* 40(3), 31–35.

Brookover, Wilbur B ., and Lawrence W. Lezotte. 1979. "Changes in School Characteristics Coincident with Changes in School Achievement." East Lansing, MI: Institute for Research on Teaching, Michigan State University.

Brookover, Wilbur B., C. Brady, P. Flood, J. Schweigen, and J. Wisenbater. 1979. *School Systems and School Achievement: Schools Can Make a Difference*. New York: Praeger.

Campbell, John P. 1977. "On the Nature of Organizational Effectiveness," in P. S. Goodman, J. M. Pennings, and Associates, Eds., *New Perspectives on Organizational Effectiveness*. San Francisco: Jossey-Bass.

Coleman, James, Ernest Q. Campbell, Carol J. Hobson, James McParland, Alexander M. Mood, Frederick D. Weinfeld, and Robert L. York. 1966. *Equality of Educational Opportunity*. 2 vol. Washington, DC: U.S. Government Printing Office, OE-38001.

Duttweiler, Patricia Cloud. 1988. "New Insights from Research on Effective Schools," *Insights*. Austin, TX: Southwest Educational Development Laboratory. No. 4.

Duttweiler, Patricia Cloud. 1990. "A Broader Definition of Effective Schools: Implications from Research and Practice," in T. J. Sergiovanni and J. H. Moore, Eds., *Target 2000: A Compact for Excellence in Texas's Schools*. Austin, TX: Texas Association for Supervision and Curriculum Development.

Edmonds, Ronald. 1979. "Some Schools Work and More Can," *Social Policy* 9(2), 28–32.

Etzioni, Amitai. 1964. *Modern Organizations*. Englewood Cliffs, NJ: Prentice-Hall.

Gerston, Russell, Douglas Carnine, and Susan Green. 1982. "The Principal as Instructional Leader: A Second Look," *Educational Leadership* 40(Dec.), 47–50.

Goodlad, John. 1983. *A Place Called School*. New York: McGraw-Hill.

Greenfield, William. 1982. *A Synopsis of Research on School Principals*. Washington, DC: National Institute for Education.

Lightfoot, Sara. 1983. *The Good High School*. New York: Basic Books.

Likert, Rensis. 1961. *New Patterns of Management*. New York: McGraw-Hill.

Likert, Rensis. 1968. *The Human Organization: Its Management and Value*. New York: McGraw-Hill.

Lipsitz, Joan. 1984. *Successful Schools for Young Adolescents*. New Brunswick, NJ: Transaction.

Meyer, John W. 1984. "Organizations as Ideological Systems," in T. J. Sergiovanni and J. E. Corbally, Eds., *Leadership and Organizational Culture*. Urbana-Champaign, IL: University of Illinois Press.

Newberg, Norman A., and Allan A. Glatthorn. Undated. "Instructional Leadership: Four Ethnographic Studies of Junior High School Principals." Washington, DC: National Institute for Education (G-81-008).

Pajak, Edward F., and Carl D. Glickman. 1989. "Dimension of School District Improvement," *Educational Leadership* 46(8), 61–64.

Prunty, John J., and Wells Hively. 1982. "The Principal's Role in School Effectiveness: An Analysis of the Practices of Four Elementary School Leaders." Washington, DC: National Institute for Education (G-8-01-10) and CEMRL, Inc.

Ravitch, Diane. 1984. "A Good School," *The American Scholar* 53(4).

Robbins, Stephen P. 1983. *Organization Theory: The Structure and Design of Organizations*. Englewood Cliffs, NJ: Prentice-Hall.

Roueche, J. E., and G. A. Baker. 1986. *Profiling Excellence in America's Schools*. Arlington, VA: American Association of School Administrators.

Rowan, Brian, David C. Dwyer, and Steven T. Bossert. 1982. "Methodological Considerations in Studies of Effective Principals." Paper presented at American Educational Research Association, New York.

Rutter, M., B. Maughan, P. Mortimore, J. Ouston, and A. Smith. 1979. *Fifteen Thousand Hours: Secondary Schools and Their Effects on Children*. Cambridge, MA: Harvard University Press.

Sergiovanni, Thomas J., and Robert J. Starratt. 1983. *Supervision: Human Perspectives*. New York: McGraw-Hill.

Silver, Paula. 1983. *Educational Administration: Theoretical Perspectives on Practice and Research*. New York: Harper & Row.

Squire, David A., William G. Huitt, and John K. Segars. 1981. "Improving Classrooms and Schools: What's Important," *Educational Leadership* 39(2).

Stedman, Lawrence C. 1987. "It's Time We Changed the Effective Schools Formula," *Phi Delta Kappan* 69(3), 215–227.

Steers, Richard. 1975. "Problems in the Measurement of Organizational Effectiveness," *Administrative Science Quarterly* 20(2), 546–558.

Torbert, William R. Undated. "Organizational Effectiveness: Five Universal Criteria." Unpublished manuscript.

Wayson, W. W. 1988. *Up From Excellence: The Impact of the Excellence Movement on Schools*. Bloomington, Indiana: Phi Delta Kappan Foundation.

Weber, George. 1971. *Inner-City Children Can Be Taught to Read: Four Successful Schools*. Occasional Paper No. 18. Washington, DC: Council for Basic Education.

Wimpelberg, Robert K., Charles Teddlie, and Samuel Stringfield. 1989. "Sensitivity to Context: The Past and Future of Effective Schools Research," *Educational Administration Quarterly* 25(1), 82–108.

APPENDIX 4-1 "Effective" and "Successful" Models of Schooling

"Effective Schools"	"Successful Schools"

1. *Definition:*

An effective school is most commonly defined by researchers as one whose students are achieving well as evidenced by achievement test scores in the basic skills areas.

A successful school is an image of schooling characterized by a strong commitment to multiple goals and within which students demonstrate by tests and other means intellectual values, high academic attainment, responsible citizenship, moral and ethical character, aesthetic expression, and emotional and physical well-being.

2. *Research Base:*

School effectiveness studies are typically conducted in elementary schools within urban school districts. Schools that are considered to be doing well (effective) are compared with those that are not (ineffective). Commonalities among effective schools are identified in such areas as instructional management, teaching methods and behaviors, curriculum and instructional design, principal behaviors, and attitudes of teachers and principals. Effective and ineffective schools are determined on the basis of student achievement test scores—typically in reading and mathematics. Weber (1971) and Edmonds (1979) would be examples of school research pioneers.

The research base for the successful schools model is comprehensive and extensive, including studies of schools at all levels. Research strategies include case studies, reflection and observations of experts, quantitative studies, and commission reports. The studies and reports are not deliberately a part of a successful schools research tradition but taken together provide common characteristics that help construct the image of a successful school. The works of Boyer (1983), Goodlad (1984), Lightfoot (1983), Ravitch (1984), and Lipsitz (1984) are examples of the breadth of literature contributing to the image of a successful school.

3. *Philosophy:*

The school effectiveness model is based on an *inclusive* philosophy that assumes that *all* students can learn the basics if the model is implemented properly. Often some form of "masterly learning" is prescribed that allows the pacing of instruction to match student learning rates. The pioneering school effectiveness research was conducted in inner city schools, as part of a commitment to extend to poor children equal educational opportunity.

Successful schools combine several characteristics of the American tradition that have endured over time: attention to the "egalitarian ideal" *balanced* with the values of hard work, competition, standards, and success; a respect for the power and intrinsic interest of the academic disciplines; a commitment to intellectual values; attention to the requirements of responsible citizenship in a democratic society; and a commitment to provide developmentally sound schooling. This agenda is best implemented under conditions that allow parents, teachers, and administrators to be in charge of schooling. The model is inclusive in that all students are believed capable of success in academically and developmentally sound schools.

APPENDIX 4-1 *(Continued)*

"Effective Schools"	"Successful Schools"

4. *Goals:*

In effective schools, teaching is primarily focused on detailed instructional objectives that emphasize cognitive learning in the basics. Disciplined coverage of the appropriate subject matter is expected of techers and students. Students are expected to demonstrate recall and comprehension competencies. Though learning rates may vary, goals, objectives and subject matter are standard for all students. High agreement exists among principal and teachers as to what the school is to accomplish and how.

Successful schools have multiple goals held together by a commitment to intellectual values (that is, providing a common core of studies, promoting the desire to learn, how to learn, critical thinking). They are both academically and developmentally sound. Goals and values comprise a common core of beliefs to which school activities and processes are aligned. Students are challenged to succeed. Success is determined by testing programs, judgments of teachers and principals, accomplishments of students, and satisfaction indicators. In successful schools, teachers and students have a clear picture of what the school believes in, hopes to accomplish, and why. This defining core of values provides direction, serves as a source of meaning and significance, and is used to evaluate decisions.

5. *Structure of Schooling:*

The work flow of teaching in effective schools is characterized by tight alignment between objectives and curriculum, curriculum and teaching methods, and teaching and testing. This tight alignment is accompanied by high expectations that students can learn the basics. The process is carefully monitored by frequent testing and close supervision. An orderly and structured environment is provided for both teachers and students.

In successful schools tight alignment exists between the defining core of values and decisions that teachers and administrators make about goals and objectives, curriculum, teaching, supervision, and evaluation. This alignment is strategic, not tactical as is the case in the effective and excellent schools models. Teachers and administrators, for example, are given a great deal of freedom to decide matters of schooling, providing that the decisions they make are consistent with the core values. In this sense successful schools combine features of tight and loose alignment.

6. *Teaching:*

Standardization and tight alignment of objectives, curriculum, teaching, and testing result in direct instruction being favored as the "best" way to teach. Direct instruction is characterized by specific learning outcomes, keeping students on task, using direct questioning of students, providing frequent practice, and testing students frequently. The teacher is dominant, and students are provided with little choice of activities.

Teaching is expected to reflect the school's basic intellectual and developmental values. No one best way of teaching is thought to be inherently better than another. Teachers are expected to draw from a rich repertoire of teaching models those that make sense for the moment. Teaching, therefore, is elevated from simplistic and bureaucratic directions-following to professional decision making. Teachers are expected to provide an

APPENDIX 4–1 *(Continued)*

"Effective Schools"	"Successful Schools"

Teachers are expected to provide an appropriate classroom climate characterized by high learning expectations, an orderly environment, positive reinforcement, and amicable relationships. Whole-class instruction is favored over small-group and independent, though this characteristic often contradicts attempts to use mastery learning. Critics maintain that students are viewed as learning products rather than as partners.

appropriate classroom climate characterized by high learning expectations, an orderly environment, positive reinforcement, and amicable relationships. Less reliance is placed on behavioral management techniques in obtaining this environment and more on providing interesting, exciting, and powerful learning. Teaching is expected to embody high intellectual values and academic standards.

7. *Supervision and Evaluation:*

Supervision and evaluation are straightforward and seek to answer two basic questions: to what extent and how well are teachers implementing the model and to what extent and how well are students achieving designated outcomes? To these ends, testing of students is ubiquitous. Though tests are intended to provide diagnostic and formative information, summative use to evaluate teachers and schools is often unavoidable. Teachers are supervised and evaluated directly by use of rating scales, analysis of teaching transcripts, and other means to ensure that proper teaching behaviors are in evidence.

Given the structure of schooling and character of teaching in successful schools, supervision and evaluation are neither technical nor routine. The emphasis is less on charting "appropriate teaching behavior" and more on ensuring that the school's basic values are embodied in teaching. Evaluation is both formative and summative. Since no one model of teaching is either prescribed or favored, no one best model of supervision and evaluation makes sense. As is the case with teaching, supervision and evaluation models are viewed metaphorically rather than prescriptively to help inform the process. Though formal systems are in place, it is the informal day-by-day interactions of teachers with teachers and administrators with teachers about teaching and learning that are deemed most important.

8. *Principal Leadership:*

In effective schools principals are instructional leaders who hold strong views about instruction and exhibit strong and highly visible managerial skills to ensure that all features of the model (objectives, curriculum, teaching, testing, expectations, and classroom climate) are properly provided and aligned. They practice close supervision and monitor carefully what teachers do and how they do it. They provide direct help to teachers to facilitate the model's implementation.

In successful schools, principals are educational leaders with strong views about schooling, teaching, and learning. They practice "purposing," defined as actions that elicit from others clarity, consensus, and commitment regarding the school's basic purposes and values. Their leadership styles range from the heroic to the ordinary. Heroic leaders often take charge personally. Ordinary leaders tend to emphasize building team leadership. Both types work within the framework of tight alignment on values and loose alignment on implementation. Style itself is less important than what the principal stands for, believes in, and communicates to others.

APPENDIX 4–1 *(Continued)*

"Effective Schools"	"Successful Schools"

9. *Results:*

Does the school effectiveness model work? The answer is yes; the model delivers what it promises. In effective elementary schools, particularly in urban settings, students learn the basics as evidenced by higher scores on achievement tests of basic skills. Many experts believe, however, that overemphasizing effective school characteristics provides a narrow conception of education, omits important learning not included in testing programs, de-emphasizes higher-order learning such as problem solving, knowledge synthesis, and evaluation, and discourages critical thinking. Some complain as well that the model, taken too literally, results in highly bureaucratic teaching that neither teachers or students find very satisfying over the long run. Questions remain as to what are the costs and benefits of using the model in high schools.

Successful schools work. Not only do they match effective schools in achievement of basic skills, but also they provide for comprehensive and higher-level learning. Further, successful schools display many of the values that are a part of America's political and educational heritage. Emphasizing high academic standards within the tradition of the discipline; promoting intellectual values such as inquiry, critical thinking, knowledge appreciation, and learning how to learn; a concern for responsible citizenship in a democratic society; active involvement of students in their own learning; responsiveness to student developmental needs and levels; improving the quality of work life of teachers; and local control are examples.

CHAPTER 5

The Forces of Leadership

Principals are important! Indeed, no other school position has greater potential for maintaining and improving quality schools. These assertions are bolstered by findings that emerge from research and from more informal observation of successful schools. It is clear that when schools are functioning especially well and school achievement is high, much of the credit typically belongs to the principal. A recent governmental study, for example, reaches the following conclusions (U.S. Senate, 1972):

> In many ways the school principal is the most important and influential individual in any school. . . . It is his leadership that sets the tone of the school, the climate for learning, the level of professionalism and morale of teachers and the degree of concern for what students may or may not become. . . . If a school is a vibrant, innovative, child-centered place; if it has a reputation for excellence in teaching; if students are performing to the best of their ability one can almost always point to the principal's leadership as the key to success. (305)

It is *potential* power, however, that characterizes the principalship. The mere presence of the principal or the ordinary articulation of the role will not automatically provide the leadership required. Often circumstances prevent the principal from fully harnessing and using this potential power. Consider, for example, what one principal has to say about constraining circumstances:

> I go almost every year to conventions for principals, and there's always a speech telling us we need to be educational leaders, not managers. It's a great idea. And yet the system doesn't allow you to be an educational leader. Everyone wants the power to run schools in one way or another—the central office, the union, the board, the parents, the special-interest groups. What's left for the principal to decide isn't always very much. There's so little we have to control or to change. The power, the authority, is somewhere else, though not necessarily the responsibility. (Boyer, 1983:219).

Still, many principals are able to rise above these and other difficulties. Key to realizing the potential for leadership in the principalship is to recognize that schools provide opportunities for expressing a *unique* form of leadership. These opportunities spring from special characteristics that schools possess.

The work of schooling is considered by most people to be important; teachers are typically a highly educated and commited group of workers; teaching itself has the potential to provide teachers with variety, interest, and challenge; schools can be fun and exciting places to work; frequently schools take on strong identities stemming from an agreed set of purposes and an agreed-upon mission; and being part of such strong identity schools can be highly motivating and exhilarating to teachers and students. Successful principals understand these unique characteristics of schools as organizations and have learned how to use them as a basis for generating forceful school leadership.

In the previous chapter we examined characteristics of successful schools and the link between this success and leadership. Included were descriptions of leadership as expressed by successful principals. The work of Blumberg and Greenfield (1980) summarizes some of those observations. They note that "principals who lead seem to be highly *goal oriented* and to have a keen sense of *goal clarity*" (246). Their research points out that successful principals are alert to opportunities or create opportunities favoring their ability to affect what is going on in the school. Although they rely heavily on operational goals of a long-term nature, they emphasize day-by-day actions as well. They have a good sense of themselves, feel secure as individuals and as principals at work, and are able to accept failure as failure of an idea rather than of them as persons. These principals have a high tolerance for ambiguity and are able to work in loosely structured environments. With respect to authority, they test the limits of the boundaries they face and do not make premature assumptions about what they can or cannot do. They are sensitive to the dynamics of power existing in the school district and school community, and they are accomplished in establishing alliances and in building coalitions that enable them to harness this power on behalf of the school. Approaching problems from an analytical perspective, they are able to remove themselves from the situation; that is, they do not become consumed by the problems and situations they face.

In this chapter the intent is to focus beneath these descriptions and to examine principal leadership as a set of forces available for improving and maintaining quality schooling. Suggestions are provided as to how principals can use these forces.

The Forces of Leadership

Leadership can be viewed as comprising a set of forces. Metaphorically speaking, each of the "forces" can be used by the principal to push the school forward toward effectiveness or to prevent it from being pushed back. Different forces have different consequences for school effectiveness.

In many schools too much attention is given to some of the forces and not enough to others. Unfortunately, as recent research reveals, it is the neglected leadership forces that are most often linked to extraordinary commitment and performance in schools. Five "forces of leadership" — technical, human, educational, symbolic, and cultural — are discussed in the following subsections.

The Technical Force

The first force available to principals is the power of leadership derived from sound management techniques. This force is concerned with the technical aspects of leadership. Principals expressing the technical force can be thought of as assuming the role of "management engineer," emphasizing such concepts as planning and time management, contingency leadership theories, and organizational structures. As management engineers, principals provide planning, organizing, coordinating, and scheduling to the school and are skilled at manipulating strategies and situations to ensure optimum effectiveness. The technical leadership force is very important because its presence, competently articulated, ensures that the school will be managed properly.

Proper management is a basic requirement of all organizations if they are expected to function properly day by day and to maintain support from external constituents. School boards and other segments of the public will not tolerate inefficient and poorly managed schools. Further, it is clear from the research that poorly managed enterprises can have debilitating effects on workers. Ray C. Hackman (1969:158), for example, found that "poor organization of work" resulted in such negative feelings among workers as frustration and aggression, anxiety, personal inadequacy, and even social rejection. It is apparent that workplaces need to be characterized by a degree of order and reliability that provides security for people *and* that frees them to focus wholeheartedly on major purposes and central work activities. The technical force of leadership serves this important need.

The Human Force

The second leadership force available to principals is the power of leadership derived from harnessing the school's social and interpersonal potential—its human resources. This force is concerned with human aspects of leadership. Principals expressing this force can be thought of as assuming the role of "human engineer," emphasizing human relations, interpersonal competence, and instrumental motivational techniques. As human engineers, principals provide support, encouragement, and growth opportunities for teachers and others.

It is hard to imagine a school functioning properly without the strong presence of this human force of leadership. Schools are, after all, human intensive, and *the interpersonal needs of students and teachers are of sufficient importance that, should they be neglected, schooling problems are likely to follow.* High student motivation to learn and high teacher motivation to teach are prerequisite for quality schooling and must be effectively addressed by principals. The development of human resources appears as either the dominant or underlying theme of each of this book's chapters.

The Educational Force

The third force available to principals is the power of leadership derived from expert knowledge about matters of education and schooling. This force is concerned with educational aspects of leadership. At one time educational aspects were dominant in the literature of educational administration and supervision. Principals were considered to be instructional leaders, and emphasis on schooling characterized university training programs. In the latter part of the 1950s and during the 1960s, advances of management and social science theory in educational administration and supervision brought to center stage technical and human aspects of leadership; indeed, educational aspects were often neglected. As a result the principalship was often viewed as a school management position separate from teaching. During this period the original meaning of principal as "principal teacher" became lost. John Goodlad (1978) has been a persistent critic of the displacement of educational aspects of leadership in favor of the technical and human. He states:

> But to put these matters (technical and human) at the center, often for understandable reasons of survival and expediency, is to commit a fundamental error which, ultimately, will have a negative impact on both education and one's own career. *Our work, for which we will be held accountable, is to maintain, justify, and articulate sound, comprehensive programs of instruction of children and youth.* (326)

He states further: "It is now time to put the right things at the center again. And the right things have to do with assuring comprehensive, quality educational programs in each and every school in our jurisdiction" (331).

Matters of education and schooling are again in the forefront. This new emphasis on the educational force of leadership is a happy result of recent school effectiveness and teaching effectiveness research and of other reports of research, such as Goodlad's *A Study of Schooling* (1983). Recent national policy studies on the present status and future of education, such as the Carnegie Foundation for the Advancement of Teaching's report *High School: A Report on Secondary Education in America* (Boyer, 1983) have also contributed to enhancing this renewed emphasis on educational aspects of leadership. The following statement regarding the preparation of principals from Boyer's book (1983) is representative of current thought:

> . . . new preparation and selection programs are required. Principals cannot exercise leadership without classroom experience. Specifically, we recommend that the preparation pattern for principals follow that of teachers. Without a thorough grounding in the realities of the classroom, principals will continue to feel uncomfortable and inadequate in educational leadership roles. Moreover, they will continue to lack credibility in instructional matters with their teachers. (223)

When expressing the educational force, the principal assumes the role of "clinical practitioner" who brings expert professional knowledge and bearing to teaching, educational program development, and supervision. As clinical practitioner, the principal is adept at diagnosing educational problems; counseling teachers; providing for supervision, evaluation, and staff development; and developing curriculum.

Sometimes the educational force takes the form of principal as strong instructional leader, and at other times principal as knowledgeable colleague or leader of leaders who engages with teachers on an equal basis on matters of teaching and learning. The first expression of this educational force might be appropriate for new teachers, teachers with less than fully developed competencies, or teachers with doubtful commitment. The second expression is appropriate for more mature, competent, and committed teachers. Though instructional leadership might be appropriate for a particular circumstance the overall goal is to become a leader of leaders.

Technical, human, and educational forces of leadership—brought together in an effort to promote and maintain quality schooling—provide the critical mass needed for basic school competence. A shortage in any of the three forces upsets this critical mass, and less effective schooling is likely to occur. Studies of excellence in organizations suggest that despite the link between technical, human, and educational aspects of leadership and basic competence, the presence of the three does not guarantee excellence. Excellent organizations, schools among them, are characterized by other leadership qualities represented by symbolic and cultural forces of leadership.

The Symbolic Force

The fourth force available to principals is the power of leadership derived from focusing attention of others on matters of importance to the school. This force is concerned with the symbolic aspects of leadership. When expressing this force, the principal assumes the role of "chief," emphasizing selective attention or the modeling of important goals and behaviors, and signaling to others what is important and valuable in the school. Touring the school; visiting classrooms; seeking out and visibly spending time with students; downplaying management concerns in favor of educational concerns; presiding over ceremonies, rituals, and other important occasions; and providing a unified vision of the school through proper use of words and actions are examples of principal activities associated with this force.

The providing of *purposing* to the school is a major aspect of symbolic leadership. Peter Vaill (1984) defines purposing as "that continuous stream of actions by an organization's formal leadership which has the effect of inducing clarity, consensus, and commitment regarding the organization's basic purposes." Leaders of the high-performing organizations he studied had in common the ability to provide purposing. The importance of purposing to school leadership and school success is supported by the research reviewed in Chapter 4 and will be expanded and illustrated in subsequent chapters.

The symbolic force of leadership derives much of its power from the needs of persons at work to have a sense of what is important and to have some signal of what is of value. Students and teachers alike want to know what is of value to the school and its leadership; they desire a sense of order and direction, and they enjoy sharing this sense with others. They respond to these conditions with increased work motivation and commitment.

The principal's behavioral style is of minimal concern with respect to this symbolic force. Instead, what the principal stands for and communicates to others is emphasized. The objective of symbolic leadership is the stirring of human con-sciousness, the integration and enhancing of meaning, the development and ex-pression of key cultural strands that identify the substance of a school, and the linking of persons involved in the school's activities to them. As Louis Pondy (1978) suggests:

> What kind of insights can we get if we say that the effectiveness of a leader lies in his ability to make activity meaningful for those in his role set—not to change behavior but to give others a sense of understanding what they are doing, and especially to articulate it so they can communicate about the meaning of their behaviors? (94)

The providing of meaning to teachers, students, and parents and the rallying of them to a common cause are the earmarks of effectiveness in symbolic school leadership.

The noted administrative theorist James G. March (1984) emphasizes the im-portance of symbolic leadership as follows:

> Administrators manage the way the sentiments, expectations, commitments and faiths of individuals concerned with the organization fit into a structure of social beliefs about organizational life. Administrative theory probably underestimates the significance of this belief structure for effective organizations. As a result, it probably underestimates the extent to which the management of symbols is a part of effective administration. If we want to identify one single way in which ad-ministrators can affect organizations, it is through their effect on the world views that surround organizational life; and those effects are managed through atten-tion of the ritual and symbolic characteristics of organizations and their administra-tion. Whether we wish to sustain the system or change it, management is a way of making a symbolic statement. (32)

Technical aspects of leadership are the managing of structures and events; human aspects are the managing of psychological factors such as needs; and educational aspects are the managing of the substance of our work. By contrast, symbolic aspects are the managing of sentiments, expectations, commitments, and faith itself. Since symbolic leadership affects the faith that people have in the school, it provides the principal with a powerful force for influencing school events.

The Cultural Force

The fifth force available to principals is the power of leadership derived from building a unique school culture and refers to cultural aspects of leadership. It is clear from reviews of the successful schools literature that the building of a *culture* that pro-motes and sustains a given school's conception of success is key. When expressing this cultural force, the principal assumes the role of "high priest," seeking to define, strengthen, and articulate those enduring values, beliefs, and cultural strands that give the school its unique identity over time. As high priest the principal is engaged in legacy building, and in creating, nurturing, and teaching an organizational saga (Clark, 1972) that defines the school as a distinct entity with an identifiable culture. The words *clan* and *tribe* come to mind as a way to think about how the school might be depicted and function.

Leadership activities associated with the cultural view include articulating school purposes and mission; socializing new members to the school; telling stories and maintaining or reinforcing myths, traditions, and beliefs; explaining "the way things operate around here"; developing and displaying a system of symbols (as exemplified in the fourth force) *over time*; and rewarding those who reflect this culture. The net effect of the cultural force of leadership is to bond together students, teachers, and others to the work of the school as believers. The school and its purposes become revered, and in some respects they resemble an ideological system dedicated to a sacred mission. It is believed that as persons become members of this strong and binding culture they are provided with opportunities for enjoying a special sense of personal importance and significance. Their work and their lives take on a new importance, one characterized by richer meanings, an expanded sense of identity, and a feeling of belonging to something special – all of which are highly motivating conditions (Peters and Waterman, 1982).

Culture can be described as the collective programming of the mind that distinguishes the members of one school from another (Hofstede, 1980:13). Cultural life in schools is constructed reality, and school principals can play a key role in building this reality. School culture includes values, symbols, beliefs, and shared meanings of parents, students, teachers, and others conceived as a group or community. Culture governs what is of worth for this group and how members should think, feel, and behave. The "stuff" of culture includes a school's customs and traditions; historical accounts; stated and unstated understandings, habits, norms and expectations; common meanings; and shared assumptions. The more understood, accepted, and cohesive the culture of a school, the better able it is to move in concert toward ideals it holds and objectives it wishes to pursue.

Practicing Symbolic and Cultural Leadership

School culture building and practicing the art of purposing in schools are the essentials of symbolic and cultural leadership forces. The expression of these forces requires vision and an understanding of the semantics of daily activities.

Expressing Symbolic Leadership. When principals are expressing symbolic aspects of leadership, they are typically working beneath the surface of events and activities; they are seeking to tap deeper meanings, deeper values. As Robert J. Starratt (1978) suggests, leaders seek to identify the roots of meaning and the flow and ebb of daily life in schools so that they can provide students, teachers, and members of the community with a sense of importance, vision, and purpose above the seemingly ordinary and mundane. Indeed, they work to bring to the school a sense of drama in human life that permits persons to rise above the daily routine that often characterizes their day-by-day activities. Symbolic leaders are able to see the significance of what a group is doing and indeed could be doing. They have a feel for the dramatic possibilities inherent in most situations and are able to urge people to go beyond the routine, to break out of the mold into something more lively and vibrant. And, finally, symbolic leaders are able to communicate their sense of vision by words and examples. They use language symbols that are easily understood but that also communicate a sense of excitement, originality, and freshness. These efforts provide opportunities for others in the school to experience this vision and to gain a sense of purpose, feeling that they share in the ownership of the school enterprise.

Lieberman and Miller (1984) found that principals often practiced symbolic leadership as opportunists and under serendipitous circumstances. They note, for example,

> when complimenting a teacher for a well-constructed and well-taught lesson, an administrator is making a statement that excellence is recognized and rewarded. When meeting with a teacher whose classroom is in revolt, the principal is expressing concern about what happens behind the closed doors of the classroom and signals a change from previous administrators who gave high marks to a teacher needing improvement. When attending department meetings that focus on curricular issues, the principal is supporting dialogue and informed action. All of these events and actions may be defined as educational leadership – not rational, linear, and planned; but ad hoc, responsive and realistic. Educational leadership happens, when it happens at all, within the cracks and around the edges of the job as defined and presently constituted. (76)

Warren Bennis (1984) finds that compelling vision is the key ingredient of leadership among heads of the highly successful organizations he studied. *Vision* refers to the capacity to create and communicate a view of a desired state of affairs that induces commitment among those working in the organization. Vision becomes the substance of what is communicated as symbolic aspects of leadership are emphasized. Tom Davis, principal of the John Muir School in the St. Louis area, speaks of vision as follows:

> I think the first thing I think I'd do real well is I have a vision about what the school should be and about what this school should be in particular . . . And I think that's essential to a number of things. I think it's important to inspire staff, both emotionally and intellectually. I think it needs to serve that function. Explicitly, I function to bring back the broader vision, the broader view . . . to bear on all the little pieces. That's something I work at very hard . . . so, because I've got all these semi-autonomous, really capable human beings out there, one major function is to keep it all going in one direction.

He continues:

> So the vision . . . has to inform the board, the parents, and staff – all the relationships. It's a whole community, so it all has to be part of it. The vision has to in-

clude not only a vision of what you do with children, but what you do in the process of doing it with children. It has to be all of one fabric. (Prunty and Hively, 1982:66)

Lieberman and Miller (1984) speak of the power of the principal as the school's "moral authority" who by actions, statements, and deeds makes symbolic statements. In describing this power from case study notes involving student discrimination, they state:

> Principals can maintain neutrality and let things progress as they always have; even that is a moral statement. Or they may take an active stance, threatening the assumptions of staff members and moving a school in more progressive or more regressive directions. Principals condone or condemn certain behaviors and attitudes; they model moral precepts as they go about the job. When the administrators at Albion took the side of minority students in the lunchroom radio incident, they gave a clear message to faculty that discrimination by race was not to be tolerated. A powerful message was transmitted. Had there been administrative apathy, an equally powerful point would have been made. (76)

Principals are cast into powerful symbolic roles whether they intend it or not and whether they like it or not. Inaction, in certain circumstances, can be as powerful a symbolic statement as is action.

The Semantics of Cultural Leadership.   To understand and practice symbolic and cultural leadership the emphasis needs to be on the semantics of leadership, not the phonetics. What the leader does represents the phonetics. What the leader's actions and behaviors mean to others represents the semantics. Focusing on semantics helps in the understanding that very often it is the little things that count. One does not have to mount a white horse and charge forward in a grand dramatic event in order to be a symbolic leader. Simple routines and humble actions properly orchestrated can communicate very important messages and high ideas.

Saphier and King (1985), for example, point out that the content of symbolic and cultural leadership need not be different from that of technical, human, and educational leadership. In their words, "Cultures are built through the everyday business of school life. It is the way business is handled that both forms and reflects the culture. . . . Culture building occurs . . . through the way people use educational, human and technical skills in handling daily events or establishing regular practices" (72). David Dwyer reaches a similar conclusion. In describing his research with Lee, Rowan, and Bossert (1983) Dwyer notes:

> Another fundamental characteristic of these principals was the routine nature of their actions. Instead of leaders of large-scale or dramatic innovation, we found men and women who shared a meticulous attention to detail. We observed an attention to the physical and emotional elements of the school environment, school-community relations, the teaching staff, schoolwide student achievement, and individual student progress. Their most essential activities included forms of monitoring,

information control and exchange, planning, direct interaction with students, hiring and staff development, and overseeing building maintenance. (1984:37)

It is through such routines that the principal focuses attention, demonstrates commitments, and otherwise "embarks on a slow but steady campaign to create a consensus of values and beliefs in a setting" (Dwyer, 1989:22).

Appendix 5–1 shows how Frances Hedges, one of the principals studied by Dwyer and his colleagues, managed to practice symbolic and cultural leadership by tending to both routine and varied aspects of her work.

The Dynamic Aspects of School Culture

All schools have cultures, but successful schools seem to have strong and functional cultures aligned with a vision of quality schooling. Culture serves as a compass setting to steer people in a common direction; it provides a set of norms defining what people should accomplish and how, and it is a source of meaning and significance for teachers, students, administrators, and others as they work. Strong and functional cultures are *domesticated* in the sense that they emerge deliberately — they are nurtured and built by the school leadership and membership.

Once shaped and established in a school, strong culture acts as a powerful socializer of thought and programmer of behavior. But the shaping and establishment of such a culture don't just happen. They are, instead, a negotiated product of the shared sentiments of school participants. When competing points of view and competing ideologies exist in the school, deciding which ones will count requires some struggling. Principals are in an advantageous position to strongly influence the outcome of this struggle. They are, for example, in control of the communications system of the school and thus can decide what information to share and with whom. Further, they control the allocation of resources and are able to reward desirable (and sanction undesirable) behavior. Bates (1981) elaborates on the principal's influence in shaping school culture:

> The culture of the school is therefore the product of conflict and negotiation over definitions of situations. The administrative influence on school language, metaphor, myths and rituals is a major factor in the determination of the culture which is reproduced in the consciousness of teacher and pupils. Whether that culture is based on metaphors of capital accumulation, hierarchy and domination is at least partly attributable to the exercise of administrative authority during the negotiation of what is to count as culture in the school. (43)

Can a culture emerge in a school based on agreements to disagree; on the maintenance of ambiguity over certainty; and on norms of variety and playfulness rather than order? Key for the concept of culture is the importance of collective ideology, shared values and sentiments, and norms that define acceptable behavior. The actual substance of culture is, by contrast, less important. Thus, not all schools with strong cultures are characterized by "harmony." Indeed, agreeing to disagree may well be the core value of a given school culture. This is often the case with respect to colleges and universities and to school research and development enterprises.

School Culture Building

Culture building requires that school leaders give attention to the informal, subtle, and symbolic aspects of school life. Teachers, parents, and students need answers to questions such as these: What is this school about? What is important here? What do we believe in? Why do we function the way we do? How are we unique? How do I fit into the scheme of things? Answering these questions imposes an order on one's school life that is derived from a sense of purpose and enriched meanings. As Greenfield (1973) states:

> What many people seem to want from schools is that schools reflect the values that are central and meaningful in their lives. If this view is correct, schools are cultural artifacts that people struggle to shape in their own image. Only in such forms do they have faith in them; only in such forms can they participate comfortably in them. (570)

What is the purpose of leadership conceived as a cultural force? "The task of leadership is to create the moral order that binds them [leaders] and the people around them," notes Thomas B. Greenfield (1984:159). James Quinn (1981) states: "The role of the leader, then, is one of orchestrator and labeler: taking what can be gotten in the way of action and shaping it—generally after the fact—into lasting commitment to a new strategic direction. In short, he makes meanings" (59). Leadership as culture building is not a new idea but one that is solidly embedded in our history and well known to successful school and other leaders. In 1957 Phillip Selznick wrote:

> The art of the creative leader is the art of institution building, the reworking of human and technological materials to fashion an organism that embodies new and enduring values. . . . To institutionalize is to *infuse with value* beyond the technical requirements of the task at hand. The prizing of social machinery beyond its technical role is largely a reflection of the unique way it fulfills personal or group needs. Whenever individuals become attached to an organization or a way of doing things as persons rather than as technicians, the result is a prizing of the device for its own sake. From the standpoint of the committed person, the organization is changed from an expendable tool into a valued source of personal satisfaction. . . . The institutional leader, then, is *primarily an expert in the promotion and protection of values.* (28)

And in 1938 the noted theorist Chester Barnard stated the following about executive functions: "The essential functions are, first to provide the system of communications; second, to promote the securing of essential efforts; and third, to formulate and define purpose." He continued: "It has already been made clear that, strictly speaking, purpose is defined more nearly by the aggregate of action taken than by any formulation in words" (vii).

Successful Schools and Central Zones

One of the findings revealed in the successful schools literature is that these schools have central zones comprising values and beliefs that take on sacred characteristics. Indeed, it might be useful to think of them as having an official "religion" that gives meaning and guides appropriate actions. As repositories of values, these central zones are sources of identity for teachers and students from which their school lives become meaningful. The focus of cultural leadership, then, is on developing and nurturing these central zone patterns so that they provide a normative basis for action within the school.

In some respects the concept of central zone suggests that successful schools are tightly structured. This means that they are closely organized in a highly disciplined fashion around a set of core ideas spelling out the way of life in the school and governing the way in which people should behave. This is in contrast to recent developments in organizational theory that describe schools as being loosely structured entities (these developments were discussed in Part I). Cohen, March, and Olsen (1972), for example, speak of educational organizations as being "organized anarchies." Similarly, Karl Weick (1982) uses the phrase "loose coupling" to describe the ways in which schools are organized. Indeed, Weick believes that one reason for ineffectiveness in schools is that they are managed with the wrong theory in mind.

Contemporary thought, Weick argues, assumes that schools are characterized by four properties: the existence of a self-correcting rational system among people who work in highly interdependent ways; consensus on goals and the means to obtain these goals; coordination by the dissemination of information; and predictability of problems and responses to these problems. He notes that, in fact, *none* of these properties is a true characteristic of schools and how they function. Principals in loosely coupled schools, he argues, need to make full use of symbol management to tie the system together. In his words: "People need to be part of sensible projects. Their action becomes richer, more confident, and more satisfying when it is linked with important underlying themes, values and movements" (675). And, he states further: "Administrators must be attentive to the 'glue' that holds loosely coupled systems together because such forms are just barely systems" (675). Finally, he notes that

> the administrator who manages symbols does not just sit in his or her office mouthing clever slogans. Eloquence must be disseminated. And since channels are unpredictable, administrators must get out of the office and spend lots of time one on one—both to remind people of central visions and to assist them in applying these visions to their own activities. The administrator teaches people to interpret what they are doing in a common language. (676)

Some commentators on the successful schools literature point out that these schools are not loosely coupled or structured at all but instead are tightly coupled (Cohen, 1983). A more careful study of this literature leads one to believe that successful schools are *both* tightly coupled and loosely coupled, an observation noted as well by Peters and Waterman (1982) in their studies of America's best-run corporations. There exists in successful schools a strong culture and clear sense of purpose that defines the general thrust and nature of life for their inhabitants. At the same time a great deal of freedom is given to teachers and others as to how these essential core values are to be honored and realized. This combination of tight structure – around clear and explicit themes representing the core of the school's culture – and of autonomy – so that people can pursue these themes in ways that make sense to them – may well be a key reason why these schools are so successful.

The combination of tight structure and loose structure matches very well three important human characteristics associated with motivation to work, commitment, enthusiasm, and loyalty to the school:

1. The need for teachers, students, and other school workers to find their work and personal lives meaningful, purposeful, sensible, and significant

2. The need for teachers, students, and other school workers to have some reasonable control over their work activities and affairs and to be able to exert reasonable influence over work events and circumstances

3. The need for teachers, students, and other school workers to experience success, to think of themselves as winners, and to receive recognition for their success

People are willing to make a significant investment of time, talent, and energy in exchange for enhancement and fulfillment of these three needs (Peters and Waterman, 1982; Hackman and Oldham, 1980). The concept of combined tight and loose coupling in schools is developed further in Chapter 7 as the importance of school goals and purposes is discussed. As part of that discussion, a balanced approach to leadership is proposed. This balance comprises both resilient and flexible leadership; resilient for the school's core of values and beliefs and flexible for the day-by-day articulation of these values in teaching and learning.

Summary

In this chapter leadership has been described metaphorically as a set of five forces: technical, human, educational, symbolic, and cultural. When the forces are brought together in expressions of the principal's leadership, they provide the basis for her or his influence. The more of these forces that come to play, the more powerful the principalship will be. Viewing the five forces within the context of school success, we can make the following assertions:

1. Technical and human leadership forces are generic; thus, they share identical qualities with competent management and leadership wherever they

are expressed. They are not, therefore, unique to the school and its enterprise regardless of how important they may be.

2. Educational, symbolic, and cultural leadership forces are situational and contextual, deriving their unique qualities from specific matters of education and schooling. These are the qualities that differentiate educational leadership, school supervision, and school administration from management and leadership in general.

3. Technical, human, and (aspects of) educational leadership forces are essential to competent schooling, and their absence contributes to ineffectiveness. The fact and strength of their presence alone, however, are not sufficient to bring about success in schooling.

4. Cultural, symbolic, and aspects of educational leadership forces are essential to success in schooling. Their absence, however, does not appear to have a negative impact on routine competence.

5. The greater the presence of educational, symbolic, and cultural leadership forces, the less important (beyond some unknown minimum presence) are technical and human forces.

As the five forces are brought together by the principal, the principalship itself becomes a powerful means for enhancing quality schooling. But the principalship also involves the enabling of others to lead; thus, the concept of *leadership density* is also important to quality schooling. As indicated earlier, leadership density means the total amount of leadership expressed on behalf of school quality by students, parents, and teachers as well as by principals. The greater the density of leadership, the more successful the school is likely to be (March, 1984). Despite the importance of leadership to the principalship, careful analysis of the successful schools research reveals that leadership is a fairly common commodity and that leadership roles are exercised freely by others in addition to the principal. Teacher leadership, for example, is particularly key—a theme to be highlighted in subsequent chapters.

The relationship between each of the forces of leadership and successful schooling is summarized in Table 5-1. Included for each force is the dominant metaphor for the principal's leadership role and behavior, important theoretical constructs from which this behavior is derived, examples of these behaviors for principals, reactions of teachers and others to the leadership forces, and links of each force to school competence and excellence.

No easy formula, set of scientific rules, or foolproof recipe exists as to how the role responsibilities suggested by the forces are to be fulfilled. By adopting a reflective stance, however, the principal increases chances of success. Reflective practice relies on findings and principles that emerge from theory and research and from careful study of the specific context of schooling that a principal faces. It does not seek to establish a "one best way" for all principals to practice or a "one best way" to account for all situations. Instead, it seeks to use knowledge from many sources to inform the intuitions of principals so that the decisions they make about

TABLE 5-1 The Forces of Leadership and Excellence in Schooling

Force	Leadership Role Metaphor	Theoretical Constructs	Examples	Reactions	Link to Excellence
Technical	"Management engineer"	Planning and time management technologies Contingency leadership theories Organizational structure	Plan, organize, coordinate, and schedule Manipulate strategies and situations to ensure optimum effectiveness	People are managed as objects of a mechanical system. They react to efficient management with indifference but have a low tolerance for inefficient management.	Presence is important to achieve and maintain routine school competence but not sufficient to achieve excellence. Absence results in school ineffectiveness and poor morale.
Human	"Human engineer"	Human relation supervision "Linking" motivation theories Interpersonal competence Conflict management Group cohesiveness	Provide needed support Encourage growth and creativity Build and maintain morale Use participatory decision making	People achieve high satisfaction of their interpersonal needs. They like the leader and the school and respond with positive interpersonal behavior. A pleasant atmosphere exists that facilitates the work of the school.	
Educational	"Clinical practitioner"	Professional knowledge and bearing Teaching effectiveness Educational program design Clinical supervision	Diagnose educational problems Counsel teachers Provide supervision and evaluation Provide inservice Develop curriculum	People respond positively to the strong expert power of the leader and are motivated to work. They appreciate the assistance and concern provided.	Presence is essential to routine competence. Strongly linked to, but still not sufficient for, excellence in schooling. Absence results in ineffectiveness.

TABLE 5-1 (Continued)

Force	Leadership Role Metaphor	Theoretical Constructs	Examples	Reactions	Link to Excellence
Symbolic	"Chief"	Selective attention Purposing Modeling	Tour the school Visit classrooms Know students Preside over ceremonies and rituals Provide a unified vision	People learn what is of value to the leader and school, have a sense of order and direction, and enjoy sharing that sense with others. They respond with increased motivation and commitment.	Presence is essential to excellence in schooling though absence does not appear to negatively affect routine competence.
Cultural	"High priest"	Climate, clan, culture Tightly structured values—loosely structured system Ideology "Bonding" motivation theory	Articulate school purpose and mission Socialize new members Tell stories and maintain reinforcing myths Explain SOPs Define uniqueness Develop and display a reinforcing symbol system Reward those who reflect the culture	People become believers in the school as an ideological system. They are members of a strong culture that provides them with a sense of personal importance and significance and work meaningfulness, which is highly motivating.	

From Thomas J. Sergiovanni (1984), "Leadership and Excellence in Schooling," *Educational Leadership* 41(5), 12.

practice are sound and effective for the unique situations and problems that they face. In this sense, theory and research are more metaphorical than real, designed to inform rather than prescribe practice.

References

Barnard, Chester I. 1938. *The Functions of the Executive.* Cambridge, MA: Harvard University Press.

Bates, Richard. 1981. "Management and the Culture of the School," in Richard Bates and Course Team, Eds., *Management of Resources in Schools: Study Guide I*, pp. 37–45. Geelong, Australia: Deakin University.

Bennis, Warren. 1984. "Transformation Power and Leadership," in Thomas J. Sergiovanni and John E. Corbally, Eds., *Leadership and Organizational Culture*, Urbana-Champaign: University of Illinois Press.

Blumberg, Arthur, and William Greenfield. 1980. *The Effective Principal: Perspectives on School Leadership.* Boston: Allyn and Bacon.

Boyer, Ernest. 1983. *High School: A Report on Secondary Education in America.* New York: Harper & Row.

Clark, Burton R. 1972. "The Organizational Saga in Higher Education." *Administrative Science Quarterly* 17(2), 178–184.

Cohen, Michael. 1983. "Instructional Management and Social Conditions in Effective Schools," in *School Finance and School Improvement; Linkages in the 1980's*, edited by Allan Odden and L. Dean Webb. Yearbook of the American Educational Finance Association.

Cohen, Michael D., James G. March, and Johan Olsen. 1972. "A Garbage Can Model of Organizational Choice." *Administrative Science Quarterly* 17(1), 1–25.

Dwyer, David. 1984. "The Search for Instructional Leadership: Routines and Subtleties in the Principal's Role." *Educational Leadership* 41(5).

Dwyer, David, Ginny Lee, Brian Rowan, and Steven Bossert. 1983. *Five Principles in Action: Perspectives on Instructional Management.* San Francisco: Far West Laboratory for Educational Research and Development.

Dwyer, David. 1989. "School Climate Starts at the Curb." *School Climate – The Principal Difference.* Monograph Series #1. The Connecticut Principals' Academy. Hartford, Conn. pp. 1–26.

Goodlad, John L. 1978. "Educational Leadership: Toward the Third Era," *Educational Leadership* 23(4), 322–331.

Goodlad, John L. 1983. *A Study of Schooling.* New York: McGraw-Hill.

Greenfield, Thomas B. 1973. "Organizations as Social Inventions: Rethinking Assumptions About Change," *Journal of Applied Behavioral Science* 9(5).

Greenfield, Thomas B. 1984. "Leaders and Schools: Willfulness and Non-Natural Order in Organization," in *Leadership and Organizational Culture*, Thomas J. Sergiovanni and John E. Corbally, Eds. Urbana-Champaign: University of Illinois Press.

Hackman, Ray C. 1969. *The Motivated Working Adult.* New York: American Management Association.

Hackman, J. Richard, and Greg R. Oldham. 1980. *Work Redesign.* Reading, MA: Addison-Wesley.

Hofstede, G. 1980. *Cultures Consequences.* Beverly Hills, CA: Sage Publications.

Lieberman, A., and L. Miller. 1984. *Teachers, Their World, and Their Work.* Arlington, VA: Association for Supervision and Curriculum Development.

March, James G. 1984. "How We Talk and How We Act: Administrative Theory and Administrative Life," in *Leadership and Organizational Culture*, Thomas J. Sergiovanni and John E. Corbally, Eds., 18–35. Urbana-Champaign: University of Illinois Press.

Peters, Thomas J., and Robert H. Waterman, Jr. 1982. *In Search of Excellence*. New York: Harper & Row.

Pondy, Louis. 1978. "Leadership Is a Language Game," in *Leadership: Where Else Can We Go?*, Morgan W. McCall, Jr. and Michael M. Lombardo, Eds. Durham, NC: Duke University Press.

Prunty, John J., and Wells Hively. 1982. "The Principal's Role in School Effectiveness: An Analysis of the Practices of Four Elementary School Leaders." National Institute of Education (G 8-01-10) and CEMRL, Inc., Nov. 30, 1982.

Quinn, James B. 1981. "Formulating Strategy One Step at a Time," *Journal of Business Strategy*, Winter.

Saphier, John, and Matthew King. 1985. "Good Seeds Grow in Strong Cultures," *Educational Leadership* 42(6).

Selznick, Phillip. 1957. *Leadership and Administration: A Sociological Interpretation*. New York: Harper & Row.

Starratt, Robert J. 1973. "Contemporary Talk on Leadership: Too Many Kings in the Parade?" *Notre Dame Journal of Education* 4(1).

United States Senate, Select Committee on Equal Educational Opportunity. 1972. "Revitalizing the Role of the School Principal," in *Toward Equal Educational Opportunity*, Senate Report No. 92-0000, 305–307.

Vaill, Peter B. 1984. "The Purposing of High Performing Systems," in *Leadership and Organizational Culture*, Thomas J. Sergiovanni and John E. Corbally, Eds., 85–104. Urbana-Champaign: University of Illinois Press.

Weick, Karl E. 1982. "Administering Education in Loosely Coupled Schools." *Phi Delta Kappan* 27(2), 673–676.

APPENDIX 5–1 Frances Hedges and Orchard Park Elementary School

The year 1982 marked Orchard Park Elementary School's 35th year in the city of Hillsdale. Surrounding the school were rows of white, grey, pale green and pastel yellow houses, whose neatly trimmed yards were, by late summer, straw-colored from lack of water. The neighborhood itself was quiet, but the noises from a nearby freeway attested to its urban setting. The community's only distinctive landmark was an old church which occupied a large corner lot adjacent to the school. Its three onion-shaped spires had for years cast a sense of permanence over the entire community.

"Permanent," however, would be a somewhat misleading description of the area. Prior to 1960, white, middle-class families of Italian descent predominated in the neighborhood. Over the next few years increasing numbers of ethnic minorities moved out of the city's poorer neighborhoods to areas like Orchard Park's community, seeking better schools and better living conditions. As a result, Orchard Park's neighborhood lost its homogeneity, and some of its quiet, as a number of racial conflicts marred the community's tranquility. The school also was affected, and staff had to find a way to adapt the program to the needs of the newer students.

The new student body at Orchard Park Elementary School was characterized by a diversity of racial groups from various ethnic backgrounds. District records showed that as many as 10 different language groups were represented in the school's student population. Fifty-nine percent of the students were black; 13 percent reflected Spanish heritage; 16 percent were Asian (Chinese, Filipino, Samoan, Laotian and Vietnamese); and 11 percent were white. Other ethnic groups composed the remaining one percent. The majority of the students' families were of low- or lower-middle income status. These students were energetic and active, frequently exhibiting aggressive behavior that stemmed more from overexuberance than from any other motivation. Groups at play were observed to be multiethnic and solicitous of affection and approval from teachers and the principal. Warm hugs exchanged between staff members and students were common occurrences on the playground.

Orchard Park employed 25 teachers, the majority of whom were very experienced. There were few signs of negativism, criticism or conflict among these teachers despite the fact that their instructional approaches differed markedly. Generally, they were supportive of the school and particularly of the principal. One teacher told us that there was only one reason for staff turnover at Orchard Park—retirement. Further evidence of their satisfaction with the status quo came at the end of the year of our study. The staff, together with the community, rallied to prevent the transfer of their principal and came together to hold a "Principal Appreciation" gathering to honor Hedges' leadership.

The center of attention at that ceremony, Frances Hedges, was a 60-year-old black woman who had served at Orchard Park for six and a half years. She conveyed to all who met her a sense of elegance through her well-matched clothes, golden earrings, oversized glasses and neatly fashioned white hair. Her appearance contrasted to the casual style adhered to by most of her staff; she was easily distinguished as the person in charge.

Long before coming to Orchard Park, Hedges had attended a teachers' college in her hometown, originally intending to become a child psychologist. But economic considerations prevented her from pursuing this goal. Instead, she spent 21 years as a classroom teacher, mostly in the district that includes Orchard Park. After receiving a Master's Degree in educational administration, she gradually climbed to her current position by working as a reading resource teacher, a district program coordinator and a vice principal.

Hedges' manner with staff and students was personable. Whether discussing professional matters or just making small talk, she conveyed warmth and friendliness through smiles and laughter. She was generous with compliments to both students and teachers. She also communicated often and comfortably through touches, hugs and embraces. As a result, she frequently was referred to by both students and teachers as Orchard Park's "mother figure."

Excerpted from David Dwyer (1989), "School Climate Starts at the Curb," *School Climate—The Principal Difference,* Hartford, Conn.: The Connecticut Principals' Academy.

both students and teachers as Orchard Park's "mother figure."

Hedges' way of acting was consistent with her philosophy. She strongly adhered to what she termed "humanistic" beliefs about education. She explained:

> My philosophy is that if we are warm and humane and nurturing, we maximize the learning of children. There is just no way to separate out those basic needs.

Believing that she was "acutely sensitive to . . . children's needs as well as adults' needs," Hedges strove to keep everyone in her learning community "reasonably happy" and worked to help everyone strengthen their self-concepts.

Attending to the basic needs of children logically led to Hedges' attention to safety and order in her school. She was a strict disciplinarian and never hesitated to reprimand children for misbehavior. Her harsh words, however, always would be followed by her efforts to help children understand their mistakes and become more responsible for their own behavior. She said:

> I believe that if we are really going to change the behavior of children, we can't just say "stop that," without going a step further and really having some kind of dialogue about what took place, why, and what are the options.

Her philosophy of education also included tenets about instruction. She strongly believed in the importance of academics, particularly reading. She pronounced:

> Reading is by far our number one priority. I believe that if children don't know how to read, they really cannot make it in this world.

Thus, Hedges' beliefs about education were related to her concerns for both the social and academic well-being of her students. It came as no surprise to find that her goals for the school reflected those convictions.

Hedges' primary goal at Orchard Park was to build a program conducive to the emotional and social growth of her students. She wanted her staff both to instill in each child a love for learning and to foster an awareness of social responsibility. She was adamant that her staff actively seek to strengthen students' self-concepts. These goals, she believed, were pre-eminent. They were a foundation upon which successful academic experiences could be built.

The principal's concern for the academic growth of her students was always stated from a "whole-child" perspective. Delineating her academic goals, she said:

> We work very hard to try to make sure that in the six or seven years that boys and girls are in elementary school, that they leave this school operating at grade level or above. . . . I'd like to see them at grade level for at least their last two years so that they can go into junior high school as much stronger and more confident children.

Hedges actively promoted both her social and academic goals to her faculty. During the year of our study with her, she utilized a district mandate to develop and implement an integrated, three-year instructional plan as a major vehicle to communicate her goals and develop her staff's commitment to them. Evidence that she had been very successful in this aspect of her work accumulated as we interviewed teachers about their beliefs and goals. In virtually all instances, their statements echoed Hedges' own.

How did Frances Hedges bring about the warm and productive climate at Orchard Park? Hedges demonstrated a propensity for direct, face-to-face interaction with participants in her setting. In total, 51 percent of her activities were verbal exchanges of varying length. The other glaring fact in the Orchard Park story is that her routine actions directly affected the climate at Orchard Park, making it conducive to teaching and learning.

Both the value she placed on students' emotional well-being and her goal to improve students' self-esteem contributed to a vision of school climate as an important end in itself. In addition, her beliefs about schools and schooling linked climate to instruction in several ways: she considered students' emotional well-being as an important precursor to their learning; she regarded an orderly, disciplined environment as a necessary condition for teaching and learning to take place; and she believed that the improvement of teachers' instructional practices was best achieved in a setting

APPENDIX 5–1 *(Continued)*

that built on the positive aspects of their skills. Thus, she strove to maintain an environment that contributed to the happiness, safety and productivity of all participants.

We see in many of Hedges' routine actions the keys to the development and maintenance of Orchard Park's social milieu. Her actions, as she supervised students in the building and on the playgrounds, attended simultaneously to the need to maintain safety and order at the school and to build students' self-esteem. She monitored their conduct and corrected them when necessary, exchanging her views about responsible behavior and reinforcing school rules. She constantly reminded students to pick up trash, bus their trays in the cafeteria, play in the correct areas of the playyard, walk instead of run in the hallways, refrain from pushing and shoving, and be quiet in the corridors and auditorium. She utilized these same actions to carry out her more social goals: she frequently stopped to talk to students, expressing delight at seeing them or remarking about the clothes they were wearing. Children often approached her to describe important events in their lives. Many of these brief interactions were concluded with a hug exchanged between the principal and the youngster.

An additional strategy Hedges used in her supervision of students was to model appropriate behavior. She might, for example, pick up a piece of trash and deposit it in a container or take a food tray to the cafeteria kitchen as she reminded students of the rules, often mentioning that they should keep the school as tidy as they would their homes.

Hedges' desire to counsel students played a large part in her interactions with children, especially those who had committed some infraction of school rules. We witnessed many instances of her counselor-like approach as she dealt with students whom she had seen misbehaving or who had been sent to her for fighting, stealing, acting inappropriately in class, or failing to complete their school work. In all instances, she carefully took the time to listen to what the students had to say about their behavior. Hedges explained this strategy in terms of her humanistic philosophy:

> *If you don't do something, [children] feel . . . that their problems are falling on deaf ears. I tell the staff all the time, "You really do have to take the time out, let a child explain what happened, and be willing to at least listen, whether it's what that particular child wants, or not . . . it's just that someone has listened."*

Students were aware that Hedges would act vigorously and appropriately if they misbehaved as well as listen to their problems. When infractions were serious, Hedges would tell students that she was going to phone their parents to report incidents . . . she always followed through. As a result Orchard Park's students understood that their principal was serious about discipline and true to her word.

We mentioned earlier the importance that Hedges placed on building on the positive aspects of people in the school. This approach was most apparent in her dealings with problem students as she implemented special plans to communicate to them that, despite misbehavior, they were still worthy human beings and could act responsibly. We observed one instance in which Hedges appointed the worst offenders in the school as "Chair Captains" and allowed them to pick their own squads who would help set up and take down chairs in the auditorium. The youngsters saw this as an important and enjoyable responsibility that gave them status among their peers. In another instance, Hedges urged that a child who had a particularly negative attitude toward school be assigned to the traffic detail. His teacher remarked that this made a dramatic improvement in the boy's classroom behavior and attitude.

When infractions were serious, Hedges often assigned offenders work projects around the school that would contribute to the school's overall welfare. She tenaciously pursued alternatives to suspension. One teacher reported of the principal's efforts to deal with problem students:

> *[Hedges] has a relationship with almost all of the children that regularly act out, the ones that are really on your blacklist. . . . If it's your child that's constantly acting out, you would almost want her to say, "Doggone! Let's give up on that kid." But she never really does.*

APPENDIX 5–1 *(Continued)*

Hedges not only worked creatively with problem students but encouraged growth in responsibility among all students at Orchard Park. For example, she taught leadership to all members of the school's student council.

Orchard Park's teachers also were encouraged to promote positive social values in the school through classroom activities. In an unusual departure from Hedges' policy of permitting a good deal of staff autonomy concerning the selection of classroom materials, for example, she established a schoolwide focus on her social goals through the introduction of a set of self-esteem materials. At the first faculty meeting of the year, Hedges presented the materials and asked staff members to use them as a regular part of their programs. Although the use of these materials was not systematically monitored, her message was clear to her staff. Subsequently, teachers were observed using an array of esteem-building activities in their classrooms, including magic circle activities, life box materials, and art projects to stimulate discussions about feelings and attitudes.

Thus Hedges aggressively pursued a positive school climate at Orchard Park. By demonstrating her values in her daily interactions and conversations, Hedges encouraged an environment in which staff members shared her child-centered approach. Participants in the setting directly and indirectly exhibited their satisfaction: there was very little vandalism by students in the school, teachers felt lucky to be at the school and left only because of retirement, and the district held a waiting list of teacher anxious to join this faculty.

Hedges also directly or indirectly manipulated such important elements of the organization as class size and composition, scheduling, staff assignments, the scope and sequence of curriculum, the distribution of instructional materials and even teaching styles. On the surface, a principal actively and successfully engaged in shaping the conditions for and of instruction in a school seems perfectly natural — principals are supposed to be instructional leaders, right? But we also know that teachers enjoy and expect autonomy in matters related to classroom instruction. It is not uncommon for teachers to actively or passively resist principals' instructional improvement campaigns.

Hedges was able to transcend this problem for two reasons. First, her own 21 years of experience as a classroom teacher and reading specialist legitimated her expertise in the eyes of her faculty. The second ingredient to Hedges' success at influencing her staff's classroom practices was her ability to establish a culture of instruction at the school, facilitated by the emphasis she placed on building on people's strengths and emphasizing the positive. Thus, experience coupled with style enabled her to provide information to teachers without alienating them. Her staff regarded her as competent and nonthreatening. They not only accepted her suggestions, but actively sought her advice and counsel.

While there many strategies that Hedges used to influence instruction both directly and indirectly at the school, the most potent and pervasive was the informal classroom visit. Hedges monitored instruction by regularly dropping into teachers' classrooms. These visits provided opportunities to make suggestions that did not carry the onus that might accompany recommendations made as the result of formal classroom evaluations. On many of Hedges' informal visits, we observed her assisting teachers by working with students and making brief constructive and supportive comments to her staff.

These often-repeated behaviors were key features in her strategy to reduce teachers' anxieties about her visits. She mentioned that she spent time building positive rapport with teachers before providing suggestions for changes in their instructional patterns:

I operate with the idea that we really are all a team. If I can just . . . give [the staff] enough strokes on those positives, then I can get [at] those areas that are not so well done.

When Hedges did feel a need to comment on teachers' deficiencies, she did so in a low-key, nonthreatening manner without embarrassing, confronting or demeaning them.

Hedges also promoted a norm of teacher-to-teacher sharing because she did not see herself as the only source of instructional expertise in the school. She often advised teachers to talk with their colleagues for assistance or ideas. Frequently this required Hedges to organize opportunities for staff members to get together. For example, she commonly arranged for the school's reading

APPENDIX 5–1 *(Continued)*

specialist to help teachers create reading centers in a classroom or help classroom teachers evaluate those students who required remedial instruction. There were many instances of Hedges arranging meetings between teachers who were successful with new methods and teachers who were less successful. In this way, she served as a "linking agent" or "information broker." Because Hedges' classroom visits were regular, her recommendations were timely and the staff found them very helpful. Hedges also used classroom visits as opportunities to impress upon children the importance she attached to academic success. By publicly complimenting students on their individual or group successes, she not only strengthened their self-esteem, but created an ethos about learning that children would want to share. . . .

Her philosophy is marked by simple tenets: all people are fundamentally good; everyone can learn and grow in a warm and nurturing environment; any successful enterprise is the result of teamwork and everyone can and must contribute to the whole. From experience, Hedges adds to these beliefs a strongly held value regarding the importance of reading as an essential skill that children must master to realize their highest potential. These humane attributes are wrapped in her tough-minded awareness about the importance of setting limits and making children and staff responsible for their own behavior.

Hedges leads her school by continually communicating her beliefs to parents, students and staff members through her routine actions. By constant word and deed she demonstrates how the vision she holds of the "good" school must work. Mostly she proceeds through patient, subtle suggestions and reminders. Occasionally, she mandates changes or additions to organizational structures, procedures and curricula. But the key to her success is the relentless pursuit of her goals and her talent in getting others to adopt those goals.

Over years at Orchard Park, staff have experimented with procedures and techniques Hedges has recommended. They have been continually bombarded with her rationale. As they experience success, the procedures and rationales become embedded in their own experiences and slowly alter their own beliefs. Slowly, a working consensus about the "right" way to teach and run a school emerges. As those beliefs fade into assumptions and become habituated, an organizational culture is born. Its progenitor, its patient nurseryman, was Frances Hedges.

CHAPTER 6

The Stages of Leadership: A Developmental View

In Chapter 5 we examined leadership as a set of forces available to principals for maintaining and improving schools. In this chapter we are concerned with the actual behaviors that make up leadership strategies and tactics as principals work firsthand with teachers and others. Four leadership strategies are identified.

1. *Bartering:* Leader and led strike a bargain within which leader gives to led something they want in exchange for something the leader wants.
2. *Building:* Leader provides the climate and interpersonal support that enhances led's opportunities for fulfillment of needs for achievement, responsibility, competence, and esteem.
3. *Bonding:* Leader and led develop a set of shared values and commitments that bond them together in a common cause.
4. *Banking:* Leader "banks the fire" by institutionalizing improvement gains into the everyday life of the school. (Sergiovanni, 1990:30)

Taken together the strategies can be thought of as developmental stages each suited to different levels of school competence and excellence. The stages are summarized below.

Stage	Leadership by	Results
1. Initiation (getting started)	Bartering (push)	Has value (helps achieve competence)
2. Uncertainty (muddling through)	Building (support)	Adds value (increases readiness for excellence)
3. Transformative (breakthrough)	Bonding (inspire)	Adds value (helps achieve excellence)
4. Routinization (remote control)	Banking (monitor)	Adds value (institutionalizes excellence)

When viewed as developmental stages the emphasis is not on which leadership strategy is best, but which of the strategies makes most sense given the stage of school improvement in question. Leadership by bartering, for example, makes most sense in schools that are not working very well. Leadership by bonding, by contrast, makes sense when basic competence is not the issue and when a healthy interpersonal climate has been established. Each of the stages and leadership strategies will be elaborated on later in this chapter. But first it is important to differentiate between leadership for competence and leadership for excellence.

Leadership for Competence and Leadership for Excellence

Principals are responsible for gaining control over the likelihood that the school's basic requirements for competence are met and for helping the school and its members transcend competence by inspiring extraordinary commitment and performance. One of the shortcomings of traditional management and its leadership practices is that they can help teachers and schools achieve a basic level of competence but cannot sustain this competence without constant monitoring. Further, traditional management and leadership are not able to encourage people and schools to transcend competence, allowing for commitment and performance beyond expectations (Burns, 1978; Bass, 1985).

In recent years the leadership practices based on traditional management have been augmented by findings from social science that suggest a more progressive human resources leadership practice (Miles, 1965; McGregor, 1960; Argyris, 1964; Likert, 1967; Sergiovanni and Starratt, 1971 and 1988). This practice seeks to enhance and uplift the intrinsic motivational structure of people, allowing them to experience higher levels of need fulfillment. The results attributed to this human resources leadership have been salutary. Given the right psychological conditions, commitment and performance exceed expectations. But human resources leadership is limited by the conditions of its psychological contract. That is, people respond enthusiastically as long as participation in work is psychologically fulfilling. When it isn't, commitment and performance become routine. When psychological fulfillment is defined in terms of higher-level needs (for example, Maslow's [1954] esteem autonomy and self-actualization or Herzberg's [1966] "motivators"), the problem is particularly troublesome. For most individuals the factors that contribute to need fulfillment have a way of escalating. Being consulted may be gratifying when a teacher is new, but as competence and recognition increase that person wants to be involved and ultimately in charge of matters of teaching that affect her or him.

The challenge of principals is to provide the leadership needed to achieve a basic level of competence and then to transcend this competence to get extraordinary commitment and performance not only when rewards are available but when they are not. Sustained commitment and performance require an approach to leadership that connects people to work for moral reasons. Moral reasons emerge from the purposes, values, and norms that form the cultural center of the school. This center bonds people together in a common cause. For this reason the leadership that is required is referred to as *bonding* leadership. The three approaches to leadership can be summarized as follows.

1. *Traditional leadership* practices emphasize hierarchy, rules, and management protocols and rely on bureaucratic linkages to connect people to work by forcing them to respond as subordinates.

2. *Human resources leadership* practices emphasize leadership styles, supportive climates, and interpersonal skills and rely on psychological linkages to motivate people to work by getting them to respond as self-actualizers.

3. *Bonding leadership* practices emphasize ideas, values, and beliefs and rely on moral linkages to compel people to work by getting them to respond as followers.

The Stages of Leadership

In 1978 James MacGregor Burns proposed a theory of leadership that has shaped the way leadership practice is now understood. According to Burns, leadership is exercised when persons with certain motives and purposes mobilize resources so as to arouse and satisfy the motives of followers. He identified two broad kinds of leadership, transactional and transformative. Transactional leadership focuses on basic and largely extrinsic motives and needs; transformative leadership focuses on higher-order, more intrinsic, and ultimately moral motives and needs. This latter point is important to understanding Burns's theory. Burns (1978:20) described transformational leadership, for example, as a process within which "leaders and followers raise one another to higher levels of morality and motivation." Transformative leadership is in two stages, one concerned with higher-order psychological needs for esteem, autonomy, and self-actualization and the other with moral questions of goodness, righteousness, duty, and obligation.

In his groundbreaking examination of the moral dimension in management and motivation, Amitai Etzioni (1988) provides a compelling case for moral authority as a source of motivation and basis for management. Etzioni acknowledges the importance of extrinsic and intrinsic motivation but points out that ultimately what counts most to people is what they believe, how they feel, and the shared norms and cultural messages that emerge from the groups and communities with which they identify. Morality, emotion, and social bonds, he maintains, are far more powerful motivators than are the extrinsic concerns of transactional leadership and the intrinsic psychological concerns of the early stages of transformative leadership.

In transactional leadership, leader and followers exchange needs and services in order to accomplish *independent* objectives. It is assumed that leader and followers do not share a common stake in the enterprise, and thus some kind of bargain must be struck. This bargaining process can be viewed metaphorically as a form of *leadership by bartering*. The wants and needs of followers and the wants and needs of the leader are traded and a bargain is struck. Positive reinforcement is given for good work, merit pay for increased performance, promotion for increased persistence, a feeling of belonging for cooperation, and so on.

In transformative leadership, by contrast, leaders and followers are united in pursuit of higher-level goals that are common to both. Both want to become the best. Both want to shape the school in a new direction. When transformative leadership is practiced successfully, purposes that might have started out being separate become fused.

Initially, transformative leadership takes the form of *leadership by building*. Here the focus is on arousing human potential, satisfying higher-order needs, and raising expectations of both leader and follower in a manner that motivates both to higher levels of commitment and performance. Leadership by bartering responds to physical, security, social, and ego needs. Leadership by building responds to esteem, achievement, competence, autonomy, and self-actualizing needs. The human resources management and leadership literature referred to earlier in this chapter provides compelling evidence supporting the efficacy of leadership by building.

Burns points out that ultimately transformative leadership becomes moral because it raises the level of human conduct and ethical aspiration of both leader and led. When this occurs, transformative leadership takes the form of *leadership by bonding*. Here the leader focuses on arousing awareness and consciousness that elevate school goals and purposes to the level of a shared covenant that bonds together leader and follower in a moral commitment. Leadership by bonding responds to such intrinsic human needs as a desire for purpose, meaning, and significance in what one does. The key concepts associated with transformative leadership by bonding are cultural and moral leadership.

Leadership by bartering, building, and bonding, when viewed sequentially, make up the stages of leadership for school improvement referred to earlier. Bartering provides the push needed to get things started; building provides the push needed to deal with uncertainty and to create the psychological support system necessary for people to respond to higher levels of need fulfillment; and bonding provides the inspiration needed for performance and commitment that are beyond expectations.

School improvement initiatives become real only when they are institutionalized as part of the everyday life of the school. To this effort, *leadership by banking* is the fourth stage of school improvement. Banking seeks to routinize school improvements, thus conserving human energy and effort for new projects and initiatives. When practicing leadership by banking, the principal *ministers* to the needs of the school and works to serve others so that they are better able to perform their responsibilities. In addition to manager, minister, and servant the leader functions as a "high priest" by protecting the values of the school. The high priest function is an expression of the cultural force of leadership discussed in Chapter 5.

Each of the stages of leadership can be thought of as comprising distinct school improvement strategies. However, tactically speaking, bartering, building, bonding, and banking can be thought of as leadership styles to be used simultaneously for different purposes or people within any of the stages. A recalcitrant teacher, for example, may well require leadership by bartering regardless of one's overall strategy.

Leadership by bartering is an especially effective strategy when the issue is one of competence. But once competence has been achieved, one needs to look to leadership by building and bonding for the strategies and tactics that will help transcend competence to inspire commitment and extraordinary performance. The stages of leadership and their relationship to school improvement are summarized in Exhibit 6-1.

Operationalizing Charismatic Leadership

Transformational leadership in the form of leadership by building and bonding sounds similar to the concept of *charisma*. This similarity can be troublesome, for depending upon how charisma is defined, one could conclude that the ability to successfully practice leadership by building and bonding is based on specific endowed gifts of birth and personality. If this is the case, then some principals have it and others don't and those who don't can't get it. This is the conclusion to be reached if one accepts the metaphysical definition that comes from the Greek language, in which *charisma* means the ability to perform miracles, to predict the future, to possess divinely inspired gifts.

In recent years the social science literature has moved away from considering charisma as having something to do with "divine personality" to more ordinary definitions themed either to one's ability to influence and inspire others or to attributions of this ability. Instead of worrying about a mysterious charismatic personality, the emphasis is on identifying behaviors that encourage people to *attribute* charismatic qualities to the leader.

Leaders thought to be charismatic have the ability to touch some people in meaningful ways. As a result these people respond to their leaders and to the ideas and values that they stand for with unusual commitment and effort. The typical result is performance that is beyond expectations.

There is growing consensus that this charismatic leadership does not exist as something concrete or objective but is a perception—indeed an attribute that cannot be separated from followership. Followers attribute charisma to the leader. Further, no leader is thought to be charismatic by everyone. There needs to be a connection between what the leader does and the meanings, if any, that followers derive. For example, to many Americans, Presidents Kennedy and Reagan were considered to be charismatic in the sense that they touched people in meaningful ways—but not necessarily the same people. By the same token large numbers of Americans view Presidents Kennedy and Reagan negatively—but not necessarily the same people. Conger (1989:23-24) points out that in order for leadership behaviors to "induce the perception of charisma, their specific character has to be seen by followers as *relevant* to their situation. If followers do not think their leader's formulation of a strategic vision matches their own aspirations, they are less likely to perceive him or her as a charismatic leader."

According to attribution theory (i.e., Kelly, 1973), followers search for the meaning of the leader's behavior. We attribute a set of generalizations to the leader based on what we see and hear and what we think it means to us. We might conclude, for example, that Bill is a wishy-washy principal, Terry is a manager but little else, and that Mary is the kind of principal who is a real leader. Our conclusions result from our own needs, our values, our conceptions of what good leadership is, and our own experiences. If there is a match between the behaviors we observe and

EXHIBIT 6–1 The Stages of Leadership and School Improvement

Leadership Type	Leadership Styles	Stages of School Improvement	Leadership Concepts	Involvement of Followers	Needs Satisfied	Effects
Value (Transactional) Leadership	Leadership as "Bartering"	*Initiation* (push) Exchanging human needs and interests that allow satisfaction of independent (leader and follower) but organizationally related objectives.	Management skills Leadership style Contingency theory Exchange theory Path-goal theory	Calculated	Physical Security Social Ego	Continual performance contingent upon parties keeping the bargain struck. "A fair day's work for a fair day's pay."
Value-added (Transformational) Leadership	Leadership as "Building"	*Uncertainty* (muddle through) Arousing human potential, satisfying higher needs, raising expectations of both leader and followers that motivate to higher levels of commitment and performance.	Empowerment Symbolic leadership "Charisma"	Intrinsic	Esteem Competence Autonomy Self-actualization	Performance and commitment are sustained beyond external conditions. Both are beyond expectations in quantity and quality.

EXHIBIT 6-1 (Continued)

Leadership as "Bonding"	*Transformative* (breakthrough) Arousing awareness and consciousness that elevate organizational goals and purposes to the level of a shared covenant and that bond together leader and followers in a moral commitment.	Cultural leadership Moral leadership Covenant Building followership	Moral	Purpose Meaning Significance
Leadership as "Banking"	*Routinization* (remote control) Turning improvements into routines so that they become second-nature, ministering to the needs of the school, being of service, guarding the values.	Procedures Institutional leadership Servant leadership Leadership by outrage Kindling outrage in others	Automatic	All needs are supported Performance remains sustained.

Source: T. J. Sergiovanni, *Value-Added Leadership: How to Get Extraordinary Performance in Schools*, New York: Harcourt Brace Jovanovich, 1990, pp. 39–40.

what we think they mean, then the attribution is a positive one, and if not it is negative. These attributions result in different kinds of commitments to the leader and different levels of effort. After an exhaustive survey of the literature on charismatic leadership and attribution theory, Yukl (1989:205) concludes: "Charisma is believed to result from follower perceptions of leader qualities and behavior. These perceptions are influenced by the context of the leadership situation and the follower's individual and collective needs."

Behavioral Dimensions of Charisma

Conger and Kanungo (1987; 1988) have proposed a theory that identifies the leadership behaviors that influence followers to attribute charismatic qualities to a leader. The dimensions identified do not constitute a personality type but rather a set of leadership behaviors that can be duplicated by principals with varying personalities. Moreover, independent of the charismatic issue, the leadership behaviors result in extraordinary levels of commitment and performance (Conger, 1989). Conger and Kanungo (1987; 1988) propose that followers are more likely to attribute charisma to leaders

who advocate a vision that challenges the status quo but still is close enough to be accepted by followers.

who demonstrate convincingly that they are willing to take personal risks, incur high costs and even make self-sacrifices to achieve their vision.

who act in unconventional ways in implementing the vision.

whose vision and actions are timely in the sense that they are sensitive to the values, beliefs, and needs of followers on the one hand and to the opportunities inherent in the situation at hand on the other.

who respond to existing dissatisfaction or, if needed, who create dissatisfaction in the status quo.

who are able to communicate confidence in themselves and their proposals and who are enthusiastic about the future prospects for successful implementation of proposals.

who rely on expert power to influence others by demonstrating that they know what they are talking about and can propose solutions that help others to be successful. (summarized from Yukl, 1989:208–209)

According to Conger (1989) the behavioral dimensions of charismatic leadership are manifested in four stages. Stage one involves sensing leadership opportunities and formulating a vision. The leader detects unexploited opportunities and deficiencies or problems in the current situation and formulates a vision that responds. Key to stage one is being sensitive to the needs of followers and other constituents. Success of the proposed vision depends on whether it helps followers and others satisfy their own needs.

Stage two involves communicating the vision in a fashion that makes it clear that the current situation is unacceptable and the proposed vision is an attractive alternative. If the proposed alternative is responsive to the needs of followers and other constituents then it is likely to be accepted even though it represents a radical departure from the present. As Conger (1989) points out, "Since the vision is a perspective shared by the followers and promises to meet their aspirations, it tends to be very acceptable despite its radical departure from the present situation" (29).

Stage three involves building trust with followers and other constituencies by demonstrating sincerity and commitment to the proposed vision. As Conger (1989) explains, "Thus the leader must build exceptional trust among subordinates in himself and in the goals he articulates. The charismatic leader does this through personal risk taking, unconventional expertise, and self-sacrifice. These qualities set the charismatic leader apart from others" (33).

Stage four involves demonstrating the means to achieve the vision through modeling, empowering others, and the use of unconventional tactics.

One of the ways to test the efficacy of the ideas Conger and Kanungo propose is to examine leaders you know from personal experience whom you consider to possess charismatic qualities. To what extent do they exhibit the behavioral dimensions just described? As you review the dimensions, which one seems to function as the lynchpin that holds the others together?

Charismatic leaders, bonding leaders, and transformative leaders share one common quality: *the ability to respond to the needs of followers.* They are able to help others reach higher levels of need fulfillment, to extract more meaning from their work lives, to see what they are doing as something that is special and significant. When these needs are addressed, followers invariably respond with higher levels of commitment, effort, and performance.

Why Leadership by Bonding Works

Bonding leadership works because:

- It is aligned with a realistic view of how schools actually work; thus its practices are practical.
- It is based on a theory of human rationality that enhances both individual and organizational intelligence and performance.
- It responds to higher-order psychological and spiritual needs that lead to extraordinary commitment, performance, and satisfaction.

In Chapter 3 it was pointed out that traditional management assumes schools, school districts, and state systems of schooling are "managerially tight and culturally loose." According to this theory what counts in improving schools is management connections, not people. When this is the case, the operation of schools represents the mechanical workings of a clock comprising cogs and gears, wheels, drives, and pins, all tightly connected in an orderly and predictable manner. This is the "Clockworks I" theory or mindscape of management.

Clockworks I leaders believe that the purpose of leadership is to gain control and regulate the master wheel and the master pin of their clockworks organization. This is sometimes done by introducing highly refined management systems to ensure that teachers will teach the way they are supposed to and students will be taught what they are supposed to learn. Unfortunately, this rarely happens, at least not on a sustained and continuous basis and not without excessive monitoring and other enforcement efforts. When such a system does work, it gets people to do what they are supposed to, but no more (leadership by bartering).

Weick's (1976) observations and those of March (1984) provide an image of schools that functions like a clockworks gone awry—a theory of cogs, gears, and pins all spinning independently of each other. Regulating for the main gear and pin as a management strategy doesn't work since they are not connected to any of the other parts. Instead, the leader must rely on "cultural cement" to provide the necessary connections for coordination and control. The ingredients for cultural cement are the norms, values, beliefs, and purposes of people. Weick (1982:675) advises school leaders to ". . . . be attentive to the 'glue' that holds loosely coupled systems together because such forms are just barely systems." March (1984:32) similarly advises:

> If we want to identify one single way in which administrators can affect organizations, it is through their effect on the world views that surround organizational life; those effects are managed through attention to the ritual and symbolic characteristics of organizations and their administration. Whether we wish to sustain the system or change it, management is a way of making a symbolic statement.

Leadership by bonding can provide the necessary cultural cement that holds people and organization together.

Theories of school management and leadership are based on different images of human rationality. When a school leader chooses a theory from which to practice, a particular image of rationality is assumed whether or not it fits the real world. A better fit between theory and practice will occur by starting the other way around. First choose the image of rationality that fits the real world, and then find a theory that fits that image of rationality.

Shulman (1989) provides three images of human rationality. All three are true to a certain extent, but some are more true than others. It makes a difference which of the three or which combination of the three provides the strategic basis for one's leadership practice. The three are provided below. Using a total of 10 points, distribute points among the three to indicate the extent to which you believe each to be true.

1. Humans are rational; they think and act in a manner consistent with their goals, their self-interests and what they have been rewarded for. If you wish them to behave in a given way, make the desired behavior clear to them and make it worth their while to engage in it.

2. Humans are limited in their rationality; they can make sense of only a small piece of the world at a time and they strive to act reasonably with respect to

their limited grasp of facts and alternatives. They must, therefore, construct conceptions or definitions of situations rather than passively accept what is presented to them. If you wish them to change, engage them in active problem solving and judgment, don't just tell them what to do.

3. Humans are rational only when acting together; since individual reason is so limited, men and women find opportunities to work jointly on important problems, achieving through joint effort what individual reason and capacity could never accomplish. If you want them to change, develop ways in which they can engage in the change process jointly with peers. (Shulman, 1989:171)

The first image of rationality fits traditional management theories and leadership by bartering practices very well. The second and third images, by contrast, are better accommodated by the clockworks-gone-awry view of management and leadership by building and bonding. Within the second and third images, rationality is achieved by helping people make sense of their world. As sense builds, some of the limits on rationality are overcome. The ability to make sense builds when people are able to construct their own definitions of situations and are involved with the leader in active problem solving. The limits, however, are typically too great for anyone to do it alone. Thus, a key strategy for sense building is the pooling of human resources and the fostering of collegial values in an effort that expands individual reason and capacity to function successfully.

Leadership as bartering responds to physical, security, social, and ego needs of people at work. In his well-known motivation-hygiene theory, Herzberg (1966) pointed out that these needs and the job factors that accommodated to them had less to do with commitment and performance beyond expectations than with meeting ordinary basic job requirements. He pointed out that should the needs not be met, worker performance and commitment are likely to fall below a satisfactory level. But when the needs are met, all that results is that workers meet basic job requirements. However, when such job factors as opportunities for achievement, challenge, responsibility, recognition for one's accomplishment, and opportunities to demonstrate competence were present, then such higher-order needs as esteem, competence, autonomy, and self-actualization were likely to be met. These factors and needs are related to leadership by building. They are the bridges that leader and followers must cross together as they move from ordinary performance to performance that is beyond expectations.

The strength of leadership by bonding is its ability to focus on arousing awareness and consciousness that elevate school goals and purposes to the level of a shared covenant that bonds together leader and led in a moral commitment. Leadership by bonding responds to such higher-order needs as the desire for purpose, meaning, and significance in what one does.

New Leadership Values for the Principalship

The discussion in the chapters of Part II is founded on a number of embedded leadership values. These values are embedded as well in much of the discussion that follows in subsequent chapters. These values involve purposing, followership, empowerment, accomplishment, collegiality, intrinsic motivation, quality control, simplicity, reflection, and outrage. Together the values provide the substance for practicing leadership by bonding. They are considered in the following subsections in the form of leadership principles.

Purposing and Shared Values

Harvard Business School professor Abraham Zaleznik (Levin, 1988) believes that "the failure of . . . management is the substitution of process for substance." The importance of management processes to school effectiveness should not be underestimated, but such processes are not substitutes for substance. It is important, for example, to know how to get from A to B, and sound management can help. However, the substance of administrative leadership is concerned with whether B is better than A and why. Furthermore, having determined the direction, substance is the means by which one brings together divergent human resources, inspires commitment, and achieves extraordinary performance.

Management processes alone turn workers into *subordinates*. Substances, by contrast, builds *followership*. Subordinates comply with manasgement rules and procedures and with the leader's directives. The job gets done. Followers, on the other hand, respond to ideas, ideals, values, and purposes; and as a result the job gets done well.

In his classic book *The Functions of the Executive* (1938), Chester Barnard stated: "The inculcation of belief in the real existence of a common purpose is an essential executive function" (87). The inculcation of belief comes from the embodiment of purposes as leaders act and behave, or from *purposing*, in the words of Peter Vaill. He defines purposing as "that continuous stream of actions by an organization's formal leadership which has the effect of inducing clarity, consensus and commitment regarding the organization's basic purposes" (1984:91). Vaill (1984) conducted extensive studies of high-performing systems from a broad spectrum of American society. He examined the characteristics held in common by these systems and the kind of leadership found within them. Key to success was the presence of purposing. "HPS's are clear on their broad purposes and on near-term objectives for fulfilling these purposes. They know why they exist and what they are trying to do. Members have pictures in their heads which are strikingly congruent" (86). He continues, "Commitment to these purposes is never perfunctory. . . . [M]otivation as usually conceived is always high" (86).

Purposing is a key characteristic found by others who have studied successful schools in the United States. This research establishes the importance of shared goals and expectations and approved modes of behavior that create a strong school culture. Important to this culture are the norms and values that provide a cohesion and identity and that create a unifying moral order from which teachers and students derive direction, meaning, and significance. One example is Joan Lipsitz's (1984) study of four successful middle schools discussed in Chapter 4. She found that the four schools achieved unusual clarity about the purposes of intermediate schooling and the students they teach and made powerful statements, both in word and in practice, about their purposes. There was little disagreement about what they believed and little discrepancy between what they said they were doing and what they were actually doing.

It is through purposing and the building of shared values and agreements that a school culture emerges.

> The concept of culture refers to the total way of life in a society, the heritage of accumulated social learnings that is shared and transmitted by the members of that society. To put it another way a culture is a set of shared plans for living, developed out of necessities of previous generations, existing in the minds of the present generation, taught directly or indirectly to new generations. (White, 1952:15)

Purposing involves both the vision of the leader and a set of agreements that the group shares. Warren Bennis (1984) describes vision as "the capacity to create and communicate a compelling vision of a desired state of affairs, a vision . . . that clarifies the current situation and induces commitment to the future" (66). Vision is an important dimension of purposing and without it the very point of leadership is missed, but the vision of the school must also reflect the hopes and dreams, the needs and interests, the values and beliefs of everyone who has a stake in the school—teachers, parents, and students. In the end it is what the school stands for that counts. In successful schools, consensus runs deep. It is not enough to have worked out what people stand for and what is to be accomplished. A binding and solemn agreement needs to emerge that represents a value system for living together and that provides the basis for decisions and actions. This binding and solemn agreement represents the school's covenant.

When both vision and covenant are present, teachers and students respond with increased motivation and commitment and their performance is beyond expectations. The affirming of values that accompanies purposing is a motivational force far more powerful than the bureaucratic and psychological transactions that characterize leadership by bartering and building. They become the very basis upon which we construct our reality and from which we derive sense and meaning. As Gardner (1986) points out,

> A great civilization is a drama lived in the minds of people. It is a shared vision; it is shared norms, expectations and purposes. . . . If we look at ordinary human communities, we see the same reality: A community lives in the minds of its members—in shared assumptions, beliefs, customs, ideas that give meaning, ideas that motivate. (7)

Building Followership

In his book *Every Employee a Manager*, Scott Meyers (1971) observed that the more managementlike jobs were, the more readily workers accepted responsibility and responded with increased motivation. By *managementlike* he meant having the freedom to plan, organize and control one's life, to make decisions, to accept responsibility, and to be held accountable for one's actions in light of this responsibility.

Every employee a manager is a goal of leadership by bonding because it contributes to leadership density. *Leadership density* refers to the extent to which leadership roles are shared and leadership itself is broadly based and exercised. To understand leadership density one needs to understand how closely leadership and followership are linked and what the differences are between being a good follower and a good subordinate. Good followers manage themselves well. They think for themselves, exercise self-control, and are able to accept responsibility and obligation, believe in and care about what they are doing, and are self-motivated, thus able to do what is right for the school, do it well, do it with persistence, and most importantly do it without close supervision (Kelly, 1988). Followers are committed people—committed perhaps to a set of purposes, a cause, a vision of what the school is and can become, a set of beliefs about what teaching and learning should be, a set of values and standards to which they adhere, a conviction.

By contrast, good subordinates do what they are supposed to but little else. They want to know specifically what is expected of them and with proper monitoring and supervision will perform accordingly. They are dependent upon their leaders to provide them with goals and objectives and the proper ways and means to achieve them. They want to know what the rules of the game are and will play the game as required to avoid problems. For them and their leaders, life is comfortable and easy. For the school and the children they teach, excellence escapes and mediocrity becomes the norm.

Subordinates are not committed to causes, values, or ideas but respond instead to authority in the form of rules, regulations, expectations of their supervisors, and other management requirements. This is a crucial distinction. Subordinates respond to authority; followers respond to ideas. The standard dictionary definition of a follower is one who is in the service of a cause or of another person who represents a cause; a follower is one who follows opinions and teachings; a disciple. Since followership is linked to ideas, it is difficult for principals to help others transcend subordinateness for followership in schools without practicing leadership by purposing.

The concept of followership proposes a number of paradoxes. It turns out that effective following is really a form of leadership (Kelly, 1988). Commitment to a cause and the practice of self-management are hallmarks of good leadership and they are hallmarks of good followership as well. The successful leader then is one who builds up the leadership of others and who strives to become a leader of leaders. A successful leader is also a good follower—one who follows ideas, values, and beliefs. When followership is established, bureaucratic and psychological authority are transcended by moral authority. A new kind of hierarchy emerges in the school, one that places purposes, values, and commitments at the apex and teachers, principals, parents, and students below in service to these purposes.

Enabling Others to Function Autonomously on Behalf of Shared Purposes

There are three dimensions to enablement: empowering principals, teachers, parents and others by giving them the discretion they need to function autonomously on behalf of school goals and purposes; providing them with the support and training they need to function autonomously; and removing the bureaucratic obstacles that keep them from being autonomous.

Bonding leaders practice the principle of power investment. They distribute power among others in an effort to get more power in return. They know that it is not power over people and events that counts, but power over the likelihood that accomplishments and shared goals and purposes will be realized. To gain control over the latter they recognize that they need to delegate or surrender control over the former. In a nonlinear and loosely connected world they are resigned to the reality that delegation and empowerment are unavoidable.

Except for the most routine of jobs, the major problem facing management in America today is the gap existing between ability and authority (Thompson, 1961). Those who have the authority to act typically don't have the necessary technical ability, and those with the ability to act typically don't have the necessary authority. Leadership by empowerment can remedy this situation by lending to those with the ability the necessary authority to act.

Empowerment without purposing is not what is intended by this value. The two must go hand in hand. When directed and enriched by purposing and fueled by empowerment, teachers and others respond not only with increased motivation and commitment but with surprising ability as well. They become smarter, using their talents more fully and growing on the job. Thus, the first question that bonding leaders ask when thinking about empowerment is, empowered to do what? The empowerment rule that they follow is *everyone is free to do the things that make sense to them providing the decisions they make about what to do embody the values that are shared.* Further, the best empowerment strategy is not to focus on teachers or to focus on any other particular role group, but to think about empowering the school site. It is principals, teachers, and parents, bonded together in a common cause, who are given the necessary discretion that they need to function effectively. Empowerment is the natural complement to accountability. One cannot hold teachers, parents, and schools accountable without giving them the necessary responsibility to make the decisions that they think are best. The mistake of equating empowerment with freedom must be avoided. Empowerment has to do with obligation and duty. One is not free to do what he or she pleases, but free to make sensible decisions in light of shared values.

Viewing Leadership as Power to Accomplish

Successful leaders know the difference between power *over* and power *to.* There is a link between leadership and power, and indeed leadership is a special form of power, power to influence. There are, however, two conceptions of power: power over and power to. Power over is controlling and is concerned with "how can I control people and events so that things turn out the way I want?" Power over is concerned with dominance, control, and hierarchy. One needs to be in a position of dominance, control, and hierarchy to exercise power over. One needs to have access to rewards and punishments, "carrots," and "bully" sticks. In reality, however, most principals don't have many carrots or bully sticks. Further, people don't like carrots or bully sticks and resist power over leadership both formally and informally. Thus, this approach is rarely effective.

The concept of power over raises certain ethical questions relating to dominance and manipulation. Power to, on the other hand, is not instrumental but facilitative. It is power to do something, to accomplish something, and to help others accomplish something that they think is important. In power to, far less emphasis is given to what people are doing, and far more emphasis is given to what they are accomplishing.

Putting Collegiality First

When combined with purposing, leadership density, and enablement, collegiality is an important strategy for bringing about the kinds of connections that make schools work and work well in a nonlinear and loosely structured world. Too often, however, collegiality is confused with congeniality (Barth, 1986). Congeniality refers to the friendly human relationships that exist among teachers and is characterized by the loyalty, trust, and easy conversation that result from the development of a closely knit social group. Collegiality, by contrast, refers to the existence of high levels of collaboration among teachers and between teachers and principal and is characterized by mutual respect, shared work values, cooperation, and specific conversations about teaching and learning. When congeniality is high, a strong, informal culture aligned with social norms emerges in the school. But the norms may or may not be aligned with school purposes. Sometimes the norms contribute to and at other times interfere with increased commitment and extraordinary performance. By contrast, when collegiality is high, a strong, professional culture held together by shared work norms emerges in the school. The norms are aligned with school purposes, contributing consistently to increased commitment and extraordinary performance.

Recent research independently reported by Little (1981) and Rosenholtz (1989) provides compelling support for the importance of collegiality and building a professional culture of teaching on the one hand and in enhancing commitment and performance on the other. Both researchers found that the kind of leadership principals provided influences the collegial norm structure of the school. Rosenholtz found that teachers in high-collegial schools described their principals as being supportive and as considering problems to be schoolwide concerns that provided opportunities for collective problem solving and learning. Teachers and principals in less collegial schools, by contrast, reported being isolated and alienated. In her research, Little found that norms of collegiality were developed when principals clearly communicated expectations for teacher cooperation; provided a model for collegiality by working firsthand with teachers in improving the school; rewarded expressions of collegiality among teachers by providing recognition, release time, money, and other support resources; and protected teachers who were willing to go against expected norms of privatism and isolation by engaging in collegial behaviors. Though norms of collegiality can be enhanced within traditionally organized school structures, these structures provide obstacles that prevent optimal expression of this value. For collegiality to be fully expressed, schools will need to be restructured differently than is now the case (one teacher working in a self-contained classroom with the same group of students following a locked, fixed schedule).

Emphasizing Intrinsic Motivation

Traditional management theory is based on the principle "what gets rewarded gets done." It makes sense to base motivational strategies and practices on this principle. But when this principle becomes the overriding framework for making decisions about how to lead and how to encourage and reward good performance, typically the result is the opposite of that which is anticipated. In the long run the job just doesn't get done. The problem with "what gets rewarded gets done" is that it results in calculated involvement of people with their work. When rewards can no longer be provided, the work no longer will be done. Work performance becomes contingent on a bartering arrangement rather than being self-sustaining because of moral principle or a deeper psychological connection. A better strategy upon which to base our efforts is "what is rewarding gets done." When something is rewarding, it gets done even when "no one is looking"; it gets done even when extrinsic rewards and incentives are scarce or nonexistent; it gets done not because somebody is going to get something in return but because it's important. The power of intrinsic motivation is well documented in both research and practice and is a key element in bonding leadership.

Understanding Quality Control

Perhaps on no issue do ordinary and highly successful leaders differ more than in their beliefs about, and concepts of, quality control. To ordinary leaders, quality control is considered to be a management problem solvable by coming up with the right controls such as scheduling, prescribing, programming, testing, and checking. Though successful leaders recognize that such managerial conceptions of quality control have their place, they are likely to view the problem of quality control as being primarily cultural rather than managerial. Quality control, they have come to learn, is in the minds and hearts of people at work. It has to do with what teachers and other school employees believe, their commitment to quality, their sense of pride, the extent to which they identify with their work, the ownership they feel for what they are doing, and the intrinsic satisfaction they derive from the work itself. It is for this reason that quality control is not viewed so much as planning, organizing, scheduling, and controlling as it is viewed as purposing, enablement, leadership density, collegiality, and intrinsic motivation as means to build identity and commitment.

Valuing Simplicity

Highly successful principals believe in lean, action-oriented, uncomplicated organizational structures. To them, "small is beautiful" and "simple is better." Smallness has the advantage of encouraging primary group relationships among teachers and students, providing more readily for empowerment, and increasing one's identity and feeling of belongingness. Simplicity is action-oriented and to the point. It places emphasis on what needs to be accomplished and how best to do it without undue emphasis on protocols and procedural matters.

Reflection in Action

Leaders of highly successful schools view with suspicion quick fixes, sure-fire remedies, and one-best-way prescriptions for teaching and learning, supervising, and evaluating. Instead, they bring to their work a more complex view of schooling (see, for example, Joyce and Weil, 1980; Brandt, 1985; Sirotnik, 1985; Glatthorn, 1984). No single model of teaching is sufficient to address all the aims of schooling. The issue, for example, is not didactic and informal versus structured and direct, but costs and benefits of various approaches to teaching and learning. What is gained and what is lost by using a particular approach? Given one's present situation, are the gains worth the losses? Similarly, no single method of supervision and evaluation is sufficient for all teachers and all situations.

Successful principals resist accepting a direct link between research and practice. They recognize instead that the purpose of research is to increase one's understanding and not to prescribe practices (Tyler, 1984). Paying close attention to theory and research, they heed well the success stories emerging from practice, but they have a conceptual rather than an instrumental view of such knowledge (Kennedy, 1984). Knowledge viewed instrumentally is evidence for directly prescribing action. Knowledge viewed conceptually is information for informing thought and enhancing professional judgment, the prerequisites for action.

Leadership by Outrage

The standard prescription that emerges from traditional management is that leaders should be cool, calculated, and reserved in everything they say or do. Studies of successful leaders (e.g., Vaill, 1984; Lipsitz, 1984; Peters and Waterman, 1983; Sergiovanni, 1990) reveal quite a different image. Indeed, successful leaders typically bring to their practice a sense of passion and risk that communicates to others that if something is worth believing in then it's worth feeling strongly about. In his extensive studies of successful leaders, Peter Vaill (1984) found that their leadership practice was characterized by *time-feeling and focus*. Successful leaders put in extraordinary amounts of time, have strong feelings about the attainment of the system's purposes, and focus their attention and energies on key issues and variables. These characteristics are key contributors to building purposing in the enterprise. According to Vaill,

> Purposing occurs through the investment of large amounts of micro- and macro-Time, through the experience and expression of very strong Feeling about the attainment of purposes and importance of the system, and through the attainment

of understanding of the key variables in the system success (Focus). All leaders of high-performance systems have integrated these three factors at a very high level of intensity and clarity. (1984:103)

Vaill noted that feeling was the important link between time and focus. His successful leaders cared deeply about the welfare of their particular enterprise, its purposes, structure, conduct, history, future security, and underlying values and commitments. They cared deeply enough to show passion; and when things were not going right this passion often took the form of outrage.

Leadership by outrage is a symbolic act that communicates importance and meaning and that touches people in ways not possible when leadership is viewed only as something objective and calculated. Leaders use outrage to highlight issues of purpose defined by the school's shared covenant, and this outrage adds considerable value to their leadership practice.

The linking of outrage to purposes is very important. Bonding leaders, for example, know the difference between real toughness and merely looking tough or acting tough. Real toughness is always principle-value based. Bonding leaders expect adherence to common values but promote wide discretion in how these values are to be implemented (they practice enablement and emphasize followership). They are outraged when they see these values ignored or violated. The values of the common core represent nonnegotiables that comprise cultural strands that define a way of life in the school. However free people may be to do and decide, they are expected to embody the values that are shared and make up the school's covenant. When this is not the case, outrage is expressed.

Kindling Outrage in Others

Outrage is not owned by the principal alone. When purposes are established, followership is understood, enabling is provided, collegiality is in place, and leadership by outrage is modeled by the designated leader, then expressing outrage becomes an obligation of every person connected with the school. When the ideals and commitments that are shared are compromised, outrage is expressed. Bonding leaders work hard at *kindling outrage in others*.

The Worth of the Leadership Values

None of the leadership values considered alone is powerful enough to make the difference in bringing about quality schooling. Indeed, a critical connectedness exists among them, and leadership is best understood as comprising interdependent parts. Practicing enabling leadership in the form of individual empowerment, for example, without practicing leadership that emphasizes purposing and the building of a covenant of shared values is more likely to result in laissez faire management than in quality schooling. Furthermore, emphasizing management at the expense of leadership by providing controls and regulations, by emphasizing authority, by attempting to regulate the flow and work of schooling will not allow the practice of convincing and meaningful empowerment. A school that builds a covenant of shared values composed of technical statements of objectives, targets, and outcomes that fail to inspire; that are lacking in symbolic representations; and that do not allow principals, parents, teachers, and students to derive sense and meaning from their school lives will not likely be characterized by extraordinary commitment and performance.

Leadership by Banking

Banking is the fourth of the stages of leadership for school improvement. Metaphorically the leader "banks the fire," thus allowing for things to run routinely. The more successful a principal is in practicing leadership by bartering, building, and bonding, the more dramatically her or his role changes. When values and beliefs become institutionalized into the everyday management life of the school, then management know-how, hierarchical authority, interpersonal skill, and personality are ultimately transcended as the leader becomes one who administers to the needs of the school and its members. The principal doesn't become less important, only differently important. On the one hand she or he becomes the guardian of the values of the school's covenant, and on the other hand a capable administrator who works hard to help others meet their commitments to the school. Once at this stage, leadership and followership become very, very close. As pointed out earlier, followers manage themselves well by thinking for themselves, exercising self-control, accepting responsibility and obligation, and believing in and caring about what they are doing (Kelley, 1988:144). Both followers and leaders are attracted to and compelled by the same things: ideas, values, and commitments. Thus, over time, leaders seek to restructure the chain of command so that followers are not connected to leaders in a hierarchical sense, but so that both leaders and followers respond to the same ideas, values, and commitments.

Traditional chain of command (hierarchical authority)	New chain of command (moral authority)
Leaders	Ideas, values, commitments
↓	↓
Followers	Leaders as followers and followers as leaders

When this happens, hierarchical authority and authority derived from one's personality give way to purpose and management. The leader is neither boss nor messiah but administrator.

The authority vested in leader as boss is organizational and hierarchical; the authority vested in leader as messiah is charismatic and interpersonal; and the authority vested in leader as administrator is obligatory, stemming from the obligations that come from serving shared values and purposes (Sergiovanni, 1990:150).

School principals are responsible for "ministering" to the needs of the schools they serve, as defined by the shared values and purposes of the school's covenant.

They minister by furnishing help and by being of service to parents, teachers, and students. They minister by providing leadership in a way that encourages others to be leaders in their own right. They minister by highlighting and protecting the values of the school. The principal as minister is one who is devoted to a cause, mission, or set of ideas and accepts the duty and obligation to serve this cause. Ultimately her or his success is known by the quality of the followership that emerges in the school. The quality of followership is a barometer that indicates the extent to which moral authority has replaced bureaucratic. When moral authority drives leadership practice, the principal is at the same time a leader of leaders, follower of ideas, minister of values, and servant to the followership.

This chapter concludes Part II, "Principal Leadership and School Success." The image of leadership proposed places the substance of leadership squarely in the middle of what is important. The argument has been that without giving prime attention to purposes and values we are likely to fall into the trap of only doing things right, neglecting doing right things. Part III picks up this theme by giving attention to the mission of schooling and how to build a covenant of shared values.

References

Argyris, Chris. 1964. *Integrating the Individual and the Organization*. New York: Wiley.

Barnard, Chester. 1938. *The Functions of the Executive*. Cambridge, MA: Harvard University Press.

Barth, Roland. 1986. "The Principal and the Profession of Teaching," *Elementary School Journal* 86(4).

Bass, Bernard. 1985. *Leadership and Performance Beyond Expectations*. New York: Harper & Row.

Brandt, Ron. 1985. "Toward a Better Definition of Teaching," *Educational Leadership* 42(8).

Burns, James MacGregor. 1978. *Leadership*. New York: Harper & Row.

Conger, Jay A. 1989. *The Charismatic Leader*. San Francisco: Jossey-Bass.

Conger, Jay A., and Rabindra N. Kanungo. 1987. "Towards a Behavioral Theory of Charismatic Leadership in Organizational Settings," *Academy of Management Review* 12(4), pp. 637–647.

Conger, Jay, and Rabindra N. Kanungo. 1988. "Behavioral Dimensions of Charismatic Leadership," in J. A. Conger and R. N. Kanungo, Eds., *Charismatic Leadership*. San Francisco: Jossey-Bass.

Etzioni, Amitai. 1988. *The Moral Dimension Toward a New Theory of Economics*. New York: The Free Press.

Gardner, John. 1986. "The Tasks of Leadership." Leadership Papers No. 2. Leadership Studies Program. Independent Sector, Washington, DC. March.

Glatthorn, Alan. 1984. *Differentiated Supervision*. Alexandria, VA: Association for Supervision and Curriculum Development.

Herzberg, Frederick. 1966. *Work and the Nature of Man*. Cleveland: The World Publishing Company.

Joyce, Bruce, and Marsha Weil. 1980. *Models of Teaching*, 2nd ed. Englewood Cliffs, NJ: Prentice-Hall.

Kelly, H. H. 1973. "The Process of Causal Attribution," *American Psychologist* 28(2), pp. 107–128.

Kelly, Robert E. 1988. "In Praise of Followers," *Harvard Business Review*, Nov.–Dec.

Kennedy, Mary. 1984. "How Evidence Alters Understanding and Decisions," *Educational Evaluations and Policy Analysis* 6(3), pp. 207–226.

Levin, Doran. 1988. "G.M. Bid to Rejuvenate Leadership." *The New York Times*. Sept. 3.

Likert, Rensis. 1967. *The Human Organization: Its Management and Value*. New York: McGraw-Hill.

Lipsitz, Joan. 1984. *Successful Schools for Young Adolescents*. New Brunswick, NJ: Transaction Books.

Little, Judith. 1981. "School Success and Staff Development in Urban Desegregated Schools." Boulder, CO: Center for Action Research.

March, James G. 1984. "How We Talk and How We Act: Administrative Theory and Administrative Life," in T. J. Sergiovanni and J. E. Corbally, Eds., *Leadership and Organizational Culture*. Urbana, IL: University of Illinois Press.

Maslow, Abraham. 1954. *Motivation and Personality*. New York: Harper & Row.

McGregor, Douglas. 1960. *The Human Side of Enterprise*. New York: McGraw-Hill.

Miles, Raymond E. 1965. "Human Relations or Human Resources?" *Harvard Business Review* 43(4), pp. 148–163.

Myers, Scott. 1971. *Every Employee a Manager*. New York: McGraw-Hill.

Rosenholtz, Susan. 1989. *Teacher's Workplace: A Social-Organizational Analysis*. New York: Longman.

Sergiovanni, Thomas J. 1990. *Value-Added Leadership: How to Get Extraordinary Performance in Schools*. San Diego, CA: Harcourt Brace Jovanovich.

Sergiovanni, Thomas J., and Robert J. Starratt. 1971. *Emerging Patterns of Supervision: Human Perspectives*. New York: McGraw-Hill.

Sergiovanni, Thomas J., and Robert J. Starratt. 1988. *Supervision: Human Perspectives*, 4th ed. New York: McGraw-Hill.

Shulman, Lee. 1989. "Teaching Alone, Learning Together: Needed Agenda for New Reforms," in T. J. Sergiovanni and J. H. Moore, Eds., *Schooling for Tomorrow Directing Reforms to Issues that Count*. Boston: Allyn and Bacon.

Thompson, Victor. 1961. *Modern Organization: A General Theory*. New York: Knopf.

Tyler, Ralph. 1984. Quoted in Philip L. Hosford, "The Problem, Its Difficulties, and Our Approaches," in P. L. Hosford, Ed., *Using What We Know about Teaching*. Alexandria, VA: Association for Supervision and Curriculum Development.

Vaill, Peter B. 1984. "The Purposing of High-Performance Systems," in T. J. Sergiovanni and J. E. Corbally, *Leadership and Organizational Culture*. Urbana, IL: University of Illinois Press.

Weick, Karl E. 1982. "Administering Education in Loosely Coupled Schools," *Phi Delta Kappan* 26.

Weick, Karl E. 1976. "Educational Organization as Loosely Coupled Systems," *Administrative Science Quarterly* 21.

White, Robert W. 1952. *Lives in Progress A Study of the Natural Growth of Personality*. New York: Dryden Press.

Yukl, Gary A. 1989. *Leadership in Organizations*, 2nd ed. Englewood Cliffs, NJ: Prentice-Hall.

PART III

THE MISSION OF SCHOOLING

CHAPTER 7

Goals of Schooling

What knowledge is of most worth? What should the purposes of schooling be? Whom should the schools serve? For what accomplishments should the schools be held accountable? These are questions being asked with increased frequency, and their answers will have significant impact on the development of local, state, and national educational policies as well as on the implementation of these policies by school principals.

This chapter examines the importance of goals to successful school leadership, reviews statements of goals that have been part of our recent history, and examines studies of the status and purposes of schooling. Its purpose is to examine what both public and professional establishments seek from schooling. Because schools and principals must select some goals and purposes from the many that are available, issues of values and beliefs about schooling will be considered. Further, the concept of educational platform, as it applies to the school and to the school principal, will be developed. Finally, some guidelines will be provided to help principals give leadership to the goal-setting process.

The Importance of Goals

Disagreement exists among those who study schools as to whether goals actually make a difference in the decisions that principals and teachers make about schooling. Many prominent organizational theorists doubt whether organizations actually have goals; for example, Perrow (1981) states: "The notion of goals may be a mystification, hiding an errant, vagrant, changeable world." (8). He continues:

> Do organizations have goals, then, in the rational sense of organizational theory? I do not think so. In fact, when an executive says, 'This is our goal' chances are that he is looking at what the organization happens to be doing and saying, 'Since we are all very rational here, and we are doing this, this must be our goal.' Organizations in this sense, run backward: the deed is father to the thought, not the other way around. (8)

Other organizational theorists have commented that schools are loosely structured (Bidwell, 1965; Weick, 1976), suggesting that parts tend to operate independently of one another. Teachers, for example, work alone in classrooms; their work is not visible to others. Close supervision under these circumstances is difficult, and continuous evaluation of teaching is impossible. No mechanism exists to ensure that school mandates, such as stated goals, are reflected in actual teaching. Coordination of the work of several teachers is difficult to achieve.

Since direct supervision and tight coordination are not possible in loosely structured schools, principals need to rely on the management of symbols to rally teachers to a common cause. Though schools may be loosely structured in the way they are organized, effective schools combine this loosely structured characteristic with a tightly structured core of values and beliefs. This core represents the cultural cement that bonds people together, gives them a sense of identity, and provides them with guidelines for their work.

But are symbols the same as goals? At one level, symbols and goals share common characteristics and similar functions. Weick's view is that symbols are more like *charters* than goals. They tell people *what* they are doing and *why* they are doing it. They reveal to people the importance and significance of their work. Goals, on the other hand, provide direction and are devices for telling people when and how well they are doing things (Weick, 1982:676).

The more generally goals are stated, the closer they approximate symbols. As goals become more precise, they tend to lose symbolic value and to resemble instrumental objectives designed to program daily school activities. They serve less to provide a sense of purpose or to instill a feeling of significance and more to guide what teachers should be doing at a given moment. Goals as symbols sacrifice precision, detail, and instrumentality to gain significance and meaning. They seek to capture the spirit of teachers at work. Objectives, on the other hand, sacrifice significance and meaning in attempting to gain instrumental power over what teachers are doing at a given moment and to provide ready measures of how well they are performing these tasks.

Experts who describe schools as being loosely structured maintain that instrumental control is difficult to achieve. Behind closed classroom doors, they argue, teachers follow the beat of a different drummer, selecting learning materials, deciding on what and how to teach not in response to objectives, but in response to available materials, their own intuitions and abilities, their perceptions of student needs, time constraints, and other situational characteristics. Tight school structures, they maintain, simply cannot reach into the classroom and challenge this de facto autonomy of the teacher no matter how detailed such structures might be or how eloquently they might be described. Since the influence of direct control is blunted by de facto teacher autonomy, the significance of goal-symbols as a means of influence in schools is increased.

Goals as Patterns

Jean Hills (1982) points out that in the real world, school administrators rarely find themselves in a position where they can pursue goals one at a time. The problem they face is that schools have multiple goals. Further, sometimes the goals conflict with each other. Making progress toward one goal may mean losing progress toward another. Always thinking in terms of discrete goals or even discrete multiple goals with each attended to sequentially by the principal, therefore, does not fit the special character of the school's unique value system. Under loosely structured conditions, schools don't achieve goals as much as they respond to certain values and tend to certain imperatives that ensure their survival over time.

Parsons (1951), for example, identified four imperatives that must be balanced against each other in such a way that each is maximized in order for the school or any other institution to survive. The neglect of any of these imperatives causes the others to decline, which means trouble for the school. The "pattern variables," as Parsons refers to them, are goal attainment; internally maintaining day-to-day stability and functions; adopting to external demands, concerns, and circumstances; and finally, tending to the cultural patterns and norms that hold the school together over time. External adoption, for example, often threatens internal stability and upsets cultural patterns. Maintaining cultural patterns often interferes with goal attainment and so on.

Rather than discrete goal attainment, Hills points out that school administrators bring to their practice what he calls "pattern rationality." They behave in response to "a conception of pattern development on a number of mutually limiting dimensions with respective gains in a given area having implications for others" (1982:7). Successful principals become surfers, skilled at riding the wave of the pattern as it unfolds. They respond to value patterns when discrete goals are in conflict with each other. Important to the concept of pattern rationality is that administrators be concerned with the costs and benefits of their actions.

Goals as Symbols

School boards, state departments of education, and other groups and institutions expect schools to have goals. Goal statements are, therefore, necessary to symbolically portray the school as being rational and therefore legitimate to outsiders. Rational schools are supposed to have goals and purposes and are supposed to pursue them deliberately. Schools, for example, are expected to behave rationally by accrediting agencies, state government, the local press, the local school board, and other groups. Thus, stated goals and purposes are necessary to obtain legitimacy from these and other groups.

It is clear that some discrepancy exists between stated goals and what schools actually do. This gap is more evident as goals take the form of actual intents (specifying exactly what we will accomplish) than the form of beliefs (specifying what is important and valued). Statements of beliefs provide the language necessary to bond people together in a common cause, to provide them with a sense of direction, and to establish a standard by which they can evaluate their actions and from which meanings for their actions can be derived. The more successful the school, the stronger is this bonding and the stronger is the link between beliefs, decisions, and actions. This assertion is supported by studies of successful schools summarized in Chapter 4.

Findings from the successful schools research parallel those of Peters and Waterman (1982) in their studies of excellent business corporations. In their words: "Every excellent company we studied is clear on what it stands for, and takes the process of value shaping seriously. In fact, we wonder whether it is possible to be an excellent company without clarity of values and without having the right sorts of values" (280). They continue:

> Virtually all of the better performing companies we looked at in the first study had a well-defined set of guiding beliefs. The less well-performing institutions, on the other hand, were marked by one of two characteristics. Many had no set of coherent beliefs. The others had distinctive and widely discussed objectives, but the only ones that they got animated about were the ones that could be quantified (the financial objectives, such as earnings per share and growth measures). (281)

Thomas Watson, Jr. (1963), in describing his many years of experience at the helm of IBM, highlights the importance of goals and symbols as statements of beliefs as follows:

> I firmly believe that any organization, in order to survive and achieve success, must have a sound set of beliefs on which it premises all its policies and actions. Next, I believe that the most important single factor in corporate success is faithful adherence to these beliefs. And, finally, I believe that if an organization is to meet the challenge of a changing world, it must be prepared to change everything about itself except those beliefs as it moves through corporate life. In other words, the basic philosophy, spirit, and drive of an organization have far more to do with its relative achievements than do technological or economic resources, organizational structure, innovation, and timing. All these things weigh heavily in success. But they are, I think, transcended by how strongly the people in the organization believe in its basic precepts and how faithfully they carry them out. (4–6)

Corporations, of course, are different from schools. They are generally considered to be more quantitative, impersonal, and instrumental. Schools, by contrast, are much more human-intensive. Though values are important to both, they are presumed to be more central to the inner workings of schools. Thus, providing examples from the corporate world illustrating the importance of goals, values, and beliefs should serve as notice to principals and other educators that such statements are even more important to schools.

Statements of beliefs provide the common cement bonding people together as they work on behalf of the school. Operationally, such beliefs form an *educational platform* for the school and principal. Eduational platforms should be thought of as encompassing the defining principles and beliefs that guide the actions of individuals and that provide a basis for evaluating these actions. Leaders of successful schools have well-defined educational platforms from which they operate. Indeed, successful schools contain fairly well-developed educational platforms serving as guides to teachers and others as they live and work in the school. Platforms are not objectives or specifications of what exactly is to be accomplished; instead, they contain guiding principles from which individuals decide what to do and how to do it. The more loosely structured the school, the more important is the concept of educational platform in bringing about cohesion and concerted action. Platforms are the means by which mission statements and broad goals and purposes are articulated into practice.

When taken together, platforms, mission statements, and broad goals and purposes constitute a covenant of shared values that functions as the cultural center of the school—the repository of that which is held sacred by all. The concept of covenant is explored further in the next chapter, "Beyond Goals: Building a Covenant of Shared Values."

In a later section of this chapter, the concept of educational platform is discussed further, and illustrations of platforms are provided. The following section provides a brief overview of the purposes of schooling as expressed by national commissions and groups since 1913. This discussion is followed by examples of current research on expectations that different groups have for schools and the goals that these expectations imply. Next examined is the problem of how principals can identify expectations and goals held by different groups and can build a reasonable consensus. This chapter concludes with a discussion of principal leadership and the effects of this leadership on building and maintaining an effective goal structure for the school.

A Review of Schooling Goals

The Cardinal Principles of Secondary Education

The first modern statement of goals and purpose of schooling in America is generally considered to be the *Cardinal Principles of Secondary Education*. This 1918 report of the National Education Association's commission on the Re-organization of Secondary Education identified seven areas considered to be essential for determining the basic objectives of education: (1) health, (2) command of fundamental processes, (3) worthy home membership, (4) vocation, (5) citizenship, (6) worthy use of leisure time, and (7) ethical character.

Health education, according to the commission, included teaching health habits, providing physical education programs, and cooperating with home and community agencies in promoting good health practices. Worthy home membership included home economics education for "girls" and home budgeting and maintenance for "boys," promoting wholesome attitudes and relationships between the sexes, and promoting proper attitudes in students toward their present home responsibilities. Vocational education was intended to decrease the student's economic dependency on family and society by developing the proper understandings, attitudes, and skills needed for employment. Citizenship education was intended to provide the skills and understandings needed for students to participate as full members of their local community, state, and nation. Worthy use of leisure time was intended to restore, for the present and future, the student's body, mind, and spirit through the development of avocational interests as a means to enhance her or his personality. Command of fundamental processes included the development of reading, writing, arithmetic, and oral expression skills. Ethical character was intended to develop "a sense of personal responsibility and initiative and, above all, the spirit of service and the principles of true democracy which would permeate the entire school."

The work of the commission, appointed in 1913, is noteworthy, for it marks the beginning of a new view of the purposes of schooling—one that stressed the importance of preparing students to function effectively in a democratic society. Prior to this time, the central focus for secondary education was on preparing students for admission to colleges and universities. The publication of the cardinal principles led to widespread debate as to the purpose of schooling. It became clear that, from this point on, schooling would be viewed more comprehensively and school goals would be more expansive.

During the next several decades many other lists of goals and purposes were published, some by local educational authorities and others by professional groups and appointed blue-ribbon committees. The *Purposes of Education in American Democracy* was issued by the Educational Policies Commission of the National Education Association in 1938. Four major aims for schools were proposed:

1. The promotion of *self-realization* by emphasizing the inquiring mind, reading, writing, aesthetic interests, and character building.
2. The promotion of *human relations* by emphasizing respect for humanity, friendships, cooperation, courtesy, and appreciation of the home.
3. The promotion of *economic efficiency* by emphasizing occupational information, occupational appreciation, work and workmanship, and consumer judgment.
4. The promotion of *civic responsibility* by emphasizing social justice, social activity, tolerance, conservation, and political citizenship.

An example of a statement of school goals and aims conceived by a local educational agency is the following, issued in 1943 by the New York City Board of Education:

1. *Character* to ensure the basis for rich, useful, ethical living in a society promoting the common welfare.
2. *Our American Heritage* to develop pride and faith in American democracy and respect for the dignity and work of individuals and peoples, regardless of race, religion, nationality, or socioeconomic status.
3. *Health* to develop and maintain a sound body and to develop wholesome mental and emotional attitudes and habits.
4. *Exploration* to discover, develop, and direct desirable individual interests, aptitudes, and abilities.

5. *Thinking* to develop reasoning based upon adequate hypotheses, supported by facts and principles.
6. *Knowledge and Skills* to develop command, in accordance with ability, of common integrating habits, knowledges, and skills.
7. *Appreciation and Expression* to develop an appreciation and enjoyment of beauty and to develop powers of creative expression.
8. *Social Relationships* to develop desirable social attitudes and relationships within the family, the school, and the community.
9. *Economic Relationships* to develop an awareness and appreciation of economic processes and of all who serve in the world of work.

In 1944 the National Association of Secondary School Principals published the influential document *The Imperative Needs of Youth of Secondary School Age.* Based on the assumptions that a free education must be planned and provided for all youth, that all youth have certain common educational needs, and that schooling should be continuous, the Association proposed 10 needs that should be addressed as schools state goals, delineate objectives, plan curriculum, and provide teaching:

1. All youth need to develop saleable skills and those understandings and attitudes that make the worker an intelligent and productive participant in economic life. To this end, most youth need supervised work experience as well as education in the skills and knowledge of their occupations.
2. All youth need to develop and maintain good health and physical fitness and mental health.
3. All youth need to understand the rights and duties of the citizen of a democratic society, and to be diligent and competent in the performance of their obligations as members of the community and citizens of the state and nation, and to have an understanding of the nations and peoples of the world.
4. All youth need to understand the significance of the family for the individual and society and the conditions conducive to successful family life.
5. All youth need to know how to purchase and use goods and services intelligently, understanding both the values received by the consumer and the economic consequences of their acts.
6. All youth need to understand the methods of science, the influence of science on human life, and the main scientific facts concerning the nature of the world and of man.
7. All youth need opportunities to develop their capacities to appreciate beauty and literature, art, music, and nature.
8. All youth need to be able to use their leisure time well and to budget it wisely, balancing activities that yield satisfactions to the individual with those that are socially useful.
9. All youth need to develop respect for other persons, to grow in their insight into ethical values and principles, to be able to live and work cooperatively with others, and to grow in the moral and spiritual values of life.
10. All youth need to grow in their ability to think rationally, to express their thoughts clearly, and to read and listen with understanding.

Contemporary Goal Statements

What seems striking about the lists of pre-1950s goals provided above (and of others from this era) is that they are remarkably contemporary. Let's compare these lists with a more recent one proposed by John Goodlad and his associates (1984). As part of his extensive study of schooling in America, Goodlad examined goal documents issued by each of the 50 states as well as those from other sources. Added to this examination was a historical review of goal statements relating to schooling. From this inquiry Goodlad and his associates were able to build a list of goals representing those appearing most commonly in the documents examined. They present the list as a guide to school board members, parents, students, and others as a means to build a common sense of direction for schooling. Four broad goal areas were identified, each with subgoals and more targeted school objectives:

A. Academic Goals
    1. Mastery of basic skills and fundamental processes
    2. Intellectual development
B. Vocational Goals
    3. Career education – vocational education
C. Social, Civic, and Cultural Goals
    4. Interpersonal understandings
    5. Citizenship participation
    6. Enculturation
    7. Moral and ethical character
D. Personal Goals
    8. Emotional and physical well-being
    9. Creativity and aesthetic expression
    10. Self-realization

Conclusions about School Goals

Several conclusions can be reached as a result of both historical and contemporary reviews of goal statements for schooling in America. First, no dearth of goal statements exists. As Goodlad points out: "There is no need to start from scratch, as though we have no goals for schooling" (51). He believes that schools should not spend time and energy in generating new lists and new statements but, should instead address such issues as the meaning and significance of existing goals and how they might be translated into curriculum and teaching programs.

Second, though some schools may wish to place more emphasis in one goal area than another, substantial consensus exists among parents and experts that schooling is a comprehensive endeavor designed to achieve multiple goals. Goodlad, for example, concludes from his research that professionals and public alike hold comprehensive expectations for school accomplishments. In discussing this aspect of his findings, he states:

The theme I pursue here is twofold. First, . . . teachers, students, and parents in the schools we studied want more than is implied by the words "intellectual development." They want some reasonably balanced attention to intellectual, social, vocational, and personal emphases in the schools' program of studies. Second, even all of these would not be enough. The school is to be also, in the eyes of parents and students, a nurturing, caring place. The parents we encountered want their children to be seen as individuals—persons and learners—and to be safe. Their children want to be known as persons as well as students. Many teachers, too, would like there to be greater school attention to students' personal attributes. (61–62)

Despite this plea for balance among the four goal areas, Goodlad found that intellectual goals were perceived as being most emphasized by students, parents, and teachers in the elementary, middle, and high schools he studied. He asked his respondents to indicate *both* the goal area they prefer to have most emphasized and the one they thought to be most emphasized. Comparisons between preferred and perceived goal areas for each of the three groups of respondents in the three levels of schooling are provided in Figure 7-1. Revealed from these data is that substantial agreement exists among students, parents, and teachers in *both* preferred and perceived goal emphases. With respect to intellectual goals, for example, only parents at the high school level reported preferring more intellectual goal emphasis than they perceived was present, but not by a wide margin. In every other case, respondents perceived greater emphasis on intellectual than they preferred. These data suggest that parents, students, and teachers are not in disagreement regarding intellectual goals. It suggests further that should a school wish to bring about greater congruence between preferred and perceived intellectual goal emphasis, some de-emphasis of intellectual goals in favor of others would be necessary. These conclusions stand in contrast to the widely held assumption, perhaps myth, that parents, teachers, and students disagree and particularly that parents desire more intellectual emphasis than do either students or teachers.

A similar analysis of the personal goal area leads to the conclusion that personal goals are not being emphasized enough. Further, Goodlad's data suggest that, should a school decide to emphasize this goal area more and thus bring about greater congruence between preferred and perceived personal emphasis, such efforts would be warmly received by parents, teachers and students alike.

Multiple Goals or No Goals?

Since the publication of the *Cardinal Principles of Secondary Education* in 1918, America's schools have been guided by a policy, albeit often implicit, of adding goals as new interests and pressures emerge. Rarely, however, do new goals replace old ones. The launching of the Soviet Sputnik in 1957, for example, resulted in increasing science and math requirements in our high schools and in adding advanced placement courses in these areas. But little was dropped from the existing curriculum. The life-adjustment curriculum movement of the 1930s and 1940s did

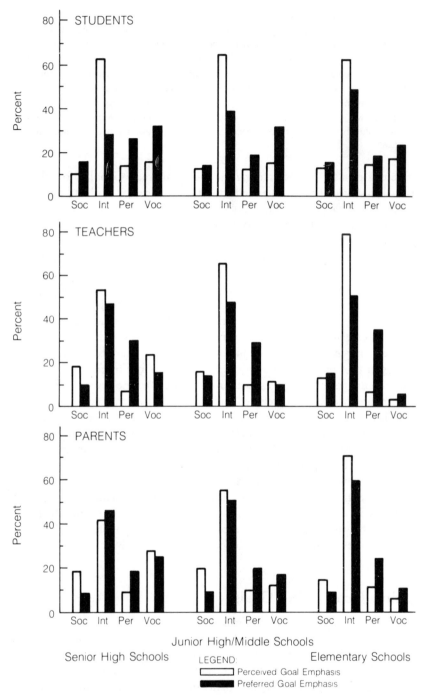

FIGURE 7-1 Comparison Between Perceived and Preferred Goal Emphasis (Social, Intellectual, Personal, and Vocational) for Students, Teachers, and Parents

From John I. Goodlad (1984), *A Place Called School* (New York: McGraw-Hill), 64.

not replace academic courses for bright students, but rather created a bulge of "more practical" and "relevant" offerings in the middle of the curriculum designed for the mass of students. Academics and life adjustment lived side by side, as did vocational education and other offerings. With the Great Society movement of the 1960s came an emphasis on special schooling for the less able. The curriculum expanded again as new goals and purposes were added. Little was given up in the existing curriculum; few, if any, goals were displaced by new ones. When dropout rates increased, "alternative" schools were developed and existed side by side (indeed sometimes within) regular schools.

Rarely have the schools made choices among goals and purposes. Instead the history of American education since at least the mid-1900s has been characterized by a policy of inclusiveness and expansion, of getting and keeping as many students as possible in schools by offering as attractive a range of choices as possible. Our schools have become something for everyone.

The reform movement of the mid-1980s began to challenge this policy of inclusiveness through expansion of offerings. Raising the issue of abuses in multiple goals, some scholars have used the metaphor "shopping mall" in describing high schools (Powell, Farrar, and Cohen, 1985). Provided a dazzling array of offerings and allowing students virtually unlimited choices, the shopping mall high school lets students pick and choose their education as it suits them. Specialty shops exist for students who desire concentrated education in particular areas; math and science boutiques and hairdressing salons would be examples. The picnic court offers an array of "foods" designed to accommodate the many ethnic cultures and requirements one finds in a multicultural society such as ours. This shopping mall conception of schooling enjoys wide acceptance among school administrators, for it enables them to avoid conflict among competing goals and values; thus, they need not suffer the consequences of making tough decisions. What knowledge is of most worth? All the knowledge that clients seek.

Many researchers have pointed out the host of problems that emerge from this inability of schools to make a statement as to what it is they stand for (Cusick, 1983; Boyer, 1983). The problem is aptly summed by Powell, Farrar, and Cohen (1985) as follows:

> Unfortunately, the flip side of the belief that all directions are correct is the belief that no direction is incorrect—which is a sort of intellectual bankruptcy. Those who study in secondary education have little sense of an agenda for studies. There is only a long list of subjects that may be studied, a longer list of courses that may be taken, and a list of requirements for graduation. But there is no answer to the query, Why these? Approaching things this way has made it easy to avoid arguments and decisions about purpose, both of which can be troublesome—especially in our divided and contentious society. But this approach has made it easy for schools to accept many assignments that they could not do well, and it has made nearly any sort of work from students and teachers acceptable, as long as it caused no trouble. (306)

Too often, multiple goals for schools means no goals. Yet highly successful schools are able to overcome this problem. They are able to build consensus as to what they are about, what they believe in, and what they hope to accomplish. Successful schools combine several characteristics of the American tradition that have endured over time: attention to the egalitarian ideal balanced with the ideals of hard work, standards, and success. They recognize the importance of making schooling attractive enough so that students will want to come, will stay, and will learn. They see no conflict between this commitment to providing developmentally sound schooling and a commitment to providing intellectually sound and academic learning for students. It is common, for example, to see an emphasis on high academic standards within the tradition of the disciplines; promoting intellectual values such as inquiry, critical thinking, knowledge appreciation, and learning how to learn; controlled choice for students; a concern for responsible citizenship in the democratic society; active involvement of students in their learning; and responsiveness to student developmental needs and levels. How is it that they are able to give attention to this array of goals and still maintain a sense of integrity and order? Successful schools are characterized by tight alignment between a defining core of values for the school and the decisions that teachers and administrators make about implementing goals and objectives, curriculum, teaching, supervision, and evaluation. But this alignment is *strategic*, not tactical. Teachers, administrators, and students are given freedom to decide matters of schooling providing that the decisions they make are consistent with the school's core values. In this sense, successful schools combine features of tight and loose alignment. These ideas were discussed in chapters 2 and 3. The shopping mall image of schooling, by contrast, is characterized by loose alignment in basic values as well as in implementing practices.

Assessing Goal Preferences

Appendix 7-1 provides a format for raising the issue of goals in your school and for building consensus. The well-known Phi Delta Kappa (1972) list of 18 goal statements is used. This format allows for the assessment of perceived needs as well as the sharing of goal preferences. Parents, board members, teachers, and other groups might, for example, first rank the statements in order of importance for their school. Then each statement could be rated to indicate perceptions of how well the school was achieving in this particular goal area. As you review the Phi Delta Kappa goal statements, sort them into one of the four major goal areas suggested by Goodlad. Now compare your goal preferences with those of parents, teachers, and students whose responses are presented in Figure 7-1. Would the parents, teachers, and students of your school agree with your assessment of goal preferences? Would they agree with your estimates of how well your school is measuring up in each of these goal areas?

Appendix 7-2, "Mistakes in Deciding Aims of Education," is excerpted from a book written in 1887. The author, James L. Hughes (1887) argued that defects in schooling of that era and faulty educational methods were the result of limited views of what schools should accomplish. The "true aims," he maintained, are comprehensive and qualitative, encompassing physical and moral as well as intellectual domains. What would the reaction of your school board, parents council, and state legislature be were they given a copy of these aims? What would a list of "mistakes" circa 1990 look like?

Educational Platform: Establishing Criteria for Action

Educational goals are symbols that provide a sense of purpose to those who work in the school and a frame of reference from which they can derive meaning. Goals also serve to specify and frame areas to be emphasized as this work unfolds. As goals become more operational, they indicate directions to be pursued and help provide rationales for curriculum content decisions and for evaluation decisions. In each of these cases, goals represent value statements that help define the unique characteristics of a particular school and that help to communicate values to be upheld by principals, teachers, and students engaged in the process of schooling.

Goals, however, are not sufficiently powerful indicators of values to provide the rallying point, common core, and critical mass of coherence needed to build a strong culture of excellence within the school. It is clear that successful schools do possess and communicate a sense of purpose, knowledge of areas to be emphasized and directions to be pursued. But they make additional value statements as well—statements that govern the ways and means of action and the building of a special environment within which this action takes place. These latter expressions of values are contained in the school's educational platform, an important component of the school's covenant.

It is helpful first to conceive of platforms on an individual basis. An individual's educational platform consists of what she or he believes is possible, true, and desirable. For some individuals, platforms are not consciously known. Some teachers, for example, may not be aware of the undergirding framework guiding their thinking about school issues and shaping the decisions they make about teaching. Others may have a vague awareness of platform, and for them it is more implicitly or tacitly known. Still, they are aware of a certain consistency in their decisions, and they can provide an operational rationale for these decisions. When formally stated and articulated in practice, an educational platform consists of a series of assumptions, theories, and beliefs usually expressed as declarative or normative statements. Statements dealing with the purposes of schooling, the ways children and young people grow, the roles they should assume in teaching and learning, the nature of learning itself, how students are to be treated, preferred teaching strategies, the worth of various kinds of knowledge, proper learning climate, and the overall climate for schooling are generally included in an educational platform.

Platform statements may take a varfiety of forms, but whatever their form, *usefulness is determined by their ability to guide the decision-making process across an array of issues relating to life in schools and classrooms and to teaching and learning.* A starting point in shaping a platform is to assess the assumptions and beliefs that one holds regarding learning and the nature of knowledge. Included in Appendix

7–3 is an assumptions inventory to help in this effort. Items in this inventory are addressed to how young children learn, but many of the items can be readily modified for reference to upper elementary, middle, and high school students. Take a moment to respond to this inventory by indicating your own "feelings" (assumptions and beliefs) about each statement. As you examine your choices across the array of statements, look for consistency in responses. From this response pattern, develop a list of about a dozen statements that reflect your beliefs about learning and knowledge. This list can now be used as a guide to decisions you make about objectives, curriculum materials, subject-matter content, classroom organization and design, and teaching practices. Further, a list similar to yours, reflecting the views of teachers with whom you work, can be used as a set of criteria to assess the worth and appropriateness of decisions they make about teaching and learning.

One approach to developing a platform statement is to consider it as a set of "agreements" for a particular group of teachers. Presented in Exhibit 7–1 is a sample set of agreements for a high school social studies department; it specifies criteria for determining if decisions that teachers make and activities that they provide for students are to be considered worthwhile. To what extent do you agree with

EXHIBIT 7–1 Educational Platform: A Sample Set of Agreements

Presented below is a set of agreements for a social studies department. Assume that the items making up this set of agreements were determined by a department faculty asking the question "All things being equal, one activity is more worthwhile than another when it . . . ?" The criteria for worthwhile activities for this set of agreements were suggested by James Raths.

- A worthwhile educational activity is one that permits students to make informed choices in carrying out the activity and to reflect on the consequences of their choices.
  Members of this department believe that students should accept responsibility for selecting objectives, and for making decisions from alternatives as to how objectives might be pursued.

- A worthwhile educational activity is one that assigns students to active learning roles rather than passive ones.
  Members of this department believe that more often than not students should assume classroom roles as researchers, panel members, reporters, interviewers, observers, and participants rather than just listeners, ditto sheet responders, and question answerers.

- A worthwhile educational activity is one that asks students to engage in inquiry into ideas, applications of intellectual processes, or current personal and social problems.
  Members of this department believe that acquainting students with ideas that transcend subject matter areas (truth, justice, self-worth), with intellectual processes such as hypothesis testing and identifying assumptions, and with writing opportunities that ask students to deal creatively and personally with social problems or human relationships are more worthwhile than focusing at the knowledge level on places, objects, dates, and names.

- A worthwhile educational activity is one that involves students with reality.
  Members of this department believe that students should have hands-on experience with ideas. Field trips, projects, community surveys, real objects, and interviews are considered more worthwhile than just relying on books and classroom discussion.

EXHIBIT 7–1 *(Continued)*

- A worthwhile educational activity is one that can be successfully accomplished by students at different levels of ability.

  Members of this department believe that students should not be subjected to only a single level of accomplishment, that youngsters should work at their own levels of ability and that comparisons should be made in terms of individuals working to capacity.

- A worthwhile educational activity is one that asks students to examine in a new setting ideas, applications, intellectual processes, and problems previously studied.

  In Raths's words, members of this department believe "an activity that builds on previous student work by directing a focus into *novel* location, *new* subject matter areas, or *different* contexts is more worthwhile than one that is completely unrelated to the previous work of the students."

- A worthwhile educational activity is one that examines topics or issues that are not normally considered by the major communication media in the nation.

  Members of this department believe that students should be generously exposed to such topics as race, religion, war and peace, the court system, fairness of the media, credibility in government, social responsibilities of public corporations, ethical standards for politicians, social class, immigration practices and effects on the economy, the representatives of lay governing groups such as school boards, labor-union practices, minority political parties, the self-interest of professional groups, such as the AMA, NEA, and Chamber of Commerce, student rights and responsibilities, drug use in professional athletics, and other topics often considered less than safe.

- A worthwhile educational activity is one that requires students to rewrite, rehearse, or polish their initial efforts.

  Members of this department believe that students should not perceive assignments as chores but as worthwhile goals requiring high standards. Students should have the opportunity to receive feedback and criticism of written work and oral work and of field projects as a means of formative evaluation. Opportunities should then be provided for revision and overhauling in light of this feedback. Fewer assignments well done are seen by this faculty as better than lots of tasks to be completed.

- A worthwhile educational activity is one that involves students in the application and mastery of meaningful roles, standards, or disciplines.

  Members of this department believe that "using standards derived from students as well as authorities, panel discussions can be disciplined by procedures; reporting of data can be disciplined by consideration of control; essays can be regulated by consideration of style and syntax." Before students conduct interviews outside the supermarket, for example, standards for a good interview should be established. Further, students should assume a key role in establishing these standards.

- A worthwhile educational activity is one that provides students with opportunities to share the planning, the carrying out of a plan, or the results of an activity with others.

  Recognizing the importance of independent study projects and of other individualized education techniques, the members of this department nevertheless believe that cooperative group activity is important and that the group setting provides numerous learning opportunities beyond group tasks.

From James Raths, *"Criteria for Worthwhile Action"* (1984), in Thomas J. Sergiovanni, Ed., *Handbook for Effective Department Leadership; Concepts and Practices in Today's Secondary Schools,* 2d. ed, 416–418, Boston: Allyn and Bacon.

the statements of this platform? Which statements would you change or delete? What additions would you make to this set of agreements?

The concept of platform for principals extends *beyond* the realm of teaching and learning to such issues as the nature and kind of leadership to be expressed, how teachers are to be treated, how teachers agree to work together, the ways in which decisions are to be made, and what constitutes an appropriate climate for a given school. Principals, therefore, are guided by strong educational platforms *and* strong management platforms. In highly successful schools, both educational and management platforms are well established and clearly articulated in practice. Key to platform development and use is that it does not detail how people will behave or what they will do. Instead, platforms are designed to provide the criteria for others to use to determine if the decisions that they make are worthwhile, given the particular culture of a school.

Providing the Necessary Leadership

Educational goals and platforms are the nerve center of a successful school. They provide the necessary signals, symbols, substance, and direction needed for coordinated action on behalf of quality in schooling. The clarity and coherence provided by goals and platform cannot be provided by close supervision, management controls, and other regulatory measures, for these latter practices require a much tighter connection among school parts, roles, and activities than is typically found in schools. Loosely structured schools achieve coordinated action by creating a powerful normative system that serves to socialize newcomers and to provide reinforcement to those already socialized. Further, this normative system provides a source of meaning and direction to those who live and work in the school.

Within the school's normative system, teachers enjoy wide discretion in making day-to-day decisions regarding teaching and learning, providing that decisions reflect dominant values. This relationship between a tightly structured value system, as expressed in the form of goals and platform, and a loosely structured decision-making structure for teachers is depicted in Figure 7–2 in the form of a target. The "bulls-eye" represents the school's core values, and the outer boundary of the target represents the larger area of discretionary decision making. This combination of tightly structured values and loosely structured decision making is the theme of a story about a misunderstanding between the president and several vice-presidents of a bank in California (Ouchi and Jaeger, 1978:309). The president and vice-presidents were accusing each other of not being able to formulate objectives. The vice-presidents meant that the president could not and would not provide them with explicitly quantified and time-framed objectives. The president meant that the vice-presidents could not see that once the bank's philosophy and platform were understood, the vice-presidents should be able to deduce for themselves appropriate objectives for *any* conceivable situation.

Tight values and loose decision making as principles of organization and leadership are often illustrated by using religious metaphors and analogies. Anthony Jay (1970), for example, states:

FIGURE 7-2 Providing Leadership in Tightly and Loosely Coupled Schools

St. Augustine once gave us the only rule of Christian conduct, "Love God and do what you like." The implication is, of course, that if you truly love God, then you will only ever want to do things which are acceptable to Him. Equally, Jesuit priests are not constantly being rung-up, or sent memos, by the head office of the Society. The long, intensive training over many years in Rome is a guarantee that wherever they go afterwards, and however long it may be before they ever see another Jesuit, they will be able to do their work in accordance with the standards of the Society. (70)

Principal leadership in tight value and loose decision-making schools is more complicated than first seems apparent. It requires the balancing of leadership style *flexibility* and *resiliency*, with the appropriate expression of each contingent upon the issues being addressed. Effective principals display a great deal of resiliency when concerned with the school's goal structure, educational platform, and overall philosophy. At the same time, they display a great deal of flexibility when concerned with the everyday articulation of these values into teaching and learning practices and designs. Before continuing with this discussion, let's examine the Style Flexibility Index (SFI) and the Style Resiliency Index (SRI) shown in Exhibits 7–2 and 7–3. The items in these indexes were suggested by W. J. Reddin's (1970) discussion of style flexibility and style resilience. Respond to each of the indexes and obtain flexibility and resilience scores. Keep in mind that both indexes suggest only how you might be perceived on these dimensions by others with whom you work.

Now let's examine the concepts of flexibility and resilience. Flexibility is perhaps best understood by understanding its relationship to drifting. As leadership concepts, both flexibility and drifting comprise the same behaviors. Yet expressions of these behaviors in one situation might result in effectiveness and in another, ineffectiveness. When the behavior expressed matches the situation, the principal will be viewed as being highly flexible. When the exact same behavior is expressed in inappropriate situations, the principal is viewed as drifting.

Reddin (1970) points out that style flexibility in leadership is characterized by high ambiguity tolerance, power sensitivity, an open belief system, and other-directedness. Highly flexible principals are comfortable in unstructured situations, are not control-oriented, bring to the work context very few fixed ideas, and display a great deal of interest in the ideas of others. These characteristics are very desirable when articulated within the loosely structured discretionary space of schools such as depicted in Figure 7–3. But, in matters of the school's goal structure and educational platform, flexibility by the principal is often viewed negatively by teachers and others. When this is the case, the principal's style can be described as drifting rather than flexible. Drifting suggests a lack of direction and an absence of commitment to a purpose or cause.

EXHIBIT 7–2 Style Flexibility Index

Think of occasions, situations, and incidents when you as school principal were interacting directly with teachers about *day-to-day and week-to-week decisions involving instructional materials, subject-matter content, classroom organization, and the provision of teaching and learning.* As a result of this interaction, indicate how teachers would describe you, using the 10 paired statements provided below.

	10	9	8	7	6	5	4	3	2	1	
Other-directed											Dogmatic
Sensitive											Unresponsive
Collaborating											Rejecting
Reality-oriented											Status-oriented
Interdependent											Authority-oriented
Involved											Inhibited
Team player											Uncooperative
Colleague oriented											Control-oriented
Open-minded											Close-minded
Practical											Intolerant
	10	9	8	7	6	5	4	3	2	1	

Scoring: Sum the scores given to each of the 10 scales of the Style Flexibility Index. Scores will range from a low of 10 to a high of 100. The higher the score, the more flexible one is perceived to be. An improved indication of style flexibility would be obtained by having teachers actually describe their principal.

EXHIBIT 7–3 Style Resilience Index

Think of occasions, situations, and incidents when you as principal were interacting directly with teachers about *general goals and purposes, educational platform, and overall philosophy of the school*. As a result of this interaction, indicate how teachers would describe you, using the 10 paired statements provided below.

	10 9 8 7 6 5 4 3 2 1	
Clear goals	_____	Inconsistent
Fulfills commitments	_____	Uncommitted
Will power	_____	Avoids conflict
Individualistic	_____	Conforming
Decisive	_____	Indecisive
Reliable	_____	Disorganized
Self-confident	_____	Avoids rejection
Simplifies issues	_____	Ambiguous
Persistent	_____	Yielding
Tough-minded	_____	Wavering
	10 9 8 7 6 5 4 3 2 1	

Scoring: Sum the scores given to each of the 10 scales of the Style Resilience Index. Scores will range from a low of 10 to a high of 100. The higher the score, the more resilient one is perceived to be. An improved indication of style resilience would be obtained by having teachers actually describe their principal.

Rigidity is the concept that Reddin suggests to understand counterproductive expressions of resilience. The resilient leadership style is characterized by will power, tough-mindedness, self-confidence, and self-discipline. Principals of effective schools display these qualities when dealing with aspects of the school's value core. Expressing these same qualities, when dealing with the day-to-day decisions that teachers make in classrooms as they work with students, would result in the principal's being perceived as rigid. The two dimensions of resilience and flexibility are illustrated in Figure 7–3 in the form of a leadership grid. Note that, at the base of the grid, resiliency ranges from a low score of 0 to a high of 100. Plot your score from the Style Resiliency Index on this dimension of the grid. To the left is the flexibility dimension, ranging from 0 to 100. Plot your score from the Style Flexibility Index on this dimension.

High resiliency scores combined with low flexibility scores would place one in the lower right-hand corner of the grid and represent the Rigid style. A flexibility score of 80 combined with a resiliency score of 30, on the other hand, would place one in the upper left-hand quadrant of the grid, representing the Drifting leadership style. High scores on both flexibility and resilience would place one in the upper right-hand quadrant—the Balanced leadership style, and low scores on both dimensions would place one in the lower left quadrant—the Monitoring style. Let's examine each of the four styles with reference to principals as they manage issues of tight and loose coupling in schools.

The Drifting style can work when important values are not at stake and might be appropriate for issues common to the school's loosely structured, high discretionary area. But when principals are flexible in dealing with the school's core of values, they appear to teachers to be drifting and are not viewed as able to provide necessary purposing and direction.

The Rigid style can work for issues relating to the school's core of values. Using

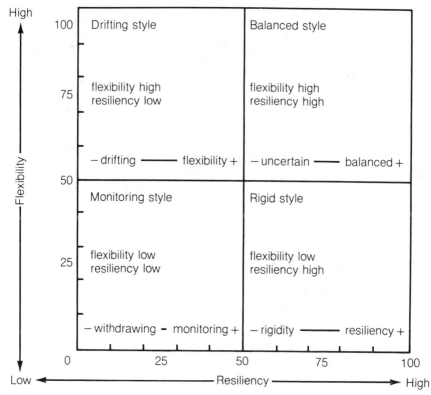

FIGURE 7-3 Styles for Flexible and Resilient Principal Leadership

this style with teachers on issues of providing for daily teaching and learning, however, is likely to be viewed negatively. Instead of appearing resilient, principals will be seen as autocratic and their style as rigid.

The Monitoring style can work in instances in which jobs can be programmed in such detail that the emphasis is less on persons and goals and more on monitoring the work flow, thus ensuring reliability. Teacher-proof designs for schooling support the Monitoring style. The enforcement of school rules and providing drill-practice work in teaching and learning might be examples appropriate for the Monitoring style. When principals use this style excessively or in the wrong instances, they are viewed as having withdrawn their concern for people as individuals and for goals and purposes.

The Balanced style provides flexible leadership in the articulation of the school's values, goals, and platform as teachers work day by day. At the same time, this style provides resilient leadership with respect to the promotion and maintenance of important values. This approach characterizes principal leadership found in successful schools. The concept of balanced leadership characteristic of successful schools should be the cornerstone of one's management platform and is an important dimension of reflective practice in the principalship.

References

Bidwell, Charles E. 1965. "The School as a Formal Organization," in James G. March, Ed., *Handbook of Organization*, 972–1022. Chicago: Rand McNally.

Boyer, Ernest L. 1983. *High School: A Report on Secondary Education in America.* New York: Harper & Row.

Cardinal Principles of Secondary Education. Commission on the Reorganization of Secondary Education, National Education Association, 1918. Bureau of Education, Bulletin No. 35.

Cusick, Philip A. 1983. *The Egalitarian Ideal and the American High School.* New York: Longman.

Educational Policies Commission. 1938. *The Purposes of Education in American Democracy.* Washington, DC: The National Education Association.

Goodlad, John I. 1984. *A Place Called School: Prospects for the Future.* New York: McGraw-Hill.

Guiding Principles in Curriculum Development. 1943. New York City Board of Education. Quoted in Ward G. Reed, *The Fundamentals of Public School Administration*, 3rd ed. New York: Macmillan, 1951.

Hills, Jean. 1982. "The Preparation of Educational Leaders: What's Needed and What's Next?" UCEA occasional paper No. 8303. Columbus, OH: University Council for Educational Administration.

Hughes, James L. 1887. *Mistakes in Teaching.* New York: E. L. Kellogg & Co.

The Imperative Needs of Youth of Secondary School Age. 1944. Washington, DC: National Association of Secondary School Principals.

Jay, Anthony. 1970. *Management and Machiavelli.* New York: Penguin Books.

Ouchi, William, and A. M. Jaeger. 1978. "Stability in the Midst of Mobility," *Academy of Management Review* 3(2), 305–314.

Parsons, Talcott. 1951. *Toward a General Theory of Social Action.* Cambridge, MA: Harvard University Press.

Perrow, Charles. 1981. "Disintegrating Social Sciences," *New York University Education Quarterly* 10(2), 2–9.

Peters, Thomas J., and Robert H. Waterman, Jr. 1982. *In Search of Excellence: Lessons from America's Best-Run Companies.* New York: Harper & Row.

Phi Delta Kappa. 1978. *Educational Planning Model.* Bloomington, IN.

Powell, Arthur G., Eleanor Farrar, and David K. Cohen. 1985. *The Shopping Mall High School: Winners and Losers in the Educational Market Place.* Boston: Houghton Mifflin.

Raths, James. 1984. "Criteria for Worthwhile Activities," in T. J. Sergiovanni, Ed., *Handbook for Effective Department Leadership: Concepts and Practices in Today's Secondary Schools*, 2nd ed., 416–418. Boston: Allyn and Bacon.

Reddin, W. J. 1970. *Managerial Effectiveness.* New York: McGraw-Hill.

Watson, Thomas J., Jr. 1963. *A Business and Its Beliefs: The Ideas That Helped Build IBM.* New York: McGraw-Hill.

Weick, Karl. 1976. "Educational Organizations as Loosely Coupled Systems," *Administrative Science Quarterly* 21(2), 1–19.

Weick, Karl. 1982. "Administering Education in Loosely Coupled Systems," *Phi Delta Kappan* 27(2), 673–676.

APPENDIX 7–1 Identifying School Needs

A needs assessment seeks to determine school priorities by comparing goals and objectives that are considered to be important to the school with estimates of how well the school is functioning in each of the goal areas. Ideally, determining needs involves a *first-hand* and comprehensive evaluation of preferences and current levels of performance in a particular school. A useful first step, nonetheless, is to examine this issue perceptually by asking various important groups from the school-community to indicate goal preferences and to rate the school's perceived performance in goal areas. Perception discrepancies between the importance of goals and the extent to which goals are emphasized or achieved constitutes a general sense of the needs for that school.

The following is an example of one set of goal statements used by many school districts in assessing needs. This set is distributed by the Phi Delta Kappa.*

Educational Goals and Goal Clarifying Statements

These are not in any order of importance.

1. *Learn how to be a good citizen*
   A. Develop an awareness of civic rights and responsibilities
   B. Develop attitudes for productive citizenship in a democracy
   C. Develop an attitude of respect for personal and public property
   D. Develop an understanding of the obligations and responsibilities of citizenship

2. *Learn how to respect and get along with people who think, dress, and act differently*
   A. Develop an appreciation for and an understanding of other people and other cultures
   B. Develop an understanding of political, economic, and social patterns of the rest of the world
   C. Develop awareness of the interdependence of races, creeds, nations, and cultures
   D. Develop an awareness of the processes of group relationships

3. *Learn about and try to understand the changes that take place in the world*
   A. Develop ability to adjust to the changing demands of society
   B. Develop an awareness of and the ability to adjust to a changing world and its problems
   C. Develop understanding of the past, identify with the present, and the ability to meet the future

4. *Develop skills in reading, writing, speaking, and listening*
   A. Develop ability to communicate ideas and feelings effectively
   B. Develop skills in oral and written English

5. *Understand and practice democratic ideas and ideals*
   A. Develop loyalty to American democratic ideals
   B. Develop patriotism and loyalty to ideas of democracy
   C. Develop knowledge and appreciation of the rights and privileges in our democracy
   D. Develop an understanding of our American heritage

6. *Learn how to examine and use information*
   A. Develop ability to examine information constructively and creatively
   B. Develop ability to use scientific methods
   C. Develop reasoning abilities
   D. Develop skills to think and proceed logically

7. *Understand and practice the skills of family living*
   A. Develop understanding and appreciation of the principles of living in the family group
   B. Develop attitudes leading to acceptance of responsibilities as family members
   C. Develop an awareness of future family responsibilities and achievement of skills in preparing to accept them

8. *Learn to respect and get along with people with whom we work and live*
   A. Develop appreciation and respect for the worth and dignity of individuals
   B. Develop respect for individual worth and understanding of minority opinions and acceptance of majority decisions
   C. Develop a cooperative attitude toward living and working with others

*From Phi Delta Kappa (1978), *Educational Planning Model* (Bloomington, IN). Used with permission.

APPENDIX 7–1 *(Continued)*

9. *Develop skills to enter a specific field of work*
   A. Develop abilities and skills needed for immediate employment
   B. Develop an awareness of opportunities and requirements related to a specific field of work
   C. Develop an appreciation of good workmanship

10. *Learn how to be a good manager of money, property, and resources*
    A. Develop an understanding of economic principles and responsibilities
    B. Develop ability and understanding in personal buying, selling, and investment
    C. Develop skills in management of natural and human resources and the environment

11. *Develop a desire for learning now and in the future*
    A. Develop intellectual curiosity and eagerness for lifelong learning
    B. Develop a positive attitude toward learning
    C. Develop a positive attitude toward continuing independent education

12. *Learn how to use leisure time*
    A. Develop ability to use leisure time productively
    B. Develop a positive attitude toward participation in a range of leisure time activities—physical, intellectual, and creative
    C. Develop appreciation and interests which will lead to wise and enjoyable use of leisure time

13. *Practice and understand the ideas of health and safety*
    A. Establish an effective individual physical fitness program
    B. Develop an understanding of good physical health and well being
    C. Establish sound personal health habits and information
    D. Develop a concern for public health and safety

14. *Appreciate culture and beauty in the world*
    A. Develop abilities for effective expression of ideas and cultural appreciation—fine arts
    B. Cultivate appreciation for beauty in various forms
    C. Develop creative self-expression through various media—art, music, writing, etc.
    D. Develop special talents in music, art, literature, and foreign languages

15. *Gain information needed to make job selections*
    A. Promote self-understanding and self-direction in relation to student's occupational interests
    B. Develop the ability to use information and counseling services related to the selection of a job
    C. Develop a knowledge of specific information about a particular vocation

16. *Develop pride in work and a feeling of self-worth*
    A. Develop a feeling of student pride in achievements and progress
    B. Develop self-understanding and self-awareness
    C. Develop the student's feeling of positive self-worth, security, and self-assurance

17. *Develop good character and self-respect*
    A. Develop moral responsibility and a sound ethical and moral behavior
    B. Develop the student's capacity for constructive discipline in work, study, and play
    C. Develop a moral and ethical sense of values, goals, and processes of free society
    D. Develop standards of personal character and ideas

18. *Develop skills in mathematics and science*
    A. Develop ability to apply skills in real-life experiences
    B. Develop a fund of information and concepts
    C. Develop special interests and abilities

First, rank each of the goal statements; then compare your rankings with others in a small-group setting. The object is to reach a consensus in the general ranking of goals and to identify major differences. Areas of general agreement represent the value core of the group or of a particular school. Major differences in ranking of goal statements suggest the importance of providing options or alternatives for those holding strong minority opinions.

APPENDIX 7–1 *(Continued)*

Another ranking approach is to write each of the goal statements on a separate card or slip of paper. Participants would then divide the goal statements into three categories—those perceived to be very important, moderately important, and less important. The goal statements would then be sorted into seven piles as follows:

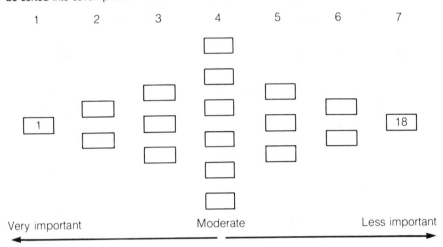

Very important   Moderate   Less important

Goal statements should now be sorted within each of the seven piles, to reflect actual rankings from 1 (most important) to 18 (least important). Keep in mind that most important and least important are relative concepts. This is a force-choice technique requiring people to make value choices among the 18 items even though at one level of abstraction all 18 might be considered important. Rankings can now be translated into needs by rating the school against each of the goal statements; that is, how well are the school's current programs and efforts meeting each of the goals? The Phi Delta Kappa program format suggests that the school should be evaluated against each goal on a 1 to 15 scale as follows:

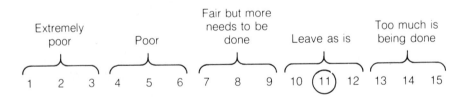

As this scale suggests, need discrepancies can take the form of deficiencies or sufficiencies. For example, it may be possible that not enough is being done in one goal area but that *too much* is being done in another goal area. Need deficiencies have more serious implications for high-ranked goals, and need sufficiencies have more serious implications for lower-ranked goals.

APPENDIX 7-2 Mistakes in Deciding Aims of Education, 1887

The defects of educational systems, and the mistakes in educational methods, have arisen from erroneous and indefinite views regarding the true aim of education. All our activities in planning, and in executing our plans are limited by our ideas. Even if our plans could be correct while our aims were not true and definite, comparatively little good would be attained. A perfect plan for the accomplishment of an imperfect purpose may produce evil instead of good results. The following are common mistakes regarding the aim of education:

1. It is a Mistake to Regard Knowledge as of Greater Importance than the Child.—This is a fundamental error. For centuries the minds of teachers have been clouded by the accepted maxim: "Knowledge is power." This is only partially true. The undue recognition of this partial truth prevents our conception of the greater truth beyond it. Knowledge in itself is not power. A single human being is worth infinitely more than all the knowledge that can be communicated to him or acquired by him. Knowledge has no power of development in itself. Man has. Man is the grandest earthly power created by God, and he should continue to grow forever. The teacher has to deal with two elements of power, the child and knowledge. The attention of educators has been directed chiefly to knowledge. This should not be the case.

2. It is a Mistake to Make the Communication of Knowledge the Great Aim of Teaching, even in the Intellectual Training of a Child.—The teacher should store the minds of his pupils. The more knowledge he communicates to them the better; provided that, in giving it, he does not cripple their power to gain knowledge independently for themselves. It would be a serious error to compel each child to attempt to acquire for himself by original experiments and investigation the accumulated knowledge of nearly sixty centuries. It would be a still greater blunder for the teacher to attempt to communicate all this knowledge to his pupils. The amount even of known truth that can be learned during school life is comparatively small. Valuable as knowledge may be, the power to acquire it independently is better. The more I value knowledge, the more carefully will I train my pupils, that they may be able to gain it for themselves after they leave school. What an advantage it will be to them to be keenly receptive to truth from books, from their fellow-men, and from the world of nature! The result of proper intellectual training should not be merely increased wisdom, but additional power to investigate known truth, and make discoveries of truths yet unrevealed.

3. It is a Mistake to Think that Education should be Completed at School.—There is very little systematic study done after school-life with a definite idea of disciplining the mind, or widening the intellectual vision. The years when men should do their best independent work are usually wasted. There is no stronger condemnation of a system of education possible, than the fact that a race of pupils trained under it leaves school without the desire as well as the ability for further study. Pupils have naturally a desire for knowledge. Like every other good tendency that desire may be developed, increased in depth and intensity. If the teacher's methods are correct this desire must so increase.

4. It is a Mistake to be Satisfied with the Development of an Aggressively Receptive Attitude of the Mind towards Knowledge.—Aggressive receptivity is good, active productivity is much better. Great as is the power to gather knowledge readily and thoroughly, the power to use it advantageously is much greater. The acquisition of knowledge in its highest development will be of little use unless accompanied by the motive and the ability to use it unselfishly and advantageously. . . . Knowledge may be used in two ways: as a basis in reasoning, and as a guide in improving our own condition, and that of our fellow-men. The teacher cannot fail to increase the readiness and the power of his pupils to use knowledge in both ways, if he remembers that knowledge should be applied as soon as it is learned, and that truth is never clear to us until we have used it; until we have in some way made it a part of ourselves by crystallizing it into a life-activity. The "rote process" of learning was abandoned

Excerpted from James L. Hughes (1887), *Mistakes in Teaching,* New York: E. L. Kellogg & Co., 5–26.

APPENDIX 7–2 *(Continued)*

for "oral teaching;" the weakness of oral teaching was recognized and an advance made when the guiding motto of teachers became "We learn through the eye;" this in turn has been given up by good teachers for the better maxim, "We learn by doing." Even this may be improved, and should be "We grow by doing."

5. It is a Mistake to Neglect the Physical Training of Pupils. — The physical nature of the child is a part, and a very important part, of its outfit of power. The physical powers may be developed as easily and as systematically as the mental powers. In the upward movement of the human race the prime essential for definite advancement is the improvement of the body. Men would be grander intellectually, and purer morally, if they had better bodies.

6. It is a Mistake to Neglect Industrial Training in Primary Classes. — The hand should be trained for three reasons:
   1. It is the chief means by which mankind earns a livelihood.
   2. It is the agency by which most of our intellectual conceptions have to be carried into execution.
   3. The intellectual powers of young children are aroused to complete activity by working with material things. Few observant parents have failed to notice that children have naturally both destructive and constructive tendencies. Both instincts are given to them for a good purpose: the first that they gain knowledge by investigation, the second that they may apply the knowledge they have gained by using, or making, or building things. A child has to use his hands in executing his intention in either case. No mind but his own can guide his hand. In order to guide his hand his mind must complete the circle of intellectual process. He must observe, think, decide, and execute.

7. It is a Mistake to Neglect a Definite Training of the Moral Nature in School. — The moral nature is susceptible to discipline. Spiritual insight may be quickened, intensified, and strengthened. Our power to control our weakening tendencies will grow stronger, by every successful effort in exercising control. It is a grievous error to give a man more physical and intellectual power, without trying to make sure that he will use his power for good purposes. It is wicked to add to the responsibilities of human beings, without at the same time strengthening their moral power. The best development of a child's physical and mental nature increases the possibilities of his moral development, but moral growth will not follow physical and intellectual growth as a necessary consequence. Increasing intelligence does not eradicate crime, or cause the general moral uplifting of the race. This could only be true, if men never did what they knew to be wrong. The moral nature itself must be trained. This training should be given early.

The true aims of education are:

1. Physically. To train the body that it may be strong, healthy, vigorous, graceful, skillful, and responsively active to the will.
2. Intellectually. To store the mind with knowledge, develop the love of knowledge, qualify for the independent acquisition of knowledge, and give regular practice in the use of knowledge.
3. Morally. To strengthen the conscience and will by forming the habit of carrying out pure feeling and good thought into immediate activity, to secure ready obedience to law as the embodiment of right, to implant a love of freedom, to give a consciousness of individual power and responsibility, and to develop in every child self-faith as the result of faith in God.

Appendix 7–3 Assumptions about Learning and Knowledge

Instructions: Make somewhere along each line a mark that best represents your own feelings about each statement.

Example: School serves the wishes and needs of adults better than it does the wishes and needs of children.

strongly agree	agree	no strong feeling	disagree	strongly disagree

I. Assumptions about Children's Learning

Motivation
    Assumption 1: Children are innately curious and will explore their environment without adult intervention.

strongly agree	agree	no strong feeling	disagree	strongly disagree

    Assumption 2: Exploratory behavior is self-perpetuating.

strongly agree	agree	no strong feeling	disagree	strongly disagree

Conditions for Learning
    Assumption 3: The child will display natural exploratory behavior if he is not threatened.

strongly agree	agree	no strong feeling	disagree	strongly disagree

    Assumption 4: Confidence in self is highly related to capacity for learning and for making important choices affecting one's learning.

strongly agree	agree	no strong feeling	disagree	strongly disagree

    Assumption 5: Active exploration in a rich environment, offering a wide array of manipulative materials, will facilitate children's learning.

strongly agree	agree	no strong feeling	disagree	strongly disagree

    Assumption 6: Play is not distinguished from work as the predominant mode of learning in early childhood.

strongly agree	agree	no strong feeling	disagree	strongly disagree

From Roland S. Barth (1971), "So You Want to Change to an Open Classroom," *Phi Delta Kappan* 53(2), 98–99.

APPENDIX 7–3 *(Continued)*

Assumption 7: Children have both the competence and the right to make significant decisions concerning their own learning.

| strongly | agree | no strong | disagree | strongly |
| agree | | feeling | | disagree |

Assumption 8: Children will be likely to learn if they are given considerable choice in the selection of the materials they wish to work with and in the choice of questions they wish to pursue with respect to those materials.

| strongly | agree | no strong | disagree | strongly |
| agree | | feeling | | disagree |

Assumption 9: Given the opportunity, children will choose to engage in activities which will be of high interest to them.

| strongly | agree | no strong | disagree | strongly |
| agree | | feeling | | disagree |

Assumption 10: If a child is fully involved in and is having fun with an activity, learning is taking place.

| strongly | agree | no strong | disagree | strongly |
| agree | | feeling | | disagree |

Social Learning
Assumption 11: When two or more children are interested in exploring the same problem or the same materials, they will often choose to collaborate in some way.

| strongly | agree | no strong | disagree | strongly |
| agree | | feeling | | disagree |

Assumption 12: When a child learns something which is important to him, he will wish to share it with others.

| strongly | agree | no strong | disagree | strongly |
| agree | | feeling | | disagree |

Intellectual Development
Assumption 13: Concept formation proceeds very slowly.

| strongly | agree | no strong | disagree | strongly |
| agree | | feeling | | disagree |

Assumption 14: Children learn and develop intellectually not only at their own rate but in their own style.

| strongly | agree | no strong | disagree | strongly |
| agree | | feeling | | disagree |

APPENDIX 7–3 *(Continued)*

Assumption 15: Children pass through similar stages of intellectual development, each in his own way and at his own rate and in his own time.

strongly agree	agree	no strong feeling	disagree	strongly disagree

Assumption 16: Intellectual growth and development take place through a sequence of concrete experiences followed by abstractions.

strongly agree	agree	no strong feeling	disagree	strongly disagree

Assumption 17: Verbal abstractions should follow direct experience with objects and ideas, not precede them or substitute for them.

strongly agree	agree	no strong feeling	disagree	strongly disagree

Evaluation

Assumption 18: The preferred source of verification for a child's solution to a problem comes through the materials he is working with.

strongly agree	agree	no strong feeling	disagree	strongly disagree

Assumption 19: Errors are necessarily a part of the learning process; they are to be expected and even desired, for they contain information essential for further learning.

strongly agree	agree	no strong feeling	disagree	strongly disagree

Assumption 20: Those qualities of a person's learning which can be carefully measured are not necessarily the most important.

strongly agree	agree	no strong feeling	disagree	strongly disagree

Assumption 21: Objective measures of performance may have a negative effect upon learning.

strongly agree	agree	no strong feeling	disagree	strongly disagree

Assumption 22: Learning is best assessed intuitively, by direct observation.

strongly agree	agree	no strong feeling	disagree	strongly disagree

APPENDIX 7–3 *(Continued)*

Assumption 23: The best way of evaluating the effect of the school experience on the child is to observe him over a long period of time.

| strongly agree | agree | no strong feeling | disagree | strongly disagree |

Assumption 24: The best measure of a child's work is his work.

| strongly agree | agree | no strong feeling | disagree | strongly disagree |

Assumptions about Knowledge

Assumption 25: The quality of being is more important than the quality of knowing; knowledge is a means of education, not its end. The final test of an education is what a man *is,* not what he *knows.*

| strongly agree | agree | no strong feeling | disagree | strongly disagree |

Assumption 26: Knowledge is a function of one's personal integration of experience and therefore does not fall into neatly separate categories or "disciplines."

| strongly agree | agree | no strong feeling | disagree | strongly disagree |

Assumption 27: The structure of knowledge is personal and idiosyncratic; it is a function of the synthesis of each individual's experience with the world.

| strongly agree | agree | no strong feeling | disagree | strongly disagree |

Assumption 28: Little or no knowledge exists which is essential for everyone to acquire.

| strongly agree | agree | no strong feeling | disagree | strongly disagree |

Assumption 29: It is possible, even likely, that an individual may learn and possess knowledge of a phenomenon and yet be unable to display it publicly. Knowledge resides with the knower, not in its public expression.

| strongly agree | agree | no strong feeling | disagree | strongly disagree |

CHAPTER 8

Beyond Goals: Building a Covenant of Shared Values

There is a growing consensus among management experts that one important key to inspiring extraordinary commitment and performance in schools is to shift the basis for what is done in schools away from bureaucratic authority and psychological authority. Certainly students, teachers, and parents respond to the requirements of bureaucratic authority to avoid penalties, and they respond as well to psychological authority to obtain rewards. But there is another, albeit neglected, source of authority that is equally powerful and perhaps even more powerful—moral authority (Selznick, 1957; Burns, 1978; Etzioni, 1988).

The Legacy of Economics

Of all the social science disciplines, management theory and practice have been most influenced by classical economics. It comes as no surprise, therefore, that most of our management principles and leadership practices emphasize bureaucratic and psychological authority at the expense of moral. The most key concept in classical economics is the "utility function," which is used to explain virtually *all* consumer behavior. In simple language the reasoning is as follows. Human beings are by their very nature selfish. They are driven by a desire to maximize their self-interest and thus continually calculate the costs and benefits of their actions choosing courses of action that either make them winners (they get rewards) or keep them from losing (they avoid punishment). So dominant is this view and so pervasive is the concept of the utility function that such emotions as love, loyalty, outrage, obligation, sense of duty, belief in the goodness of something, dedication to a cause, and a desire to help make things better count very little in determining a course of action. For the most part, classical economics views these emotions as mere currency that one uses to get something. The soldier hero, for example, storms the hill and sacrifices life not out of a sense of duty or obligation but to gain a medal or receive honors, even if given posthumously. A loving relationship is a contract within which two people exchange sentiments and commitments in order to gain benefits and services not as easily available outside such a relationship.

Another important concept underlying economic theory is that it is the individual that counts, not the group or community to which she or he belongs. The individual is the prime decision maker who calculates costs and benefits and chooses courses of action that are personally beneficial. The decisions of groups or societies are acknowledged but explained merely as the aggregate of many individual decisions.

Like management, the field of economics is undergoing a radical change, challenging its basic assumptions and developing new understandings that explain human behavior more fully. Amitai Etzioni (1988), for example, provides compelling evidence that people are driven not only by self-interest but by values and emotions as well. Values have to do with what people believe to be morally right, and emotions are the pleasure or intrinsic satisfaction they derive from doing something. Further, the idea of the individual decision maker determining all human behavior is now thought to be suspect. Individuals typically make decisions that reflect collective attributes and processes in response to the norms and values of the groups and communities with which they identify. As Etzioni (1988:4) explains:

> The neoclassical assumption that people render decisions rationally . . . is replaced by the assumption that people typically select means, not just goals, first and foremost on the basis of their values and emotions. Far from always "intruding on" or "twisting" rational deliberations, values and emotions render some decision-making more effective. This holds not just for social behavior, such as courtship, but also for economic behavior, say relationships with one's employees or superiors. . . .
>
> The neoclassical assumption that the individual is the decision-making unit is changed here to assume that social collectivities (such as ethnic and racial groups, peer groups at work, and neighborhood groups) are the prime decision-making units. Individual decision-making often reflects, to a certain extent, collective attributes and processes. Individual decisions do occur, but largely within the context set by various collectivities.

The new economics does not dismiss the important roles of self-interest or individual decision making in understanding why people decide to behave the way they do, but it enlarges this view by including two other powerful reasons, emotions and values. This discovery matches very well the evidence that emerges from studies of successful schools and other enterprises reviewed in Chapter 4 and the leadership practices that contribute to success reviewed in chapters 5 and 6. These studies and practices reveal that schools and other enterprises have something that metaphorically might be described as "cultures." As pointed out in Part II, at the heart of any culture is what the noted sociologist Edward A. Shils (1961) calls the "central zone." He believes that all societies and organizations within societies have central zones that provide a sense of order and stability and a source for the development of norms that give meaning and significance to the lives of people. The school's central zone represents a repository for the emotions and values that become the basis for moral authority.

Centers evolve naturally in schools in response to human needs. But if left unattended they can take the form of "wild cultures." Wild cultures are driven by emotions and values that may or may not be compatible with school goals, may or may not be supportive of improved teaching and learning, may or may not be growth oriented, may or may not be good for students. One of the jobs of the principal is to try to unravel and make manifest the wild culture so that it can be examined and understood. Doing so helps those involved come to grips with what is in relation to the values and beliefs that are desired. The idea is to "domesticate" this culture so that it emerges as a system of shared values and beliefs that define for all a way of life that is committed to quality teaching and learning.

When domesticated, the center that defines the school culture becomes the basis for collective decision making and the basis for moral action. The actions and behaviors of parents, teachers, students, and others are driven less by self-interest and more by what the school community considers to be right and good. In this chapter, *center* is referred to as the *covenant* of shared values that determines for the school what is right and good, points to the school's mission, defines obligations and duties, and spells out what must be done to meet commitments. The topic of school culture, a recurrent theme in this book, will be treated more specifically in Part IV.

Purposing Is the Lynchpin

Key to domesticating the culture of the school is the building of a covenant of shared values that replaces more implicit and informal norms. Abraham Zaleznik (1988) believes that "the failure of American management is the substitution of process for substance." He attributes this substitution to an exaggerated belief that schools can be improved by perfecting management systems, structures, and programs and by emphasizing human relationships in order to better control what people do (Zaleznik, 1988). Too often, process and relationship means become ends in themselves, resulting in vacuous school improvement strategies (Sergiovanni and Duggan, 1990).

To Zaleznik, "leadership is based on a compact that binds those who lead and those who follow into the same moral, intellectual and emotional commitment" (1988:15). Purposing is what principals do to develop this compact. Purposing involves both the vision of the leader and the covenant that the group shares.

Vision in school leadership needs to be understood differently than the way it emerges from the corporate sector. Peters and Austin (1985), for example, point out that vision should start with a single person and suggest that one should be wary of "committee visions." There is some truth to this observation, but there are problems as well. Principals and superintendents have a responsibility and obligation to talk openly and frequently about their beliefs and commitments. They are responsible for encouraging a dialogue about what the school stands for and where it should be headed. But vision should not be construed as a strategic plan that functions like a road map charting the turns needed to reach a specific reality that the leader has in mind. It should, instead, be viewed more as a compass that points the direction to be taken, that inspires enthusiasm, and that allows people to buy into and take part in the shaping of the way that will constitute the school's mission (Bricker, 1985). The fleshing out of this vision requires the building of a shared consensus about purposes and beliefs that creates a powerful force bonding people together around common themes. This bonding provides them with a sense of what is important and some signal of what is of value. *With bonding in place the school is transformed from an organization to a community.*

Often overlooked is the importance of the personal visions of teachers. As Roland Barth (1986) points out:

> All of us who entered teaching brought with us a conception of a desirable school. Each of us had a personal vision and was prepared to work, even fight, for it. Over time our personal visions became blurred by the visions, demands, and requirements of others. Many teachers' personal visions are now all but obliterated by external prescriptions. (478)

Vision is a noun that describes what principals and others bring to the school. *Purposing* is a verb that points to what principals do to bring about a shared consensus tight enough and coherent enough to bond people together in a common cause and to define them as a community but loose enough to allow for individual self-expression.

The realm of purposing, vision, and covenant is that of the high ground that inspires and provides moral leadership. This realm should not be confused with the stating of technical objectives and the development of tactical plans for their implementation. The technical and high ground mix in purposing and planning are illustrated below.*

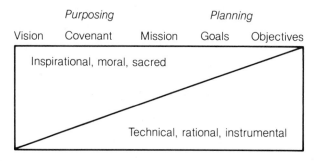

*Diagram is from T. J. Sergiovanni, *Value-Added Leadership: How to Get Extraordinary Performance in Schools*, New York: Harcourt Brace Jovanovich, 1990, p. 58.

Purposes in Action

Purposes let people know where the school is going, why, and how. Sometimes purpose statements contain bedrock beliefs that comprise value assumptions about the nature of people. The following four beliefs, for example, are based on Purkey and Novak's (1988) proposal for an approach to schooling they call *invitational education*:

1. Teachers, parents, students, and everyone else with whom the school works are able, valuable, and responsible and should be treated accordingly.

2. Education should be a collaborative, cooperative activity.

3. Teachers, parents, students, and everyone else with whom the school works possess untapped potential in all areas of human endeavor.

4. Human potential can best be realized by places, policies, and processes that are designed to invite development and by the actions and behaviors of people that are intentionally inviting.

When adopted, the four beliefs become a policy platform from which decisions are made about how to organize the school and its curriculum, how people are to work together, and the tone of teaching expected. The first belief, for example, frames policies about success and failure. If principal and teachers believe that every parent is worthy of respect and can learn, then they will find ways for parents to improve their parenting skills, to learn about how to help their children at home with their lessons, and so on. Excuses such as "they are barely literate themselves" and "they don't speak English" would not be acceptable. This formula applies as well to student success.

Similarly, the second belief frames policies in the direction of cooperation rather than competition. Good policies and practices in a school committed to those beliefs are those that do things *with* people rather than *to*. They give parents, teachers, and students voices and they listen to these voices. Similar guidelines for action can be derived from beliefs three and four.

Sometimes purposes take the form of a set of common principles that combine beliefs with understandings and expectations. "The Common Principles" of the Coalition of Essential Schools, a national effort to restructure secondary schools founded by Theodore Sizer, is an example of this approach. Sizer believes that no two good schools are quite alike. Instead, each should be a creation of its unique school-community. Thus, advocating common principles rather than proposing a model to be emulated makes sense (Sizer, 1988). The principles of the coalition are as follows:

1. An Essential school should focus on helping adolescents learn to use their minds well. Schools should not attempt to be "comprehensive" if such a claim is made at the expense of the school's central intellectual purpose.

2. The school's goals should be simple: that each student master a limited number of essential skills and areas of knowledge. While these skills and areas will, to varying degrees, reflect the traditional academic disciplines, the program's design should be shaped by the intellectual and imaginative powers and competencies that students need, rather than by "subjects" as conventionally defined. The aphorism "less is more" should dominate. Curricular decisions should be guided by the aim of thorough student mastery and achievement rather than by an effort merely to "cover content."

3. The school's goals should apply to all students, although the means to these goals will vary as those students themselves vary. School practice should be tailor made to meet the needs of every group or class of adolescents.

4. Teaching and learning should be personalized to the maximum feasible extent. Efforts should be directed toward a goal that no teacher have direct responsibility for more than 80 students. To capitalize on personalization, decisions about the course of study, the use of students' and teachers' time, and the choice of teaching materials and specific pedagogies must be unreservedly placed in the hands of the principal and staff.

5. The governing practical metaphor of the school should be student-as-worker, rather than the more familiar metaphor of teacher-as-deliverer-of-instructional-services. A prominent pedagogy will be coaching, to provoke students to learn how to learn and thus to teach themselves.

6. Students entering secondary school studies should be those who can show competence in language and elementary mathematics. Students of traditional high school age but not yet at appropriate levels of competence to enter secondary school studies should be provided intensive remedial work to help them meet these standards. The diploma should be awarded upon a successful final demonstration of mastery for graduation — an "exhibition." This exhibition by the student of his or her grasp of the central skills and knowledge of the school's program may be jointly administered by the faculty and by higher authorities. The diploma is awarded when earned, so the school's program proceeds with no strict age grading and with no system of credits collected by time spent in class. The emphasis is on the students' demonstration that they can do important things.

   The tone of the school should stress values of unanxious expectation ("I won't threaten you but I expect much of you"); of trust (until abused); and of decency (the values of fairness, generosity, and tolerance). Incentives appropriate to the school's particular students and teachers should be emphasized, and parents should be treated as essential collaborators.

7. The principal and teachers should perceive themselves as generalists first (teacher and scholars in general education), and specialists second (experts in one particular discipline). Staff should expect multiple obligations (teacher-counselor-manager), and demonstrate a sense of commitment to the entire school.

8. Ultimate administrative and budget targets should include, in addition to total student loads per teacher of 80 or fewer pupils, substantial time for collective planning by teachers, competitive salaries for staff, and an ultimate per pupil cost not to exceed that at traditional schools by more than 10 percent. To accomplish this, administrative plans might include the phased reduction or elimination of some services now provided students in many traditional comprehensive secondary schools (Sizer, 1989:2–4).

Sometimes the substance of a school's covenant comprises a commitment to a set of ideals and beliefs or "theory" about the nature of schooling. This is the case in the Key School in the Indianapolis, Indiana, School District. This school is attempting to organize itself around Howard Gardner's (1983) theory of multiple intelligences. Gardner proposes that people are possessed by seven relatively autonomous intellectual competencies: linguistic and mathematical (the two now emphasized almost exclusively in schools), musical, spatial, bodily-kinesthetic, and two personal intelligences (one focusing on self-understanding and the other on the understanding of others). The Key School is attempting to give all seven of these intelligences equal emphasis through the use of an interdisciplinary curriculum. Belief in a common approach to teaching and a common conception of human potential is the core element that bonds together the Key School faculty into a common cause.

Relying on purposing, bonding leadership, and other characteristics of values-oriented leadership as the cornerstone of one's school improvement strategy can cause discomfort among some administrators. These are, after all, "soft" concepts in a otherwise hard-nosed world of management. One way to respond to this uneasiness is to point to corporate America. If values-oriented leadership is accepted in that "dog-eat-dog" world, then perhaps its use within the more humanistic and friendly confines of schooling is equally if not more appropriate.

Many of America's blue ribbon companies (e.g., Johnson and Johnson, IBM, Procter and Gamble, Hewlett-Packard) have long used credos or belief statements as ways to define their essential purposes and as guides to decision making. Newly established companies also seem to be moving in this direction. One of the first things that newcomer Perot Systems did was to come to grips with its basic beliefs about what it hoped to accomplish and how. Consider, for example, the Johnson and Johnson credo:

> We believe our first responsibility is to the doctors, nurses, and patients, to mothers, and all others who use our products and services. In meeting their needs, everything we do must be of high quality. We must constantly strive to reduce our costs in order to maintain reasonable prices. Customers' orders must be serviced promptly and accurately. Our suppliers and distributors must have an opportunity to make a fair profit.
>
> We are responsible to our employees, the men and women who work with us throughout the world. Everyone must be considered as an individual. We must respect their dignity and recognize their merit. They must have a sense of security in their jobs. Compensation must be fair and adequate, and working conditions clean, orderly, and safe. Employees must feel free to make suggestions and complaints. There must be equal opportunity for employment, development, and advancement for those qualified. We must provide competent management, and their actions must be just and ethical.
>
> We are responsible to the communities in which we live and work and to the world community as well. We must be good citizens—support good works and charities and bear our fair share of taxes. We must encourage civic improvements and better health and education. We must maintain in good order the property we are privileged to use, protecting the environment and natural resources.
>
> Our final responsibility is to our stockholders. Business must make a sound profit. We must experiment with new ideas. Research must be carried on, innovative programs developed, and mistakes paid for. New equipment must be purchased, new facilities provided, and new products launched. Reserves must be created to provide for adverse times. When we operate according to these principles, the stockholders should realize a fair return.

As Badaracco, Jr. and Ellsworth (1989) point out, Johnson and Johnson clearly spells out its priorities by the order in which it lists its responsibilities: "first customers, next employees, then communities, and finally shareholders. Shareholders are not only last, they are expected to receive a fair, not maximum, return" (77–78). These authors point out that Johnson and Johnson CEO James Burke credits the company's quick and successful response to the Tylenol crises of 1982 and 1986 to widespread acceptance of belief in the credo.

Appendix 8-1, "Harnessing the Power of Beliefs in Restructuring Schools," provides an example of how coming to grips with "bedrock beliefs" can be used to develop a policy structure for improving schools not only at the local but at the state level as well. Appendix 8-2, "Tips on How to Create a Covenant," provides a perspective that might be useful to a school community that is seeking to develop or refine its purposes. The ideas and examples included in these appendices represent deeply held value positions that are not meant to be "cookie cutters" for direct imitation, but rather to be aids to reflection and debate as local school-communities determine what they believe and why.

Characteristics of Purpose Statements

There is no recipe for developing a covenant of shared values. It is a "personal" statement that is developed and owned by a particular school-community. There are, however, some general characteristics of covenants that might be helpful to school communities as they seek to develop ones that are useful and meaningful:

1. They should be clear enough so that you know you are achieving them.
2. They should be accessible enough so that they can be achieved with existing resources.
3. They should be important enough to reflect the core values and beliefs that are shared by those with a stake in the school.
4. They should be powerful enough that they can inspire and touch people in a world that is managerially loose and culturally tight.
5. They should be focused and few in number so that it is clear as to what is important and what isn't.
6. They should be characterized by consonance. The purposes should "hang together" as a group. It should be clear that contradictory purposes can be managed.
7. They should be difficult enough to evoke challenge and cause people to persevere, to persist.
8. They should be resilient enough to stand the test of time and thus not easily changed.
9. They should be flexible enough to be changed after careful consideration.

Taken together, a good set of purposes should encourage cooperation within the school, and not competition. Cooperative purposes encourage people to work together by allowing each member to share in what the group achieves or attains. Everyone benefits when anyone is successful. Competitive purposes, by contrast, pit one person against another. Each member receives rewards independent of the success of the group and contingent only upon his or her own performance, regardless of how well the group does. This view of cooperation and competition parallels the view widely accepted in corporate America. Emphasize competition between organizations but cooperation within.

Is Outcome-Based Education a Model?

To what extent are such ideas as vision, purposing, and covenant similar to statements of outcome and to designs for schooling linked tightly to outcomes? The answer to this question depends upon one's interpretation of "outcome-based education."

There is a difference between viewing outcome-based education as a prepackaged program comprising predetermined steps and scripts and as a more general way of doing business. When viewed more generally as a value, the idea has considerable merit. Advocates of outcome-based education believe that the essential value to the approach is "focusing and organizing all the school's programs and instructional efforts around clearly designed outcomes we want all students to demonstrate when they leave school" (Spady, 1989). Advocates are committed to providing all students with the knowledge competencies and orientation they need for future success and to implementing the programs and conditions that maximize learning success for all students. According to Spady the premises behind outcome-based education are that all students can learn and succeed, success breeds success, and schools control the conditions of success. Key to the outcome-based approach is what advocates call "designing down." It is the outcomes that determine everything else, and not vice versa. Outcomes determine the curriculum, its content and structure; the instruction; approaches to teaching and learning; student placement; and student assessment.

There are some problems with the concept of outcome-based education, none of which are beyond fixing. To begin with, if goals are stated generally enough so that there is some flexibility for objectives to emerge day by day and if the concept is not viewed so narrowly that only stated outcomes count, thus allowing for the discovery of worthwhile outcomes along the way, then the approach is viable. A great deal depends on how one defines outcomes. Secondly, outcomes provide only one, albeit important, dimension of a school covenant. Equally important are overarching values and beliefs and agreements about how people will work together. Adding these to one's commitment to certain outcomes increases the viability of this approach.

Taking a values approach and viewing issues of purposing and mission as something more than clearly defined and readily measured educational objectives has important implications for how principals understand evaluation—the topic of the next chapter.

References

Badaracco, Jr., Joseph L., and Richard R. Ellsworth. 1989. *Leadership and the Quest for Integrity*. Boston: Harvard Business School Press.

Barth, Roland. 1986. "The Principal and the Profession of Teaching," *Elementary School Journal* 86(4).

Block, Peter. 1987. *The Empowered Manager: Positive Political Skills at Work*. San Francisco: Jossey-Bass, pp. 109–121.

Bricker, H. 1984. As quoted in Robert H. Hayes, "Strategic Planning Forward in Reverse?" *Harvard Business Review*, Nov.–Dec.

Burns, James McGregor. 1978. *Leadership*. New York: Harper & Row.

Etzioni, Amitai. 1988. *The Moral Dimension Toward a New Economics*. New York: The Free Press.

Gardner, Howard. 1983. *Frames of Mind: The Theory of Multiple Intelligences*. New York: Basic Books.

Peters, Tom, and Nancy Austin. 1985. *A Passion for Excellence*. New York: Random House.

Purkey, William W., and J. M. Novak. 1988. *Education: By Invitation Only*. Bloomington, IN: Phi Delta Kappan Foundation.

Selznick, Philip. 1957. *Leadership in Administration A Sociological Interpretation*. Berkeley, CA: University of California Press.

Sergiovanni, Thomas J. 1990. *Value-Added Leadership: How to Get Extraordinary Performance in Schools*. San Diego, CA: Harcourt Brace Jovanovich.

Sergiovanni, Thomas J., and Brad Duggan. 1990. "Moral Authority: A Blueprint for Managing Tomorrow's Schools," in T. J. Sergiovanni and J. H. Moore, Eds., *Target 2000 A Compact for Excellence in Texas's Schools*. The 1990 Yearbook of the Texas Association for Supervision and Curriculum Development. San Antonio, TX: Watercress Press.

Shils, Edward A. 1961. "Centre and Periphery," in *The Logic of Personal Knowledge: Essays Presented to Michael Polanyi*. London: Routledge and Kegan Paul.

Sizer, Theodore R. 1989. "Diverse Practice, Shared Ideas: The Essential School," in Herbert J. Walberg and John J. Lane, Eds., *Organizing for Learning: Toward the 21st Century*. Reston, VA: National Association of Secondary School Principals.

Spady, William. 1989. "Applying the Power and Principles of Outcome-Based Education in Your Schools." Annual Conference of the Minnesota Association of School Administrators. Brainerd, Minnesota, October 2.

Zaleznik, Abraham. 1988. Quoted in Doran P. Levin, "G.M. Bid to Rejuvenate Leadership." *The New York Times*. Sept. 3.

APPENDIX 8–1 Harnessing the Power of Beliefs in Restructuring Schools

The Texas Organizing for Excellence Partners, a group sponsored by the Southwest Educational Development Laboratory in Austin, Texas, has developed a statement of beliefs that they believe can serve as a foundation for restructuring schools. The beliefs are a personal statement of the partners offered as a model to school districts as they develop belief statements of their own. The partners also propose a set of criteria for identifying "bedrock beliefs."

Statements of Belief

Acting on the conviction that vision is needed to define "the right thing to do" in providing for the education of our children, members of the partners group developed and tested each belief statement using the following five criteria:

1. Relevance: Is this a fundamental, core belief?
2. Importance: Can we answer the question, "What difference does this statement make?"
3. Common Meaning: Can this statement be understood by the average person? Is it clearly stated?
4. Context: Does the statement "fit" within the context of the whole set? Does it contribute to the whole meaning?
5. Universality: Can this belief be applied at all levels (school, district, state); to all involved (students, teachers, administrators, parents, school board members, etc.); and in all areas (curriculum, instruction, staff development, budgeting, etc.)?

A future goal of the partners group is to develop the implications of each belief, as part of the whole set of statements, for a restructured educational system. The set of beliefs and implications will provide that "mechanism" suggested by Drucker for identifying and systematically eliminating those policies, programs, or activities that are unproductive,- dysfunctional, or obsolete. Such a set of belief statements can provide both a frame for evaluating the current organizational structure and a starting point for building a new structure.

A Declaration of Educational Intent

Every individual in Texas has a vested interest in the success of schooling. To ensure that success, we must build a system based on vision and moral purpose. Our intent is to promote a restructuring of the educational system into a learning community that supports, affirms, and reflects in its every operation the following fundamental beliefs.

1. Every person has equal value and worth.
2. Every person can learn and realize success.
3. Together, the family, school, and community control the conditions for success.
4. Schools must develop knowledge, skills, thinking processes, and attitudes for successful living today and for tomorrow's world.
5. In a democratic society, schools must ensure the opportunities necessary for all individuals to reach their potential.
6. Schools must enable individuals to assume responsibility for their own behavior and performance.
7. Schools that honor courtesy, mutual respect, obligation, and shared commitment provide the best conditions for success.
8. Collaboration and cooperation are essential for arriving at the best decisions and for implementing successful solutions.

APPENDIX 8–1 *(Continued)*

9. Individuals and schools must be empowered with sufficient authority to carry out responsibilities for which they are held accountable.

10. Successful schools require a climate that encourages creativity and innovation.

Rationale for Belief Statements

1. *Every person has equal value and worth.*

   The educational system must be designed to affirm the dignity and worth of all who participate in it. Though an individual's behavior will affect the degree to which he or she is held in esteem by others, the basic humanity shared by all must be acknowledged and respected. This must be the basis for all educational decision-making in a highly heterogeneous society.

   The value placed on education for all in the U.S. must be matched with a commitment to value each person's language and ethnic identity. Students must be assured that their ethnic and cultural heritage is viewed as equal to any other. Parents/guardians must be assured that their thoughts and feelings are given equal consideration regardless of their ethnic, educational, or socioeconomic background. Teachers, other staff, and administrators at all levels of the system must be assured that their contributions to the educational process are of equal value to those of all others. Full and enthusiastic participation in the educational system is stimulated through an active and ongoing affirmation of the inherent worth of each individual.

2. *Every person can learn and realize success.*

   The system must be prepared to deal with students at the levels of knowledge, skills, and attitudes with which they enter the system. The schooling experience must be structured so that every student can move from where he or she "is at" to where they need to be to experience success in learning and in life.

   The inclusion of "every person" in this belief statement promotes the idea that learning is an ongoing process for adults as well as children. Each individual can continue to learn and attain greater success. The system must be prepared to provide parents/guardians with opportunities to understand the purpose of schooling and to contribute to their children's success. The system must provide teachers, other staff, and administrators with the professional growth opportunities they need to succeed in their work with students.

3. *Together, the family, the school, and the community control the conditions for success.*

   The success of learning, teaching, school administration, and family welfare is an interdependent endeavor. It requires the coordinated efforts of the separate forces of family, school, and community. Together, the family, the school, and the community must forge a "learning community" that unites spheres of responsibility, areas of interest, resources, and common goals to create conditions for success. The weaving of these three forces into such a "learning community" will invalidate all excuses for failure. There must be a recognition that much of our learning occurs outside of the school, and that both the family and the community provide valuable learning resources.

4. *Schools must develop knowledge, skills, thinking processes, and attitudes for successful living today and for tomorrow's world.*

   Schools promote the development of the whole person in the present and in the future. The educational system must be designed to provide students with the basic knowledge required to function in a technological society; with the ability to analyze problems, to access information, and to develop alternatives; and with the understanding that learning is a continuing process. Schools must deal with the cognitive and the affective, the vocational and the avocational, the realities and the possibilities.

APPENDIX 8–1 *(Continued)*

Learning is a lifelong process; therefore, students must be prepared to learn throughout life. In addition, the definition of "student" must be expanded to include people of any age with a desire to learn. The educational system must provide parents/guardians with an appreciation of the need for continued learning and for analytical thinking. It must provide teachers, other staff, and administrators with the opportunity to acquire new knowledge and to develop new skills and attitudes required in a changing world so that they can better address the needs of students.

5. *In a democratic society, schools must insure the opportunities necessary for all individuals to reach their potential.*
   A democracy requires the full participation of its citizenry. Full participation depends on all individuals achieving their full potential to contribute to the economy and culture of the nation. Webster's Dictionary defines "potential" as "something that can develop or become actual." This means that each individual has an array of possibilities limited only by innate physical or genetic factors. Schools must ensure conditions that encourage these possibilities to develop to their fullest.
   We can no longer afford a system that meets the needs of only a certain percentage of our students. The educational system must be structured so that students from all ethnic groups, from all socioeconomic levels, and those with special needs are ensured the opportunity to reach their potential. While individual acceptance of those opportunities is necessary, the realization of full potential is contingent on the educational system developing within the individual the skills and attitudes that enable learning.
   In addition, all parents/guardians should have the opportunity to participate as part of the learning community. They should have a chance to learn what they need to know to reach their own potential as well as to help their children. Teachers, other staff, and administrators should have staff development opportunities to grow and develop.

6. *Schools must enable individuals to assume responsibility for their own behavior and performance.*
   The educational system must be redesigned from a system focused on external control to one that encourages individuals to develop a sense of responsibility for their own behavior and performance. To "enable" is to provide the means or the opportunity that makes something possible. Therefore, skills and knowledge necessary to assume responsibility must be identified and learned. Responsibility must be both given and accepted. Barriers to responsibility must be recognized and overcome, and mutual support for all individuals must be provided.

7. *Schools that honor courtesy, mutual respect, obligation, and shared commitment provide the best conditions for success.*
   The educational system must foster an atmosphere in which courtesy and respect are observed in all interactions between people; where everyone feels free to express their ideas; where individuals fulfill their obligation to accept responsibility for the success of the whole; and where everyone is committed to working together toward common goals.

8. *Collaboration and cooperation are essential for arriving at the best decisions and for implementing successful solutions.*
   The educational system must be redesigned so that every level provides opportunities for input into the decision-making process by those who will be involved in carrying out the decisions. Because the best decisions emerge from a consideration of viable options, it is important to include those individuals who have the experience and the information needed to identify the options. Collaboration—the joining together—of those who are concerned about an issue produces the quality of information needed to gain insight into the possibilities; cooperation—working together for mutual benefit—

APPENDIX 8-1 *(Continued)*

generates the best options from which to choose. The inclusion of teachers, other staff, and administrators in decision-making processes reflects an enlightened leadership philosophy that promotes a sense of "ownership" in the decision. This sense of ownership, in turn, generates a commitment to the successful implementation of decisions and encourages individuals to harmonize their respective professional judgments and responsibilities.

9. *Individuals and schools must be empowered with sufficient authority to carry out responsibilities for which they are held accountable.*
Accountability is an essential ingredient at all levels of the educational system. Staff at each level of the system should be held accountable for those areas for which they are responsible, but accountability should be coupled with sufficient control over the conditions for success. Empowerment—giving legal authority or official sanction—provides the opportunity to effectively carry out responsibilities.

10. *Successful schools require a climate that encourages creativity and innovation.*
In a world where change is rapid and information doubles in geometric proportions, the educational system must encourage creativity and innovation. While care must be taken to avoid jumping onto each new and untested bandwagon, there also must be an acceptance of the risks involved in trying new ideas and new ways of doing things. Within the "learning community," people at all levels must recognize that fear of failure will effectively stifle both creativity and innovation.

APPENDIX 8–2 Tips on Creating a Covenant

In *The Empowered Manager,** Peter Block gives some helpful tips on how to begin to tackle the job of creating a vision. He uses the term *vision* broadly, as *covenant* is used to communicate not only the leader's vision but the amalgamation of visions that exist among members throughout the organization and that bonds them together in a common cause. Block's tips, in italics, and a discussion of his advice follow.

"Tip No. 1: Forget about Being No. 1."
Block believes that a vision statement should express "the contribution we want to make to the organization, not what the external world is going to bestow upon us." He believes that a vision of greatness needs to comprise a statement of what the organization intends to offer to the clients or customers it serves and to the people who work in the organization. For example, when the Psychological Corporation launched two new companies, Learning and Teaching and HBJ Leadership, it did so with the intent that the two would become the best of their kind. But in describing his vision for the companies the president, Tom Williamson, didn't say "It is our goal to be number one in the field, to make more money than anyone else, to dominate the market" and so on. Instead, his vision was "to increase the number of competent people in the United States by 10 percent." He wasn't concerned about recognition for the companies, but about their contribution to society. Williamson agrees with Block's statement: "If we get rewarded for making the vision happen, we will accept the recognition gracefully—but this is not why we pursue it."

"Tip No. 2: Don't Be Practical."
Block points out that in our pragmatic culture we are apt to think about vision in terms of the setting of specific and measurable objectives. It has already been noted that purposing is a concept different from planning. One's vision statement is not a road map but a compass. In Block's words, "A vision of greatness expresses the spiritual and idealistic side of our nature. It is a preferred future that comes from the heart, not from the head." He believes that a practical statement acts as a restraint when the idea is to make a statement about what we want to create or become.

"Tip No. 3: Begin with Your Customers."
Our customers in schools are the students and parents we seek to serve, and ultimately our society. Staying in touch with the customer was one of the most important lessons taught by Thomas J. Peters and Robert H. Waterman's best-seller *In Search of Excellence,* and it has become one of the fundamental principles of management among successful corporations and businesses. We should expect nothing less from schools. Block makes the point that it is equally important to give attention to "internal customers": the teachers, custodians, cooks, bus drivers, and others who do the work of the school. It is fair to say that students are not likely to be treated any better than are teachers and others.

Here are some examples of vision statements from Block's book that give us some idea as to what greatness looks like when an enterprise is dealing effectively with its customers. They are readily transferable to the school.

> *We act as partners with our customers (parents and teachers).*
> *We are committed to our customers' success and we encourage them to teach us how to do business with them.*
> *Our customers leave us feeling understood.*
> *The purpose of a sales call (student conference, parent-teacher conference) is to help the customer make a good decision.*
> *We fulfill every promise, meet every requirement.*
> *We have the courage to say no.*
> *We choose quality over speed.*
> *We don't cover up bad news.*
> *We want everyone involved to express real feelings and stay engaged.*

*Block, Peter. 1987. The Empowered Manager: Positive Political Skills at Work. San Francisco: Jossey-Bass, pp. 109–121.

APPENDIX 8–2 *(Continued)*

> *We want to understand the impact of our actions on our customers.*
> *We offer forgiveness to and expect forgiveness from our customers.*
> *Our customers are as important as our shareholders (school board). We exceed their expectations.*
> *We don't force solutions on our customers.*
> *Our dissatisfied customers teach us how to sell to (work with) those who currently do not use our service or product.*

"Tip No. 4: You Can't Treat Your Customers Any Better than You Treat Each Other."
A covenant should not only communicate what is important and provide a sense of direction, but it should also indicate how people are to work together and treat each other within the school. There are many reasons for this, with the most important being that students are not likely to be treated any better than are teachers. As Block points out, "If we, as customers, are being ignored, they as employees are probably being ignored. If they are cold, indifferent, and unresponsive, we have some very good clues as to the management style of their supervisors." The point is that teachers and other school employees need to be treated in the very same way that we want our students and parents to be treated.

"Tip No. 5: If Your Vision Statement Sounds like Motherhood and Apple Pie and Is Somewhat Embarrassing, You Are on the Right Track."
Block believes that a great vision is characterized by three qualities: It comes from the heart; the enterprise alone can make the statement and it is personal enough to be recognizably part of that enterprise; and it is dramatic and compelling. Visions are statements of hope and idealism. They are simple, moral in quality, and compelling.

CHAPTER 9

Reflecting on Program Development and Evaluation

Among the array of leadership roles and responsibilities for the principalship, none is more important than educational program development, administration, and evaluation. An important characteristic of principals of successful schools is their greater understanding of the complexity of educational programs and their ability to reflect this complexity in the leadership they provide. A school's educational program is more than the formally stated curriculum and the content of this curriculum. It includes the spectrum of educational activities of the school that influence teaching and learning: curricular and extracurricular, formal and informal, intended and unintended, known and unknown.

The curriculum that matters in a school is the curriculum expressed in the actual activities of teaching and learning. Concerned with the *curriculum in use*, principals of successful schools conceive of curriculum as something more dynamic and inclusive than a collection of written goals, subject-matter content, unit plans, and suggested teaching activities. The curriculum in use includes, as well, the setting for learning, patterns in influence that characterize student and teacher interactions, objectives actually achieved and meanings actually derived from learning regardless of intents, and reasons why students choose to learn. Often these aspects of the curriculum in use are more influential in determining the type and quality of teaching and learning than is the subject-matter content taught. Subject matter, for example, is *both* something to teach and something to teach with. Far more is learned in any lesson or unit than intended subject matter; this learning, too, should be planned for and accounted for in the administration and evaluation of educational programs.

How principals think about schooling, the curriculum, teaching, and learning influences how they act. Such thoughts, however, are not randomly arranged in one's mind. Instead, they are organized into implicit and explicit mental frames of reference. These frames, one's educational mindscape, provide the necessary rationale that enables principals to make sense of, and to justify, their decisions and actions.

Metaphors for Schooling

Mindscapes are often revealed by thinking metaphorically. Metaphors are figures of speech that help us to express complex ideas more simply. They are aids to communication and shortcuts to providing meaning for ideas. Educational metaphors are drawn from our social and personal experiences in schools. They shape our current thinking about schools and frame educational issues in ways that help us to make decisions according to a perceived logical process.

Two metaphors for schooling have dominated the thinking of curriculum theorists and workers. Herbert Kliebard (1972), referring to them as the metaphor of "production" and the metaphor of "growth," describes them as follows:

The Metaphor of Production

The curriculum is the means of production and the student is the raw material which will be transformed into a finished and useful product under the control of a highly skilled technician. The outcome of the production process is carefully plotted in advance according to rigorous design specifications, and when certain means of production prove to be wasteful, they are discarded in favor of more efficient ones. Great care is taken so that raw materials of a particular quality or composition are channeled into the proper production systems and that no potentially useful characteristic of the raw material is wasted. (403)

The Metaphor of Growth

The curriculum is the greenhouse where students will grow and develop to their fullest potential under the care of a wise and patient gardener. The plants that grow in the greenhouse are of every variety, but the gardener treats each according to its needs, so that each plant comes to flower. This universal blooming cannot be accomplished by leaving some plant unattended. All plants are nurtured with great solicitude, but no attempt is made to divert the inherent potential of the individual plant from its own metamorphosis or development to the whims and desires of the gardener. (403)

Production and growth images of schooling compete with each other for attention among curriculum theorists and workers. The growth metaphor, for example, dominated thinking during the progressive education era of the 1920s and 1930s and more recently during the open education movement (see, for example, Featherstone, 1967; James, 1968; and Weber, 1971). During the first half of the 1980s several national reports critical of American education appeared (see, for example, A Nation at Risk, 1983). Many of the recommendations contained in these reports reflected the production view of schooling.

The production view relies heavily on developing an educational program that resembles a detailed instructional delivery system. In a sense, the school is conceived as a factory within which students are processed in accordance with the specifications of this system. Sometimes schools are conceived as production "pipelines" with students being at the end of this line awaiting the flow of knowledge to be learned. The pipeline is constructed in a form that facilitates the effective flow of knowledge. Curriculum activities, subject-matter content, textbooks, and other educational means and devices are carefully selected, planned, and designed to fit the input end and to travel smoothly through the line. Once this flow is begun, the instructional delivery system is carefully monitored. Tests are conducted periodically. Should blockages in the line be discovered, input adjustments are made or the line itself is adjusted or purged. Thus, diagnostic troubleshooting is considered very important in schooling conceived as a pipeline.

The growth view of schooling relies heavily on developing a responsive and nurturing educational program. Student-defined needs and interests are paramount, and schooling is conceived as an enriched setting within which students unfold into intellectual, social, and emotional maturity. Emphasis is placed on developing a personable learning environment, and teaching is designed to facilitate the natural unfolding of students' potential.

Neither the production nor growth metaphor for schooling seems adequate in actual practice. One places too much emphasis on planning educational experiences for students in accordance with specifications determined by adults in advance. The other places too much emphasis on providing for student choice and interests. One places too much emphasis on rationality and detailed specifications. The other places too much emphasis on intuition and serendipity. One relegates students to passive roles as consumers of knowledge and responders to directions. The other relegates teachers to passive roles as facilitators of learning and responders to student initiatives.

The Metaphors in Practice

In current practice the production metaphor is expressed as a concern for the primacy of fundamentalism, adult authority, and formal structure in schooling. By contrast, the growth metaphor is expressed as a concern for the primacy of freedom, student participation, and informal structure in schooling (Frazier, 1972).

Dimensions of the two views are contrasted in Exhibit 9-1. Note that fundamentalism relies heavily on a curriculum characterized by carefully detailed lessons in the basic skills and subject-matter content areas geared to specific student outcomes, highly sequenced placement of this context, and diagnostic testing as a means to monitor student progress and to provide remedial assistance. Mastery learning, individualized instruction, behavioral objectives, tutorials, and prescriptive teaching are all important to this view. Growth, by contrast, relies heavily on a curriculum that provides for student options, unanticipated learning outcomes, and student interests. The teacher's role is that of guide and helper; the emphasis is on learning by doing; student satisfaction and personal growth are viewed as important.

As you review Exhibit 9-1, try to imagine what schooling would be like if only one view were used exclusively. Can you think of instances in which the two views can be blended? Can you think of specific learning situations in which one view would be decidedly superior or inferior to the other as a guide to educational decision making? An overall view of schooling is important and necessary to provide purposing, to achieve clarity, and to bring about coherence. But within this overall view, dimensions of both production and freedom should be incorporated into

EXHIBIT 9-1 Contrasting Production and Growth Views of Schooling

Growth	Elements	Production
Many options and choices for children Use of unexpected incident to lead into group undertakings Much attention to interest, sense of need, current concerns Emphasis on large or global goals Structure for learning exists chiefly in heads of teachers, not paper	1 Curriculum	Carefully worked out lessons in basic skills and content areas Stress on scientifically determined placement of content Sequences of work very carefully planned Evaluation geared to specific content and its learning
Many resources of all kinds—may have media center easily available Live animals—garden—pond Junk or nonstructured stuff Few textbooks in sets—more trade and reference works in or close to wherever study takes place	2 Resources	Boxes, programs, learning packets, multimedia packages: super textbooks Diagnostic devices Assignments highly explicit in terms of study materials to go through Much testing of progress
More emphasis on learning than on teaching Teacher as guide and helper Planning done by children Emphasis on learning by doing—centered on activities Stress on satisfaction and sense of growth in personal competence	3 Instruction	Mastery of the goal Individualized instruction seen as ideal Ends exemplified in behavioral terms—highly explicit Tutoring relationship valued Much small group target teaching Remediation continuous concern Prescriptive teaching
May plan and teach together May be assigned to large group of children as a staff rather than to 25 or 30 Paid and volunteer layworkers part of mix	7 Staff	Paraprofessionals to handle routine tasks High level of accountability for getting desired results Teachers coached to ensure greater effectiveness (increased inservice education)

EXHIBIT 9-1 (Continued)

Growth	Elements	Production
No bells—few fixed time divisions Work going on in many aspects of study at same time Individual pupils planning own use of time within some limits Relatively few occasions for work in large groups—mostly small group and individual or independent study	4 Time schedules	Flexible scheduling related to needs Regular attention, however, to major skills and content areas Individual pacing in progress through study sequences Large amounts of time devoted to individual study
Walls in the school pushed out Learning areas equal in floor space to several classrooms Expansion out of doors—field trips Use of public facilities as study space Community-centered study projects Some space may be structured as interest or work	5 Space	Large study areas—may be several classrooms opened up to form study space Smaller spaces for discussion groups Specialized facilities such as studios, laboratories, workshops Provisions for individual study: carrels, stations, computer terminals
Larger units—like 75 to 125 May be called learning communities, schools within schools, subschools Grouping may be interage, vertical, family-type Children may remain with same teacher or teachers several years	6 Classification of pupils	Pupils handled as individuals Grouping as such not regarded as too important Grouping for instruction on basis of achievement or need level Regrouping for instruction in basic skills

From Alexander Frazier (1972), *Open Schools for Children*, Washington, DC: Association for Supervision and Curriculum Development, 60–61.

practice, with the appropriateness of each determined situationally. For example, a distinction is often made between training objectives and teaching formats and educational objectives and teaching formats (see Chapter 13). Generally, when the intent of schooling is to train students in the mastery of a given set of skills or information, the production image of schooling may be superior. But for educational outcomes that emphasize the linking and synthesis of concepts, critical thinking, problem solving, imagination, and judgment, curriculum and teaching approaches in the growth image will very likely be superior (Stallings and Kaskowitz, 1974; Wallberg, Schiller, and Haertel, 1979).

The perennial struggle that reflective principals face, as they give leadership to the process of educational program development, is how to achieve balance between the two emphases suggested by production and growth metaphors of schooling. The metaphor of *travel*, as proposed by Kliebard (1972), provides a third view of schooling that can bring about this needed balance:

> **The Metaphor of Travel**
> The curriculum is a route over which students must travel under the leadership of an experienced guide and companion. Each traveler will be affected differently by the journey since the effect is at least as much a function of the predilections, intelligence, interest, and intents of the traveler as it is to the contours of the route. This variability is not only inevitable, but wondrous and desirable. Therefore, no effort is made to anticipate the exact nature of the effect on the traveler; but a great effort is made to plot the routes so that the journey will be as rich, as fascinating, and as memorable as possible.

If an educational program is conceived as a route to learning traveled by students under the direction and guidance of the principal and teachers, then a great deal of planning will be required. But this planning cannot be simplistic. Instead, it needs to specify the general route to be traveled while allowing the flexibility necessary for principals and teachers to provide meaningful teaching and learning for students.

What other metaphors come to mind as you think about how educational programs might be developed and put into place? What are the implications of each of the metaphors discussed for how one thinks about evaluation?

Thinking about Evaluation

The technical details of evaluation are important and indispensable, but it is how principals think about evaluation that makes the major difference. Their mental frameworks shape what they see, say, and do; provide guidance and direction to evaluation efforts; and determine evaluation reality for their schools. Principals are in a unique position to frame the thinking of others about evaluation in the school. Their position of power and influence enables them to take the lead in defining evaluation issues and in setting parameters. A principal who equates school evaluation with a simple problem of comparing grade-level scores on standard achievement tests with national grade-level scores creates a different reality with respect to curriculum choices, teaching and learning methods, and student evaluation than does a principal with a more comprehensive view.

Many experts point out that language is a source of power and whoever is in control of the language of evaluation controls the thinking and behavior of others as they engage in evaluation (Greenfield, 1984). Since principals are in a position of control and their evaluation stance can influence the thinking of others, this chapter emphasizes not how to evaluate but how to think about evaluation. Principals provide leadership to the evaluation process not so much by "doing," but rather by providing the proper frames of reference within which evaluation will take place.

The Ordinariness of Evaluation

Who evaluates? What is evaluated? Where does evaluation take place? Everyone, everything, every place are the answers to these questions. Evaluation is such a natural part of our human existence that we rarely think about it. Ordinary individuals value certain things, express preferences, and make choices constantly. Evaluation involves making judgments about the worth of things, events, options, activities and achievements. In our ordinary lives such judgments are typically made "on the spot" and on the basis of our "common sense." Judgments become informed when we take the time to reflect on the process of evaluation and when we gather information, beyond common sense, about the evaluation issues we face. But this reflection and the information we collect do not replace our judgment. We are not put on hold while some process does the evaluation for us. Instead, reflection and information serve our judgment—*inform our intuition*—as we decide what we prefer, what is of worth, and what to do. Informed intuition is the key to reflective practice in any profession and an essential ingredient in effective school evaluation.

Measurement and Evaluation Are Different

Most of us have become pretty good at making judgments in our daily lives. In fact, whether we realize it or not we are already experienced and fairly accomplished evaluators. Evaluating school programs, however, seems to be another issue entirely. Often, much of the confidence and reasonableness that characterize evaluation in our ordinary lives is forgotten. Very often, what we call *evaluation* with respect to school programs turns out not to be evaluation at all, but *measurement*. Measurement and evaluation are different. Measurement requires that a "goodness of fit" or "worth" be determined against a fixed standard. In measurement this standard and the rules of thumb, procedures, protocols, and data-collection strategies used are more important than the person doing the measuring. Ideally, measurement procedures should be "person-proof" in the sense that each person who does the measuring should reach the same conclusion.

Often, measurement and evaluation go together. When this is the case, the two processes still maintain separate identities. For example, suppose you are interested in buying blinds for a window in your home. You would first need to know the size of the window. Let's say the window is 22 inches wide by 60 inches long. This set of figures is now your standard. Your friend who has some extra blinds in the attic offers them to you. Using a ruler, you carefully measure the blinds and learn that none "measures up" to your standard of 22″ × 60″. Though you had a role to play in this process, it was really the ruler that counted. Someone else using the same ruler would very likely have reached the same conclusion. Though measurements need to be accurate and some skill is involved in the process, the standard against which measurements are weighed and the measuring device are more important than the person doing the measuring.

Where does evaluation fit into your blinds purchase? You locate several blinds that measure up to your standard of 22″ × 60″. Now the emphasis shifts from measurement to evaluation. Which of the blinds that fits will you choose? Will they be metal or wood, half or full inch, yellow or blue? We are now dealing with matters of taste and other "softer" aspects of decorating. Some of the options available to you will be better than others, and the more informed you are about decorating and the more information you have and use about the particulars of the room and window you are decorating, the better your choice (evaluation) will be. To find out how well you did in decorating your window, both measurement and evaluation would be involved. The measurement part is easier – do the blinds fit? The evaluation part is more complex – are the blinds aesthetically pleasing given the room and window setting, and are the blinds functional given your intents?

The root word in evaluation is *value*, and valuing requires a human response from an individual or group. The more informed the response is, the more meaningful the evaluation will be. Unfortunately, when it comes to evaluating school programs, the processes used and the results obtained are often not as meaningful as they might be.

When Does a Measurement Stance Make Sense?

Typically, measurement and evaluation go hand in hand as principals and teachers think about and make decisions about school programs. Still, whether one takes a measurement stance given a particular problem or issue or whether one takes an evaluation stance can make a difference in how the evaluation turns out. A measurement stance does not exclude evaluation concerns and methods, but does bring to the forefront of the process methods and issues different from those of an evaluation stance. A measurement stance makes sense

1. When the emphasis is on the individual rather than on a group or program and when the intent is to make decisions about that individual's educational present or future.

2. When the emphasis is on outcomes comprising specific and measurable objectives and other readily fixed standards considered to be important by a school.

In the first instance, aptitude tests such as the Scholastic Aptitude Tests (SAT) and achievement tests such as the Iowa Test of Basic Skills are examples of available measurement tools. Aptitude tests are designed to predict a student's future performance. Achievement tests provide insights into what and how much a student has learned. Both can help make useful decisions about a student's educational present and future; however, these tests are not very useful for evaluating specific school programs or teaching practices. it is hard to pinpoint programmatic educational causes for rises and dips in such test scores. Further, aptitude and achievement scores are greatly influenced by nonschool considerations such as socioeconomic background of students, basic intelligence, and enriched home environment. These considerations make it difficult to evaluate the effects of particular school programs.

Standardized test scores are particularly sensitive to response patterns, and often a small change in pattern results in a large change in score. Harnischfeger and Wiley (1975), for example, point out that the 42-point drop in the average performance on the verbal part of the SAT over a recent 12-year period was caused by missing only five additional questions. Three additional misses on the math section resulted in a 26-point drop in the average score.

Aptitude and achievement tests such as the SAT and the Iowa Test of Basic Skills are norm-referenced, as opposed to criterion-referenced. Norm-referenced achievement tests are standardized in the sense that items are based on subject-matter content and objectives considered to be common for schools across the country, and items are concerned with comprehensive knowledge across an array of general concepts and topics. Such comprehensiveness and commonness make these tests ideally suited for making comparisons. To facilitate such comparisons, standard tests provide norms for various groups broadly representative of performance across the country. This enables the comparison of a student's score with the norm group to determine how well she or he is doing. Sometimes it is useful to compare average test scores for a larger group, such as a class or school, with a similar group to see how well each did when compared with the norm. School A or State A may score higher on a given test than did School B or State B when each is compared with the norm group.

Though these comparisons of groups against the norm can often be useful, certain risks are involved in making interpretations. Often, grade norms are viewed as objectives. For example, all third-grade students should read at the third-grade level. Considering norms as objectives is a fallacy that results in perpetual failure for schools (Dyer, 1973). Grade norms represent the average of all test scores for that grade level. It is not possible for the half of the student population that is below average to reach the average without raising the average. Norm-referenced tests always have "winners" and "losers." As student achievement gains result in higher scores, the average is adjusted upward to reflect this higher achievement. Half of the student population, however, always remains below "average."

Criterion-referenced tests differ from norm-referenced tests in that they are designed to measure the extent to which students achieve specific objectives considered to be important to particular school programs and teachers. The emphasis in criterion-referenced testing is on local objectives and outcomes linked to local school programs. Test items and other measurement rods are developed by local teachers associated with specific programs. Such tests are used to determine how well students have achieved. Important in constructing such tests is having fairly specific objectives and outcomes in mind. If a school is unsure of its objectives or if there is difficulty in stating the objectives in fairly measurable terms, it will be difficult to develop accurate and useful measurement tools. When faced with this problem, principals and teachers have three alternatives: They can abandon the measurement stance for an evaluation stance; they can concentrate only on objectives that are easily specified and lend themselves toward measurement (and thus overlook or neglect other objectives); or they can combine both approaches. When combining both, it is important that evaluation information be given weight equal to measurement information in making decisions and reaching conclusions.

Goals, Objectives, and School Evaluation

Schools should be accountable, and being concerned with purposes, goals, and objectives is one way to reflect this accountability. As leaders, principals need to be concerned both with what *should be* and *is being* accomplished in their schools. Concern for objectives is, therefore, important but should not be limited only to thinking that is characteristic of the measurement stance. Too often, principals assume that a statement of purpose accompanied by clearly defined objectives stated in the form of measurable student behaviors is a necessary first step in the evaluation process. Evidence is then accumulated from which judgments are made to determine how well the objectives have been accomplished. As indicated previously, this view represents an appropriate procedure in many instances but as an exclusive view of evaluation seems unnecessarily tidy and rigid. Indeed, this simplistic view of evaluation can result in a number of problems, including:

- *Substituting precision for accuracy.* When this occurs, there is a tendency to select, fit, or force objectives, activities, and events to be evaluated into forms and structures that match the technologies required for precise evaluation. The methods and procedures of evaluation determine what it is that will be evaluated rather than the other way around.

- *Honoring ends over means.* When this occurs, there is a tendency to focus on evaluating prespecified student behaviors, thus slighting what it is that the teacher does, the context or environment for learning, and unanticipated outcomes. Evaluating only for ends without evaluating the means does not provide enough clues and ideas for starting and carrying out school improvement efforts.

- *Erosion of professional confidence.* There is a tendency toward loss of confidence among teachers and principals in their own abilities to make judgments, to assess, to evaluate. Tests and measurements becomes substitutes for, rather than supplements to, professional observations and judgments.

Let's consider, for example, the issue of accuracy and precision in evaluation. Collecting objective evidence to determine the extent to which objectives are being met can sometimes result in misplaced emphasis. When this occurs, one risks trading accuracy for precision. *Accuracy* refers to the importance or value of an educational activity or goal. *Precision*, on the other hand, refers to the scientific rigor with which the educational activity or goal can be pursued or measured. A fairly accurate set of objectives relating to a unit on family life in a social science or literature class, for example, might include:

- Helping students understand that families everywhere fulfill similar functions although customs and traditions differ among societies.
- Helping students to compare, understand, and appreciate how their own family functions and what their roles are in this functioning.
- Helping students to be better family members as their roles change from child to adult and to understand the adult roles of partner and parent.

These objectives leave much to be desired with respect to ease of evaluation. To the extent that they are considered important, they are accurate but not precise. More precise objectives dealing with the same topic might include:

- List the various roles "father" plays in three named cultures.
- Given a list of 10 family functions, identify 5 common across the three named cultures, 3 that are dissimilar, and 2 that are not appropriate.
- Identify the main characters and family order they assume in three short stories. Match the character with the correct role and both character and role with the correct story.

This group of objectives is more precise than the first but less accurate. Students could, and many do, study for and pass a test construed to determine if objectives have been met, without really understanding much about family life, what it means to them, and how they might function in present and future family roles.

Accuracy and Precision in Evaluation

The relationships between accuracy and precision are illustrated in Figure 9-1 in the form of a grid. Note that the four quadrants of the grid are formed by comparing the emphases given to accuracy and precision in evaluation. The abscissa of the grid represents the extent to which accuracy is emphasized from low to high, and the ordinate represents the emphasis given to precision.

Quadrant 2 represents situations characterized by high accuracy and high precision. Here the events, activities, and objectives being evaluated are important in their intellectual potency or with respect to other school intents. Further, the evaluation methods and procedures are efficient and readily implemented. This is the ideal setting for a measurement stance in evaluation.

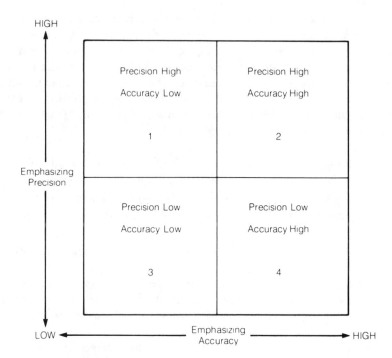

FIGURE 9-1 Emphasizing Accuracy and Precision in Educational Evaluation

Quadrant 4 represents situations characterized by high accuracy with low precision. Quadrant 1 represents situations characterized by low accuracy but high precision. Quadrant 3 represents situations characterized by both low accuracy and low precision.

Principals should work to ensure that evaluation efforts take place within the context of quadrants 2 and 4. In each case the emphasis is on pursuing important objectives, activities, and events with whatever measurement and evaluation tools are available. Sometimes the tools will be precise, but at other times they will be ambiguous. Sometimes evaluation will put people on remote control, and standardized measureurement rods will be used profitably and effectively. At other times one will have to rely on judgment, consensus, and hunch in making assessments. Unfortunately, in today's educational environment, principals are under a great deal of pressure to emphasize the measurement stance whether it fits or not. They will need to resist these pressures if they wish to avoid succumbing to the plight of the cowboy who placed in a crooked poker game because it was the only one in town.

An Expanded View of Objectives

Key to determining whether a measurement or evaluation stance makes sense in a particular instance is one's view of the nature of educational objectives. Though most people agree that a goal focus is needed, controversy exists over what is a legitimate objective and how it should be stated. Behavioral objectives advocates often fight the battle on one extreme, insisting that all objectives be predetermined and stated in the form of measurable expected student outcomes. Those opposed to behavioral objectives insist that no place exists for such objectives, but rather that goals should be stated more generally or derived incidentally from learning experiences. To do otherwise, this latter group argues, results in rigid instructional experiences, insensitivities to the individual needs of students, and so on.

Both sides on this argument are right and wrong. Behavioral objectives (referred to here as instructional objectives) are worthwhile and important in some situations but hinder effectiveness and indeed border on triviality in other situations. On the other hand, many teaching and learning situations lend themselves to general or to incidentally derived objectives, but in some instances their use is inefficient and irresponsible. Objectives come in a variety of forms and types. Each is a tool that, when properly used, can help principals and teachers develop more effective learning experiences. At least four types of objectives can be identified and should be used in planning for teaching and learning and in evaluating teaching and learning programs:

1. *Instructional objectives.* These are outcomes and solutions that are provided and specified before teaching in the form of student behaviors. Expected student behavior is specified in advance of the learning encounter or teaching activity (Popham and Baker, 1970).

2. *Expressive objectives.* These are actual outcomes of an educational encounter or activity. The educational encounter or activity is not designed to lead to specific objectives but to a range of objectives not specifically determined beforehand. Evaluation involves looking back to assess what value occurred from the encounter or activity. Almost any worthwhile objective discovered is considered to be acceptable. Since expressive objectives are not "real" objectives, some prefer to term them *expressive outcomes* (Eisner, 1979).

3. *Middle-range objectives.* These do not define the outcomes or solutions expected from students beforehand but rather the problems with which the student will deal. The student is not free to come up with any worthwhile solution, but one that meets the specifications of the problem under study. Sometimes these are referred to as *problem-solving outcomes* (Eisner, 1979).

4. *Informal objectives.* These focus less deliberately on content and concepts per se and more deliberately on processes and other informal objectives that accompany formal objectives.

Instructional Objectives.   Typically, instructional objectives are concerned with expected student behaviors or desired student behaviors. The objectives do not speak to what the teacher does, the methods used, or the nature of the educational encounter directly. Instead, these objectives are intended to define measurable outcomes in order to facilitate direct evaluation. Used properly these objectives can help teachers select learning experiences, materials, and educational settings that will best lead students to the desired behavior. An example of an instructional objective is the following:

> The student will be able to measure her or his own height, weight, arm length, foot span, foot size, and leg stretch to the nearest metric unit.

One of the problems with instructional objectives is that they tend to place too much emphasis on identification and description skills at the knowledge-recall and comprehension levels of the hierarchy of educational objectives and not enough emphasis on application, analysis, synthesis, and evaluation levels. Further, instructional objectives tend not to emphasize affective learnings. More advanced kinds of learning and many affective learning outcomes simply do not lend themselves well to the rigor of being predetermined for each learner and the rigor of being behaviorally stated. Nonetheless, instructional objectives are very important and should play a role in the planning of educational programs and in their evaluation. Indeed, they become even more important where inferior teaching exists or where educational program designs are weakly conceived. Instructional objectives permit fairly close supervision and at least guarantee that certain minimum outcomes will be attended to. But too rigid or exclusive use of instructional objectives can often stifle superior teaching and often results in lack of sensitivity to the individual needs of learners. For these reasons, instructional objectives should be viewed as only one, albeit important, kind to be balanced with other kinds of objectives.

Expressive Objectives — Outcomes. The use of expressive objectives requires that principals and teachers focus less on specific expected outcomes for students and more on the arrangement of potent, high-quality educational encounters or activities that will stimulate the emergence of a number of worthwhile outcomes. Expressive outcomes are the consequences of curriculum and teaching activities. Instead of focusing on student behaviors, expressive outcomes describe more what it is that the teacher is to do and emphasize more the specific nature of learning activities.

Examples of expressive outcomes might include these:

- To arrange for students to participate in a mock trial
- To have students interview shoppers exiting from the supermarket about their opinions on the freedom of assembly, redress of grievances, and right to bear arms provisions of the Bill of Rights

In each case the emphasis is not on what the student will specifically learn but on developing and arranging a learning encounter. Any number of important outcomes can result from students who are involved in a mock trial. Differentiating fact from conjecture, learning roles and functions of those involved in the judicial process, evaluating the rules of operation of our court system, preparing written and oral arguments, analyzing the evidence, experiencing firsthand how one's values affect one's opinions, and analyzing the content and issues of the court case are examples of highly significant potential learning outcomes for students. The expressive outcome is any worthwhile activity of the trial simulation planned by the teacher. The simulation is not designed to lead students to a specific goal or predetermined form of behavior but to forms of thinking, feeling, and behaving that are of their own choice.

Emphasizing expressive outcomes reflects the reality that takes place in America's classrooms. Though teachers do indeed teach to instructional objectives, the vast majority of their teaching tends to focus on the provision of potent learning activities that they believe will produce meaningful outcomes for students. But the outcomes are typically not decided beforehand. An examination of lesson plans reveals that expressive outcomes represent the dominant mode of thinking about teaching and learning among teachers. Rarely are instructional objectives listed. Instead, teachers make planning notations describing what it is that they and students will be doing (for example, "set up a debate for and against states' rights").

Middle-Range Objectives.   Middle-range objectives provide much more freedom to teachers and students than instructional objectives do for determining what will be learned, but less freedom than expressive objectives do. In instructional objectives the solution is provided. In expressive objectives the setting is provided and the student discovers his or her own solutions from a range of possibilities. In middle-range objectives the problem is provided, along with specifications for its solution. The student then discovers her or his solution not from a wide range but from a range that conforms to the specifications. The following is an example of a middle-range objective that a teacher might sketch in a plan book:

> Using data from an actuarial table of life expectancies for individuals in selected occupational groups, students will develop a series of visual aids explaining the data. The visuals to be developed should be understood by average fifth-grade students without the assistance of accompanying verbal or oral text. In other words, the visuals should be so labeled and keyed that they are self-explanatory to this group.

In this case the student is provided with a problem to solve and is free to develop any solution to the problem that meets the specification. "What the teacher looks for in evaluating achievement is not a preconceived fit between a known objective and a known solution but an appraisal, after inquiry, of the relative merit of solution to the objective formulated" (Eisner, 1972:575).

Middle-range objectives describe best the ways in which many professionals work. As Eisner (1979) points out, designers are typically given a set of criteria or set of specifications and asked to create products that will satisfactorily meet these criteria. This is also true of the engineering profession. In architecture, clients provide architects with sets of specifications (budget, personal lifestyle, tastes, and so on) and the builder presents the architect with still further specifications, such as the municipal code and so on. Given these parameters, the architect is then free to work toward a solution. The work of laboratory scientists evolves similarly. As in the case of expressive outcomes, problem-solving outcomes associated with middle-range objectives tend not to lend themselves toward the measurement stance as much as they do toward the evaluation stance. Indeed, there is a measurement aspect: To what extent did the student, the architect, the engineer, the scientist meet problem-solving specifications? But the worth and value of the solution generated within those specifications cannot be determined by measurement but by evaluation.

Informal Objectives.   Informal objectives differ from the others in that they focus less deliberately on content and concepts than on processes. Informal objectives include the development of personal meanings, intrinsic satisfaction, joy in learning, interpersonal competencies, and love of self found in the affective domain of objectives as well as more cognitively oriented processes such as exploring, feeling, sensing, comparing, sorting, clarifying, and creating. Informal objectives add the necessary balance of how something is learned to what is learned.

The content learned by comparing and categorizing various types of mental illness, for example, may be important, but the processes of comparing and categorizing are important, too, in their own right. The outcome of a social science group report on the geography of world poverty is important, but so are informal learnings that occur as students work in a group—learnings having to do with leadership, values, cooperation, and group processes. Teachers and principals need to plan educational experiences and curriculum formats with high emphasis on informal objectives and to provide for evaluation of informal outcomes.

The extent to which each of the four types of objectives or outcomes is provided in the curriculum and the emphasis given to each in teaching are important considerations in evaluating the school's educational program, texts, materials, and the work of teachers in the classroom.

A Comprehensive View of Evaluation

John Tukey's admonition "Far better an approximate answer to the right question, which is often vague, than an exact answer to the wrong question, which can always be made precise" (quoted in Rose, 1977:23) takes us to the heart of reflective practice in school evaluation. Pressures for easy and precise answers to how well schools are doing are difficult to resist.

Why do instructional objectives and outcomes so often dominate the evaluation process? Because they allow for easy and precise evaluation. Why do measurement conceptions tend to dominate the evaluation process? Because they allow for clear-cut answers to simple evaluation questions. Norm- and criterion-referenced achievement tests are important, and measuring how well students do in a given school by comparing their scores to those of various reference groups can also be useful. But not all desired student outcomes can be accounted for by such tests, and not all such desired student outcomes can be specified with precision. There is, after all, more to life and school than can be inferred from achievement tests (Sirotnik, 1984). Further, if evaluation is too concerned with measuring student achievements as compared with standards such as objectives and average grade-level scores, its power as a tool for informing the decision-making process is weakened. An exclusive outcome focus does not provide clues as to cause and effect. Thus, schools are not able to determine whether what they are doing, the materials they are using, or how they are organizing for teaching and learning makes sense. Few clues are available to help determine what of present practice to keep, change, or delete.

Why bother to evaluate something, anyway? This is an important question for principals to ask. If the answer includes to help make judgments, facilitate dialog, inform decisions, and guide actions, then more will be required than outcome-based evaluation. One well-known evaluation expert, Daniel Stufflebeam (1971), suggests that evaluation can help us determine what our objectives ought to be as well as how well we have achieved our intents. He suggests further that evaluation must also be justified in terms of how well it informs our planning, implementing, and refining decisions about teaching and learning and other school processes.

Robert Stake (1967), another well-known evaluation expert, has proposed a comprehensive evaluation model that gives attention to interactions between antecedent, transactional, and outcome variables affecting the schooling process. He views evaluation as a continuous process rather than as something that occurs at the end.

Antecedent variables include student abilities and interests, previous educational experiences, levels of skill development, and other indicators that provide a portrait of where students are before they study. Teaching goals and intents and available curriculum and teaching materials are also included as antecedents. Antecedent variables are evaluation benchmarks that become the basis for making decisions about appropriate teaching and learning experiences and encounters and about the curriculum and instructional choices that will need to be made to support teaching.

Stake refers to teaching and learning decisions and encounters as *transactional variables*. Since transactional variables describe the actual teaching and learning taking place, they provide the clues to what must be changed in improving instruction. *Outcome variables* refer to change in student understandings, attitudes, skills, and achievement. Stake believes that changes in teacher understandings and behaviors are also outcome variables that require attention in an evaluation design. Since evaluation is continuous, outcome information feeds back to antecedents that influence transactions and so on. Stake suggests that the following strategies and tactics be used to evaluate each of the three categories:

- *Antecedent:* Norm- and criterion-referenced achievement tests, student interviews, previous evaluations of students by teachers, consultation with students and teachers
- *Transactional:* Student evaluations of teaching, learning experiences, and curriculum materials; checklists; classroom visits and teacher observations

- *Outcome:* Norm- and criterion-referenced tests, student evaluations as above, inventories, and judgments of teachers and others familiar with the program

Responsive Evaluation

Stake (1975) has been an advocate of making evaluations more responsive to groups and individuals and the needs they identify. In evaluating he would ask: What information does a particular group need about a school program? Why does it need this information? How can the evaluation be responsive to this need? This approach is in contrast with outcome approaches, which respond to impersonal and predetermined objectives rather than to personal information requirements of a particular group. In responsive evaluation the emphasis is on communicating with people as information is exchanged to serve needs. Goals and tests may be part of the needed information requirements, but they are not ends in themselves. The "steps" in responsive evaluation include:

1. Identifying the audience for the evaluation
2. Determining what is valued by this audience and what its information requirements are
3. Keeping in mind why the audience needs this information
4. Deciding on a framework for evaluation
5. Eliciting topics, issues, and questions of concern from the audience
6. Formulating initial questions to facilitate getting started
7. Conceptualizing issues and problems as the process is underway
8. Identifying informational needs
9. Selecting observers, judges, instruments, and checklists
10. Collecting information from among antecedent, transactional, and outcome categories
11. Preparing an interim report and sharing with the audience
12. Identifying and investigating a narrower range of dominant issues and questions for further and fuller inquiry
13. Validating, confirming, and disconfirming information
14. Preparing to report the results in a narrative form to the audience
15. Providing information that illuminates issues and answers questions raised by the audience (Stake, 1975:32–33; Stake and Pearsol, 1981:25–33)

The Principal's Role

As is often the case with other school leadership responsibilities, the principal is in a unique position to influence school evaluation thinking, planning, and doing. Key in this process is the evaluation stance the principal communicates by her or his words and actions. Reflective practice in school evaluation requires a far more complex view than is associated with simple outcome-based conceptions and with the measurement stance.

Complexity has its price in time and effort, but its benefits for the school are meaningful and *useful* evaluations—evaluations that help one understand what is going on, facilitate planning, inform choices, and provide for school improvement.

Central to the principal promoting a concern for useful and meaningful evaluation is her or his ability to compellingly communicate the inherent subjective and value-laden nature of evaluation. After all, *value* is the root word in evaluation. Every evaluation finding is in reality subjective. Take, for example, a faculty that wants to evaluate its school climate, the adequacy of its discipline practices, the effectiveness of its student mentoring program, or the efficiency of its reading program. These evaluations all require implicit or explicit criteria of "effectiveness." Further, decisions need to be made about what information to collect and how. In the end the criteria and the decisions are articulations of human preferences and judgment. Different preferences and judgment result in different criteria, different decisions, and ultimately different standards of effectiveness. In every case these important characteristics of the evaluation are creations of the people who are doing the evaluation. Evaluation facts are products of normative assertions.

As Paul W. Taylor (1961) points out, normative assertions are true only because we decide to accept certain standards, rules, and conditions as being applicable to what we are making the assertions about. He states: "Our adoption of a standard or rule on which the truth or falsity of our assertion depends does not itself depend on the way things are. We must decide what ought to be the case. We cannot *discover* what ought to be the case by investigating what is the case" (248).

In addressing these issues as they affect the validity of different models of teaching, Jerome Bruner (1985) states:

> Any model of learning is right or wrong for a given set of stipulating conditions, including the nature of the tasks one has in mind, the form of the attention one creates in the learner, the generality or specificity of the learning to be accomplished, and the semiotics of the learning situation itself—what it means to be the learner. (5)
>
> Yet the model of the learner is not fixed but varies. A choice of one reflects many political, practical, and cultural choices. Perhaps the best choice is not a choice of one, but an appreciation of the variety that is possible. The appreciation of that variety is what makes the practice of education something more than a scripted exercise in cultural rigidity. (8)
>
> In a word, the best approach to models of the learner is a reflective one that permits you to "go meta," to inquire whether the script being imposed on the learner is there for the reason that was intended or for some other reason. (8)

Reflective principals recognize that easy answers to questions of evaluation may not be the best ones. They are willing to struggle with the issues and to involve others in the struggle in an effort to make evaluation something honest, useful, and meaningful. Perhaps most important, reflective principals do not confuse evaluation processes with the substance of evaluation. While the process of evaluation (i.e., how information is collected) may at times be objective, issues of substance (i.e., what to collect) are always subjective.

References

Bruner, Jerome. 1985. "Models of the Learner," *Educational Researcher* 14(5).

Dyer, Henry S. 1973. *How to Achieve Accountability in the Public Schools.* Bloomington, IN: Phi Delta Kappan Educational Foundation.

Eisner, Elliott. 1972. "Emerging Models for Educational Evaluation," *School Review* 80(4), 573–589.

Eisner, Elliot. 1979. *The Educational Imagination on the Design and Evaluation of School Programs.* New York: Macmillan.

Featherstone, Joseph. 1967. "Schools for Children," *The New Republic*, August 1967, 17–21.

Frazier, Alexander. 1972. *Open Schools for Children.* Washington, DC: Association for Supervision and Curriculum Development.

Greenfield, Thomas B. 1984. "Leaders and Schools: Willfulness and Nonnatural Order in Organization," in Thomas J. Sergiovanni and John E. Corbally, Eds., *Leadership and Organizational Culture*, 142–169. Urbana-Champaign, IL: University of Illinois Press.

Harnischfeger, Annegret, and David E. Wiley. 1975. "Schooling Cutbacks and Achievement Declines: Can We Afford Them?" *Administrators' Notebook* 24(1).

James, Charity. 1968. *Young Lives at Stake.* London: Collins Press.

Kliebard, Herbert M. 1972. "Metaphorical Roots of Curriculum Design," *Teachers College Record* 73(3), 403–404.

A Nation at Risk: The Imperative for Educational Reform. 1983. Washington, DC: U.S. Department of Education, National Commission on Excellence in Education, David P. Gardner, Chairperson.

Popham, W. James, and Eva L. Baker. 1970. *Systematic Instruction.* Englewood Cliffs, NJ: Prentice-Hall.

Rose, R. 1977. "Disciplined Research and Undisputed Problems," in Carol H. Weiss, Ed., *Using Social Research in Public Policy Making.* Lexington, MA: Heath.

Sirotnik, Kenneth A. 1984. "An Outcome-Free Conception of Schooling: Implications for School-Based Inquiry and Information Systems," *Educational Evaluation and Policy Analysis* 6(3), 227–239.

Stake, Robert E. 1967. "The Countenance of Educational Evaluation," *Teachers College Record* 68(2), 523–540.

Stake, Robert E. 1975. *Program Evaluation, Particularly Responsive Evaluation.* Occasional Paper No. 5. Kalamazoo, MI: Evaluation Center of Western Michigan University.

Stake, Robert E., and James A. Pearsol. 1981. "Evaluating Responsively," in Ronald S. Brandt, Ed., *Applied Strategies for Curriculum Evaluation*, 25–33. Alexandria, VA: Association for Supervision and Curriculum Development.

Stallings, Jane A., and David Kaskowitz. 1974. *Follow-through Classroom Observation Evaluation 1972–1973.* SRI Project URU-7370. Menlo Park, CA: Stanford Research Institute. ERIC Accession no. ED 104 969.

Stufflebeam, Daniel L., et al. 1971. *Educational Evaluation and Decision Making.* Itasca, IL: F. E. Peacock.

Taylor, Paul W. 1961. *Normative Discourse.* Englewood Cliffs, NJ: Prentice-Hall.

Walberg, Herbert J., Diane Schiller, and Geneva D. Haertel. 1979. "The Quiet Revolution in Educational Research," *Phi Delta Kappan* 61(3).

Weber, Lillian. 1971. *The English Infant School and Informal Education.* Englewood Cliffs, NJ: Prentice-Hall.

PART IV

THE DEVELOPMENT
OF HUMAN RESOURCES

CHAPTER 10

The Importance
of School Climate
and Culture

Reflect on a school in your experience that worked particularly well – one in which teachers and students seemed to thrive and grow. Why was this school such an exciting place for teaching and learning? How did it function? How did people relate to one another? What characteristics of this school stand out? As you describe this school, you are likely to refer to principal leadership, warmth and support among teachers, the amount of emphasis put on getting the work done, sense of purpose, expectations teachers and principal shared, and the number of responsibilities teachers assumed.

These descriptors are dimensions of the school's climate. Seven such descriptors appear persistently in the writings of organizational climate theorists and researchers (see, for example, Campbell et al., 1970; DuBrin, 1984; Likert, 1967; and Payne and Pugh, 1976). The seven are arrayed in Exhibit 10-1 in the form of an organizational climate inventory. As schools differ on these descriptors, they take on different personalities and operating styles. Take a moment to use the inventory for describing the school you recalled as functioning particularly well. Now describe a school in your experience that was not functioning very well. Your inventory responses for each of these schools provide a hint at differences in climate typically found when more and less effective schools are contrasted.

Why Is Climate Important?

School climate has obvious implications for improving the quality of work life for those who work in schools. But what is the link between climate and teacher motivation, school improvement efforts, student achievement, and other school effectiveness indicators? No easy answer exists, for the relationship is indeed complex. Schools characterized by a great deal of togetherness, familiarity, and trust among teachers may not be more effective – and indeed may be less effective – than schools in which this familiarity does not exist. In this sense, climate is a form of organizational *energy* whose telling effects on the school depend on how this energy is channeled and directed.

Principals can play key roles in directing climate energy into productive channels. Teachers, for example, often form closely knit and highly familiar groups or

EXHIBIT 10–1 Organization Climate Questionnaire

For each of the seven organization climate dimensions described below, place an (A) above the number that indicates your assessment of the organization's current position on that dimension and an (I) above the number that indicates your choice of where the organization should ideally be on this dimension.

1. *Conformity.* The feeling that there are many externally imposed constraints in the organization; the degree to which members feel that there are many rules, procedures, policies, and practices to which they have to conform rather than being able to do their work as they see fit.

Conformity is not character- istic of this organization.	1 2 3 4 5 6 7 8 9 10	Conformity is very character- istic of this organization.

2. *Responsibility.* Members of the organization are given personal responsibility to achieve their part of the organization's goals; the degree to which members feel that they can make decisions and solve problems without checking with superiors each step of the way.

No responsibility is given in the organization.	1 2 3 4 5 6 7 8 9 10	There is a great emphasis on personal responsibility in the organization.

3. *Standards.* The emphasis the organization places on quality performance and outstanding production, including the degree to which the member feels the organization is setting challenging goals for itself and communicating these goal commitments to members.

Standards are very low or nonexistent in the organiza- tion.	1 2 3 4 5 6 7 8 9 10	High, challenging standards are set in the organization.

4. *Rewards.* The degree to which members feel that they are being recognized and rewarded for good work rather than being ignored, criticized, or punished when something goes wrong.

Members are ignored, pun- ished, or criticized.	1 2 3 4 5 6 7 8 9 10	Members are recognized and rewarded positively.

5. *Organizational clarity.* The feeling among members that things are well organized and that goals are clearly defined rather than being disorderly, confused, or chaotic.

The organization is disor- derly, confused and chaotic.	1 2 3 4 5 6 7 8 9 10	The organization is well or- ganized with clearly defined goals.

6. *Warmth and support.* The feeling that friendliness is a valued norm in the organization, that members trust one another and offer support to one another. The feeling that good relation- ships prevail in the work environment.

There is no warmth and sup- port in the organization.	1 2 3 4 5 6 7 8 9 10	Warmth and support are very characteristic of the organization.

7. *Leadership.* The willingness of organization members to accept leadership and direction from qualified others. As needs for leadership arise, members feel free to take leadership roles and are rewarded for successful leadership. Leadership is based on expertise. The organization is not dominated by, or dependent on, one or two individuals.

Leadership is not rewarded; members are dominated or dependent and resist leader- ship attempts.	1 2 3 4 5 6 7 8 9 10	Members accept and re- ward leadership based on expertise.

From David A. Kolb, Erwin M. Rubin, and James M. McIntyre (1984), *Organizational Psychology: An Experiential Approach*, 4th ed. Englewood Cliffs, NJ: Prentice-Hall, 343.

cliques. Some of these groups use their climate energy to help make the school work better, but other groups may use the same energy to promote and cause school problems and difficulties. Key is whether the group identifies with, and is committed to, the school and its purposes. The good feeling that typically results from identification and commitment is referred to by Halpin and Croft (1962) as *esprit*. Quality of togetherness among teachers is referred to as *intimacy*. The school climate research of Halpin and Croft (1962) found that the intimacy quality was characteristic of both "open" and "closed" school climates. Esprit, however, was found to be high in open climates and low in closed. What conclusions might we reach about the relationship between school climate and school effectiveness? If one views climate as a condition representing a school's capacity to act with efficiency, enthusiasm, and vigor, then the following generalizations can be made:

1. School improvement and enhanced school effectiveness will not likely be accomplished on a sustained basis without the presence of a favorable school climate.

2. However, favorable school climates alone cannot bring about school improvement and enhanced school effectiveness.

3. Favorable school climates can result in more or less effective schooling depending on the quality of educational leadership that exists to channel climate energy in the right directions.

4. Favorable school climates combined with quality educational leadership are essential keys to sustained school improvement and enhanced school effectiveness. Corollary: Unfavorable school climates hinder sustained school improvement efforts and enhanced school effectiveness regardless of the quality of educational leadership.

It is in this sense that climate should be considered as a process variable and should not be confused with school effectiveness itself.

How does the concept of climate fit into the five forces of leadership discussed in Chapter 5 and depicted in Table 5-1? Climate conceived psychologically as the shared perceptions of organizational life in the school is a concept related primarily to the human leadership force. Climates are largely built, shaped, and channeled as a result of effective interpersonal leadership by the principal. Climate conceived as potential energy to act — the capacity to change, improve, and achieve — is a concept primarily related to the educational leadership force. School improvement and enhanced effectiveness are products of the proper channeling of this potential capacity to act. Sound educational leadership provides the necessary know-how and direction.

The Concept of School Culture

In every school there are observable behavioral regularities defined by the rules of the game for getting along. These rules are norms that define for people what is right and correct to do, what is acceptable, and what is expected. Norms are expressions of certain values and beliefs held by members of the work group. When trying to understand how norms emerge and work, the metaphor of culture can be helpful. Some experts may debate whether schools really have cultures or not. But the issue is less the reality of culture and more what can be learned by thinking about schools as cultures. The metaphor school culture helps direct attention to the symbols, behavioral regularities, ceremonies, and even myths that communicate to people the underlying values and beliefs that are shared by members of the organization.

School Climate and School Culture

How are school climate and school culture linked? Both have similar characteristics, but climate is more interpersonal in tone and substance and is manifested in the attitudes and behaviors of teachers, supervisors, students, and principals at work. It is a concept that enables the charting and interrelating of commonalities and consistencies of behavior that define, for better or for worse, the operating style of a school. Climate is concerned with the process and style of a school's organizational life rather than its content and substance.

School culture, by contrast, is more normative than school climate in the sense that it is a reflection of the shared values, beliefs, and commitments of school members across an array of dimensions that include but extend beyond interpersonal life. What the school stands for and believes about education, organization, and human relationships; what it seeks to accomplish; its essential elements and features; and the image it seeks to project are the deep-rooted defining characteristics shaping the substance of its culture.

External Adoption and Internal Integration

Edgar Schein believes that the term culture "should be reserved for the deeper level of *basic assumptions* and *beliefs* that are shared by members of an organization, that operate unconsciously, and that define in a basic 'taken-for-granted' fashion an organization's view of itself and its environment" (Schein, 1985:6). The concept of culture is very important, for its dimensions are much more likely to govern what it is that people think and do than is the official management system. Teachers, as suggested earlier, are much more likely to teach in ways that reflect the shared assumptions and beliefs of the faculty as a whole than they are in ways that administrators want, supervisors say, or teacher evaluation instruments require.

Following Parsons (1951), Merton (1957), and Argyris (1964), Schein (1985) points out that schools and other organizations must solve two basic problems if they are to be effective: external adoption and survival and internal integration. The problems of *external adoption and survival* are themed to:

1. Mission and strategy (how to reach a shared understanding of the core mission of the school, and its primary tasks)

2. Goals (developing a consensus on goals that are linked to the core mission)

3. Means (reaching consensus on the managerial and organizational means to be used to reach goals)

4. Standards (reaching consensus on the criteria to be used to determine how well the group is doing in fulfilling its goals and whether it is meeting its commitments to agreed upon processes)

5. Correction (reaching consensus on what to do if goals are not being met) (Schein, 1985).

The problems of *internal integration* are themed to:

1. Developing a common set of understandings that facilitates communication, organizes perceptions, and helps to categorize and make common meanings.

2. Developing criteria for determining who is in and out and how one determines membership in the group.

3. Working out the criteria and rules for determining who gets, maintains, and loses power.

4. Working out the rules for peer relationships and the manner in which openness and intimacy are to be handled as organizational tasks are pursued.

5. "Every group must know what its heroic and sinful behaviors are; what gets rewarded with property, status and power; and what gets punished in the form of withdrawal of the rewards and, ultimately, excommunication" (Schein, 1985:66).

6. Dealing with issues of ideology and sacredness: "Every organization, like every society, faces unexplainable and inexplicable events, which must be given meaning so that members can respond to them and avoid the anxiety of dealing with the unexplainable and uncontrollable" (Schein, 1985:66).

As issues of external adaption and internal integration are solved, schools and other organizations are better able to give full attention to the attainment of their goals and have the means for allowing people to derive sense and meaning from their work lives—to see their work as being significant. In summarizing his stance, Schein (1985) notes that culture is *"a pattern of basic assumptions—invented, discovered or developed by a given group as it learns to cope with its problems of external adaptation and internal integration—that has worked well enough to be considered valid and, therefore, to be taught to new members as the correct way to perceive, think, and feel in relation to those problems"* (9). Since the assumptions have resulted in decisions and behaviors that have worked repeatedly, they're likely to be taken for granted. This point is important because the artifacts of culture, such as symbols, rites, traditions, and behaviors, are different from the actual content and substance of culture; the basic assumptions that govern what is thought to be true, what is right, and for all intents and purposes what is reality for the school. As mentioned in earlier discussions of culture, the central zone that Shils (1961) speaks of is composed of assumptions, values, and beliefs. The values and beliefs are often manifest, but the assumptions are typically tacit.

Levels of Culture

Since assumptions and basic beliefs are typically tacit, they are inferred from manifestations of cultures such as the school's climate (Dwyer, 1989) and the rites and rituals of the school's organizational life (Deal, 1985). To account for both, it is useful to think about dimensions of school culture as existing at at least four levels (Schein, 1981; Dyer, 1982; Schein, 1985). The most tangible and observable level is represented by the *artifacts* of culture as manifested in what people say, how people behave, and how things look. Verbal artifacts include the language systems that are used, stories that are told, and examples that are used to illustrate certain important points. Behavioral artifacts are manifested in the ceremonies and rituals and other symbolic practices of the school. The interpersonal life of the school as represented by the concept of school climate is an important artifact of culture.

Less discernible but still important is the level of *perspectives*. Perspectives refer to the shared rules and norms to which people respond, the commonness that exists among solutions to similar problems, how people define the situations they face, and what are the boundaries of acceptable and unacceptable behavior. Often, perspectives are included in statements of the school's purposes or its covenant when these include ways in which people are to work together as well as the values that they share.

The third level is that of *values*. Values provide the basis for people to judge or evaluate the situations they face, the worth of their actions and activities, their priorities, and the behaviors of people with whom they work. Values not only specify what is important but often the things that are not important. In schools the values are arranged in a fashion that represents the covenant that the principal, teachers, and others share. As discussed in Chapter 8, this covenant might be in the form of an educational or management platform, statements of school philosophy, mission statements, and so on.

The fourth level is that of *assumptions*. Assumptions are "the tacit beliefs that members hold about themselves and others, their relationships to other persons, and the nature of the organization in which they live. Assumptions are the non-conscious underpinnings of the first three levels—that is, the implicit, abstract axioms that determine the more explicit system of meanings" (Lundberg, 1985:172).

Identifying the Culture of Your School

The four levels provide a framework for analyzing the culture of a school. Since assumptions are difficult to identify firsthand, they often must be inferred from what is found at the artifacts, perspectives, and values levels. Much can be learned from examining the school's history. Terence E. Deal (1985) points out, for example, that

[e]ach school has its story of origin, the people or circumstances that launched it, and those who presided over its course thereafter. Through evolutionary development – crises and resolutions, internal innovations and external pressures, plans and chance occurrences – the original concept was shaped and reshaped into an organic collection of traditions and distinctive ways. Throughout a school's history, a parade of students, teachers, principals, and parents cast sustaining memories. Great accomplishments meld with dramatic failures to form a potentially cherishable lore. (615)

The following questions might be helpful in uncovering a school's history:

How does the school's past live in the present? What traditions are still carried on? What stories are told and retold? What events in the school's history are overlooked or forgotten? Do heroes and heroines exist among teachers and students whose idiosyncracies and exploits are still remembered? In what ways are the school's traditions and historical incidents modified through reinterpretation over the years? Can you recall, for example, a historical event that has evolved from fact to myth? Believing that an organization's basic assumptions about itself can be revealed through its history, Schein (1985) suggests that the organization's history be analyzed by identifying all major crises, crucial transitions, and other times of high emotion. For each event identified reconstruct how management dealt with the issue, how it identified its role, what it did and why. Patterns and themes across the various events identified should then be analyzed and checked against current practices. The next step is to identify the assumptions that were behind the actions taken in the past and check whether those assumptions are still relevant for present actions.

To uncover beliefs, ask what are the assumptions and understandings that are shared by teachers and others, though they may not be explicitly stated. These may relate to how the school is structured, how teaching takes place, the roles of teachers and students, what is believed about discipline, the relationship of parents to the school. Sometimes assumptions and understandings are written down somewhere in the form of a philosophy or other value statements. Whether that is the case or not, beliefs can best be understood by being inferred from examples of current practices.

According to Schein, one important set of basic assumptions revolves around the theme of what is believed about human nature and how these beliefs then affect policies and decisions. To address this issue, he suggests that an attempt be made to identify organizational heroes and villains, successful people and those who are less successful, and compare the stories that are told about them. He recommends as well that recruitment selection and promotion criteria be examined to see if indeed they are biased toward selecting a certain type of person into the organization and promoting that type. An analysis of who gets rewarded and who gets punished can also be revealing. Do patterns emerge from this sort of analysis? Are there common assumptions about people that begin to emerge?

Values can be identified by asking what things the school prizes. That is, when teachers and principals talk about the school, what are the major and recurring value themes underlying what they say? When problems emerge, what are the values that seem to surface as being relied upon in developing solutions?

Norms and standards can be identified by asking what are the oughts, shoulds, do's, and don'ts that govern the behavior of teachers and principals, and examining what behaviors get rewarded and what behaviors get punished in the school. What are the accepted and recurring ways of doing things, the patterns of behavior, the habits and rituals that prevail?

Corwith Hansen (1986) suggests that teachers discuss the following questions when seeking to identify the culture of their school: Describe your work day both in and outside of the school. On what do you spend your time and energy? Given that most students forget what they learn, what do you hope your students will retain over time from your teaching? Think of students that you are attracted to — those that you admire, respect, or enjoy. What common characteristics do these students share? What does it take for a teacher to be successful in your school? What advice would you give to new teachers who wanted to be successful? What do you remember about past faculty members and students in your school? If you were to draw a picture or take a photo or make a collage that represented some aspect of your school, what would it look like? How are students rewarded?

The Power of Culture

School culture represents a double-edged sword for principals. If allowed to emerge and progress informally, principals cannot be sure whether basic assumptions and ensuing practices will be aligned with goals and purposes that support teaching and learning. Sometimes informal or wild cultures actually result in the development of a norm system that forces teachers to work in ways that compromise official goals and purposes. When domesticated, however, the school culture can replace detailed plans and systems of monitoring as quality-control measures. Further, culture provides a means for coordinating the efforts of people even though structurally the school may be loosely connected. As Bresser and Bishop explain:

> If values, beliefs, and exemplars are widely shared, formal symbolic generalizations (such as detailed plans, monitoring systems and other controls) can be parsimonious. In effect, a well developed organizational culture directs and coordinates activities. By contrast, if an organization is characterized by many different and conflicting values, beliefs, and exemplars, those whose authority dominates the organization cannot expect that their preferences for action will be carried out voluntarily and automatically. Instead, considerable direction and coordination will be required, resulting in symbolic generalizations formalized in plans, procedures, programs, budgets and so on. (quoted in Weick, 1985:383)

When wild cultures are in place or when beliefs and values emerge either in idiosyncratic ways or are in conflict with each other, more emphasis needs to be given to detailed planning and the other management functions.

> There is also a greater probability that the detailed plans will not be implemented as intended, because they will be interpreted in diverse ways and lead to divergent

actions. Thus the substitutability of culture for strategic plans may be asymmetrical. Culture can substitute for plans more effectively than plans can substitute for culture. (Weick, 1985:383)

The Dark Side of School Culture

The benefits of a strong school culture are clear. Culture represents an effective means of coordination and control in a loosely connected and nonlinear world. Its covenant or center of purposes and shared values represents a source of inspiration, meaning, and significance for those who live and work in the school. These qualities can lead to enhanced commitment and performance that are beyond expectations. And as a result the school is better able to achieve its goals.

But there is a dark side to the concept of school culture, as well. Weick (1985) points out, for example, that

> a coherent statement of who we are makes it harder for us to become something else. Strong cultures are tenacious cultures. Because a tenacious culture can be a rigid culture that is slow to detect changes and opportunities and slow to change once opportunities are sensed, strong cultures can be backward, conservative instruments of adaptation. (385)

Further, the presence of a strong norm system in a school can collectively program the minds of people in such a way that issues of reality come into question. If this is carried to the extreme, the school might come to see reality in one way but its environment in another. And, finally, there is the question of rationality. As commitment to a course of action increases, people become less rational in their actions (Staw, 1984). Strong cultures are committed cultures, and in excess, commitment takes its toll on rational action.

Schein points out that as organizations mature, the prevailing culture becomes so entrenched that it becomes a constraint on innovation. Culture preserves the glories of the past and hence becomes valued as a source of self-esteem and as a means of defense rather than for what it represents and the extent to which it serves purposes (Schein, 1985).

The Importance of a Loyal Opposition

If the purposes and covenants that constitute cultural centers are highly dynamic and fluid, school cultures are likely to be weak and ineffectual. By the same token, if they are cast in granite they can squelch individuality and innovation. The alternative is to build a resilient culture—one that can bend to change here and there but not break, that can stretch in a new direction and shrink from an old but still maintain its integrity, a culture that is able to bounce back and recover its strength and spirit, always maintaining its identity. Key to resiliency is the cultivation of a small but energetic loyal opposition made of people with whom we enjoy an honest, high-trusting relationship but who have conflicting visions, goals or methods. . . . The task of the (loyal opposition) is to bring out the best in us. We need to be grateful for those who oppose us in a high-trust way, for they bring the picture of reality and practicality to our plans. (Block, 1987:135–136)

Block believes that it is important when working with the loyal opposition that the leader communicate the extent to which they are valued. Leaders can do this, in his view, by reaffirming the quality of the relationship and the fact that it's based on trust. They should be clear in stating their positions and the reasons why they hold them. They should also state in a neutral way what they think positions of the loyal opposition are. The leader reasons as follows:

We disagree with respect to purpose, goals, and perhaps even visions. Our task is to understand their position. Our way of fulfilling that task is to be able to state to them their arguments in a positive way. They should feel understood and acknowledged by our statement of their disagreement with us. (Block, 1987:137)

With this kind of relationship in place, the leadership and the loyal opposition are in a position to negotiate differences in good faith.

References

Argyris, Chris. 1964. *Integrating the Individual and the Organization.* New York: Wiley.

Block, Peter. 1987. *The Empowered Manager.* San Francisco: Jossey-Bass.

Bresser, R. K., and R. C. Bishop. 1983. "Dysfunctional Effects of Formal Planning: Two Theoretical Explanations," *Academy of Management Review* 8, 588–599.

Campbell, John P., Marvin D. Dunnette, Edward E. Lawler, and Karl E. Weick. 1970. *Managerial Behavior, Performance, and Effectiveness.* New York: McGraw-Hill.

Deal, Terrance E. 1985. "The Symbolism of Effective Schools," *The Elementary School Journal* 85(5).

Dubrin, Andrew J. 1984. *Foundations of Organizational Behavior.* Englewood Cliffs, NJ: Prentice-Hall.

Dyer, W. G., Jr. 1982. *Patterns and Assumptions: The Keys to Understanding Organizational Culture.* Office of Naval Research, Technical Report TR-O NR-7.

Dwyer, David C. 1989. "School Climate Starts at the Curb," in *School Climate – the Principal Difference.* Hartford, CN: The Connecticut Principals' Academy.

Halpin, Andrew W., and Donald B. Croft. 1962. *The Organizational Climate of Schools.* Washington, DC: U.S. Office of Education, Research Project, Contract #SAE543-8639, August.

Hansen, Corwith. 1986. "Department Culture in a High-Performing Secondary School." Unpublished dissertation, Teachers College, Columbia University.

Likert, Jane G., and Rensis Likert. 1977. "Profile of a School." Ann Arbor, MI: Rensis Likert Associates.

Likert, Rensis. 1961. *New Patterns of Management.* New York: McGraw-Hill.

Likert, Rensis. 1967. *The Human Organization: Its Management and Value.* New York: McGraw-Hill.

Lundberg, Craig C. 1985. "On the Feasibility of Cultural Intervention in Organizations," in Peter J. Frost, Larry F. Moore, Meryl Reis Louis, Craig C. Lundberg, and Joanne Martin, *Organizational Culture*. Beverly Hills, CA: Sage.

Merton, Robert K. 1957. *Social Theory and Social Structure*. New York: The Free Press.

Parsons, Talcott. 1951. *The Social System*. New York: The Free Press.

Payne, Roy L., and Derek S. Pugh. 1976. "Organization Structure and Climate," in Marvin Dunnette, Ed., *Handbook of Organizational and Industrial Psychology*. Chicago: Rand McNally.

Schein, Edgar H. 1985. *Organizational Culture and Leadership*. San Francisco: Jossey-Bass.

Schein, Edgar H. 1981. "Does Japanese Management Style Have a Message for American Managers?" *Sloan Management Review*, 24(1), 55–68.

Shils, Edward A. 1961. "Centre and Periphery," in *The Logic of Personal Knowledge: Essays Presented to Michael Polanyi*. London: Routledge and Kegan Paul.

Weick, Karl E. 1985. "The Significance of Culture," in Peter J. Frost, Larry F. Moore, Meryl Reis Louis, Craig C. Lundberg, and Joanne Martin, *Organizational Culture*. Beverly Hills, CA: Sage.

APPENDIX 10–1 Studying the Climate of Your School

The pioneering work of Rensis Likert and his colleagues at the Institute for Social Research, University of Michigan, from the late 1950s through the 1960s, placed the concept in the mainstream of management thought. This research introduced into practice the idea that principals and other school administrators needed to focus not only on "end results" indicators of effectiveness of their policies, actions, and decisions but on the "mediating" indicators as well (Likert, 1961; 1967).

Mediating Variables

According to Likert's theory, school policies, standard operating procedures, and accompanying administrative actions and decisions do not influence school effectiveness and other end results variables directly. Instead, they influence how teachers, students, and others perceive and feel, the attitudes and values they share, the trust and support binding them together, and the degree to which they are motivated to work and are committed to school goals and purposes. It is these mediating indicators that in turn influence school effectiveness.

Initiating → mediating → school effectiveness variables

Likert reached these conclusions by studying the characteristics of more and less effective work groups and organizations. He found that differences in the mediating variables of these group and organization types followed consistent patterns. He was able to identify four distinct patterns of management: Systems 1, 2, 3, and 4. System 1 resembles a rigid bureaucracy and is characterized by little mutual confidence and trust among supervisors and workers, direct supervision, high control, centralized decision making, detailed rules and regulations and work operating procedures, top-down communications, and routine work regulation by inspection. System 4 reflects a commitment to the development and use of human resources and is characterized by trust, supportive relationships, goal clarity and commitment, autonomy with responsibility, group decision making, authority more closely linked with ability, team work, social interaction, and controls linked to agreed-upon goals and purposes. Systems 2 and 3 are at intermediate positions on this continuum. Though they represent a distinct improvement over the rigid bureaucratic management of System 1, they do not recognize human potential as fully as does System 4.

The basic features of Likert's theory are illustrated in Figure 10–1, "How Management Systems 1 and 4 Influence Mediating and School Effectiveness Variables." The principal's assumptions and resuting behavior with regard to leadership, control, organization, goals and purposes, and the motivation of teachers and students provide a specific pattern of management that can be described on a continuum from System 1 to 4. This management system elicits a predictable response from teachers at work that influences their motivation and performance. Teacher attitudes and behavior, it follows, have predictable consequences on school effectiveness. The effects of management systems 2 and 3 on mediating and school effectiveness variables would fall somewhere between the indicators provided in Figure 10–1.

Evaluating the Climate of Your School

Likert (1967) developed the Profile of Organizational Characteristics (POC) as a tool for measuring and charting system characteristics of the organizations he studied. The POC provides an indication not only of which management system characterizes a particular organization but of that organization's climate as well. Hall (1972) found that a form of the POC designed specifically for schools (Profile of a School, Likert and Likert, 1971) was correlated with Halpin and Croft's Organizational Climate Description Questionnaire (OCDQ). His research led him to conclude that Likert's management systems are conceptually similar to Halpin and Croft's conception of organizational climate. In reviewing this research, Hoy and Miskel (1982) state that "a safe conclusion is that both measures are getting at important aspects of organizational life that are similar in some respects and different in others" (198).

APPENDIX 10–1 *(Continued)*

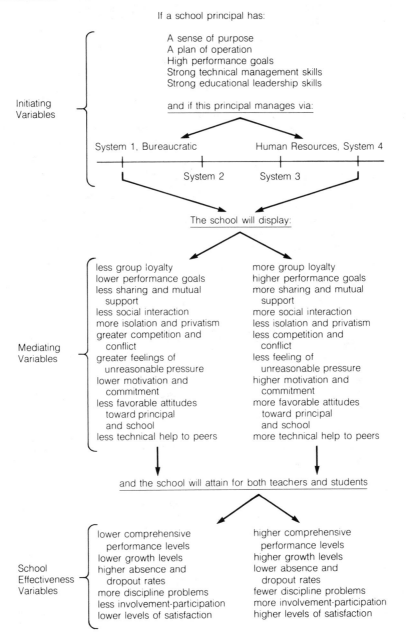

FIGURE 10–1 How Management Systems 1 and 4 Influence Mediating and School Effectiveness Variables

Summarized from Rensis Likert (1961), *New Patterns of Management,* New York: McGraw-Hill, and Rensis Likert (1967), *The Human Organization: Its Management and Value,* New York: McGraw-Hill.

APPENDIX 10–1 *(Continued)*

The POC was adopted for school use in the form of The Profile of a School (Likert and Likert, 1977). An important advantage of the POS over the OCDQ is that it provides a richer and more detailed and operational description of the components and dimensions of organizational climate with more direct implications for practice. An abbreviated version of the profile appears in Figure 10–2. Use it to evaluate your school or another school you know very well. Try to imagine how most of the teachers who work in this school would respond if they had the chance. Following the directions, plot your scores on the answer sheet and draw a profile depicting your perceptions of that school's climate. You can develop a profile grid for connecting responses for each item by using an answer sheet as shown in Figure 10–3.

There are limitations in evaluating a school "secondhand"; nonetheless, comparing your responses with those of others who know this school should reveal some similarities. Chances are your profile line reveals that this school can be characterized as System 2 or 3. Consistencies are likely in your ratings as you move from item to item, though probably your profile line has certain peaks toward System 4 and dips toward System 1. Peaks represent unusually strong qualities of the school's climate. Dips, by contrast, suggest areas where improvements are needed. Analyzing peaks and dips on the profile line allows principals and teachers to diagnose their school climate.

Dips can also be used as benchmarks for evaluating school climate improvement efforts. Imagine a school with relatively low climate scores on dimensions describing the extent to which students trust teachers and feel free to consult with them on academic and nonacademic matters. Principals and teachers might agree on a plan to improve this situation. Perhaps they decide to initiate voluntary open forum sessions for students and teachers on a weekly basis. They might agree as well to conduct weekly "that was the week that was" sessions in home rooms, in which students are free to summarize their academic week, pointing out highs and lows. More informally, teachers might resolve to be more sensitive to this issue as they interact with students. After several months a second reading of the school climate might be taken; new responses could be compared with benchmark responses to detect improvements.

One implicit benefit of the POS and other climate instruments is that they provide handy structures for encouraging conversation and dialog about events and conditions that ordinarily are difficult to discuss. It is much easier, for example, for teachers and principals to discuss items and item responses and their meanings than to engage in more unstructured conversations about school conditions and school improvements.

Take a moment to reflect on the climate of the school that you just evaluated. Using the POS, evaluate the climate by first indicating how you would like it to be. What discrepancies do you note between your ideal and real responses? Assume that your responses represent average responses for the entire faculty. Based on the scoring profile that you prepare, what improvements need to be made in the climate of this school?

An important strength of the POS is that climate is not conceived as the product of only the principal's behavior or of any other single source. As one reads the items, it becomes clear that climates are based on a mix of attitudes, beliefs, and behaviors of everyone who lives and works in the school. They are manifestations of the school's culture. This being the case, school improvement efforts require that teachers and principals work together. Striving towards a System 4 climate, for example, requires a shared commitment. As you review the climate profile of the school you evaluated, what ideas come to mind as to how you as principal (and the faculty, whose responses are represented by your responses) can plan to work together to improve the school?

Organizational Variable	System 1	System 2	System 3	System 4
A. Leadership Processes used:	RARELY	SOMETIMES	OFTEN	VERY OFTEN
1. How often is your behavior seen by students as friendly and supportive?	① ②	③ ④	⑤ ⑥	⑦ ⑧
How often does the principal seek and use your ideas about:				
2. academic matters	① ②	③ ④	⑤ ⑥	⑦ ⑧
3. non-academic school matters	① ②	③ ④	⑤ ⑥	⑦ ⑧
4. How often do you see the principal's behavior as friendly and supportive?	① ②	③ ④	⑤ ⑥	⑦ ⑧
	VERY LITTLE	SOME	QUITE A BIT	A VERY GREAT DEAL
5. How much confidence and trust does the principal have in you?	① ②	③ ④	⑤ ⑥	⑦ ⑧
6. How much confidence and trust do you have in the principal?	① ②	③ ④	⑤ ⑥	⑦ ⑧
	NOT FREE	SOMEWHAT FREE	QUITE FREE	VERY FREE
7. How free do you feel to talk to the principal about school matters?	① ②	③ ④	⑤ ⑥	⑦ ⑧
	VERY LITTLE	SOME	QUITE A BIT	A VERY GREAT DEAL
8. How much confidence and trust do you have in students?	① ②	③ ④	⑤ ⑥	⑦ ⑧
9. How much confidence and trust do students have in you?	① ②	③ ④	⑤ ⑥	⑦ ⑧
	NOT FREE	SOMEWHAT FREE	QUITE FREE	VERY FREE
10. How free do students feel to talk to you about school matters?	① ②	③ ④	⑤ ⑥	⑦ ⑧
How often are students' ideas sought and used by the principal about:	RARELY	SOMETIMES	OFTEN	VERY OFTEN
11. academic matters	① ②	③ ④	⑤ ⑥	⑦ ⑧
12. non-academic school matters	① ②	③ ④	⑤ ⑥	⑦ ⑧
13. How often does the principal use small group meetings to solve school problems?	① ②	③ ④	⑤ ⑥	⑦ ⑧
B. Character of Motivational Forces:	DISLIKE IT	SOMETIMES DISLIKE IT, SOMETIMES LIKE IT	USUALLY LIKE IT	LIKE IT VERY MUCH
14. What is the general attitude of students toward your school?	① ②	③ ④	⑤ ⑥	⑦ ⑧
How often do you try to be friendly and supportive to:	RARELY	SOMETIMES	OFTEN	VERY OFTEN
15. the principal	① ②	③ ④	⑤ ⑥	⑦ ⑧
16. other teachers	① ②	③ ④	⑤ ⑥	⑦ ⑧
	USUALLY A WASTE OF TIME	SOMETIMES A WASTE OF TIME	OFTEN WORTH-WHILE	ALMOST ALWAYS WORTH-WHILE
17. In your job is it worthwhile or a waste of time to do your best?	① ②	③ ④	⑤ ⑥	⑦ ⑧
	NOT SATISFYING	SOMEWHAT SATISFYING	QUITE SATISFYING	VERY SATISFYING
18. How satisfying is your work at your school?	① ②	③ ④	⑤ ⑥	⑦ ⑧
To what extent do the following feel responsible for seeing that educational excellence is acheved in your school:	VERY LITTLE	SOME	CONSIDER-ABLE	VERY GREAT
19. principal	① ②	③ ④	⑤ ⑥	⑦ ⑧
20. department heads	① ②	③ ④	⑤ ⑥	⑦ ⑧
21. teacher	① ②	③ ④	⑤ ⑥	⑦ ⑧
22. To what extent do students help each other when they want to get something done?	① ②	③ ④	⑤ ⑥	⑦ ⑧
23. To what extent do students look forward to coming to school?	① ②	③ ④	⑤ ⑥	⑦ ⑧
24. To what extent do students feel excited about learning?	① ②	③ ④	⑤ ⑥	⑦ ⑧
25. To what extent do you look forward to your teaching day?	① ②	③ ④	⑤ ⑥	⑦ ⑧
26. To what extent are you encouraged to be innovative in developing more effective and efficient educational practices?	① ②	③ ④	⑤ ⑥	⑦ ⑧
C. Character of Communication Process:	VERY LITTLE	SOME	QUITE A BIT	A VERY GREAT DEAL
27. How much do students feel that you are trying to help them with their problems?	① ②	③ ④	⑤ ⑥	⑦ ⑧
28. How much accurate information concerning school affairs is given to you by students?	① ②	③ ④	⑤ ⑥	⑦ ⑧
D. Character of Interaction-Influence:				
How much influence to the following *have* on what goes on in your school:	VERY LITTLE	SOME	QUITE A BIT	A VERY GREAT DEAL
29. principal	① ②	③ ④	⑤ ⑥	⑦ ⑧
30. teachers	① ②	③ ④	⑤ ⑥	⑦ ⑧
31. central staff of your school system	① ②	③ ④	⑤ ⑥	⑦ ⑧

FIGURE 10–2 Profile of a School: Teacher Form

Organizational Variable	System 1	System 2	System 3	System 4
32. students	① ②	③ ④	⑤ ⑥	⑦ ⑧
How much influence do you think the following *should have* on what goes on in your school:				
33. principal	① ②	③ ④	⑤ ⑥	⑦ ⑧
34. teachers	① ②	③ ④	⑤ ⑥	⑦ ⑧
35. central staff of your school system	① ②	③ ④	⑤ ⑥	⑦ ⑧
36. students	① ②	③ ④	⑤ ⑥	⑦ ⑧
37. How much influence do students *have* on what goes on in your school?	① ②	③ ④	⑤ ⑥	⑦ ⑧
38. How much influence do you think students *should have* on what goes on in your school?	① ②	③ ④	⑤ ⑥	⑦ ⑧
	USUALLY IGNORED	APPEALED BUT NOT RESOLVED	RESOLVED BY PRINCIPAL	RESOLVED BY ALL THOSE AFFECTED
39. In your school, how are conflicts between departments usually resolved?	① ②	③ ④	⑤ ⑥	⑦ ⑧
	VERY LITTLE	SOME	QUITE A BIT	A VERY GREAT DEAL
40. How much do teachers in your school encourage each other to do their best?	① ②	③ ④	⑤ ⑥	⑦ ⑧
	[EVERY ONE FOR SELF]	LITTLE COOPER-ATIVE TEAMWORK	A MODERATE AMOUNT OF COOPER-ATIVE TEAMWORK	A VERY GREAT AMOUNT OF COOPER-ATIVE TEAMWORK
41. In your school, is it "every man for himself" or do principals, teachers, and students work as a team?	① ②	③ ④	⑤ ⑥	⑦ ⑧
	VERY LITTLE	SOME	QUITE A BIT	A VERY GREAT DEAL
42. How much do different departments plan together and coordinate their efforts?	① ②	③ ④	⑤ ⑥	⑦ ⑧
E. Character of Decision-Making Processes:				
	RARELY	SOMETIMES	OFTEN	VERY OFTEN
43. How often do you seek and use students' ideas about academic matters, such as their work, course content, teaching plans and methods?	① ②	③ ④	⑤ ⑥	⑦ ⑧
44. How often do you seek and use students' ideas about non-academic school matters, such as student activities, rules of conduct, and discipline?	① ②	③ ④	⑤ ⑥	⑦ ⑧
	VIEWED WITH GREAT SUSPICION	SOME VIEWED WITH SUSPICION, SOME WITH TRUST	USUALLY VIEWED WITH TRUST	ALMOST ALWAYS VIEWED WITH TRUST
How do students view communications from				
45. you	① ②	③ ④	⑤ ⑥	⑦ ⑧
46. the principal	① ②	③ ④	⑤ ⑥	⑦ ⑧
	NOT WELL	SOMEWHAT WELL	QUITE WELL	VERY WELL
47. How well do you know the problems faced by students in their school work?	① ②	③ ④	⑤ ⑥	⑦ ⑧
	VERY LITTLE	SOME	CONSIDER-ABLE	VERY GREAT
48. To what extent is the communication between you and your students open and candid?	① ②	③ ④	⑤ ⑥	⑦ ⑧
49. To what extent does the principal give you useful information and ideas?	① ②	③ ④	⑤ ⑥	⑦ ⑧
	FROM THE TOP DOWN	MOSTLY DOWN	DOWN AND UP	DOWN, UP AND LATERALLY
50. What is the direction of the flow of information about academic and non-academic school matters.	① ②	③ ④	⑤ ⑥	⑦ ⑧
	VIEWED WITH GREAT SUSPICION	SOME VIEWED WITH SUSPICION, SOME WITH TRUST	USUALLY VIEWED WITH TRUST	ALMOST ALWAYS VIEWED WITH TRUST
51. How do you view communications from the principal?	① ②	③ ④	⑤ ⑥	⑦ ⑧
	USUALLY INACCURATE	OFTEN INACCURATE	FAIRLY ACCURATE	ALMOST ALWAYS ACCURATE
52. How accurate is upward communication to the principal?	① ②	③ ④	⑤ ⑥	⑦ ⑧
	NOT WELL	SOMEWHAT WELL	QUITE WELL	VERY WELL
53. How well does the principal know the problems faced by the teachers?	① ②	③ ④	⑤ ⑥	⑦ ⑧
	VERY LITTLE	SOME	CONSIDER-ABLE	VERY GREAT
To what extent is communication open and candid:				
54. between principal and teachers	① ②	③ ④	⑤ ⑥	⑦ ⑧
55. among teachers	① ②	③ ④	⑤ ⑥	⑦ ⑧

FIGURE 10–2 (*Continued*)

Organizational Variable	System 1		System 2		System 3		System 4	
56. How much help do you get from the central staff of your school system?	VERY LITTLE ①	②	SOME ③	④	QUITE A BIT ⑤	⑥	A VERY GREAT DEAL ⑦	⑧
57. How much are students involved in major decisions affecting them?	VERY LITTLE ①	②	SOME ③	④	QUITE A BIT ⑤	⑥	A VERY GREAT DEAL ⑦	⑧
58. Are decisions made at the best levels for effective performance?	AT MUCH TOO HIGH LEVELS ①	②	AT SOMEWHAT TOO HIGH LEVELS ③	④	AT QUITE SATISFAC-TORY LEVELS ⑤	⑥	AT THE BEST LEVELS ⑦	⑧
59. To what extent are you involved in major decisions related to your work?	VERY LITTLE ①	②	SOME ③	④	CONSIDER-ABLE ⑤	⑥	VERY GREAT ⑦	⑧
60. To what extent are decision makers aware of problems, particularly at lower levels?	①	②	③	④	⑤	⑥	⑦	⑧
F. Character of goal setting:								
61. To what extent does the principal make sure that planning and setting priorities are done well?	①	②	③	④	⑤	⑥	⑦	⑧
G. Character of control processes: What is the administrative style of:	HIGHLY AUTHORI-TARIAN		SOMEWHAT AUTHORI-TARIAN		CONSUL-TATIVE		PARTICI-PATIVE GROUP	
62. the principal	①	②	③	④	⑤	⑥	⑦	⑧
63. the superintendent of schools	①	②	③	④	⑤	⑥	⑦	⑧
How competent is the principal:	NOT COMPETENT		SOMEWHAT COMPETENT		QUITE COMPETENT		VERY	
64. as an administrator	①	②	③	④	⑤	⑥	⑦	⑧
65. as an educator	①	②	③	④	⑤	⑥	⑦	⑧
H. Performance goals:								
66. To what extent does the principal try to provide you with the materials, equipment and space you need to do your job well?	VERY LITTLE ①	②	SOME ③	④	CONSIDER-ABLE ⑤	⑥	VERY GREAT ⑦	⑧
67. How much do you feel that the principal is interested in your success as a teacher?	VERY LITTLE ①	②	SOME ③	④	QUITE A BIT ⑤	⑥	A VERY GREAT DEAL ⑦	⑧
68. How much interest do students feel you have in their success as students?	①	②	③	④	⑤	⑥	⑦	⑧
69. How much does the principal try to help you with your problems?	①	②	③	④	⑤	⑥	⑦	⑧
70. To what extent do students accept high performance goals in your school?	①	②	③	④	⑤	⑥	⑦	⑧
71. How adequate are the supplies and equipment the school has?	INADEQUATE ①	②	SOMEWHAT INADEQUATE ③	④	QUITE ADEQUATE ⑤	⑥	VERY ADEQUATE ⑦	⑧
72. How high are the principal's goals for educational performance?	LOW ①	②	ABOUT AVERAGE ③	④	QUITE HIGH ⑤	⑥	VERY HIGH ⑦	⑧

FIGURE 10–2 *(Continued)*

Items and scoring formats are from The Profile of a School, Form 3, Teacher Form. Items have been regrouped and renumbered, and system designations have been added. The original questionnaire contains additional items that enable evaluation of high school departments, grade levels, or teaching teams. Used by permission of Rensis Likert Associates, Inc., Ann Arbor, Michigan 48104. Copyright © 1977 by Jane Gibson Likert and Rensis Likert. Distributed by Rensis Likert Associates, Inc. All rights reserved. No further reproduction in any form authorized without written permission of Rensis Likert Associates, Inc., Ann Arbor, Michigan 48104.

FIGURE 10-3 Profile of a School Scoring Sheet

Item	System 1		System 2		System 3		System 4	
1	1	2	3	4	5	6	7	8
2	1	2	3	4	5	6	7	8
3	1	2	3	4	5	6	7	8
4	1	2	3	4	5	6	7	8
5	1	2	3	4	5	6	7	8
6	1	2	3	4	5	6	7	8
7	1	2	3	4	5	6	7	8
8	1	2	3	4	5	6	7	8
9	1	2	3	4	5	6	7	8
10	1	2	3	4	5	6	7	8
11	1	2	3	4	5	6	7	8
12	1	2	3	4	5	6	7	8
13	1	2	3	4	5	6	7	8
14	1	2	3	4	5	6	7	8
15	1	2	3	4	5	6	7	8
16	1	2	3	4	5	6	7	8
17	1	2	3	4	5	6	7	8
18	1	2	3	4	5	6	7	8
19	1	2	3	4	5	6	7	8
20	1	2	3	4	5	6	7	8
21	1	2	3	4	5	6	7	8
22	1	2	3	4	5	6	7	8
23	1	2	3	4	5	6	7	8
24	1	2	3	4	5	6	7	8
25	1	2	3	4	5	6	7	8
26	1	2	3	4	5	6	7	8
27	1	2	3	4	5	6	7	8
28	1	2	3	4	5	6	7	8
29	1	2	3	4	5	6	7	8
30	1	2	3	4	5	6	7	8
31	1	2	3	4	5	6	7	8
32	1	2	3	4	5	6	7	8
33	1	2	3	4	5	6	7	8
34	1	2	3	4	5	6	7	8
35	1	2	3	4	5	6	7	8
36	1	2	3	4	5	6	7	8
37	1	2	3	4	5	6	7	8
38	1	2	3	4	5	6	7	8
39	1	2	3	4	5	6	7	8
40	1	2	3	4	5	6	7	8
41	1	2	3	4	5	6	7	8
42	1	2	3	4	5	6	7	8
43	1	2	3	4	5	6	7	8
44	1	2	3	4	5	6	7	8
45	1	2	3	4	5	6	7	8
46	1	2	3	4	5	6	7	8

FIGURE 10–3 *(Continued)*

Item	System 1		System 2		System 3		System 4	
47	1	2	3	4	5	6	7	8
48	1	2	3	4	5	6	7	8
49	1	2	3	4	5	6	7	8
50	1	2	3	4	5	6	7	8
51	1	2	3	4	5	6	7	8
52	1	2	3	4	5	6	7	8
53	1	2	3	4	5	6	7	8
54	1	2	3	4	5	6	7	8
55	1	2	3	4	5	6	7	8
56	1	2	3	4	5	6	7	8
57	1	2	3	4	5	6	7	8
58	1	2	3	4	5	6	7	8
59	1	2	3	4	5	6	7	8
60	1	2	3	4	5	6	7	8
61	1	2	3	4	5	6	7	8
62	1	2	3	4	5	6	7	8
63	1	2	3	4	5	6	7	8
64	1	2	3	4	5	6	7	8
65	1	2	3	4	5	6	7	8
66	1	2	3	4	5	6	7	8
67	1	2	3	4	5	6	7	8
68	1	2	3	4	5	6	7	8
69	1	2	3	4	5	6	7	8
70	1	2	3	4	5	6	7	8
71	1	2	3	4	5	6	7	8
72	1	2	3	4	5	6	7	8

CHAPTER 11

Teacher Motivation and Commitment

The theoretical and research base for policy development within the principalship is not as strong as that existing for other professions such as medicine and engineering. And yet, in the area of motivation to work, extensive literature is available for informing the policy process and for guiding practice. None of this research is universal or a one-best-way to motivate everyone—the requirements and behavior of people are too idiosyncratic and the nature of circumstances faced too varied for that. Another problem with the research is that for the most part it was conducted by men using men as subjects. For this reason the research may be biased and accompanying practice prescriptions, at least if taken literally, may not apply to women. In a later section of this chapter some of this research is discussed and interpreted in a manner that takes into account the experiences of women.

Still, much is known about how to arrange job dimensions and work conditions within schools so that teachers are more personally satisfied and are inspired to work harder and smarter on behalf of effective teaching and learning. Further, few topics are more important. High teacher motivation to work and strong commitment to work are essential requirements for effective schooling. When these characteristics are absent, teachers are likely to consider their commitment as being a "fair day's work for a fair day's pay" (Sergiovanni, 1968). Instead of exceeding minimums and giving their best, teachers emphasize meeting basic work requirements in exchange for material and other extrinsic benefits. Should teachers experience considerable work dissatisfaction, their performance is likely to fall below even this fair day's work level (Brayfield and Crockett, 1955; Vroom, 1964). Should teachers experience considerable loss of meaning and significance with what they are doing, they are likely to become detached, even alienated, from their jobs (Argyris, 1957; Durkheim, 1947). Perhaps it is too much to ask for all teachers to exceed the fair day's work commitment, but it is clear that excellence will remain elusive unless many teachers are willing to make this commitment.

Despite what is known about how to improve teacher motivation and commitment and the links between such improvement and effective schooling, this knowledge base typically does not inform policy development and administrative practice. More alarming is the fact that state and local policy makers frequently mandate changes in school organizational patterns, curriculum, and teacher evaluation in ways that contradict the motivation research. Though well intended, these policy initiatives can actually inhibit—even lower—teacher motivation and commitment, with predictable effects on effective schooling.

Problems and Contradictions in Policy and Practice

Two examples of policies and practice that contradict motivation theory and research are examined in this section: mandating and implementing highly structured, prescriptive, and standardized curriculum and teaching formats that result in increasing bureaucracy in the classroom; and school organizational patterns that encourage isolation, privatism, and lack of social interaction among teachers.

Bureaucracy in the Classroom

Exhibit 11-1 contains an instrument entitled "Quality of Work Life in Teaching," adapted from a more general scale developed by Marshall Sashkin and Joseph J. Lengerman (Pfeiffer and Goodstein, 1984). The instrument is designed to assess perceptions of job conditions in one's work setting. Please respond to the questions following the directions. Response patterns indicate the extent to which one perceives her or his job to be growth-oriented on a number of dimensions considered important by job-enrichment theorists and researchers. Later in this chapter the instrument will be scored, and response patterns will be examined as the concept of job enrichment is discussed.

The instrument can also be used to assess the extent to which one's job is bureaucratized. Responses to items 1, 3, 4, 6, 8, 11, and 24 will hint at the extent to which the teaching job you describe is bureaucratic. The more prevalent are the job characteristics described in the items, the more bureaucratic is that job likely to be.

It is generally assumed that teaching is a profession, though perhaps a fledgling one. Professionals and bureaucrats operate quite differently at work. The work of bureaucrats is programmed for them by their work system. The work of professionals emerges from an interaction between available professional knowledge and individual client needs. Webster, for example, describes a bureaucrat as "a government official following a narrow, rigid, formal routine." In contrast, professionals are assumed to command a body of knowledge enabling them to make informed judgments in response to unique situations and individual client needs. Essential to professionalism is sufficient freedom for professionals to use informed judgment as they practice.

In recent years there has been a trend toward greater centralization in deciding what will be taught in schools: when, with what materials, to whom, and for how long. During the 1970s approximately two-thirds of the states enacted policies that sought to standardize and regulate teacher behavior (Darling-Hammond, 1984). States were even more active during the 1980s. There are many legitimate and desirable reasons for the state to be involved in matters of education, and many alternatives are open to states as they set standards, provide guidelines, promote

EXHIBIT 11–1 Quality of Work Life in Teaching

Directions: The following questions ask you to describe the objective characteristics of your job, as well as the activities of your co-workers and supervisor. Try not to use these questions to show how much you like or dislike your job; just be as factually correct as possible – imagine what an outside observer would say in response to these questions. Circle the appropriate letter.

(A)ll of the time, (M)ost of the time, (P)art of the time, (N)ever

1. Teachers in my school are allowed to make some decisions, but most of the decisions about their work have to be referred to their supervisor or are shaped by rules, curriculum requirements, or testing requirements.   A   M   P   N

2. Teachers in my job normally move on to better jobs as a direct result of the opportunities my job offers.   A   M   P   N

3. Teachers in my school are required to produce or cover a specific amount of work each day or each week.   A   M   P   N

4. Teachers in my school perform tasks that are repetitive in nature.   A   M   P   N

5. My work requires me to coordinate regularly with other teachers.   A   M   P   N

6. Teachers in my school have a great deal of control over their work activities.   A   M   P   N

7. Teachers in my job have the opportunity to learn new skills in the course of their work.   A   M   P   N

8. Teachers in my school must work according to a fixed schedule; it is not possible to let the work go for a time and then catch up on it later.   A   M   P   N

9. Teachers in my job are required to follow certain procedures in doing their work that they wouldn't choose if it were up to them.   A   M   P   N

10. Teachers in my position work alone, on their teaching, with little or no contact with other teachers.   A   M   P   N

11. When they encounter problems in their teaching, teachers in my school must refer these problems to their supervisor; they cannot take action on their own.   A   M   P   N

12. My work requires me to learn new methods in order to keep up with changes and new developments.   A   M   P   N

13. Teachers in my position must work very rapidly.   A   M   P   N

14. My work involves completing a "whole" task.   A   M   P   N

15. Teachers in my position are able to help out one another as they teach.   A   M   P   N

16. My principal acts on some of the suggestions of teachers in my school.   A   M   P   N

17. Teachers in my position are encouraged to try out methods of their own when teaching.   A   M   P   N

18. Teachers in my position have considerable control over the pace or scheduling of work.   A   M   P   N

19. Jobs at my level fail to bring out the best abilities of teachers because they are designed too simply.   A   M   P   N

20. Teachers in my position must interact with other teachers as they teach.   A   M   P   N

EXHIBIT 11–1 *(Continued)*

21. Teachers at my level can make their own decisions without checking with anyone else or without consulting approved teaching and curriculum requirements.	A	M	P	N
22. Teachers at my level have the opportunity to learn about the teaching that is occurring at other grade levels and in other departments.	A	M	P	N
23. My work must be completed on a set schedule.	A	M	P	N
24. Teachers in my position perform the same series of tasks all day.	A	M	P	N
25. My work requires a great deal of contact with other teachers.	A	M	P	N

The QWLT Instrument is adapted from a more general job-enrichment instrument developed by Marshall Sashkin and Joseph J. Longerman entitled "Quality of Work Life Scale," in J. William Pfeiffer and Leonard D. Goodstein, Eds., *The 1984 Annual Handbook for Group Facilitators*, San Diego, CA: University Associates.

equity, and ensure accountability. But the problem lies in how far the state should go and the consequences of going too far. Providing leadership to local districts is an important responsibility of the state. Legislating learning to the point of installing a system of bureaucratic teaching is quite another matter (Wise, 1979).

When curriculum and teaching decisions are programmed in a way that diminishes the influence of students and teacher in making teaching and learning decisions, then impersonal, standard, and formal learning goals dominate; teaching and learning become "teacher proof" and "student proof"; instructional leadership is discouraged as the teacher spends more time managing the learning process by monitoring, inspecting, regulating, and measuring; and commitment to teaching and learning by both teacher and students is lessened. For students the consequences can be more emphasis on learnings and meanings defined by the school (Coombs, 1959; MacDonald, 1964) and less emphasis on intrinsic motivation for learning. Student learning is enhanced when teaching is characterized by a balanced emphasis on personally and school-defined meanings and learning outcomes and on students being intrinsically motivated to learn. These characteristics are not encouraged by bureaucratic teaching.

Teachers as "Origins" and "Pawns"

What are the consequences of legislated learning and bureaucratic teaching on motivation and commitment of teachers? Is there a link between teacher motivation and commitment and school effectiveness? In successful schools, teachers are more committed, are harder workers, are more loyal to the school, and are more satisfied with their jobs. The research on motivation to work (Herzberg, 1966; Hackman and Oldham, 1980; Peters and Waterman, 1982) suggests that these highly motivating conditions are present when teachers:

- Find their work lives to be *meaningful*, purposeful, sensible and significant, and when they view the work itself as being worthwhile and important.

- Have reasonable *control over their work activities* and affairs and are able to exert reasonable influence over work events and circumstances.
- Experience *personal responsibility* for the work and are personally accountable for outcomes.

Meaningfulness, control, and personal responsibility are attributes of teachers functioning as "Origins" rather than as "Pawns." According to De Charms (1968); "An Origin is a person who perceives his behavior as determined by his own choosing: a Pawn is a person who perceives his behavior as determined by external forces beyond his control." He continues:

> An Origin has a strong feeling of personal causation, a feeling that the locus for causation of effects in his environment lies within himself. . . . A Pawn has a feeling that causal forces beyond his control, or personal forces residing within others, or in the physical environment determine his behavior. This constitutes a strong feeling of powerlessness or ineffectiveness. (274)

Personal causation is an important dimension of motivation. People strive to influence the events and situations of their environment, to be Origins of their own behavior.

Legislated learning and bureaucratic teaching threaten personal causation by creating work conditions more associated with Pawn feelings and behavior. In referring to Pawn feelings and behavior among teachers, the economist and Nobel laureate Theodore Schultz (1982) states:

> Most of these attitudes of school teachers should have been anticipated in view of the way schools are organized and administered. The curriculum is not for them to decide; nor is the content of the courses to be taught and the plans to be followed. . . . In assessing the performance of teachers, it is a dictum of economics that incentives matter. School teachers are responding to the much circumscribed opportunities open to them. They are not robots but human agents who perceive, interpret, and act in accordance with the worthwhile options available. (43)

There is a paradox at play here. On the one hand, clear mandates, mission statements, goals and purposes, and high achievement expectations for teachers provide them with a needed sense of direction and clear signal of what is important and significant. This realization was an important leadership theme of earlier chapters, which discussed the concepts of purposing and symbolic and cultural aspects of leadership. On the other hand, if such mandates are described and prescribed in such detail that teachers come to feel and behave like Pawns rather than Origins, problems in motivation arise. Mandates that provide direction, define meaning, and promote significance in one's work are motivating and contribute to building commitment. Mandates that reduce the decision-making prerogatives of teachers and make teaching "teacher-proof" discourage motivation and contribute to detachment, even alienation, rather than to commitment.

Principals are responsible for monitoring this delicate balance by ensuring that mandates are sensibly interpreted and articulated into administrative, supervisory, and teaching practices that promote Origin feelings and behaviors among teachers. They must ask whether interpretation and implementing decisions will promote professionalism or bureaucracy in teaching. Responsive to unique situations, professionals take their cues from the problems they face and the clients they serve. They draw upon the wealth of knowledge and technology available to them as they create professional knowledge in use in response to client needs. Bureaucrats, by contrast, are not driven by client problems but by the technology itself. They are appliers of rules, regulators of formats, direction followers, and managerial implementers. They strive for a one-best-way to treat all cases, and, pursuing standard outcomes, they apply formal procedures in standardized ways. It is in this sense that legislated learning and bureaucratic teaching encourage Pawn feelings and behaviors among teachers and students, contributing to less effective teaching and learning. Legislated learning and bureaucratic teaching are related to teacher job dissatisfaction and to teacher motivation to work. Appendix 11-1 contains excerpts from a Rand Corporation report on the problem of teacher job dissatisfaction. Many of the identified factors contributing to dissatisfaction can be attributed to increased bureaucracy in teaching.

Isolation in Teaching

Teaching can be aptly described as a lonely profession. Typically teachers work alone. As a result, no one else in the school knows what they are doing or how well they are doing it (Waller, 1932; Bidwell, 1975; Lortie, 1975). Related to isolation in teaching are tendencies to encourage the value of privatism and the consequences of this value on social interaction. Privatism forces teachers to look inward, discourages sharing, and encourages competition; further, it promotes feelings of inadequacy and insecurity. Lack of social interaction deprives teachers of opportunities to help and seek help from others, to give feedback and to get feedback from others—both essential ingredients in most motivation to work models. These conditions not only contradict what is known about sound management practices but also impede professional growth and effective teaching. Despite the debilitating effects of isolation in teaching, schools persist in organizational structures and supervisory and evaluation practices that encourage these conditions. Let's examine further the effects of isolation, privatism, and lack of social interaction in teaching.

Susan Rosenholtz (1984) identifies isolation as one of the major impediments to school improvement. Her recent review of the research on this topic leads to the following conclusions:

> In isolated settings, teachers come to believe that they alone are responsible for running their classrooms and that to seek advice or assistance from their colleagues constitutes an open admission of incompetence.
> Teacher isolation is perhaps the greatest impediment to learning to teach, or to

improving one's existing skills, because most learning by necessity occurs through trial and error. One alarming consequence of trial and error learning is that teachers' limits for potential growth depend heavily on their own personal ability to detect problems and to discern possible solutions.

Another consequence is that teachers in isolated settings have few role models of good teaching to emulate. As a matter of fact, it is more typical of teachers in isolated settings to use role models that they recall from their own student days than to seek models of teaching excellence among their contemporaries.

. . . in interpreting and formulating solutions to classroom problems, teachers realize little benefit from the advice, experience, or expertise of colleagues with whom they work. That is, any pre-existing practical knowledge is seldom passed along to new recruits, who must then, of their own accord, sink or swim.

For teachers restricted to trial-and-error learning then, there is a limit to their capacity to grow in the absence of others' professional knowledge. . . . Teachers teach their prime after about four or five years and thereafter, perhaps because of little teaching input, their effectiveness with students actually begins to decline. (4–6)

Lieberman and Miller (1984) point out that being private means not sharing experiences about teaching, classes, students, and learning. By being private, teachers forfeit the opportunity to share their successes with colleagues but gain the security of not having to disclose shortcomings. Having worked in isolation and not having accurate knowledge of the teaching of others, teachers tend to assume that they are not measuring up to colleagues.

Isolation and privatism contribute to fewer social interaction opportunities among teachers. The three conditions combine to force teachers to look inward for sources of feedback and rewards. Indeed, teachers rely almost exclusively on interactions with students as sources of satisfaction in teaching (Waller, 1932; Lortie, 1975). The question, though, is whether the satisfaction derived from student social interaction enough to provide the kind of motivation and commitment needed for effective schooling. How does social interaction with adults fit into the picture?

Social interaction is a key ingredient in the supervisory process. Contrary to myth, teachers report increases in satisfaction as supervision increases moderately (Dornbush and Scott, 1975). Moderate increases in supervision seem also to be related to increases in teaching effectiveness. From his research, Natriello (1984) concludes: "Teachers who report more frequent evaluation activities also report being markedly more effective in teaching tasks" (592). Social interaction, as a form of feedback about one's teaching, is a contributor to these findings. Social interaction is also the medium by which recognition is given and received. Further, social interaction seems to be a key factor in evoking the achievement, power-influence, and affiliation motives of persons at work and is an integral part of most motivation-to-work and job-enrichment models emerging from the research (Hackman and Oldham, 1980).

Many experts believe that social interaction among teachers, and between teachers and supervisors, is essential for promoting and institutionalizing change in schools and is related as well to successful staff-development efforts. With respect to institutionalizing changes, Clark, Lotto, and Astuto (1984) point out that the focus of staff development must reach beyond the development of new teaching skills to the development of new concepts and behaviors within a supportive school climate. Their review of the research on effective school improvement efforts leads them to conclude that interaction among teachers, and between teachers and administrators, provides the needed opportunities for technical and psychological support that enhances effective implementation. "Teachers report that they learn best from other teachers. Teacher-teacher interactions provide for technical and psychological support as well as personal reinforcement" (Clark, Lotto, and Astuto, 1984:58). Though more than social interaction opportunities may be necessary for school improvement efforts to be successful, success will not be likely without social interaction. Informal professional development efforts are also linked to social interaction among teachers. When provided with opportunity and encouragement, teachers learn a great deal from one another and trust one another as sources of new ideas and as sharers of problems they face (Keenan, 1974; Glatthorn, 1984).

Legislated learning and bureaucratic teaching, isolation in the work place, the tradition of privatism, and lack of social interaction are problems that principals and their faculties must address as they work to improve the quality of work life in schools, to encourage professional development, and to increase teacher motivation and commitment.

Using Motivation Theory and Research to Inform Practice

In Chapter 6 it was pointed out that leadership practice might usefully be understood through use of the metaphor "developmental stages." Four stages were discussed: leadership by bartering, building, bonding, and banking. Virtually all the available research on motivation addresses the first two stages, leadership by bartering and building. As you recall, leadership by bartering makes the assumption that the interests of leaders and led are different, and therefore a bargain needs to be struck whereby the leader gives to the led something they want in return for their compliance with the leader's wishes. For the most part the trading that takes place in leadership by bartering focuses on extrinsic factors. Tradeoffs occur in leadership by building as well, though they tend to address higher-order need factors and intrinsic motives of the led.

These ideas are captured by the theorizing of the psychologist Abraham Maslow (1943) and by the research of Frederick Herzberg (1966). These experts make the assumption that people have many needs and that the needs stem from at least two human desires—avoidance of pain, hardship, and difficulty; and the desire for growth and development in an effort to realize one's potential (e.g., Herzberg, 1966:56). Perhaps most well known is the need classification scheme proposed by Maslow (1943). He proposed that human needs could be classified into five broad categories: physiological, security-safety, social-belonging, esteem, and self-actualization. Key to Maslow's theory is that the need categories are arranged in a hierarchy of prepotency, with individual behavior motivated to satisfy the need most important at the time. Further, according to theory, the strength of this need depends on its position in the hierarchy and the extent to which lower-order needs are met or satiated. The press from esteem needs, for example, will not be very great for individuals whose security needs are not met. Maslow's ideas form much of the basis for the material and psychological bartering that takes place between leader and led as each seeks an accommodation of their needs. The leader needs to get work done in a certain way. The led needs to get certain needs met. One is traded for the other.

The work of Frederick Herzberg (1966) and his colleagues (Herzberg, Mausner, and Snyderman, 1959) provides a more sophisticated set of ideas for engaging in this kind of bartering. Herzberg's approach, often referred to as *two-factor theory*, is based on the premise that job characteristics contributing to work motivation are different from those contributing to work dissatisfaction. He called the first set of factors *motivators* and the second *hygienic*. According to the theory, if hygienic factors are not attended to by principals, poor work hygiene will occur, with corresponding feelings of teacher job dissatisfaction and poor performance. However, tending to these factors and eliminating job dissatisfaction will not result in increased teacher commitment or job performance. On the other hand, the motivation factors that contributed to increased teacher performance when present seemed not to result in job dissatisfaction or work performance that was below par when absent. According to the theory, if principals do not attend to the motivation factors, teachers will not be motivated to work, but they will not be dissatisfied either. They will perform up to a certain level considered satisfactory but will make little or no effort to exceed this level (Sergiovanni, 1966).

The factors identified by Herzberg and his associates as being related to work hygiene included interpersonal relationships with students, teachers, and supervisors; quality of supervision; policy and administration; working conditions; and personal life. The factors related to work motivation were achievement, recognition, work itself, responsibility, and advancement.

Two-factor theory suggests that job satisfaction and motivation to work are related to two decision possibilities for teachers: participation and performance (Sergiovanni, 1968). The decision to participate in one's job is associated with the fair day's work concept. When participating, one takes a job and does all that is necessary to meet minimum commitments; in return, one receives "fair pay" in the form of salary, benefits, social acceptance, courteous and thoughtful treatment, and reasonable supervision. Since these dimensions are *expected* as part of fair pay, they tend not to motivate a person to go beyond. The decision to perform, however, results in exceeding the fair day's work for a fair day's pay contract. This decision is voluntary, since all that school districts can require from teachers is fair work. Rewards associated with the fair day's work are for the most part extrinsic, focusing on the conditions of work. Rewards associated with the performance investment tend to be more intrinsic (e.g., recognition, achievement, feelings of competence, exciting and challenging work, interesting and meaningful work).

Principals need to be concerned with both extrinsic and intrinsic rewards. Schools cannot function adequately unless the participation investment is made and continued by teachers. But schools cannot excel unless the majority of teachers make the performance investment as well. Two-factor theory can provide principals with a cognitive map for ensuring that administrative, organizational, curricular, and teaching practices provide for both levels of work investment by teachers. But a map is different than a recipe. Not everything will work for everyone. Much trial and error will be necessary as principals practice leadership by bartering.

The Potential of Work Itself as a Motivator

A major problem with leadership by bartering is that it relies heavily on making deals. At the heart of the deals are bureaucratic and psychological authority as the means to obtain compliance. Bureaucratic authority promises sanctions and punishments if compliance is not forthcoming. Psychological authority gives rewards in exchange for compliance. Both forms of authority are limited in two ways. First, they lead to calculated involvement. A person's compliance is contingent on either the avoidance of penalties or the obtaining of rewards. When neither is forthcoming, continued compliance is often chancey and sometimes nonexistent.

Both rewards and penalties are based on the economic concept of utility function, as discussed in Chapter 8. Human beings are driven by a desire to maximize their self-interests and thus continually calculate the costs and benefits of all their options, choosing the course of action that either makes them a winner or keeps them from losing. In Chapter 3 it was pointed out that the concept of utility function is now being successfully challenged by a new economics that does not dismiss the importance of self-interest but gives equal weight to emotions and values—to expressive and moral authority as motivators (Etzioni, 1988). Leadership by bartering is based on the principle that "what gets rewarded gets done." Leadership by building, by contrast, is based on the principle "what *is* rewarding gets done." Here the emphasis is on intrinsic returns and expressive reasons for involvement in one's work. To these Etzioni would add the principle "what is right and good gets done." He has in mind the addition of moral authority as a means to understand why people choose to do something and to do it well.

Flow Theory

Mihaly Csikszentmihalyi (1975) proposes *flow theory* as a way to understand the potential of work itself as a source of motivation. He studied highly accomplished and motivated experts (such as rock climbers, composers, surgeons, authors) in a number of different fields. Though the work of these experts differed, each experienced a certain flow that Csikszentmihalyi attributes to intrinsic motivation. Flow is characterized by opportunity for action; the merging of action and awareness; focused attention characterized by concentration, narrowing of consciousness, and being absorbed in what one is doing; loss of self-consciousness as one works; clarity of goals and norms; direct and immediate feedback; and feelings of competence and of being in control of what one does. He concludes that the satisfaction derived from this total absorption in one's work provides a powerful source of motivation.

Csikszentmihalyi is convinced that experiencing flow can be a very common experience under the right conditions. One must first be faced by a *challenge* that is not too great for the *skills* needed to meet it but great enough for a person to meet the challenge with enjoyment on the one hand and to grow in competence, confidence, and/or skill on the other. Should one's skills be greater than the challenge, then boredom is likely to result. One can speculate, for example, that when teachers are bored with their work their available skills may not be used fully enough. Some experts maintain that this is the likely consequence of teachers who are subjected to curriculum and supervisory mandates that specify unduly what it is they must do and how. Such specification can lead to work simplification and the subsequent "de-skilling" of teachers (McNeil, 1987).

Sometimes teachers are faced with levels of challenge that far exceed their skills, with the result being feelings of anxiety. When neither level of challenge or level of skill is very high, the response is likely to be one of apathy, another version of the de-skilling hypothesis. It might be useful at this point to inventory one's own personal experience with teachers and with students. Compare occasions when they responded to work with apathy, boredom, anxiety, or total absorption (flow). What are the mixes of challenge and skills levels that seemed to contribute to these states?

The message of flow theory for principals is that maintaining the right balance between level of skill and level of challenge makes good motivational sense. When challenge is up, principals need to provide the necessary support on the skill dimension to avoid frustration and fear of failure. In areas where teacher skill levels are high, challenging opportunities will need to be provided. Successful matching of challenge and skill, according to the theory, is likely to result in flow—total absorption in one's work.

Job-Enrichment Theory

Another window through which one might view the potential of the work itself to motivate is provided by the research of Richard Hackman and Greg Oldham (1980). These scholars have developed a theory of job enrichment—the Job Characteristics model—that has been successfully applied in practice. Key to the model is the presence of three psychological states found to be critical in determining a person's work motivation and job satisfaction:

- *Experience meaningfulness*, which is defined as the extent to which an individual perceives her or his work as being worthwhile or important by some system of self-accepted values
- *Experience responsibility*, which is defined by the extent to which a person believes that she or he is personally accountable for the outcomes of efforts
- *Knowledge of results*, which is defined as the extent to which a person is able to determine, on a fairly regular basis, whether or not performance is satisfactory and efforts lead to outcomes (Hackman, et al., 1975:57).

According to the Job Characteristics model, when these psychological states are experienced, one feels good and performs better – internal work motivation occurs. Internal work motivation means how much an individual experiences positive feelings from effective performance. Hackman and Oldham have found that the content of one's job is an important critical determiner of internal work motivation. Further, when certain characteristics of one's job are improved or enhanced, internal work motivation can be increased. They found, for example, that experience meaningfulness of work was enhanced by jobs characterized by skill variety, task identity, and task significance. Autonomy was the job characteristic related to experience responsibility, and feedback was related to knowledge of results.

The Job Characteristics model suggests that in teaching, jobs that require: 1. different activities in carrying out the work and the use of a variety of teacher talents and skills (skill variety); 2. teachers to engage in tasks identified as whole and comprising identifiable pieces of work (task identity); 3. teachers to have substantial and significant impact on the lives or work of other people (task significance); 4. substantial freedom, independence, and direction be provided to teachers in scheduling work and in deciding classroom organizational and instructional procedures (autonomy); and 5. teachers be provided with direct, clear information about the effects of their performance (feedback) are likely to evoke the psychological states of meaningfulness, responsibility, and knowledge of results. Hackman and Oldham's research reveals that these conditions result in high work motivation, high-quality performance, high job satisfaction, and low absenteeism among teachers.

Figure 11-1 illustrates the Job Characteristics model. Besides job dimensions, psychological states, and personal and work outcomes, an "implementing concepts" panel is included. Implementing concepts are suggestions the researchers offer to principals interested in building more of the job dimensions into the work of the school. The principle of combining tasks, for example, suggests that as much as possible, fractionalized aspects of teaching should be put together into larger, more holistic modules. Comprehensive curriculum strategies, interdisciplinary teaching approaches, and team-group teaching modes all contribute to the combining of teaching and curriculum tasks. Combining teaching tasks increases not only skill variety for teachers but their identification with the work as well.

Although establishing close relationships with students ("clients") is a natural part of teaching and learning, some patterns of school organization and teaching encourage impersonal relationships between teachers and students. Forming "natural work units" has interesting implications for schooling. The intent of such units would be to increase one's sense of ownership and continuing responsibility for identifiable aspects of the work. The self-contained elementary school classroom comes closer to this concept than does the departmentalized and quick-moving secondary school teaching schedule. But even in the elementary setting, the building of teaching teams that plan and work together and whose members share a common responsibility for students is often lacking. "Vertical loading" suggests strategies that bring together actual teaching and planning to teach. Providing teachers with more control over schedules, work methods, evaluation, and even the training and supervision of less experienced teachers might be examples of vertical loading.

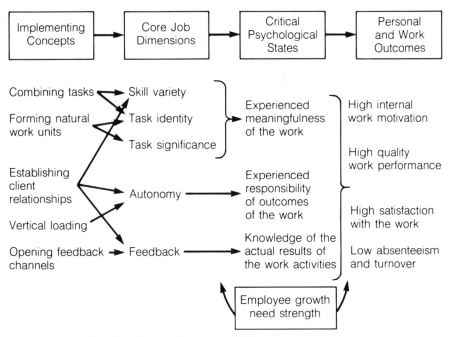

FIGURE 11-1 Job Enrichment Concepts and Practices

From J. R. Hackman, G. Oldham, R. Johnson, and K. Purdy, "A New Strategy for Job Enrichment,"
© 1975 by The Regents of the University of California. Reprinted from *California Management Review*,
Vol. XVII, no. 4, p. 64, by permission of The Regents.

"Opening feedback channels" is another way of saying that the more principals
are able to let teachers know how well they are doing, the more highly motivated
they will be. Indeed, motivation and satisfaction are neglected benefits of teacher-
evaluation supervisory programs designed to provide teachers with helpful feedback. Examples of helpful programs would be those that include clinical supervision, peer supervision, target settings, and similar formats. Principals should strive
to create ways in which feedback to teachers occurs naturally from their day-to-
day activities and from working closely with colleagues.

The Job Characteristics model suggests that virtually every decision principals
make about schooling, classroom organization, curriculum development and implementation, and the selection of materials and teaching itself has implications
for building motivation and commitment of teachers. Principals need to assess the
consequences of a particular decision on promoting job-enrichment opportunities
for teachers.

Friendship opportunities and opportunities to work with others are two other
dimensions identified in the Job Characteristics model (Sashkin and Morris, 1984).
"Friendship opportunities" refers to the extent to which the work setting provides
for the development of close contacts among teachers and the development of
friendly patterns of interaction. "Working with others" refers to the extent to which

the accomplishment of tasks requires that teachers interact with other teachers in order to complete the work successfully. These dimensions seem related to the extent to which workers are involved in their jobs, experience satisfaction, and report improvements in work quality (Sashkin and Morris, 1984).

In sum, the Job Characteristics model provides principals with a conceptual framework allowing them to make informed decisions about the nature and structure of the work of teaching to help teachers feel that their job is meaningful, to enable them to learn the actual outcomes of their efforts, to provide them with feelings of control and responsibility for results, and to help them become part of a social unit. These conditions are related to high intrinsic work motivation, increases in quality performance, high job satisfaction, and lower absence and turnover rates.

Appendix 11-2 contains a scoring key allowing you to score your responses to the Quality of Work Life in Teaching form. Please score by following the directions provided. Note that five subscores are provided, each corresponding to an important dimension of most job-enrichment models. With the exception of work speed and routine, the higher the score, the more enriched is the job and the greater are the possibilities for increased motivation and commitment.

Women as a Special Case

At the beginning of this chapter the issue of male bias in the motivation research and accompanying prescriptions for practice was raised and the reader was cautioned that literal use of the findings may not apply to women. The problem, according to Shakeshaft (1987) is androcentrism defined as "the practice of viewing the world and shaping reality from a male perspective. . . . the elevation of the masculine to the level of the universal and the ideal and honoring of men and the male principle above women and female" (94). Maslow's theory, two-factor theory and job enrichment theory, for example, give heavy emphasis to competition, the setting of task goals, individual achievement, the building of self competence and esteem, individual autonomy and self actualization. Women, by contrast, give emphasis to such themes as cooperation, intimacy, affiliation, the construction of interpersonal networks and community building. In using teamwork as an example Shakeshaft (1987) points out that men tend to view the concept in terms of goals, roles and responsibilities. A team must first define what needs to be done and then allocate responsibilities to roles making clear not only what is expected but how one person's niche fits that of others who comprise the team. The metaphor for team, in this context, is sport in the form of baseball, basketball or football. For women teamwork is not the parallel play of men but the meshing of individual identities to create a new configuration and the bonding together of people in a common cause.

Key in applying the concepts from traditional motivation theory is redefining concept indicators. Achievement, for example, can mean the accumulation of a series of individual successes on the one hand or the successful constructing of a learning community on the other. Application of the motivation theory and research, therefore, should be idiosyncratic. If you want to know what motivates people start by asking them.

The Power of Beliefs

In this and other chapters the adding of moral authority to bureaucratic and psychological was recommended. Doing so depends on schools being able to develop a set of shared values and beliefs that spells out who they are, what they want to accomplish, and how. Centers or covenants (see, for example, Chapter 8) provide the basis for bonding people together as members of a learning community that knows why it exists and detail as well what the community owes its members and what its members in turn owe the community. This theme was at the heart of earlier discussions of leadership and school culture and will be returned to in the final chapter, "Administering as Moral Craft." The challenge to principals is as follows.

Interpreted properly, the theory and research in the area of teacher motivation and commitment can be helpful. Often, policy mandates, administrative directives, and out own complacency in insisting on "business as usual" present conditions and practices at odds with this knowledge base. School practices, for example, too often encourage bureaucratic teaching, promote isolationism among teachers, encourage privatism, and discourage social interaction. These conditions are typically associated with decreases in teacher motivation and commitment. Effective teaching and learning and other school improvement efforts are enhanced as teachers work harder and smarter and as their commitment to the school and its success is increased. This gap between present practice and what we know represents a test of leadership for principals.

Even more challenging is the attempt to broaden present conceptions of the nature of human potential. Without dismissing the importance of self-interest, principals and faculties must give far more attention to expressive and moral reasons for determining courses of action. As expressive and moral authority gain acceptance as legitimate ways of working with teachers, attention will need to be given to applying these same ideas to students as well.

References

Argyris, Chris. 1957. *Personality and Organization.* New York: Harper & Row.

Bidwell, Charles E. 1975. "The School as a Formal Organization," in James G. March, Ed., *Handbook of Organizations,* 972–1022. Chicago: Rand McNally.

Brayfield, A. H., and W. H. Crockett. 1955. "Employee Attitudes and Employee Performance," *Psychological Bulletin* 52(1), 415–422.

Clark, David L., Linda S. Lotto, and Terry A. Astuto. 1984. "Effective Schools and School Improvement: A Comparative Analysis of Two Lines of Inquiry," *Educational Administration Quarterly* 20(3), 41–68.

Coombs, Arthur W. 1959. "Personality Theory and Its Implication for Curriculum Development," in Alexander Frazier, Ed., *Learning More About Learning.* Washington, DC: Association for Supervision and Curriculum Development.

Csikszentmihalyi, Mihaly. 1975. *Beyond Boredom and Anxiety.* San Francisco: Jossey-Bass.

Darling-Hammond, Linda. 1984. *Beyond the Commission Reports: The Coming Crisis in Teaching*. Santa Monica, CA: The Rand Corporation.

De Charms, Richard. 1968. *Personal Causation*. New York: Academic Press.

Dornbush, S. M., and W. R. Scott. 1975. *Evaluation and the Exercise of Authority*. San Francisco: Jossey-Bass.

Durkheim, Emil. 1947. *The Division of Labor in Society*. Translated by G. Simpson. New York: The Free Press.

Etzioni, Amitai. 1988. *The Moral Dimension Toward A New Economics*. New York: The Free Press.

Glatthorn, Allan A. 1984. *Differentiated Supervision*. Alexandria, VA: Association for Supervision and Curriculum Development.

Hackman, J. R., and G. R. Oldham. 1980. *Work Redesign*. Reading, MA: Addison-Wesley.

Hackman, J. R., G. Oldham, R. Johnson, and K. Purdy. 1975. "A New Strategy for Job Enrichment," *California Management Review* 17(4).

Herzberg, F. 1966. *Work and the Nature of Man*. New York: World Publishing.

Herzberg, Frederick, B. Mausner, R. D. Peterson, and D. F. Capwell. 1957. *Job Attitudes: A Review of Research and Opinion*. Pittsburgh, PA: Psychological Service of Pittsburgh.

Herzberg, F., B. Mausner, and B. Snyderman. 1959. *The Motivation to Work*. New York: Wiley.

Keenan, Charles. 1974. "Channels for Change: A Survey of Teachers in Chicago Elementary Schools." Doctoral dissertation, Department of Educational Administration, University of Illinois, Urbana.

Lieberman, Ann, and Lynne Miller. 1984. *Teachers, Their World, and Their Work*. Alexandria, VA: Association for Supervision and Curriculum Development.

Lortie, Dan. 1975. *School Teacher*. Chicago: University of Chicago Press.

MacDonald, James. 1964. "An Image of Man: The Learner Himself," in Ronald R. Doll, Ed., *Individualizing Instruction*. Washington, DC: Association for Supervision and Curriculum Development.

Maslow, A. H. 1943. "A Theory of Human Motivation," *Psychological Review* 50(2), 370–396.

McNeil, Linda M. 1987. "Exit Voice and Community: Magnet Teachers Responses to Standardization," *Educational Policy* 1(1).

Peters, Thomas J., and Robert H. Waterman, Jr. 1982. *In Search of Excellence*. New York: Harper & Row.

Pfeiffer, J. William, and Leonard D. Goodstein. 1984. *The 1984 Annual: Developing Human Resources*. San Diego, CA: University Associates.

Rosenholtz, Susan J. 1984. "Political Myths about Educational Reform: Lessons from Research on Teaching." Paper prepared for the Education Commission of the States, Denver, CO.

Sashkin, Marshall, and William C. Morris. 1984. *Organizational Behavior Concepts and Experiences*. Reston, VA: The Reston Co.

Schultz, Theodore W. 1982. "Human Capital Approaches in Organizing and Paying for Education," in Walter McMahan and Terry G. Geste, Eds., *Financing Education: Overcoming Inefficiency and Inequity*. 36–51. Urbana, IL: University of Illinois Press.

Sergiovanni, Thomas J. 1966. "Factors Which Affect Satisfaction and Dissatisfaction of Teachers," *Journal of Educational Administration* 5(1), 66–82.

Sergiovanni, Thomas J. 1968. "New Evidence on Teacher Morale: A Proposal for Staff Differentiation," *The North Central Association Quarterly* 62(3), 259–266.

Shakeshaft, Charol (1987). *Women in Educational Administration*. Beverly Hills, CA: Sage.

Vroom, V. H. 1964. *Work and Motivation*. New York: Wiley.

Waller, Willard. 1967. *Sociology of Teaching*. New York: Wiley.

Wise, Arthur E. 1979. *Legislated Learning: The Bureaucratization of the American Classroom*. Berkeley, CA: University of California Press.

APPENDIX 11-1 Factors Contributing to Dissatisfaction in Teaching

This appendix, excerpted from a report issued by the Rand Corporation and prepared by Linda Darling-Hammond,* describes factors contributing to dissatisfaction in teaching. To what extent are these the result of increases in legislated learning and bureaucratic teaching? The Rand report points out that teachers are feeling more like "Pawns" in an impersonal system of schooling that is increasingly beyond their control. Changes in schooling are needed to restore teachers to "Origin" status. How can two-factor and job-enrichment theory and research help in rethinking ways in which schools are organized and the ways in which work settings and conditions of teachers are arranged? What can school principals do to help improve the quality of work life for teachers? The Rand report excerpt begins below:

> For several decades, the National Education Association has polled several thousand teachers annually about their teaching conditions and views. One question asked in each poll is, If you could go back and start all over again, would you still become a teacher? Chart 1 shows the dramatic change in responses to that question over twenty years. Between 1971 and 1981 the proportion of respondents saying they would not teach again more than tripled, rising from about 10 percent to nearly 40 percent. Less than half of the present teaching force say they plan to continue teaching until retirement.[1]
>
> It is easy to summarize the factors that contribute to teacher dissatisfaction. Teachers feel that they lack support—physical support in terms of adequate facilities and materials; support services such as clerical help for typing, duplicating, and paperwork chores; and administrative support that would provide a school environment in which their work is valued and supported rather than obstructed by interruptions and a proliferation of

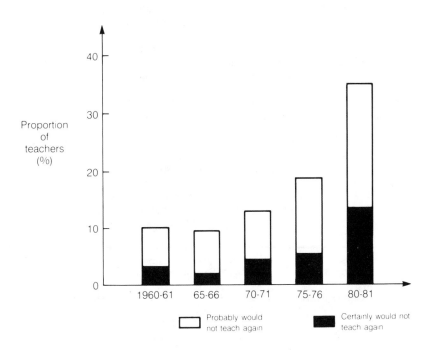

* Linda Darling-Hammond (1984). *Beyond the Commission Reports: The Coming Crisis in Teaching*, Santa Monica, CA: The Rand Corporation, 11–13.

1. National Education Association, *Status of the American Public School Teacher, 1980–81*, 1982, 73–76.

APPENDIX 11–1 *(Continued)*

non-teaching tasks. They see their ability to teach hampered by large class sizes and non-teaching duties. And they feel that they are not treated as professionals. They have limited input to decisions that critically affect their work environment, and they see few opportunities for professional growth.[2]

Let us translate these categories into more concrete terms. Imagine that you are a high-school English teacher. You have at least a master's degree (as do most teachers today) and you would like to impart to your students the joys of great literature and the skills of effective communication. You have at your disposal a set of 100 textbooks for your 140 students. You cannot order additional books so you make copies of some plays and short stories, at your own expense, and you jockey with the 50 other teachers in your school for access to one of the two available typewriters so that you can produce other materials for your class. You stand in line after school to use the secretary's telephone to call parents of students who have been absent or are behind in their work.

You spend roughly 12 hours each week correcting papers, because you believe your students should write a theme each week. You feel guilty that this allows you to spend only 5 minutes per paper. You spend another 6 hours each week preparing for your five different sections, mostly writing up the behavioral objectives required by the system's curriculum guide, which you find meaningless and even counterproductive to your goals for your students. You do all of this after school hours, because your one preparation period is devoted to preparing attendance forms, doing other administrative paperwork, and meeting with students who need extra help. Between classes, you monitor hallways and restrooms, supervise the lunch room, and track down truants.

You are frustrated that the district's new competency-based curriculum is forcing you to spend more and more of your time teaching students to answer multiple-choice questions about the mechanics of grammar. Meanwhile, your efforts to teach writing and critical thinking are discouraged, as they do not seem to fit with the district's mandated curriculum and testing program. You have no input into decisions about curriculum, teaching methods, materials, or resource allocations. You will, of course, never get a promotion; nor will you have an opportunity to take on new responsibilities. You receive frequent feedback about public dissatisfaction with schools and teachers, but little reinforcement from administrators or parents that your work is appreciated. Sometimes you wonder whether your efforts are worth the $15,000 a year you earn for them.

This description is not an overdramatization. It reflects the modal conditions of teaching work in this country today. The importance of professional working conditions to teacher satisfaction and retention has recently been recognized in a number of studies at Rand and elsewhere. Conditions that undermine teacher efficacy, i.e., the teacher's ability to do an effective job of teaching, are strongly related to teacher attrition. These conditions include lack of opportunity for professional discourse and decisionmaking input; inadequate preparation and teaching time; and conflict with or lack of support from administrators.[3]

2. Ibid., pp. 76–78; National Education Asociation, *Nationwide Teacher Opinion Poll, 1983,* p. 9; American Federation of Teachers, *Schools as a Workplace: The Realities of Stress,* Vol. 1, 1983, 15–17.

3. See, for example, Linda Darling-Hammond and Arthur E. Wise, "Teaching Standards or Standardized Teaching?," *Educational Leadership,* October 1983, pp. 66–69; Susan J. Rosenholtz and Mark A. Smylie, *Teacher Compensation and Career Ladders: Policy Implications from Research,* Paper commissioned by the Tennessee General Assembly's Select Committee on Education, December 1983; D. W. Chapman and S. M. Hutcheson, "Attrition from Teaching Careers: A Discriminant Analysis," *American Educational Research Journal,* Vol. 19, 1982, pp. 93–105; M. D. Litt and D. C. Turk, *Stress, Dissatisfaction, and Intention to Leave Teaching in Experienced Public High School Teachers,* Paper presented at the annual meeting of the American Educational Research Association, Montreal, April 1983.

APPENDIX 11–2 Quality of Work Life in Teaching Scoring Form

Instructions: Transfer your answers to the questions on the QWLinT instrument to the scoring grid below, circling the number below the letter of the answer you selected. When you have transferred all answers and circled the appropriate numbers, add up all the numbers circled in each of the columns and enter the total in the empty box at the bottom of the column. Each of these totals refers to one of the scales of the QWLinT. Note that high scores for autonomy, personal growth, work complexity, and task-related interaction indicate a strong presence of these characteristics and suggest high job-enrichment opportunities in one's job. High scores for work speed and routine indicate a weak presence of this characteristic and low job enrichment.

Q.1 A M P N 1 2 3 4	Q.2 A M P N 4 3 2 1	Q.3 A M P N 1 2 3 4	Q.4 A M P N 1 2 3 4	Q.5 A M P N 4 3 2 1
Q.6 A M P N 4 3 2 1	Q.7 A M P N 4 3 2 1	Q.8 A M P N 1 2 3 4	Q.9 A M P N 1 2 3 4	Q.10 A M P N 1 2 3 4
Q.11 A M P N 1 2 3 4	Q.12 A M P N 4 3 2 1	Q.13 A M P N 1 2 3 4	Q.14 A M P N 4 3 2 1	Q.15 A M P N 4 3 2 1
Q.16 A M P N 4 3 2 1	Q.17 A M P N 4 3 2 1	Q.18 A M P N 4 3 2 1	Q.19 A M P N 1 2 3 4	Q.20 A M P N 4 3 2 1
Q.21 A M P N 4 3 2 1	Q.22 A M P N 4 3 2 1	Q.23 A M P N 1 2 3 4	Q.24 A M P N 1 2 3 4	Q.25 A M P N 4 3 2 1
Autonomy	Personal Growth Opportunity	Work* Speed and Routine	Work Complexity	Task Related Interaction

Scale Score Interpretation:

 5 to 9, low job enrichment
10 to 15, moderate job enrichment
16 to 20, high job enrichment
*High scores for work speed and routine indicate low job enrichment

CHAPTER 12

The Change
Process

School improvement does not occur by happenstance. Someone must decide to do something to change the status quo for the better. Sometimes the decision to embark on school improvement efforts emerges from a teacher or group of teachers; generally, though, such efforts result from deliberate action by the school principal. As Harold Geneen (1984) might put it, when it comes to school improvement efforts, it is clear that principals must manage, manage, manage and lead, lead, lead.

Management involves the marshaling of financial and other resources, the planning and implementing of structures, and the providing of actions, arrangements, and activities needed for the school to reach its school improvement goals. Management is the means to get to point B from point A. Leadership is concerned with an issue such as, Why go to Point B anyway? What school improvement goals are worth pursuing? How can agreement be reached among the faculty and among school constituencies regarding these goals? What levels of motivation and commitment are needed for people to work together energetically on school improvement? In essence, leadership deals with how one can provide the necessary purposing and inspiration to school improvement efforts. Leadership without management can lead to mere rhetoric and disappointment. Management without leadership rarely results in sustained changes in teaching and learning practices.

More Than Adoption,
More Than Implementation

Much of the literature on change in schools assumes that adoption is the same as implementation. The two, however, are different (Gaynor, 1975). Schools frequently adopt innovations that are not implemented or, if implemented, innovations are shaped to the way things were to the point that the "change" is hardly noticeable. The open-space concept, popular during the late 1960s and early 1970s, is an example. "Implementation" of open space was characterized by carving schools into traditional classrooms through the use of bookcases, room dividers, lockers, and other partitions. Goodlad and Klein (1970) make a similar observation with respect to the adoption of team teaching and the ungraded classroom concept. Frequently implementation was characterized by "turn" teaching and the creation of grades within grades. From your own experiences you probably know of a junior high school that has adopted, but not really implemented, the middle school concept.

Even successful implementation of a change in schooling is not enough. School improvement requires that such implementation be sustained over time; this, in turn, requires that the change be institutionalized. Institutionalization means that the change is "built in" to the life of the school (Miles, 1983). As Huberman and Crandall point out: "New practices that get built into the training, regulatory, staffing, and budgetary cycles survive, others don't. Innovations are highly perishable goods" (cited in Miles, 1983:14). Institutionalization is a process of making a change routine; it becomes part of the ordinary life of the school. Changes requiring new dollars, for example, become institutionalized when these new dollars become regularly budgeted dollars. Changes requiring new structural arrangements become institutionalized when regular school policies are revised to reflect these arrangements. Changes requiring new patterns of behavior become institutionalized when the regular reward system (salary, promotions, psychological rewards) is adjusted to reflect these patterns. Institutionalization cannot be taken for granted. School improvement, therefore, requires that adoption, implementation, *and* institutionalization become the principal's goals.

The "One-Best-Way" Problem

For every successful school improvement effort, one hears horror stories about unsuccessful efforts. The major reason for failure, beyond lack of management and leadership effort by the principal, is a limited view of what the process of change involves. Unsuccessful school improvement efforts tend to put "all their eggs in one basket" by using a one-best-way to approach the problem.

Some experts advocate engineering the social and political context within which the school exists in an effort to provide the necessary support and momentum for change (see for example, Gaynor, 1975; Baldridge, 1971). Other experts emphasize the development of favorable school climates that provide the necessary interpersonal support for change. In recent years, scholars from this group have focused on the concept of school culture and have emphasized the importance of developing values and norms that include the proposed changes (Likert, 1967; Sergiovanni and Corbally, 1984). Still other experts concentrate almost exclusively on the individual and her or his needs, dispositions, stages of concern for the proposed change, and the driving and restraining forces that pull and tug, causing resistance to the change (Bennis, Benne, and Chin, 1969; Reddin, 1970). Finally, some experts give primary attention to engineering the work context as a means to program and structure teacher behavior to ensure that the school improvement effort is implemented properly (Hunter, 1984). All these concerns are important, but none alone is an adequate model for school improvement.

A Systems View of Change

When one brings together each of these concerns, a systems view begins to emerge—one that provides a dynamic, integrative, and powerful view of change. Within this view the unit of change is not limited to the individual teacher, the school, the workflow of teaching and schooling, or the broader political and administrative context. Instead, the four are viewed as interacting units of change, all requiring attention. When attended to properly, these units of change are the roads to successful school improvement.

The systems view is depicted in Figure 12–1. Note that the direct road to changes relating to teaching and learning is through structuring the workflow of schooling. But teaching is human-intensive. This means that regardless of how hard one might try to introduce change, teachers cannot be ignored. They count whether one wants them to or not. They make the day-to-day and minute-to-minute decisions influencing what happens to students. For changes in the workflow of teaching to count they must be directly linked to changes in teaching behavior, and this inevitably means changes in the attitudes and beliefs of individual teachers and the faculty as a whole.

Teachers typically work alone. This isolation has telling negative consequences on teaching effectiveness and school improvement (Rosenholtz, 1989). Still, teachers are members of social groups that make up the larger school faculty. Social groups create norms, customs, and traditions that define ways of living. School culture is the term often used to refer to the sense of order and being that emerges. School culture defines what is of worth for teachers, specifies acceptable limits of behavior and beliefs, and is a powerful factor in promoting or resisting school improvement efforts (Saronson, 1971).

Schools do not exist in isolation; thus, another dimension of importance in the school improvement process is the broader administrative, social, and political environment. School climates, for example, are influenced by actions and attitudes of the teachers' union, the school board, and central office school district administrators (Kirst, 1984). Influences from this political system trickle down from the school level to the individual teacher and finally to the workflow. All four levels—individual, school, workflow, and political context—are, therefore, interacting units of change needing attention as principals promote school improvement. In the following sections, each of the four units of change is examined more closely.

The Individual as the Unit of Change

When considering the individual teacher as the unit of change, needs, values, beliefs, and levels of readiness are important. Change is often frightening. So much is at stake as present circumstances, norms, and ways of operation are threatened. Before most teachers are able to examine the worth of a proposed new idea for improving teaching and learning, they are apt to view this idea selfishly. The first reaction is likely to be, "How will this proposed change affect me?" For example, the prospect

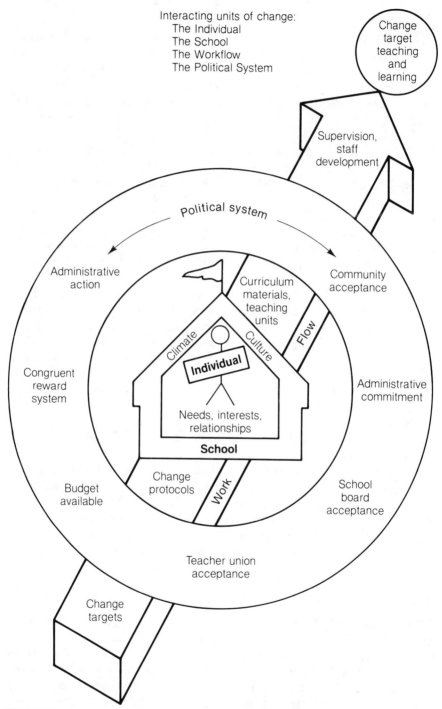

Interacting units of change:
The Individual
The School
The Workflow
The Political System

Change target teaching and learning

Supervision, staff development

Political system

Administrative action

Community acceptance

Congruent reward system

Administrative commitment

Curriculum materials, teaching units

Flow

Climate

Culture

Individual

Needs, interests, relationships

School

Change protocols

Work

Budget available

School board acceptance

Teacher union acceptance

Change targets

FIGURE 12–1 Interacting Units: A Systems View of Change

of family grouping, team teaching, or a new pattern of organization (such as school within the school or middle school) raises such questions in teachers' minds as: How will my relationship with other teachers change? How will my view of myself change? How will my authority over students and influence in the school change? How will the amount of work I do change? How will my relationship with parents and administrators change? Will I be more or less successful as a teacher? Who will be the team leader or master teacher? What will other teachers think of me as a person? What will other teachers think of me as a teacher?

These questions reflect concerns that are normal and deserve answering. Unless these human concerns are adequately resolved, continued emphasis on educational and other job-related aspects of the change will likely increase anxiety and promote skepticism. Principals react similarly when faced with the prospects of change; so do professors and superintendents. Healthy individuals are naturally concerned with how changes will affect them, their work, their relationships with others; all these concerns require attention.

For some time, researchers have been interested in the concerns of teachers and how these concerns focus their attention on a limited range of issues relating to change (Fuller, 1969; Hall and Louckes, 1978; Hord, et al., 1987). This work has led to the development of the "concern-based adoption model," which describes the changing feelings of people as they learn about a proposed change, prepare to use it, use it, and modify it as a result. The model proposes seven stages of concern as follows (Hall and Loucks, 1978).

1. Awareness	I am not concerned about it.
2. Informational	I would like to know more about it.
3. Personal	How will using it affect me?
4. Management	I seem to be spending all my time getting material ready.
5. Consequence	How is my use affecting kids?
6. Collaboration	I am concerned about relating what I am doing with what other teachers are doing.
7. Refocusing	I have some ideas about something that would work even better.

The developers of the model do not maintain that every teacher marches through all the stages beginning with awareness and ending with refocusing or that the stages are mutually exclusive with only one being tended to at a time. The stages do, however, represent the general kind of development that takes place as changes are adopted and used on a continuous basis. They are therefore developmental *in nature* rather than being strictly developmental.

The progression of concerns seems to follow this pattern. In the early stages of a change effort, teachers are likely to have self concerns that center on learning more about the proposed change and how the change will affect them personally. Once these concerns are taken care of, they tend next to focus on the management problems they are likely to face as they begin to implement the change. Next their attention shifts to the impact the change is likely to have on their students and, as this change is remediated, to issues of collaboration with other teachers in an effort to implement the change and to improve its effects. Finally, since teachers are different and their situations are varied, adaptions are made in the change in an effort to improve its fit.

Principals and others who are interested in promoting change can use the concern-based model as a general framework for evaluating where various individuals are with respect to change concerns and for matching their own strategies to these levels. It makes little sense, for example, to spend an inordinate amount of time worrying about management concerns or consequences that a particular change is likely to have for students when teachers are still pretty much focused on such personal concerns as whether they will indeed be able to successfully adopt the change, how it will affect their relationships with other teachers, and so on.

Resistance to change occurs when one's basic work needs are threatened. Though individual differences among teachers exist in the relative importance of specific work needs, four fairly universal needs can be identified (Mealiea, 1978):

1. *The need for clear expectations.* Most of us require fairly specific information about our jobs to function effectively. We need to know what is expected of us, how we fit into the total scheme of things, what our responsibilities are, how we will be evaluated, and what our relationships with others will be. Without such information our performance is likely to decline and our job satisfaction will be lessened (Katz and Kahn, 1978). Change upsets this "equilibrium" of role definition and expectations.

2. *The need for future certainty.* Closely related to knowing how we fit into the job system is being able to predict the future. We need to have some reliability and certainty built into our work lives to provide us with security and allow us to plan ahead (Coffer and Appley, 1964). Change introduces ambiguity and uncertainty, which threaten our need for a relatively stable, balanced, and predictable work environment.

3. *The need for social interaction.* Most of us value and need opportunities to interact with others. This interaction helps us to define and build our own self-concepts and to reduce anxiety and fear we experience in the work environment. We seek support and acceptance from others at work. Change is often perceived as threatening to these important social interaction patterns, and the prospects of establishing new patterns can present us with security problems.

4. *The need for control over our work environment and work events.* Most of us want and seek a reasonable degree of control over our work environment (Argyris, 1957). We do not wish to be at the mercy of this system. We want to be Origins and not Pawns (De Charms, 1968) when it comes to making decisions that affect our work lives.

When control is threatened or reduced, the net effect for teachers is not only less job satisfaction but also a loss of meaning in work that can result in job indifference and even alienation. Change efforts that do not involve teachers and changes that threaten to lessen their control over teaching, learning, and other aspects of schooling can have serious consequences for school effectiveness.

Teachers vary in the intensity with which the four universal needs are held. The greater the intensity, the more likely will change threats be felt. Still, for all teachers, change will likely create some disturbance in their present situation. Principals can help get teachers back onto a more comfortable and stable course by providing as much relevant information as possible about the change and how it affects the work of teaching. Teachers need to know what will be expected of them as the change is put into operation. This theme will be discussed further, when the workflow as the unit of change is considered. Allowing—indeed, welcoming—teacher participation in planning the proposed change will help to provide for these needs and will very likely result in ideas about how to improve the proposal. Keeping the proposed change simple and implementing aspects of the change gradually will increase teachers' confidence in themselves as successful implementers.

Mealiea (1979) suggests that changes be accompanied by a nonevaluation period during which the teacher's performance cannot have a negative effect on income, career ladder promotion, or other school benefits. During this period the emphasis would be solely on providing feedback to teachers to help them learn more about the change and to increase proficiency in implementing the change. Directing change efforts first to teachers who might be considered as role models and who optimally would become early adopters of the change can be helpful to successful school improvement. If teachers who are widely respected by others are moving ahead with the change, a certain confidence and calm are likely to occur and resistance is likely to be lessened.

The School as the Unit of Change

Concentrating on individual teachers as units of change is important, but many experts maintain that too much emphasis has been given to this level. The well-known social psychologists Daniel Katz and Robert Kahn (1978) state: "Attempts to change organizations by changing individuals have a long history of theoretical inadequacy and practical failure. Both stem from a disregard of the systematic properties of organizations and from the confusion of individual changes with modifications in organizational variables" (658).

Katz and Kahn believe that individuals and individual behavior remain important in change considerations but take on different qualities and meanings when viewed within the context of the group. Consider, for example, recent interactions you had with your supervisor one to one and in a group context. In many respects you were two different persons. Many individuals, for example, feel more an equal of supervisors when interacting within a group context rather than interacting on a one-to-one basis.

The school as a community needs to be considered as an important unit of change. This theme was one of the concerns of Chapter 10, which examined the concepts of school culture and school climate and their relationships to school effectiveness. Schools with more open climates and schools whose management systems could be described as more 4 than 1 were better able to initiate changes, respond to changes, accept changes, and implement changes. Changes that are consistent with the school's value system as defined by its shared purposes and covenant are likely to be accepted more easily.

The Workflow as the Unit of Change

Change experts who focus their efforts almost entirely on the individual and school as units of change are often successful in promoting adoption of a school improvement idea but not in implementing it. Adoption goals create the necessary readiness and enthusiasm for change and result from a bit of salespersonship on the one hand and psychological reassurance on the other. Too often, however, enthusiasm wanes, teachers experience frustration with implementation attempts, and the proposed change is modified to resemble the familiar "business as usual" or abandoned entirely. Focusing almost exclusively on the individual or the school or the two in combination results in "up-front" commitment (Crandall, 1983:7), but this commitment may not be expanded or sustained as teachers begin to put the change into practice. Up-front commitment, of course, is important because it gets us into the water. Now we need help learning how to swim differently, and this requires that we focus on the workflow as the unit of change.

Workflow focus builds commitment during and after teachers are actually engaged in new practices (Crandall, 1983). No secrets are involved in focusing on the workflow. The process is simple and direct. It involves making known specifically what is to be accomplished; defining carefully how this will be accomplished, giving specific attention to what teachers will actually be doing that is different; providing the necessary teaching apparatus, equipment, and curriculum materials; and providing the necessary ongoing training, assistance, supervision, and evaluation for ensuring that teachers' attempts to implement the change will be successful.

The dimensions of the workflow requiring attention from principals can be summarized as follows:

1. *The Change Goal* — This is what the school wants to accomplish.
2. *The Change Targets* — These are practical and operational definitions, descriptions, and examples of the goal.
3. *The Change Protocols* — These are practical and operational definitions, descriptions, and examples of arrangements and behaviors that need to be provided or articulated to reach targets.
4. *The Curriculum and Teaching Requirements* — These are the curriculum and teaching materials and units that teachers will need for them to work differently and successfully.

5. *The Supervisory and Staff Development Support* — This is the help teachers will need before they begin the process of change and while the process of change continues.

Expectancy theory of motivation can help us understand the importance of the dimensions of the workflow described above. According to expectancy theory, before motivation to change occurs, teachers need answers to the following questions:

1. Do I know what it is that needs to be accomplished?
2. Are the benefits of accomplishment important to me and desired by me?
3. Do I have a clear idea of exactly what it is that I need to do to accomplish this?
4. Should I attempt accomplishment; will I be successful?

A "no" answer to any of these questions means that teachers will not be motivated to participate in the school improvement effort. "Yes" answers that result in motivation depend on the attention principals give to the workflow as the unit of change. Particularly key is the supervisory support available to teachers to ensure successful implementation.

The Political System as the Unit of Change

Adoption and implementation are not the same as institutionalization of a change. Institutionalization occurs when the change is no longer viewed as an innovation; instead, it is considered part of the regular pattern of operation within the school and school district. Institutionalization requires changes in school district policies, rules, and procedures; actual budget allocations; school structural and administrative arrangements; and the official reward system that is made available to teachers. In school settings very few change attempts ever reach the institutional level; this explains, in part, why changes tend not to stick.

Principals are the main characters in bringing about adoption and implementation goals. They play key roles in planning and providing leadership for changes addressed to individuals, the school, and the workflow as units of change. But when it comes to institutionalizing changes, they do not have much power. The reality is that principals will need the help of the superintendent and central office staff and, at the very least, the acquiescence of the school board and teachers' union. There is no way around this reality. The best of ideas and the most enthusiastic of responses to these ideas at the school level are not enough to make an adopted and implemented school improvement attempt a permanent fixture of the school.

It is common practice among the best school districts in the country for the superintendent and the central office staff to meet regularly with school principals. These meetings are typically held monthly, but often more frequently. They can last for a full day and often well into the evening. The purpose of the meetings is to exchange information and ideas about what is occurring in each of the schools. Principals are given an opportunity to update the superintendent and other administrators, including peers, on the last month's happenings in each school and to share plans for the next month. Superintendents and principals do not view these sessions as evaluation and review but as communication and assistance. Good ideas from schools become better ones as other principals and central office staff consider them. More importantly, these sessions allow the superintendent to "buy in" to local school improvement initiatives, and this buying in is the first step to ensure that the necessary support for institutionalization will be forthcoming.

Michael Fullan (1982) points out that adoption of a change does not occur without an advocate, and one of the most powerful advocates is the superintendent of schools with her or his staff and in combination with the school board. This conclusion is supported by many other studies (e.g., Berman and McLaughlin, 1977; 1979).

Leadership for School Improvement

The systems view of change depicted in Figure 12–1 emphasizes interactions among individual teachers, the school, the workflow of teaching and learning, and the broader political context as units of change. This view represents a strategy map for planning school improvement efforts and for increasing the possibility that such efforts will be not only adopted but also implemented and institutionalized. But the question remains: What should the principal do to help things along as each of the units of change is addressed? What are the *specific* principal behaviors associated with successful school improvement efforts?

Change Facilitator Styles

Let's begin our inquiry into this topic by describing the behavior of a principal whose school is, or has recently been, involved in a change effort. It is hard to separate all the aspects of a principal's change facilitator style from his or her general style or orientation; thus, you will want to focus on both the general style and the change style as we begin our analysis. What kind of leadership does the principal bring to the school? What does the leader stand for, and how effective is she or he in communicating these standards to teachers? What kind of interpersonal leader is the principal? How does the principal work to facilitate change that will result in school improvement? Before continuing further, turn to the Change Facilitator Styles Inventory (CFSI), which appears as Appendix 12–1; following the directions, describe the principal you have been thinking about.

The CFSI is based on an extensive research program investigating links between principal behaviors and successful school improvements (Hall, et al., 1983). This research was conducted at the Research and Development Center for Teacher Education at the University of Texas, Austin. The investigators were able to group principal leadership behaviors into three general change facilitator styles: Responder,

Manager, and Initiator. These three styles correspond to the R, M, and I response categories on the CFSI and are described in the following extract (Hall and Rutherford, 1983):

> *Responders* place heavy emphasis on allowing teachers and others the opportunity to take the lead. They believe their primary role is to maintain a smooth-running school by focusing on traditional administrative tasks, keeping teachers content, and treating students well. Teachers are viewed as strong professionals who are able to carry out their instructional role with little guidance. Responders emphasize the personal side of their relationships with teachers and others. Before they make decisions they often give everyone an opportunity to have input so as to weigh their feelings or to allow others to make the decision. A related characteristic is the tendency toward making decisions in terms of immediate circumstances rather than in terms of longer-range instructional or school goals. This seems to be due in part to their desire to please others and in part to their limited vision of how their school and staff should change in the future.
>
> *Managers* represent a broader range of behaviors. They demonstrate both responsive behaviors in answer to situations or people and they also initiate actions in support of the change effort. The variations in their behavior seem to be linked to their rapport with teachers and central office staff as well as how well they understand and buy into a particular change effort. Managers work without fanfare to provide basic support to facilitate teachers' use of the innovation. They keep teachers informed about decisions and are sensitive to teacher needs. They will defend their teachers from what are perceived as excessive demands. When they learn that the central office wants something to happen in their school, they then become very involved with their teachers in making it happen. Yet, they do not typically initiate attempts to move beyond the basics of what is imposed.
>
> *Initiators* have clear, decisive long-range policies and goals that transcend but include implementation of the current innovation. They tend to have very strong beliefs about what good schools and teaching should be like and work intensely to attain this vision. Decisions are made in relation to their goals for the school and in terms of what they believe to be best for students, which is based on current knowledge of classroom practice. Initiators have strong expectations for students, teachers, and themselves. They convey and monitor these expectations through frequent contacts with teachers and clear explication of how the school is to operate and how teachers are to teach. When they feel it is in the best interest of their school, particularly the students, Initiators will seek changes in district programs or policies or they will reinterpret them to suit the needs of the school. Initiators will be adamant but not unkind, they solicit input from staff and then decisions are made in terms of the goal of the school even if some are ruffled by their directness and high expectations. (84)

Which of these general change facilitator styles best corresponds with your response patterns on the CFSI? Can you estimate which of these styles were most and least associated with successful school improvement efforts? Hall and Rutherford (1983) found that Initiator principals were more likely to be successful than were Manager and Responder principals. Responders were least likely to be successful. As you review the principal behavior descriptions on the CFSI associated with each of these styles, note that Initiators have a clear sense of what needs to be accomplished and take more active roles in planning, prodding, encouraging, advising, participating, checking, stimulating, monitoring, and evaluating change efforts. Further, they assume more direct roles in obtaining and providing the necessary material and psychological support for successful change efforts.

Levels of Leadership Behavior

As a result of their research on principals at work, Kenneth A. Leithwood and Deborah J. Montgomery (1986) identified four levels of leadership behavior, each with a different focus and style and each with different consequences for principal effectiveness. They found that the "higher" the level of principal behavior the more effective the school. Effectiveness was defined as gains in student achievement in the "basics" and increases in student self-direction and problem solving.

Each of the levels represents increasingly complex and effective principalship behaviors. Principals functioning at level one, the *Administrator*, believe that it is the teacher's job to teach and the principal's job to run the school. Principals functioning at level two, the *Humanitarian*, believe that the basis of a sound education is a good interpersonal climate. Principals functioning at level three, the *Program Manager*, believe that their job is to provide the best possible programs for students. Principals functioning at level four, the *Systematic Problem Solver*, are committed to doing whatever is necessary by way of invention and delivery in order to give students the best possible chance to learn. Program Managers and Systematic Problem Solvers both bring to their practice a focus on students, but Program Managers are largely committed to proper implementation of officially sanctioned goals and programs. They are more dependent on established guidelines, resources, and procedures than are Systematic Problem Solvers.

> Systematic Problem Solvers are 'bottom liners' virtually all the time; bottom line is the goals for students by their school. Their focus is largely unconstrained by established practice and their client orientation leads them to the invention and delivery of whatever legitimate services are likely to realize the goals held by their school for students. (Leithwood and Montgomery, 1986:83)

Important to Liethwood and Montgomery's formulation is the concept of level. What administrators do at level one is not necessarily ineffective, only less effective than the other three levels if this behavior pattern is dominant. Humanitarians at level two carry with them some of the Administrator's style but focus primarily on more complex behaviors that emphasize human relationships. Though more effective than Administrators, Humanitarians are not as effective as Program Managers. Program Managers bring aspects of the Administrator and Humanitarian style to their practice but focus primarily on more complex matters of educational program development and implementation. And, finally, the strategic Problem Solvers focus primarily on students' success. This entrepreneurial stance is supported, nonetheless, by competent administrative, human relations, and program management skills.

Leithwood and Montgomery's research suggests that as principals come to view their jobs in more complex ways they become more effective operating at higher levels of practice. They recognize, of course, the important management demands in their job and the need to provide an environment that supports and enhances human relationships. But neither management nor human relations processes are viewed as ends in themselves. They believe that process always serves substance. The substance of the school is defined by its educational programs and levels of commitment to teaching and learning. But neither process nor substance can be viewed as something static. They are, instead, pursued in a context characterized by an array of demands, constraints, and choices. Realizing that expanding choices results in better schooling, principals at level four work for this expansion by taking a problem-solving, even entrepreneurial approach to their leadership practice.

Some Ethical Questions

Principals often feel uncomfortable when they are asked to assume fairly direct roles in bringing about change. Change is, after all, a form of "social engineering"; and, as one becomes more skilled at bringing about change, ethical issues are naturally raised. Are we talking about leadership, or are we really talking about manipulation? No easy answer exists to this question, but one thing is certain. Principals have an obligation to provide leadership to the school, and this involves following a course of action leading to school improvement. The change agent role is therefore unavoidable.

Kenneth Benne (1949) proposes a set of guidelines for principals to ensure that their change behavior is ethical. He believes that the engineering of change and the providing of pressure on groups and organizations to change must be collaborative. Collaboration suggests that principals and teachers form a change partnership, with each being aware of the intentions of others. Change intents are honest and straightforward. Teachers, for example, do not have to endure being "buttered up" today for the announced change of tomorrow.

The engineering of change should be educational to those involved in the process. "Educational" suggests that principals will try to help teachers to become more familiar with the process of problem solving and changing so that they are less dependent on her or him. Giving a teacher a solution is not as educational as helping the teacher muddle through a problem.

The engineering of change should be experimental. "Experimental" implies that changes will not be implemented for keeps but will be adopted tentatively until they have proven their worth or until a better solution comes along.

The engineering of change should be task-oriented; that is, controlled by the requirements of the problem and its effective solution rather than oriented to the maintenance or extension of prestige or power of the principal and others who are encouraging changes. Task orientation refers to one's primary motive for change. The principal should have job-related objectives in mind first—objectives that are concerned with improving teaching and learning for students. If such school improvement efforts are successful, the principal and others responsible for the change enjoy personal success and a certain amount of fame as well. These are the rewards for hard work, but they are not the reasons for bringing about the change in the first place. Principals who emphasize change to get attention from their supervisors or to improve their standing or influence in the school district may well be violating this ethical principle.

The Change Facilitating Team

This is a book for principals; thus it is natural to emphasize the principal's role and its significance in school improvement efforts. But the principal can't do it alone. In highlighting this issue, Hord, Hall, and Stiegelbauer (1983:1) point out: "This rhetoric, abundant in literature, quite obviously hangs like a heavy mantle on the principal. However, what is becoming equally certain and abundantly clear is that the principal does not bear the weight of leadership responsibility alone." Their research reveals that often one or two other key people in the school emerge as key change facilitators. As a result of their research on school improvement and analysis of the change literature, Loucks-Horsley and Hergert (1985:ix) conclude: "The principal is not *the* key to school improvement. Although the principal is important so are many other people." Teachers and supervisors have important roles to play, as do superintendents and specialists at the central office.

The research suggests that it may be more useful to view the principal as the leader of the change facilitating team (Hall, 1988), with as many as four change facilitators serving on the team. The principal, for example, might be viewed as the primary change facilitator. Very often a second change facilitator (assistant principal, department chairperson, resource teacher, or teacher on a special assignment) was identified by the researcher. Frequently a third level of change facilitator existed. Typically facilitators at this level were teachers whose roles were less formalized but whose help was substantial and sought by their peers (Hord et al., 1987). This group of facilitators served the process of change primarily by modeling the use of the new practices, disseminating information to other teachers, cheerleading, and providing support. The principals who were most effective in implementing change were team-oriented, working closely with these other levels of change facilitators. Often, structures were built that allowed them to work together as a change facilitator team.

> In some schools, they may meet each week to review data about the school improvement process, generate ideas, and plan who will do what during the ensuing week. When they meet again, they debrief to ascertain what went well and what needs more attention. In other schools we observe a more hierarchical organization of facilitators: the first CF (the principal) appeared to interact only with the second CF, who in turn related to the third CF. All communications flowed through this "chain of command." Whether the team of CFs has a "flat" or horizontal collegial structure or a more hierarchical one, however, the important aspects to remember are what they need to do as group. (Hord et al., 1987:85).

These researchers identified even a fourth category, the *external facilitator*. Frequently this role was filled by someone from the central office who served as a facilitative link between the office resources and the school.

The Meaning of Educational Change

One theme emerges from this discussion of the process of change. Though principals are important and their visions key in focusing attention on change and in successfully implementing the process of change, what counts in the end is bringing together the ideas and commitments of a variety of people who have a stake in the success of the school. As this process unfolds, principals can often find themselves on thin ice. They need to be clear about what it is that they want but cannot be so clear that they are providing people with road maps. They need to allow people to have an important say in shaping the direction of the school and deciding on the changes needed to get there, but they cannot be so detached that these individual aspirations remain more rhetorical than real. Michael Fullan (1982), after reviewing Lighthall's (1973) work, points out that there is strong support for the assertion that

> leadership commitment to a particular version of a change is negatively related to ability to implement it . . . educational change is a process of coming to grips with the *multiple* realities of people who are the main participants in implementing change. The leader who presupposes what the change should be and acts in ways which preclude others' realities is bound to fail. (82)

Key, of course, are the visions of teachers. If change is not responsive to the world of teaching as teachers experience it, it is likely to be viewed as irrelevant if not frivolous (Lortie, 1975). Fullan (1982) believes that the assumptions that principals and others make about change are key because they represent powerful, though frequently unconscious, sources of one's actions. His analysis of the process of change leads him to identify certain do's and don'ts assumptions as being basic to the successful implementation of educational change:

1. Do not assume that your version of what the change should be is the one that should or could be implemented. On the contrary, assume that one of the main purposes of the process of implementation is to exchange your reality of what should be through interaction with implementers and others concerned. Stated another way, assume that successful implementation consists of some transformation or continued development of initial ideas.
2. Assume that any significant innovation, if it is to result in change, requires individual implementers to work out their own meaning. Significant change involves a certain amount of ambiguity, ambivalence, and uncertainty for the individual about the meaning of the change. Thus, effective implementation is a *process of clarification*.
3. Assume that conflict and disagreement are not only inevitable but fundamental to successful change. Since any group of people possess multiple realities, any collective change attempt will necessarily involve conflict.

4. Assume that people need pressure to change (even in directions which they desire), but it will only be effective under conditions which allow them to react, to form their own position, to interact with other implementers, to obtain technical assistance, etc. Unless people are going to be replaced with others who have different desired characteristics, resocialization is at the heart of change.

5. Assume that effective change takes time. It is a process of "development in use." Unrealistic or undefined time-lines fail to recognize that implementation occurs developmentally.

6. Do not assume that the reason for lack of implementation is outright rejection of the values embodied in the change, or hard-core resistance to all change. Assume that there are a number of possible reasons: value rejection, inadequate resources to support implementation, insufficient time elapsed.

7. Do not expect all or even most people or groups to change. The complexity of change is such that it is totally impossible to bring about widespread reform in any large social system. Progress occurs when we take steps (e.g., by following the assumptions listed here) which *increase* the number of people affected. Our reach should exceed our grasp, but not by such a margin that we fall flat on our face. Instead of being discouraged by all that remains to be done, be encouraged by what has been accomplished by way of improvement resulting from your actions.

8. Assume that you will need a *plan* which is based on the above assumptions and which addresses the factors known to affect implementation (see the section below on guidelines for action). Knowledge of the change process is essential. Careful planning can bring about significant change on a fairly wide scale over a period of two or three years.

9. Assume that no amount of knowledge will ever make it totally clear what action should be taken. Action decisions are a combination of valid knowledge, political considerations, on-the-spot decisions, and intuition. Better knowledge of the change process will improve the mix of resources on which we draw, but it will never and should never represent the sole basis for decisions.

10. Assume that change is a frustrating, discouraging business. If all or some of the above assumptions cannot be made (a distinct possibility in some situations for some changes), do not expect significant change *as far as implementation is concerned* (Fullan, 1982:91–92).

School improvement may not be easy, but it is well within reach of most schools. Successful efforts depend on the principal's taking a comprehensive view of the problem. This view acknowledges the importance of leadership density and emphasizes implementation and institutionalization of change as well as adoption. Further, successful change efforts are directed to the four levels of the school's interacting system: individual, school, workflow, and administrative-political context.

References

Argyris, Chris. 1957. *Personality and Organizations.* New York: Harper & Row.

Baldridge, Victor A. 1971. "The Analysis of Organizational Change: A Human Relations Strategy Versus a Political Systems Strategy." Stanford, CA: R & D Memo #75, Stanford Center for R & D in Teaching, Stanford University.

Benne, Kenneth D. 1949. "Democratic Ethics and Social Engineering," *Progressive Education* 27(4).

Bennis, Warren, Kenneth D. Benne, and Robert Chin. 1969. *The Planning of Change*, 2d ed. New York: Holt, Rinehart and Winston.

Berman, Paul, and Milbrey Wallin McLaughlin. 1977. *Federal Programs Supporting Educational Change. Vol. VII Factors Affecting Implementation and Continuation.* Santa Monica, CA: Rand Corporation.

Berman, Paul, and Milbrey Wallin McLaughlin. 1979. *An Exploratory Study of School District Adaptations.* Santa Monica, CA: Rand Corporation.

Coffer, C. N., and M. H. Appley. 1964. *Motivation: Theory and Research.* New York: Wiley.

Crandall, David P. 1983. "The Teacher's Role in School Improvement," *Educational Leadership* 41(3), 6–9.

De Charms, Richard. 1968. *Personal Causation: The Internal Affective Determinants of Behavior.* New York: Academic Press.

Fullan, Michael. 1982. *The Meaning of Change.* New York: Teachers College Press.

Fuller, Frances F. 1969. "Concerns of Teachers: A Developmental Conceptualization," *American Educational Research Association Journal* 6(2).

Gaynor, Alan K. 1975. "The Study of Change in Educational Organizations: A Review of the Literature." Paper presented at the University Council for Educational Administration, Ohio State University Career Development Seminar, Columbus, March 27–30.

Geneen, Harold. 1984. *Managing.* Garden City, NY: Doubleday.

Goodlad, John I., and Frances M. Klein. 1970. *Behind the Classroom Door.* Worthington, OH: Charles A. Jones.

Hall, Gene E. 1988. "The Principal as Leader of the Change Facilitating Team," *Journal of Research and Development in Education* 22(1).

Hall, Gene E., and Susan F. Loucks. 1978. "Teacher Concerns as a Basis for Facilitating Staff Development," *Teachers College Record* 80(1).

Hall, Gene E., and William L. Rutherford. 1983. "Three Change Facilitator Styles: How Principals Affect Improvement Efforts." Paper presented at the Annual Meeting of the American Educational Research Association, Montreal, Canada, April.

Hall, Gene E., Shirley M. Hord, Leslie L. Huling, William L. Rutherford, and Suzanne M. Stiegelbauer. 1983. "Leadership Variables Associated with Successful School Improvement." Papers presented at the Annual Meeting of the American Educational Research Association, Montreal, Canada, April.

Hord, Shirley M., Gene E. Hall, and Suzanne Stiegelbauer. 1983. "Principals Don't Do It Alone: The Role of the Consigliere." Paper presented at the Annual Meeting of the American Educational Research Association, Montreal, Canada, April.

Hord, Shirley M., William L. Rutherford, Leslie Huling-Austin, and Gene E. Hall. 1987. *Taking Charge of Change.* Alexandria, VA: Association for Supervision and Curriculum Development.

Huberman, A. M., and D. P. Crandall. 1982. *People, Policies and Practices: Examining the Chain of School Improvement. Vol. IX: Implications for Action.* Andover, MA: The Network.

Huling, Leslie L., Gene E. Hall, Shirley M. Hord, and William L. Rutherford. 1983. "A Multi-Dimensional Approach for Assessing Implementation Success." Paper presented at the Annual Meeting of the American Educational Research Association, Montreal, Canada, April.

Hunter, Madeline. 1984. "Knowing, Teaching and Supervising," in Philip L. Hosford, Ed., *Using What We Know about Teaching.* Alexandria, VA: Yearbook of the Association for Supervision and Curriculum Development.

Katz, Daniel, and Robert L. Kahn. 1978. *The Social Psychology of Organizations*, 2d ed. New York: Wiley.

Kirst, Michael W. 1984. *Who Controls Our Schools?* New York: Freeman.

Leithwood, Kenneth A., and Deborah J. Montgomery. 1986. *Improving Principal Effectiveness: The Principal Profile.* Toronto: Ontario Institute for Studies in Education Press.

Lighthall, F. 1973. "Multiple Realities and Organizational Nonsolutions: An Essay on the Anatomy of Educational Innovations," *School Review*, February.

Likert, Rensis. 1967. *The Human Organization: Its Management and Value.* New York: McGraw-Hill.

Lortie, Dan. 1975. *Schoolteacher: A Sociological Study.* Chicago: University of Chicago Press.

Loucks-Horsley, Susan, and Leslie F. Hergert. 1985. *An Action Guide to School Improvement.* Arlington, VA: Association for Supervision and Curriculum Development and The Network.

Mealiea, Laird W. 1978. "Learned Behavior: The Key to Understanding and Preventing Employee Resistance to Change," *Group and Organizational Studies* 3(2), 211–223.

Miles, Matthew B. 1983. "Unraveling the Mystery of Institutionalization," *Educational Leadership* 41(3), 14–19.

Reddin, W. J. 1970. *Managerial Effectiveness.* New York: McGraw-Hill.

Rosenholtz, Susan J. 1989. *Teachers Workplace: A Social-Organizational Analysis.* New York: Longman.

Saronson, Seymour B. 1971. *The Culture of the School and the Problem of Change.* Boston: Allyn and Bacon.

Sergiovanni, T. J., and John E. Corbally, Eds. 1984. *Leadership and Organizational Culture.* Urbana-Champaign, IL: University of Illinois Press.

APPENDIX 12-1 Change Facilitator Styles Inventory

This inventory contains descriptions of principal behavior grouped by style. The items are drawn from actual research comparing more and less effective principals involved in school improvement. The inventory provides an opportunity for you to describe a principal you know (or perhaps yourself) and to compare your responses with the change facilitator styles of these principals.

Each item comprises three different descriptors of principal behavior. Using a total of 10 points, distribute points among the three to indicate the extent to which each describes your principal's behavior. Record your responses on the score sheet provided.

Score Sheet

Principal Behaviors		R	M	I	Totals
A. Vision	1.	___	___	___	10
	2.	___	___	___	10
	3.	___	___	___	10
B. Structuring the	4.	___	___	___	10
school as a	5.	___	___	___	10
work place	6.	___	___	___	10
	7.	___	___	___	10
	8.	___	___	___	10
C. Structuring	9.	___	___	___	10
involvement	10.	___	___	___	10
with change	11.	___	___	___	10
	12.	___	___	___	10
	13.	___	___	___	10
	14.	___	___	___	10
D. Sharing of	15.	___	___	___	10
responsibility	16.	___	___	___	10
	17.	___	___	___	10
E. Decision making	18.	___	___	___	10
	19.	___	___	___	10
	20.	___	___	___	10
F. Guiding and	21.	___	___	___	10
supporting	22.	___	___	___	10
	23.	___	___	___	10
	24.	___	___	___	10
	25.	___	___	___	10
	26.	___	___	___	10
G. Structuring	27.	___	___	___	10
his/her	28.	___	___	___	10
professional	29.	___	___	___	10
role	30.	___	___	___	10
	31.	___	___	___	10
	32.	___	___	___	10
	33.	___	___	___	10
	34.	___	___	___	10
	35.	___	___	___	10
	36.	___	___	___	10
	37.	___	___	___	10
	TOTALS				370

Score	Style Emphasis
0- 39	Very Low
40-136	Low
137-233	Medium
234-330	High
331-370	Very High

Change Facilitator Styles Inventory (CFSI)

Principal Behaviors

	R	M	I
A. Vision	1. Accepts district goals as school goals	Accepts district goals but makes adjustments at school level to accommodate particular needs of the school	Respects district goals but insists on goals for school that give priority to this school's student need
	2. Future goals/direction of school are determined in response to district level goals/priorities	Anticipates the instructional and management needs of school and plans for them	Takes initiative in identifying future goals and priorities for school and in preparing to meet them
	3. Responds to teachers', students' and parents' interest in the goals of the school and the district	Collaborates with others in reviewing and identifying school goals	Establishes framework of expectations for the school and involves others in setting goals within that framework
B. Structuring the school as a work place	4. Maintains low profile relative to day-by-day operation of school	Very actively involved in day-by-day management	Directs the ongoing operation of the school with emphasis on instruction through personal actions and clear designation of responsibility
	5. Grants teachers autonomy and independence, provides guidelines for students	Provides guidelines and expectations for teachers and students	Sets standards and expects high performance levels for teachers, students, and self
	6. Ensures that district and school policies are followed and strives to see that disruptions in the school day are minimal	Works with teachers, students, and parents to maintain effective operation of the school	First priority is the instructional program; personnel and collaborative efforts are directed at supporting that priority
	7. Responds to requests and needs as they arise in an effort to keep all persons involved with the school comfortable and satisfied	Expects all involved with the school to contribute to effective instruction and management in the school	Insists that all persons involved with the school give priority to teaching and learning
	8. Allows school norms to evolve over time	Helps establish and clarify norms for the school	Establishes, clarifies, and models norms for the school
C. Structuring involvement with change	9. Relies on information provided by other change facilitators, usually from outside the school, for knowledge of the innovation	Uses information from a variety of sources to gain knowledge of the innovation	Seeks out information from teachers, district personnel, and others to gain an understanding of the innovation and the changes required

APPENDIX 12–1 *(Continued)*

Principal Behaviors

	R	M	I
10.	Supports district expectations for change	Meets district expectations for change	Accommodates district expectations for change and pushes adjustments and additions that will benefit his/her school
11.	Sanctions the change process and strives to resolve conflicts when they arise	Involved regularly in the change process, sometimes with a focus on management and at other times with a focus on the impact of the change	Directs the change process in ways that lead to effective use by all teachers
12.	Expectations for teachers, relative to change, are given in general terms	Tells teachers that they are expected to use the innovation	Gives teachers specific expectations and steps regarding application of the change
13.	Monitors the change effort principally through brief, spontaneous conversations and unsolicited reports	Monitors the change effort through planned conversations with individuals and groups and from informal observations of instruction	Monitors the change effort through classroom observation, review of lesson plans, reports that reveal specific teacher involvement, and specific attention to the work of individual teachers.
14.	May discuss with the teacher information gained through monitoring	Discusses information gained through monitoring with teacher in relation to teacher's expected behavior	Gives direct feedback to teacher concerning information gained through monitoring, which includes a comparison with expected behaviors and a plan for next steps, possibly including improvements
D. Sharing of responsibility			
15.	Allows others to assume the responsibility for the change effort	Tends to do most of the intervening on the change effort but will share some responsibility	Will delegate to carefully chosen others some of the responsibility for the change effort
16.	Others who assume responsibility are more likely to be outside the school, e.g., district facilitators	Others who assume responsibility may come from within or from outside the school	Others who assume responsibility are likely to be from within the school

APPENDIX 12–1 (Continued)

Principal Behaviors

		R	M	I
E. Decision making	17.	Others who assume responsibility have considerable autonomy and independence in which responsibilities they assume and how they carry them out	Coordinates responsibilities and stays informed about how others are handling these responsibilities	First establishes which responsibilities will be delegated and how they are to be accomplished, then works with others and closely monitors the carrying out of tasks
	18.	Makes decisions required for ongoing operation of the school as deadlines for those decisions approach	Actively involved in routine decision making relative to instructional and administrative affairs	Handles routine decisions through established procedures and assigned responsibilities, thereby requiring minimal time
	19.	Makes decisions influenced by the immediate circumstances of the situation and formal policies	Makes decisions based on the norms and expectations that guide the school and the management needs of the school	Makes decisions based on the standard of high expectations and what is best for the school as a whole, particularly learning outcomes and the longer-term goals
	20.	Willingly allows others to participate in decision making or to make decisions independently	Allows others to participate in decision making but maintains control of the process through personal involvement	Allows others to participate in decision making and delegates decision making to others within carefully established parameters of established goals and expectations
F. Guiding and supporting	21.	Believes teachers are professionals and leaves them alone to do their work unless they request assistance or support	Believes teachers are a part of the total faculty and establishes guidelines for all teachers to be involved with the change effort	Believes teachers are responsible for developing the best possible instruction, so expectations for their involvement with innovation is clearly established
	22.	Responds quickly to requests for assistance and support in a way that is satisfying to the requester	Monitors the progress of the change effort and attempts to anticipate needed assistance and resources	Anticipates the need for assistance and resources and provides support as needed as well as sometimes in advance of potential blockages
	23.	Checks with teachers to see how things are going and to maintain awareness of any major problems	Maintains close contact with teachers involved in the change effort in an attempt to identify things that might be done to assist teachers with the change	Collects and uses information from a variety of sources to be aware of how the change effort is progressing and to plan interventions that will increase the probability of a successful, quality implementation

Principal Behaviors

	R	M	I
24.	Relies on whatever training is available with the innovation in order to aid in the development of teacher's knowledge and skill relative to the innovation	In addition to the regularly provided assistance, seeks out and uses sources within and outside the school to develop teacher knowledge and skills	Provides increased knowledge or skill needed by the teachers through possible utilization of personnel and resources within the building
25.	Provides general support for teachers as persons and as professionals	Provides support to individuals and to subgroups for specific purposes related to the change as well as to provide for their personal welfare	Provides direct programmatic support through interventions targeted to individuals and to the staff as a whole
26.	Tries to minimize the demands of the change effort on teachers	Moderates demands of the change effort to protect teacher's perceived overload	Keeps ever-present demands on teachers for effective implementation
G. Structuring his/her professional role			
27.	Sees role as administrator	Sees role as avoiding or minimizing problems so instruction may occur	Sees role as one of ensuring the school has a strong instructional program with teachers teaching students so they are able to learn
28.	Believes others will generate the initiative for any school improvement that is needed	Engages others in regular review of school situation to avoid any reduction in school effectiveness	Identifies areas in need of improvement and initiates action for change
29.	Relies primarily on others for introduction of new ideas into the school	Is alert to new ideas and introduces them to faculty or allows others in school to do so	Sorts through new ideas presented from within and from outside the school and implements those deemed to have high promise for school improvement
30.	Is concerned with how others view him	Is concerned with how others view the school	Is concerned with how others view the impact of the school on students
31.	Accepts the rules of the district	Lives by the rules of the district but goes beyond minimum expectations	Respects the rules of the district but determines behavior by what is required for maximum school effectiveness
32.	Opinions and concerns of others determine what will be accomplished and how.	Is consistent in setting and accomplishing tasks and does much of it himself/herself	Tasks determined and accomplished are consistent with school priorities but responsibility can be delegated to others

APPENDIX 12–1 *(Continued)*

Principal Behaviors

	R	M	I
33.	Maintains a general sense of "where the school is" and of how teachers are feeling about things	Is well informed about what is happening in the school and who is doing what	Maintains specific knowledge of all that is going on in the school through direct contact with the classroom, with individual teachers, and with students
34.	Responds to others in a manner intended to please them	Responds to others in a way that will be supportive of the operation of the school	Responds to others with concern but places student priorities above all else
35.	Develops minimal knowledge of what use of the innovation entails	Becomes knowledgeable about general use of the innovation and what is needed to support its use	Develops sufficient knowledge about use to be able to make specific teaching suggestions and to troubleshoot any problems that may emerge
36.	Indefinitely delays having staff do tasks if perceiving that staff are overloaded	Contends that staff are already very busy and paces requests and task loads accordingly	Will knowingly sacrifice short-term feelings of staff if doing a task now is necessary for the longer-term goals of the school
37.	Ideas are offered by each staff member, but one or two have dominant influence	Some ideas are offered by staff and some by the principal; then consensus is gradually developed	Seeks teachers' ideas as well as their reactions to her/his ideas; then priorities are set

The items on this inventory were identified as a result of an extensive research program investigating the relationship between principal behavior and successful school improvement. This program was conducted at the Research and Development Center for Teacher Education, University of Texas, Austin. The items are from Gene E. Hall and William L. Rutherford (1983), "Three Change Facilitator Styles: How Principals Affect Improvement Efforts," paper presented at the Annual Meeting of the American Educational Research Association, Montreal, April. Available from the RDCTE, Austin, TX, document number 3155. See also "Leadership Variables Associated with Successful School Improvement" (Austin, TX: RDCTE, 1983).

THE HEART
OF THE MATTER:
TEACHING AND
SUPERVISION

CHAPTER 13

Reflecting on Teaching and Supervision

Language is a form of power that can frame thoughts and shape meanings. Because of their thought-framing ability, words with metaphorical overtones are more powerful than ordinary words. The word *supervision*, for example, conjures thoughts of authority, control, hierarchy, and inspection in the minds of teachers. Borrowed from industrial settings, this word communicates role definitions and meanings typically not intended by principals, and these interpretations often hinder the development of helpful and useful supervisory programs. The word *supervision* is too much a part of our history for it to be wished away. Its negative overtones would be lessened considerably, however, if principals were clearer as to its intent, more specific as to its definition, less dogmatic about how it is to be implemented, more appreciative of its complexities, and more accepting of teachers as partners in its implementation.

Typically, successful schools are characterized by lively and diverse programs of supervision that are accepted as a natural part of the school's way of life. Principals and teachers are clear as to the purposes of the supervisory program and share responsibility for its implementation. Supervision is not defined narrowly as one best way uniformly applied to all. Instead, individual competency levels, needs, interests, professional maturity levels, and personal characteristics of teachers are all taken into account as supervisory strategies are developed and implemented. Further, supervision is viewed not as something done to teachers but as a process in which teachers participate as partners. In successful schools the emphasis in supervision is on understanding and improving teaching and learning, not on sorting or grading teachers. And, finally, the primary concern of principals is on building a viable, workable, and meaningful supervisory program. Attention is given to what is practical and what works rather than to building a system of supervision that takes too much time, talent, effort, and too many resources to be implemented in a useful and meaningful way.

A first step in building a practical and meaningful supervisory program is willingness by the principal and by teachers to face up to, struggle with, and accept a more complex view of supervision and evaluation. Required next is dealing with the negative stereotypes of supervision emerging from its history of hierarchy, dominance, and control. Both issues are of concern. Chapters 14 and 15 begin by clarifying definitions of supervision and examining its many purposes. Then, an analysis of what is involved in improving teaching and learning is provided by identifying critical teaching competency areas and knowledge domains. These dimensions are used to develop a framework for a supervisory program and for analyzing and describing supervision presently taking place in schools.

No one-best-way strategy, model, or set of procedures for supervision is provided. Instead, a differentiated system of supervision more in tune with growth levels, personality characteristics, needs and interests, and professional commitments of teachers is proposed. Within this differentiated system, consideration is given to the actual time available to the principal for supervision and to the purposes and tasks of supervision that are to be attended. Appropriate supervisory strategies are viewed in light of teacher needs and dispositions, time available to the principal, the task at hand or purpose intended for supervision, and professional competency level of teachers. Teaching modes and instructional strategies are additional concerns. As these change, appropriate supervisory strategies often need changing. Direct instruction formats, for example, call for different supervisory techniques than would be used in more informal teaching and learning approaches. A sound supervisory system reflects these differences by being flexible and by offering options to teachers. As teachers became more professionally confident and competent, the supervision they receive should change to reflect this growth.

Teachers differ, too, with respect to their work styles and needs. Those who prefer to work alone, who require more structure in their work, and who are highly "task-oriented," for example, may not respond as well to collegial or team-based supervision as might teachers with higher social interaction needs or higher tolerances for ambiguity in their work. Typically, these teachers find a more structured and direct approach, or a more structured and independent approach, to supervision to be more satisfying and useful—strategies that teachers with higher social interaction needs may not view as suitable. This prelude is intended to accent the themes of Part V. Reflective practice in supervision is sensitive to a wide array of differences existing among teachers; unless these differences are accommodated, teachers will not consider the supervision they receive to be very helpful.

Supervision and Evaluation

When the focus of supervision is on teaching and learning, evaluation is an unavoidable aspect of the process. The literature is filled with reports and scenarios highlighting the disdain with which teachers regard evaluation (see, for example, Blumberg, 1980). One reason for such attitudes is that evaluation has been too narrowly defined in both purpose and method. Evaluation is, and will remain, an integral part of the process of supervision, and this reality cannot be ignored by principals and teachers. Attempts to mask evaluation aspects of supervision by avoiding use of the term, by denying that evaluation occurs, or by declaring that evaluation is reserved only for the annual administrative review of one's teaching performance will not be helpful. Such claims are viewed suspiciously by teachers and for good reason—evaluation cannot be separated from supervision.

Principals can help shift the focus of attention from whether or not evaluation does or should exist to expanding the meaning of evaluation within supervision. Evaluation, for example, is often defined narrowly as a process for calculating the extent to which educational programs (see Chapter 9) or teachers measure up to *preexisting standards*. Standards might be a program goal or teaching intent, or perhaps a list of "desirable" teaching competencies or performance criteria. Broader conceptions of evaluation include describing what is going on in a particular classroom, discovering learning outcomes actually achieved, and assessing their worth. In broader conceptions, the focus of evaluation is less on measuring and more on describing and illuminating teaching and learning events as well as on identifying the array of meanings that these events have for different people. Evaluation broadly conceived involves *judgment* more than measurement. Judgments of teaching and learning are less fixed, more personal, and are embedded in a particular context or situation (Dewey, 1958). Of interest in judgmental evaluation are *particular* teachers and students, *specific* teaching situations and events, and the *actual* teaching and learning issues, understandings and meanings emerging from teaching. Though measuring against preexisting standards has its place in the process of supervision and evaluation, the present onerous view of evaluation will be greatly lessened if principals emphasize judgmental aspects.

Using the word *evaluation* in its ordinary, rather than technical, sense will also help dissipate its negative effects among teachers. Commonplace in our ordinary lives, evaluation is an inescapable aspect of most of what we do. Whether we are buying a pair of shoes, selecting a recipe for a dinner party, rearranging the living-room furniture or enjoying a movie, baseball game, or art show, evaluation is part of the process. In its ordinary sense, evaluation means to discern, understand, and appreciate, on the one hand, and to value, judge, and decide on the other. These very same natural and ordinary processes are at play in evaluating teaching. As in ordinary life, these processes serve to heighten our understanding and appreciation of teaching and to inform our intuition as we make decisions about teaching. Heightened sensitivity and informed intuition are the trademarks of accomplished practice in all the major professions. It is by increasing and informing their sensitivities and intuitions that attorneys, architects, and physicians make better practice decisions and improve their performance. Professional practice in teaching, supervision, and the principalship improve similarly.

In reflective practice, supervision and evaluation of teaching look for answers to the following questions:

What is actually going on in this classroom?

What is the teacher and what are students actually doing?

What are the actual learning outcomes?

What ought to be going on in this classroom given our overall goals, educational platform, knowledge of how youngsters learn, and understandings of the structure of the subject matter to be taught

What do these events and activities of teaching and learning mean to teachers, students, and others?

What are the personal meanings that students accumulate regardless of teacher intents?

How do teacher and principal interpretations of teaching reality differ?

What actions should be taken to bring about even greater understanding of teaching and learning and better congruence between our actions and beliefs?

These questions provide a broader and more complex conception of the supervisory process than that implied just in rating teachers or in measuring outcomes for comparison with stated intents.

Purposes

The multifaceted nature of teacher supervision and evaluation can be illustrated by providing a framework for describing and bringing together key dimensions of the process. Included in this framework will be general purposes of supervision and evaluation, specific perspectives that stem from these purposes, key competency areas that serve as benchmarks for evaluation, and critical knowledge areas that help define and describe teaching competence. This framework is designed to help principals analyze supervisory problems and plan supervisory strategies.

What is supervision for? Who is to be served? Why evaluate? How one answers such questions determines how one approaches the tasks of supervision and evaluation and influences the relationships emerging among teachers and between teachers and the principal. Supervision and evaluation have many purposes. These range from ensuring that minimum standards are being met and that teachers are being faithful to the school's overall purposes and educational platform, to helping teachers grow and develop as persons and professionals.

Purposes can be grouped into three major categories:

1. *Quality control.* The principal is responsible for monitoring teaching and learning in her or his school and does so by visiting classrooms, touring the school, talking with people, and visiting with students.

2. *Professional development.* Helping teachers to grow and to develop in their understanding of teaching and classroom life, in improving basic teaching skills, and in expanding their knowledge and use of teaching repertoires is the second purpose of supervision.

3. *Teacher motivation.* Often overlooked, but important nonetheless, is a third purpose of supervision—building and nurturing motivation and commitment to teaching, to the school's overall purposes, and to the school's defining educational platform.

One hallmark of a good supervisory system is that it reflects these multiple purposes. No supervisory system based on a single purpose can succeed over time. A system that focuses only on quality control invites difficulties with teachers and lacks needed expansive qualities. By the same token, a supervisory system concerned *solely* with providing support and help to teachers (and thus, by omission, neglects teaching deficiencies and instances where overriding purposes and defining platforms are ignored) is not sufficiently comprehensive. Quality control and teacher improvement are, therefore, basic purposes that should drive any system of supervision and evaluation. A third purpose, often neglected but important in the long run, is that of teacher motivation. Overwhelming evidence exists suggesting that "knowledge of results" is an important ingredient in increasing a person's motivation to work and in building commitment and loyalty to one's job (Hackman and Oldham, 1976; Hackman et al., 1975).

Different Purposes, Different Standards

Different teacher-evaluation purposes require different teacher-evaluation standards and criteria. When the purpose is quality control to ensure that teachers measure up, standards, criteria, expectations, and procedures take one form. When the purpose is professional improvement to help increase teachers' understanding and enhanced teaching practice, standards, criteria, expectations, and procedures take on a different form. In evaluation for quality control the process is formal and documented; criteria are explicit and standards are uniform for all teachers; criteria are legally defensible as being central to basic teaching competence; the emphasis is on teachers meeting requirements of minimum acceptability; and responsibility for evaluation is in the hands of administrators and other designated officials. When the purpose of teacher evaluation is professional improvement, the process is informal; criteria are tailored to the needs and capabilities of individual teachers; criteria are considered to be appropriate and useful to teachers before they are included in the evaluation; the emphasis is on helping teachers reach agreed-upon professional development goals; and teachers assume major responsibility for the process by engaging in self-evaluation and collegial evaluation, and by obtaining evaluation information from students.

The outcome of evaluation for quality control is the protection of students and the public from incompetent teaching. Unquestionably this is an important outcome and a highly significant responsibility for principals and other supervisors. The outcome of evaluation for professional improvement is quite different. Rather than ensuring minimum acceptability in teaching, professional improvement guarantees quality teaching and schooling for the students and the public.

The *80/20 quality rule* spells out quite clearly what the balance of emphasis should be as schools engage in teacher evaluation. *When more than 20 percent of the principal's time and money is expended in evaluation for quality control or less than 80 percent of the principal's time and money is spent in professional improvement, quality schooling suffers.* The 80/20 quality rule provides a framework for those responsible for evaluation of teachers to evaluate whether their efforts are indeed directed toward quality schooling. In making this assessment, one should give less attention to the rhetoric that one hears (that is, to what those responsible for teacher evaluation say their purposes are) but more to the standards and procedures that they use. The standards and procedures associated with each of the two purposes of evaluation are outlined in Exhibit 13–1. If the standards at the left side of the exhibit are emphasized, quality control is the purpose of the evaluation regardless of what is claimed.

Teaching Competency Areas

The typical evaluation program puts the emphasis on the wrong thing. It relies almost exclusively on classroom observations of teaching behaviors and recording the presence or absence of these behaviors on instruments and forms. This results in placing the emphasis on whether the teacher can do the job as required while being observed. Even if it were possible to identify the correct list of teaching behaviors, the approach is still narrow. A good evaluation is not only concerned with "can do" but with other teaching competency areas as well.

What are the major competency areas for which teachers should be accountable? Teachers should *know how* to do their jobs and to keep this knowledge current. The areas of knowledge for professional teaching include purposes, students, subject matter to be taught, and teaching techniques. But knowing and understanding are not enough; teachers should be able to put this knowledge to work—to

EXHIBIT 13–1 Purposes and Standards for Evaluation

Purposes	
Quality control (ensuring that teachers meet acceptable levels of performance)	Professional improvement (increasing understanding of teaching and enhancing practice)

Standards	
The process is formal and documented.	The process is informal.
Criteria are explicit, standard, and uniform for all teachers.	Criteria are tailored to needs and capabilities of individual teachers.
Criteria are legally defensible as being central to basic teaching competence.	Criteria are considered appropriate and useful to teachers.
Emphasis is on meeting minimum requirements of acceptability.	Emphasis is on helping teachers reach agreed-upon professional development goals.
Evaluation by administrators and other designated officials counts the most.	Self-evaluation, collegial evaluation, and evaluation information for students count the most.

Outcome	
Protects students and the public from incompetent teaching.	Guarantees quality teaching and schooling for students and the public.

The 80/20 Quality Rule: When more than 20 percent of supervisory time and money is expended in evaluation for quality control *or* less than 80 percent of supervisory time and money is expended in professional improvement, quality schooling suffers.

From T. J. Sergiovanni and R. J. Starratt (1988), *Supervision Human Perspectives,* 4th ed., p. 383.

demonstrate that they *can do* the job of teaching. Demonstrating knowledge, however, is a fairly low-level competency. Most teachers are competent enough and adept enough to come up with the right teaching performance when they are required to do so. More important is whether they *will do* the job well consistently and on a sustained basis. Finally, all professionals are expected to engage in a lifelong commitment to self-improvement. Self-improvement is the *will-grow* competency area. Self-employed professionals, such as physicians and attorneys, are forced by competition and by more visible performance outputs to give major attention to the will-grow dimension. Teachers are "organizational" professionals whose "products" are difficult to measure, and they have not felt as much external pressure for continued professional development. Increasingly, however, school districts are making the will-grow dimension a significant part of their supervision and evaluation program. As teachers strive for further professionalism, they too recognize the importance of this dimension.

A comprehensive system of supervision and evaluation is, therefore, concerned with all four professional development competency areas: knowledge about teaching, ability to demonstrate this knowledge by actual teaching under observation, willingness to sustain this ability continuously, and demonstration of a commitment to continuous professional growth. Though each of the competency areas represents a discrete category that suggests different evaluation strategies, the four remain largely interdependent in practice. When observing classrooms, principals naturally are interested in the knowledge base exhibited by teachers. Most observations, in turn, lead to issues and ideas that form the basis for informing continuing growth plans and more formal staff development programs.

Substantive Aspects of Professional Development

When one speaks of knowledge about teaching, demonstrating this knowledge, and improving one's teaching, what substance areas are of concern? Rubin (1975) has identified four critical areas in good teaching that he believes can be improved through supervision:

- The teacher's sense of purpose
- The teacher's perception of students
- The teacher's knowledge of subject matter
- The teacher's mastery of technique

Sense of purpose and perception of students represent values, beliefs, assumptions, and action theories that teachers hold about the nature of knowledge, how students learn, appropriate relationships between students and teachers, and other factors. Composing the teacher's educational platform, they thus become the basis for decisions made about classroom organization and teaching. For example, a teacher who views teaching as primarily the dissemination of information will likely rely heavily on direct instruction as a teaching methodology and on formally structured classroom arrangements as a method of organizing for teaching. A teacher who views youngsters as being basically trustworthy and interested in learning is likely to share responsibility for decisions about learning, and so on. A principal who was interested in reducing the amount of teacher talk in a given classroom or in increasing the amount of student responsibility in another would have to contend with the critical considerations of purposes and perceptions as key components of the teachers' educational platforms.

The third factor in good teaching is the teacher's knowledge of subject matter to be taught. Rubin (1975) notes:

> There is considerable difference between the kind of teaching that goes on when teachers have an intimate acquaintance with the content of the lesson and when the acquaintance is only peripheral. When teachers are genuinely knowledgeable, when they know their subject well enough to discriminate between the seminal ideas and the secondary matter, when they go beyond what is in the textbook, the quality of pedagogy becomes extraordinarily impressive. For it is only when a teacher has a consummate grasp of, say arithmetic, physics, or history, that their meaning can be turned outward and brought to bear upon the learner's personal experience. Relevancy lies less in the inherent nature of a subject than in its relationship to the child's frame of reference. In the hands of a skilled teacher, poetry can be taught with success and profit to ghetto children. (47)

Though content versus process arguments continue in teaching, both aspects are necessary. The less a teacher knows about a particular subject, the more trivial is teaching likely to be. Content is important. Still, one can have a great appreciation of a particular field of study and not be able to disclose its wonder and excitement effectively. Shulman (1989) believes that teaching what one knows to someone else represents a distinct level of knowledge different from each of the other five levels of Bloom's taxonomy. The substance of this level is the ability to create a bridge between what a teacher knows and the students' experiences. To Shulman, content and pedagogy are inseparable. Mastery of technique, knowing how this technique relates to the subject matter one wants to teach (Stodolsky, 1988), classroom organization and management, and other pedagogical skills make up the fourth critical dimension of effective teaching. A comprehensive system of supervision and evaluation is concerned with all four substance areas: the teacher's conception of purpose, sensitivities to students, intimacy with subject matter, and basic repertoires of teaching techniques.

Figure 13–1 combines professional development competency areas and teaching substances areas to provide an "angle" for appreciating the complexity involved in supervision and evaluation, for analyzing existing supervisory programs, and for planning future strategies. Professional competency areas represent the range that should be included in a comprehensive supervision and evaluation system. Substance areas represent the content concerns to be included.

In sum, supervision and evaluation are concerned with the extent to which teachers demonstrate they know how, can do, will do, and will grow in such teaching knowledge areas as purpose, students, subject matter, and teaching techniques. The

Professional Development Competency Areas

Teaching Substance Areas	Knows how	Can do	Will do	Will grow
Purpose				
Students				
Subject Matter				
Teaching Techniques				

FIGURE 13-1 Competency and Substance Areas in Supervision and Evaluation

following questions provide examples of evaluation concerns raised in Figure 13-1. Within each substance area, *know how, can do, will do,* and *will grow* questions are provided:

1. *Sense of purpose.* To what extent does a teacher know and understand how management strategies such as Gordon's TET technique and behavior modification techniques work, what the philosophical base of each is, what the advantages and disadvantages of each are, and under which circumstances would each be more or less effective? Can and will the teacher demonstrate these two approaches to classroom management? Is there evidence that the teacher is growing in knowledge and skill in using these and other classroom management techniques?

2. *Knowledge of students.* Is the teacher sensitive to, and does the teacher know about, problems of peer identity among students and pressures for conformity that students face at certain ages and grade levels? Does the teacher understand how peer pressure can affect student motivation, classroom attention, voluntary participation in class, and other activities? Does the teacher exhibit knowledge about how to cope with peer pressure? Can and will the teacher demonstrate this knowledge by effective planning and teaching? Does the teacher show a commitment to increasing competence and skill in this area?

3. *Knowledge of subject matter.* Does the teacher have a firm grasp of the subject matter in the area she or he is teaching? Is there evidence, for example, that the teacher has an adequate cognitive map of the subject, appreciates the structure of knowledge inherent in the disciplinary base of the subject, and understands the major concepts undergirding this structure? Does the teacher demonstrate this mastery in her or his teaching? Is there evidence that concept attainment and other higher-level cognitive concerns are continuously emphasized? In what ways does the teacher keep up with expanding knowledge in her or his field?

4. *Mastery of technique.* Is the teacher knowledgeable about an array of teaching methods and strategies? Does the teacher show sensitivity to the conditions under which each is more or less effective? Can the teacher demonstrate a variety of techniques in teaching? Does this ability to demonstrate variety occur continuously? Is there evidence that the teacher expands her or his repertoire of teaching over time? Is there evidence that the teacher is becoming more effective in matching teaching strategies to circumstances? What is the link between the subject being taught and how it is taught? Do methods change when content changes? How successful is the teaching in building bridges between the teacher's knowledge and student experiences?

When one takes into account different evaluation purposes and perspectives and different teaching competence and substance areas, it becomes clear that limiting one's supervision and evaluation strategy to only classroom observation, rating scales, paper and pencil tests, target setting, clinical supervision, portfolio development, or any other *single* strategy does not account for the complexities involved in providing a comprehensive, meaningful, and useful system of evaluation. In sum, principals are responsible for the school's supervisory program. At the very minimum, this responsibility includes ensuring that a helpful, useful, and comprehensive system of supervision is operating. Teachers should report that they find the system helpful and satisfying. The following are questions that can reasonably be asked in evaluating a school's supervisory program:

- Are teachers involved in shaping, implementing, and evaluating the supervisory program?
- Are multiple purposes provided for? Does the program, for example, address issues of quality control, professional development, and teacher motivation and commitment? Are formative, summative, and diagnostic perspectives all included in the program?
- Is the program sufficiently comprehensive to include *know how, can do, will do,* and *will grow* as basic teaching performance expectations?
- Does the program focus on improving knowledge and skill in such basic teaching essentials as purpose, student needs and characteristics, subject matter, and teaching techniques?

These questions highlight the importance of including formal and informal staff development programs as part of the school's overall design for supervision. The major emphasis in supervision should be on professional growth and development; thus, its link to staff development is inseparable. Supervision is a form of staff development, and staff development programs are often extensions of supervision. Both should be planned and provided as *interdependent* parts of a school's overall commitment to striving for quality.

The Clinical Mind in Teaching and Supervision

If supervision is to work well, it must accommodate to the clinical mind of teachers. Don Hogben (1981) maintains that teachers and other professional practitioners view their work quite differently than do theoreticians or researchers. They have, he concludes, a different world view. He draws his conclusions from Freidson's (1972) extensive examination of the profession of medicine and accepts for teachers the concept of "clinical mentality" as advanced by Freidson. Professionals, he maintains, are possessed by a clinical mentality that provides them with a view of work at odds with theoretical views.

In comparing clinically minded medical professionals with medical researchers and theoreticians, Hogben (1981) identifies four major differences. First, *professionals aim at action*, not at knowledge. Doing something, indeed anything, is always preferable to doing nothing. As they practice, teachers and supervisors are more likely to take action when faced with a problem they do not understand very well than to wait for theory and research to unravel the problem. They prefer action over inaction even when such action has little chance of success. In this action process, supervisors and teachers are more likely to seek "useful" than "ideal" knowledge. They want to understand the immediate problem they face, and they want help with its resolution. Useful knowledge and increased understanding are prized because they support action.

It is clear that scientific knowledge verified by theory and research does exist and is of great interest to professionals as a basis for determining courses of action. It would be irresponsible, for example, for teachers and supervisors to ignore the findings from the teaching effectiveness–school effectiveness research. Nonetheless, the unique situations that professionals face make it difficult for them to simply apply such scientific knowledge. Within the medical specialty of ophthalmology, for example, it is estimated that 80 percent of the cases of patient complaints do not fall into the available standard categories of diagnosis or treatment. Physicians are grateful for occasions when standard treatment repertoires *do* fit the problems they face, but they must take action, nonetheless, in the vast majority of other cases. By taking action, they seek to make sense of the problems they face and to *create knowledge in use*. They rely heavily on *informed* intuition to fill in the gaps between what is known and unknown. Informed intuition and creating knowledge in use are the hallmarks of accomplished practice in any profession.

Despite exaggerated claims to the contrary, a single concept of good teaching cannot be established empirically, and such a concept cannot exist in an absolute sense. Indeed, different versions of good teaching exist, each depending on a different world view, different interests, and different purposes. It is possible to agree on a version of good teaching. Disagreement would depend not so much on facts or on empirically established reality but on a process of justification. Justification, in turn, is a product of our values and interests.

The second characteristic of the clinical mind is that professionals *need to believe in what they are doing* as they practice. They need to believe that their actions do more good than harm and that they are effective in solving problems and serving clients. Teachers, Hogben (1981:2) concludes, "must strongly believe in what they are doing because their daily practices and decisions are rarely followed by pupil improvement which can be tied unequivocally to those practices and decisions." The theoretical perspective in supervision and teaching encourages detachment and healthy skepticism, but the world of practice is characterized by close attachment and commitment to one's course of action.

The third characteristic is the heavy reliance of professionals on their own *firsthand experiences* and on the experiences of other professionals in similar settings with whom they work. They rely more on results than on theory. They trust their own accumulated experiences in making decisions about practice than they do abstract principles. It is not surprising, therefore, that researchers such as Haller (1968) and Keenan (1974) found teachers to rely primarily on other teachers as sources of new ideas and sources of help in solving problems they faced.

The final characteristic of the clinical mind is that "the practitioner is very prone to emphasize the idea of *indeterminancy* or uncertainty, not the idea of regularity of lawful, scientific behavior" (Hogben, 1981:2). The issue may be less whether professionals want to emphasize uncertainty than that they must. Using medicine as an example again, a recent review of the research reveals that only about 15 percent of medical procedures in common use are validated by scientific studies (Gross, 1984). The figure in education would be even less. How incongruous it would be to ignore the complexities of the problems faced in schools and the fragility of the scientific base for teaching by abandoning indeterminancy and uncertainty in favor of a single conception of teaching or a one best way to supervise and evaluate.

Reflective Practice Issues

A practical approach to supervision seeks to build professional knowledge that promotes understanding, is useful in solving problems, and guides professional action. Professional knowledge is created in use as professionals, faced with ill-defined, unique, and constantly changing problems, decide courses of action. Teachers create knowledge in use, and the process of supervision should help in this effort.

Many issues emerge as supervision becomes more practical. Who, for example, is being evaluated and what is being evaluated as supervision unfolds? Identifying the *object* of evaluation and the *subject* who conducts the evaluation may be more difficult than is first apparent. Traditionally, the supervisor has been the subject who evaluates the teacher as the object of the evaluation. Teaching itself is of concern, but no distinction is made between the teacher and teaching. An improved conception of the process of supervision places the emphasis on teaching itself as the object of evaluation. Of course, teacher and teaching can never be actually separated, nor is that desirable, but "teacher" can be temporarily "suspended" as both teacher and supervisor look together at teaching. Supervision of this type typically seeks to develop a portrait, map, record, or data display to represent and describe the teaching and learning that are taking place. The emphasis is on collecting information to be used *conceptually* for informing judgments about teaching.

This is in contrast to collecting information as *evidence* to prescribe and justify decisions about teaching (Kennedy, 1984).

A second issue is the matter of objectivity. Supervisors don't come to the classroom as neutral parties. Being blessed with human qualities and linked to traditions, preferences, and beliefs, they have a preunderstanding of teaching. This preunderstanding, perhaps in the form of a bias, comes to play in every facet of the evaluation, from deciding what issues will be included in the evaluation to what methods will be used in the evaluation and finally to what information will be collected. In fact, this preunderstanding by the supervisor helps in deciding how the evaluation will be conducted and what its findings mean. A principal who identifies with direct instruction, for example, will find some observed teaching issues to be of more significance than others and, as a result, will choose certain data collection methods over others. Whatever one's view of teaching, it leads to certain decisions that "stack the deck" in determining what will happen, how it will happen, and what it means after it happens. The nature and characteristics of evaluation knowledge are determined by the way in which the supervisor understands them; this understanding weighs heavily in determining the outcome of the evaluation. To understand an evaluation, therefore, one must understand the evaluator, and every evaluation reflects the professional history of the evaluator.

The use of ordinary versus technical language is yet another important issue that must be addressed. What is the role of language in the process of supervision? How is language a source of power for the supervisor? The language of supervisory conferences is frequently theoretical, abstract, and remote. Sometimes this language is a function of having used rating scales, personality inventories, technical data collection strategies, and other devices. These highly theoretical devices introduce into the process of supervision an abstract language system that often has little to do with the actual teaching and learning that have occurred in a particular classroom or in a particular context. Few teachers are likely to find the generic lists of teaching behaviors found on instruments such as the Tennessee Instructional Model, the Florida Performance Measurement System, or the Texas Teacher Appraisal System as being specifically and particularly relevant to their teaching, their students, their purposes, their conceptions of the subject matter, the unique problems they face, and other idiosyncratic characteristics of the teaching situation. The resulting conversation with supervisors, therefore, is likely to be technical and abstract, indeed pedantic rather than real. As Greenfield (1982:8) points out: "Language is power. It literally makes reality appear and disappear. Those who control language control thought—and thereby themselves and others." Since the supervisor is typically in command of the data and is the person who chooses the methods of observation, she or he has an inordinate supremacy over the language system used. A teacher in this situation can be heavily dominated by this technical language, by the ordinary authority of the supervisor, and by the information monopoly the supervisor possesses from controlling the method of evaluation and having collected the evaluation information. Sometimes teachers react to this situation by joining with the supervisor and also use abstract language. When this happens, the process of supervision is intellectualized away in a sea of verbiage, with neither meaning or change likely.

An alternative to highly abstract and technical language is to use more ordinary and practical language, the language of classrooms and teachers, the language of particular instances and specific occasions. For this to be accomplished, much less reliance needs to be placed on deciding instruments to be used and criteria to be applied in an evaluation *beforehand* and on supervisors remaining in control of the evaluation process. Instead, what will be evaluated and how evaluation will take place should be decided on by teachers and supervisors together. They should rely on information collection devices, schedules, and other means that grow out of this sharing. Teachers should be equal partners in the process of supervision and evaluation.

These issues can be summarized in the form of assertions as follows:

- Since situations of practice are characterized by unique events, uniform answers to problems are not likely to be very helpful.
- Since teachers, supervisors, and students bring to the classroom beliefs, assumptions, values, opinions, preferences, and predispositions, objective and value-free supervisor strategies are not likely to address issues of importance.
- Since uncertainty and complexity are normal aspects of the process of teaching, intuition becomes necessary to fill in the gaps between what can be specified as known and what is not known.
- Since reality in practice does not exist separate from persons involved in teaching and supervising, the process of knowing cannot be separated from what is to be known and from those involved in knowing.
- Since evaluation reality is linked to the observer and to decisions she or he makes about methods of observation, it is reality constructed as an artifact of the supervisory situation.
- Since supervision is context-bound and situationally determined, the language of actual classroom life and actual teaching events will be listened to, rather than theoretical language or the language of rating scales and other measurement devices.

Ordinary practice is typically characterized by a uniform system of supervision based on a single conception of "good" teaching and a narrow view of educational program. By contrast, reflective practice in supervision is characterized by the view that *no one best way exists to teach*. Instead, appropriate teaching strategies and tactics depend on goals and objectives being pursued and the desired curriculum context for learning. Accomplished practice within teaching is characterized by using an array of teaching repertoires. Reflective teachers select from this array specific strategies suitable to intentions and contexts. Thus, teaching strategies ranging from highly direct, teacher-controlled, and narrowly focused to very indirect, student-centered, and widely focused have appropriate roles to play in teaching and learning.

The principal's supervisory strategies should reflect differences in teaching formats. One approach to accommodating differences is the establishment of a differentiated system of supervision (Glatthorn, 1984) that provides teachers with an array of options and formats from which they may choose. Options are a reflective response to differences in personality, needs, professional development levels, and learning styles. Included in this range would be options allowing teachers who are so inclined to engage in collegial or peer supervision and allowing other teachers to select a highly individualized option characterized by self-pacing and working alone, should this option be viewed as more suitable.

A differentiated system of supervision should function within, and be consistent with, an overarching framework. This framework would comprise the school's purposes, educational and management platforms, and other defining dimensions of the school's culture, all of which should be reflected in supervising and teaching. Thus, *in differentiated supervision, not anything goes.* In schools where active learning is prized, for example, this characteristic should be present in the vast majority of teaching strategies observed. In schools committed to the concept of leadership density and to the sharing of professional responsibility for growth and improvement, selected supervisory strategies should be characterized by high teacher involvement. Other values of the school's overarching framework would be reflected similarly. Chapter 14 provides examples of supervisory options available to principals who opt for differentiated supervision. Of concern also is how one matches options for supervision to the needs, learning styles, and developmental levels of teachers.

Moreover, all educational settings, regardless of teaching approach, purpose, or desired curriculum context, should be characterized by a certain caring and warmth toward students and a sensitive recognition of their personhood. Advocating variety in teaching does not belie the necessity for all approaches to contain these nurturing characteristics. Despite stereotypes to the contrary, informal, discussion-oriented, and student-centered classrooms have no monopoly on warmth. Many informal settings do result in warmth for students, but more effective structured and teacher-centered classrooms can also be characterized by warmth. Tikunoff, Berliner, and Rist (1975), for example, found higher-achieving, structured, and teacher-centered classes to be cooperative, democratic, and warm, whereas low-achieving, structured, and teacher-centered classes were characterized by belittling and shaming of students and by teacher use of sarcasm. Solomon and Kendall (1976) report that criticisms of student behavior, such as scolding, ridicule and sarcasm, were consistently and negatively related to student achievement in the classrooms they studied. Despite the fact that certain settings for learning and certain teaching approaches may have greater *potential* for providing warmth and support of classroom climates, teaching approaches and student climates are relatively independent, with no one approach ensuring warmth or excluding warmth. It is the teacher who makes the critical difference. Warmth in a given classroom is more a function of the teacher than of a particular teaching strategy or technique.

References

Blumberg, Art. 1980. *Supervisors and Teachers: A Private Cold War.* 2d ed. Berkeley, CA: McCutchan.

Dewey, John. 1958. *Art as Experience.* New York: Putnam.

Filley, Alan C., and Robert J. House. 1969. *Managerial Process and Organizational Behavior*. Glenview, IL: Scott, Foresman.

Freidson, E. 1972. *Profession of Medicine: A Study of the Sociology of Applied Knowledge*. New York: Dodd Mead.

Glatthorn, Allan A. 1984. *Differentiated Supervision*. Alexandria, VA: Association for Supervision and Curriculum Development.

Goldhammer, Robert. 1969. *Clinical Supervision: Special Methods for the Supervision of Teachers*. New York: Holt, Rinehart and Winston.

Greenfield, Thomas B. 1982. "Against Group Mind: An Anarchistic Theory of Education," *McGill Journal of Education* 17(1).

Gross, Stanley J. 1984. "On Contrasting Rates of Diffusion of Professional Knowledge: A Response to McGuire and Tyler," in Philip L. Hosford, Ed., *Using What We Know About Teaching*, 26–29. Alexandria, VA: Association for Supervision and Curriculum Development.

Hackman, J. R., G. Oldham, R. Johnson, and K. Purdy. 1975. "A New Strategy for Job Enrichment," *California Management Review* 17(4).

Hackman, J. R., and Greg Oldham. 1976. "Motivation Through the Design of Work: Test of a Theory," *Organizational Behavior and Human Performance* 16(2), 250–279.

Haller, Emil. 1968. *Strategies for Change*. Toronto: Ontario Institute for Studies in Education, Department of Educational Administration.

Hogben, Donald. 1981. "The Clinical Mind: Some Implications for Educational Research and Teaching Training," *South Pacific Journal of Education* 10(1).

Kennan, Charles. 1974. "Channels for Change: A Survey of Teachers in Chicago Elementary Schools." Doctoral dissertation, Department of Educational Administration, University of Illinois, Urbana-Champaign.

Kennedy, Mary M. 1984. "How Evidence Alters Understanding and Decisions," *Educational Evaluation and Policy Analysis* 6(3), 207–226.

Rubin, Louis. 1975. "The Case for Staff Development," in Thomas J. Sergiovanni, Ed., *Professional Supervision for Professional Teachers*, 33–49. Washington, DC: Association for Supervision and Curriculum Development.

Shulman, Lee. 1989. "Teaching the Disciplines Liberally." The Third Annual Meeting of The Holmes Group, Atlanta, January 28.

Solomon, D., and A. J. Kendall. 1976. *Final Report: Industrial Characteristics and Children's Performance in Varied Educational Settings*. Chicago: Spencer Foundation. May.

Stodolsky, Susan S. 1988. *The Subject Matters*. Chicago: University of Chicago Press.

Tikunoff, William J., David C. Berliner, and Ray C. Rist. 1975. *An Ethnographic Study of the Forty Classrooms of the Beginning Teacher Evaluation Study Known Sample*. Technical Report No. 75-10-5. San Francisco: Far West Lab for Educational Research and Development.

CHAPTER 14

Options for Supervision

What are the options for a differentiated system of supervision? How does a principal decide which options would be best for a particular teacher? This chapter describes four possible options for supervision: clinical, collegial, individual, and informal and considers how these options can be successfully matched to teacher needs, professional development levels, and personality characteristics. The rationale for a differentiated system of supervision is simple; teachers are different and respond differently to various supervisory options (Glickman, 1981; Glatthorn, 1984).

Clinical Supervision

In the late 1950s Robert Goldhammer (1969), Morris Cogan (1973), and their colleagues at Harvard University began to develop the clinical supervision concept as they sought more effective ways to supervise graduate students enrolled in the Master of Arts in Teaching program. Since then, this idea has been further developed to accommodate not only preservice supervision of teachers but also inservice supervision of beginning teachers and of seasoned professional teachers. Cogan (1973) defines clinical supervision as follows:

> The rationale and practice is designed to improve the teacher's classroom performance. It takes its principal data from the events of the classroom. The analysis of these data and the relationships between teacher and supervisor form the basis of the program, procedures, and strategies designed to improve the students' learning by improving the teacher's classroom behavior. (54)

Clinical supervision is considered by many experts (Goldhammer, Anderson, and Krajewski, 1980; Garman, 1982) to be a very effective strategy for bringing about improvements in teaching. It requires a more intense relationship between supervisor and teacher than typically is found in supervisory strategies. The perspective for clinical supervision is basically formative. Its focus is on building teacher motivation and commitment, on the one hand, and on providing for "on-line" staff development for teachers, on the other. Since teachers assume active roles in the process, they often find this a satisfying approach. Further, clinical supervision need not be hierarchical; that is, it lends itself to peer and collegial relations among teachers.

The purpose of clinical supervision is to help teachers to modify existing patterns of teaching in ways that make sense to them. Evaluation is, therefore, responsive to the needs and desires of the teacher. It is the teacher who decides the course of a clinical supervisory cycle, the issues to be discussed, and for what purpose. Obviously, principals who serve as clinical supervisors will bring to this interaction a considerable amount of influence; but, ideally, this should stem from their being in a position to provide the help and clarification needed by teachers. The supervisor's job, therefore, is to help the teacher select goals to be improved, teaching issues to be illuminated, and to understand better her or his practice. This emphasis on understanding provides the avenue by which more technical assistance can be given to the teacher; thus, clinical supervision involves, as well, the systematic analysis of classroom events.

The Cycle of Clinical Supervision

Most authorities (e.g., Goldhammer, 1969) suggest that a sequence of clinical supervision contain five general steps or stages, as follows:

1. Preobservation conference
2. Observation of teaching
3. Analysis and strategy
4. Postobservation conference
5. Postconference analysis

Preobservation Conference.   No stage is more important than the preobservation conference. It is here that the framework for observations is developed and an agreement is reached between supervisor and teacher governing the process that subsequently unfolds. After a brief warm-up period, the supervisor needs to become familiar with the class and with the teacher's way of thinking about teaching. How does the teacher view this class? What are the qualities and characteristics of this class? What frames of reference regarding purposes, models of teaching, classroom management, and so on does the teacher bring to teaching? Getting into the teacher's "corner" and understanding the class from her or his perspective should help the supervisor to understand what the teacher has in mind for the particular teaching sequence that will be observed. How the particular lesson in question fits into the teacher's broader framework of purposes and view of teaching is also essential to provide the supervisor with a perspective beyond the particular lesson at hand.

The supervisor is now ready to engage the teacher in a mental or conceptual *rehearsal* of the lesson. The teacher provides an overview of her or his intents, outcomes not formally anticipated but likely or possible, and problems likely to be encountered. An overview of how teaching will unfold, what the teacher and students will be doing, and anticipated responses from students should also be provided. The supervisor might wish to raise questions for clarification and, depending on the relationship existing between supervisor and teacher, to make suggestions for improving the lesson before it unfolds.

Typically, this conceptual rehearsal by the teacher identifies an array of teaching issues of interest. Clinical supervision is selective in the sense that an intense and detailed study is made of only a handful of issues at a time. Thus, supervisor and teacher must decide what aspects of teaching will be considered, with the teacher assuming major responsibility for setting the supervisory agenda. What would the teacher like to know about this class and the teaching that will take place? On what aspects of teaching would she or he like feedback? Teachers inexperienced with clinical supervision may have initial difficulty in suggesting agenda items, but careful prodding and guiding by the supervisor usually help to elicit meaningful issues that become the basis for a particular cycle of supervision. This phase of the conference concludes with the teacher and supervisor reaching a fairly explicit agreement or "contract" about the reasons for supervision, along with the teaching and learning agendas to be studied. The contract might contain, as well, some indication of the information to be collected, how this information will be collected, what the supervisor will be doing, and what the supervisor should not do. Clinical supervision advocates feel that the teacher should have as complete as possible a picture of events to occur as the process of supervision unfolds.

Observation of Teaching.   The second stage in a clinical supervision cycle— and basic to it—is the actual and systematic observation of teaching. Attention is given to the teacher *in action* and to the classroom story unfolding as a result of this action. Clinical supervision purists would argue that "canned" or standardized devices, or scales for ratings of general teaching characteristics, may well be useful but in themselves are not sufficient; and when used, they should stem from, and be related to, the actual observation of teaching and learning at issue. It is what the teacher actually says and does, how students react, and what actually occurs during a specific teaching episode under study that remains the center of evaluation to advocates of clinical supervision. Student interviews, collections of classroom artifacts and the development of evaluation portfolios, bulletin board and classroom arrangements, photo essays, inventories of lessons accomplished by youngsters or books read, and other evaluative data collection strategies should supplement and illuminate this actual teaching.

The teacher will know what to expect because of the preobservation conference. The teacher should understand that the supervisor wishes to make an unobtrusive entrance and to remain as unobtrusive as possible. During the observation the clinical supervisor may take copious notes attempting to record all classroom events. Notes should be descriptive—that is, free from inferences; for example, the supervisor would avoid writing "during the questioning of students on the use of microscopes by criminologists, the students were bored" in favor of something like "John and Mary both did not hear the question when it was asked" and "two students were looking out the window; a third was playing with materials in his desk during the microscope questioning time." Sometimes the information collected is focused on a particular issue such as cognitive level of questions, attention spans of youngsters, time on task, or cooperative relationships among students. Then, instead of attempting to record everything that takes place during the lesson, the supervisor might record and rate each question asked on the Bloom Taxonomy of Educational Objectives or collect similar, more detailed information. Many clinical supervision purists insist on a written transcript or the collection of firsthand data by the supervisor, and many supervisors using clinical methods have been successful by using television and videotaping equipment or by using audiotaping equipment to record actual teaching. At the conclusion of the observation, the supervisor leaves the classroom as unobtrusively as possible.

Analysis and Strategy. The third step in the cycle of clinical supervision is the analysis of teaching and the building of a supervisory strategy. The analysis stage requires that the supervisor convert the raw data or information collected from the observation into a manageable, meaningful, and sensible form. Clinical supervision advocates recommend that the analysis yield significant teaching patterns and that critical incidents be identified for use in the supervisory conference. Of paramount importance is the contract initially struck with the teacher. What was the purpose of the observation? How did the information collected illuminate this purpose? Can the supervisor arrange this information in a fashion that communicates clearly to the teacher the feedback she or he seeks but at the same time does not prejudge the teaching? This process identifies teaching patterns: recurring teacher verbal and nonverbal behaviors discovered in the course of teaching. Critical incidents are those occurrences that have a particularly noticeable positive or negative effect on the teaching and learning.

Having organized the information, the supervisor now gives attention to building a strategy for working with the teacher. The supervisor takes into account the nature of the contract originally struck, the evaluation issues uncovered during the observation and analysis, the quality of interpersonal relationships existing between teacher and supervisor, the authority base from which she or he is operating, and the competency or experience level of the teacher in deciding on this strategy.

The Postobservation Conference. The fourth stage in the cycle of clinical supervision is the supervisory conference. The supervisor uses the specific information gathered to help the teacher analyze the lesson. Typically, this postobservation conference focuses on a handful of issues previously agreed upon by the teacher and supervisor. It is appropriate as well for the supervisor to introduce new issues as circumstances warrant, but these issues should be few and cautiously introduced. The emphasis remains on providing information to the teacher for fulfilling the contract that was the basis for the observation cycle. Further, the emphasis is not on providing evaluative information but on providing *descriptive* information. The process of making sense of this information is a joint one shared by teacher and supervisor.

Let's assume that the most important issue identified and agreed to in the preconference is "level of cognitive questioning" used by the teacher and cognitive level of assignments given to the students. The teacher uses objectives that span all six levels of the taxonomy of educational objectives but wishes to emphasize the higher-level objectives of analysis and synthesis. Perhaps this teacher is not confident that actual teaching emphasizes these levels; or perhaps the supervisor, suspecting that teaching is not matching teacher intents, suggests that level of cognitive questionings be examined. In either event, teacher and supervisor agree to use the Classroom Question Classification inventory (which appears in Appendix 14–1) to collect information on this issue. During the observation of teaching, each question asked by the teacher is classified into an appropriate level. A transcript of actual questions asked could be prepared. During the analysis and strategy stage of the supervisory cycle, the supervisor tallies questions and computes percentages. The supervisor then decides on a strategy whereby the teacher is asked to restate her or his purposes for the lesson and indeed for the unit of which this lesson is a part. The cognitive level of questioning information is then presented and compared with the teacher's intents. The supervisor is careful to avoid drawing conclusions or to elaborate on possible discrepancies, considering these conclusions to be the responsibility of the teacher. The teacher and supervisor might decide that it would be helpful to collect homework assignments given for other lessons in this particular teaching unit and indeed to examine questions on tests that have been used. These assignments and test questions could also be categorized into the cognitive level of questioning format. Throughout the process, the supervisor's role is not to condemn, cajole, or admonish but to provide information useful to the teacher and in a supportive atmosphere. Some suggestions for providing helpful feedback to teachers are provided in Exhibit 14–1.

Postconference Analysis. The fifth and final stage in a cycle of clinical supervision is the postconference analysis. The postconference phase is a natural springboard to staff development for both teacher and supervisor. The supervisor evaluates what happened in the supervisory conference and throughout the supervisory cycle, for purposes of improving her or his own efforts. Was the integrity of the teacher protected? Did the teacher participate in the process as a cosupervisor? Was feedback given in response to the teacher's needs and desires? Was the emphasis more on teaching and the improvement of teaching than on teacher and evaluating the teacher? What can the supervisor do to improve her or his skills in clinical supervision? A typical outcome of the first four phases of clinical supervision is agreement on the kinds of issues to be pursued next as further cycles are undertaken. The postconference analysis is, therefore, both the end of one cycle and the beginning of another.

Is Clinical Supervision for Everyone?

Clinical supervision is demanding in the time it requires from both supervisor and teachers. Principals who have difficulty finding the time to use this approach with all teachers might reserve it for working with two or three teachers at a time. Should it be desirable for more teachers to be involved, then using collegial or peer

EXHIBIT 14–1 Some Suggestions for Providing Helpful Feedback to Teachers

1. *When giving feedback to teachers, be descriptive rather than judgmental:* Clinical supervision is designed to help teachers improve ongoing teaching and should not be used as a device for summative evaluation designed to determine the value of a person or program. For example, instead of saying to a biology teacher, "You are spending too much time in lecture and not enough time with students engaged in field work and laboratory," try "Your time log shows that you spent 85 percent of class time these past two weeks in lecture. Let's look at your objectives and plans for this unit and see if this is what you intended."

2. *When giving feedback to teachers, be specific rather than general:* General statements tend to be misunderstood more than specific statements. Instead of saying to a teacher, "You interrupt students and tend not to listen to what they are saying," try, "When you asked John a question, you interrupted his response and seemed uninterested in what he had to say." A cassette transcript of the question, response attempt, and interruptions would be helpful.

3. *When giving feedback to teachers, concentrate on things that can be changed:* A teacher may have little control over a nervous twitch or voice quality, but much can be done about arranging seats, grouping students, improving balance between knowledge level and other objectives, and disciplining students.

4. *When giving feedback to teachers, consider your own motives:* Often feedback is given to impress teachers with one's knowledge or for some other reason that builds the supervisor's status. Feedback is intended for only one purpose—to help the teacher know and understand her or his actual behavior as a teacher and consequences of this behavior on teaching and learning.

5. *Give the teacher feedback at a time as close to the actual behavior as possible:* Details of events are likely to be forgotten easily. Further, fairly prompt attention is likely to upgrade and personalize the importance of clinical supervision.

6. *When giving feedback to teachers, rely as much as possible on information whose accuracy can be reasonably documented:* Photographs of bulletin boards, audio- and videotapes of teachers and students at work, a portfolio of classroom tests, a record of books borrowed from the class library, the number of students who return to shop during free periods or after school, a tally of questions asked by the teacher sorted into the hierarchy of educational objectives are examples of documented feedback. It will not always be possible or desirable to provide this type of highly descriptive feedback, but it is important, nevertheless, as a technique, for clinical supervision cannot be overemphasized.

clinical supervision may be the answer. Here teachers take turns assuming the role of clinical supervisor as they help each other. Collegial clinical supervision, however, often results in teachers' being burdened with additional time demands. Further, participation requires much more training in conferencing, information collecting, interpreting, and other supervisory techniques than is typically necessary for other forms of supervision. If teachers are to be clinical supervisors, they will need to receive the proper training; this, too, can present problems because training takes time and is expensive.

A further issue is that *clinical supervision may be too much supervision for some teachers.* Though all teachers would profit from clinical supervision from time to time, it does not appear that this strategy should be used all the time for all teachers. Going through this process every second, third, or fourth year may be less burdensome and tiresome for some. Unfortunately, this supervisory process can become too routinized and ritualized if overused. And, finally, teacher needs and dispositions as well as work and learning styles vary. Clinical supervision may be suitable for some teachers but not for others, when these concerns are taken into consideration.

Collegial Supervision

Allan Glatthorn (1984) uses the phrase *cooperative professional development* to describe a collegial process within which teachers agree to work together for their own professional development. He prefers this term over *peer supervision* or *collegial supervision*, fearing that these labels might suggest that teachers are supervising one another in a management sense. Cooperative professional development is a nonevaluative strategy for teachers to help one another as equals and professional colleagues. Glatthorn (1984:39) defines this approach as a "moderately formalized process by which two or more teachers agreed to work together for their own professional growth, usually by observing each other's classroom, giving each other feedback about the observation, and discussing shared professional concerns."

Cooperative professional development, or in the terms of this book, *collegial supervision*, can take many different forms. In some schools, teachers might be organized into teams of three. In forming such teams, teachers would have an opportunity to indicate with whom they might like to work. Often at least one member of the team is selected by the principal or the supervisor, but there are no rigid rules for selecting teams. Once formed, the teams may choose to work together in a number of ways ranging from clinical supervision to less intensive and more informal processes. They may, for example, simply agree to observe each other's classes, providing help according to the desires of the teacher being observed. The teachers then might confer, giving one another informal feedback and otherwise discussing issues of teaching that they consider to be important. An approach relying on Hunter's teaching steps and elements of lesson design might be used on another occasion. In this case the emphasis on teaching might be narrowly focused on specific issues identified by the teacher. On still another occasion the emphasis might be quite unfocused in order to provide a general feel or rendition of teaching. All that is needed is for team members to meet beforehand to decide "the rules and issues" for the observation and for any subsequent conversations or conferences.

It is a good idea for collegial supervision to extend beyond classroom observation. It should provide a setting in which teachers can informally discuss problems they are facing, share ideas, help one another in preparing lessons, exchange tips, and provide other support to one another. Some suggestions for principals seeking to implement collegial supervision are provided in Exhibit 14-2.

Self-Directed Supervision

Another option suggested by Glatthorn (1984) in establishing a differentiated system is what he calls *self-directed development*. Here teachers working alone assume

EXHIBIT 14–2 Guidelines for Implementing Cooperative or Collegial Supervision

1. Teachers should have a voice in deciding with whom they work.

2. Principals should retain final responsibility for putting together collegial supervisory teams.

3. The structure for collegial supervision should be formal enough for the teams to keep records of how and in what ways time has been used and to provide a general *nonevaluative* description of collegial supervisory activities. This record should be submitted annually to the principal.

4. The principal should provide the necessary resources and administrative support enabling collegial supervisory teams to function during the normal range of the school day. The principal might, for example, volunteer to cover classes as needed, or to arrange for substitutes as needed, or to provide for innovative schedule adjustments enabling team members to work together readily.

5. If information generated within the team about teaching and learning might be considered even mildly evaluative, it should stay with the team and not be shared with the principal.

6. Under no circumstances should the principal seek evaluation data from one teacher about another.

7. Each teacher should be expected to keep a professional growth log that demonstrates that she or he is reflecting on practice and growing professionally as a result of collegial supervisory activities.

8. The principal should meet with the collegial supervisory team at least once a year for purposes of general assessment and for sharing of impressions and information about the collegial supervisory process.

9. The principal should meet individually at least once a year with each collegial supervisory team member to discuss her or his professional growth log and to provide any encouragement and assistance that may be required.

10. Generally, new teams should be formed every second or third year.

responsibility for their own professional development. They develop a yearly plan comprising targets or goals derived from an assessment of their own needs. This plan is then shared with the supervisor, principal, or other designated individual. Teachers are allowed a great deal of leeway in developing the plan, but supervisors should ensure that the plan and selected targets are both realistic and attainable. At the end of a specified period, normally a year, the supervisor and teacher meet to discuss the teacher's progress in meeting professional development targets. Teachers are expected to provide some form of documentation (such as time logs, reflective practice diaries, schedules, photos, tapes, samples of students' work, and other artifacts) illustrating progress toward goals. This conference then leads to the generation of new targets for subsequent individual professional development cycles.

A number of problems are associated with approaches to supervision that rely heavily on target setting. Supervisors, for example, sometimes rigidly adhere to prespecified targets and sometimes impose targets on teachers. Rigidly applying a target-setting system unduly focuses the evaluation and limits teachers to the events originally anticipated or stated. When this happens, teaching energies and concerns are directed to a prestated target, and other areas of importance not targeted can be neglected. Target setting is meant to help and facilitate, not to hinder, the self-improvement process.

Individual approaches to supervision are ideal for teachers who prefer to work alone or who, because of scheduling or other difficulties, are unable to work with other teachers. This supervisory option is efficient in use of time, less costly, and less demanding in its reliance on others than is the case with other options. For these reasons self-directed supervision is a feasible and practical approach. This approach is ideally suited to competent and self-directed teachers. Some guidelines for implementing self-directed supervision are provided in Exhibit 14–3.

Informal Supervision

Included in every differentiated system of supervision should be a provision for *informal supervision*. Informal supervision is a casual encounter by supervisors with teachers at work and is characterized by frequent but brief and informal observations of teachers. Typically no appointments are made and visits are not announced. Successful informal supervision requires that certain expectations be accepted by teachers. This approach, for example, assumes that principals and supervisors are indeed first and foremost lead or principal-teachers and thus have a right and responsibility to be a part of all the teaching that takes place in the school. They

EXHIBIT 14–3 Guidelines for Implementing Individualized Supervision

1. *Target setting.* Based on last year's observations, conferences, summary reports, clinical supervision episodes, or other means of personal assessment, teachers develop targets or goals that they would like to reach in improving their teaching. Targets should be few, rarely exceeding five or six and preferably limited to two or three. Estimated time frames should be provided for each target, which are then shared with the supervisor, along with an informal plan providing suggested activities for teacher engagement.

2. *Target-setting review.* After reviewing each target and estimated time frame, the principal provides the teacher with a written reaction. Further, a conference is scheduled to discuss targets and plans.

3. *Target-setting conference.* Meeting to discuss targets, time frames, and reactions, the teacher and principal revise targets if appropriate. It may be a good idea for the principal to provide a written summary of the conference to the teacher. Teacher and principal might well prepare this written summary together.

4. *Appraisal process.* Appraisal begins at the conclusion of the target-setting conference and continues in accordance with the agreed-upon time frame. The specific nature of the appraisal process depends on each of the targets and could include formal and informal classroom observations, an analysis of classroom artifacts, videotaping, student evaluation, interaction analysis, and other information. The teacher is responsible for collecting appraisal information and arranges this material in a portfolio for subsequent discussion with, and review by, the principal.

5. *Summary appraisal.* The principal visits with the teacher to review the appraisal portfolio. As part of this process, the principal comments on each target, and together the teacher and principal plan for the next cycle of individual, self-directed supervision.

are instructional partners to every teacher in every classroom for every teaching and learning situation. When informal supervision is properly in place, principals and supervisors are viewed as relatively common fixtures in classrooms, coming and going as part of the natural flow of the school's daily work.

The general management literature refers to informal supervision as "management by wandering around" (MBWA). This practice is commonly found among leaders of highly successful business firms and is discussed at great length in the writings of such business authorities as Deal and Kennedy (1982), Peters and Waterman (1982), and Peters and Austin (1985).

Informal supervision should not be considered as a sole option for teachers. Glatthorn (1984), for example, believes that a differentiated system of supervision should require all teachers to participate in informal supervision. In addition to informal supervision they would be involved in one additional approach such as clinical, collegial, or individual supervision. In selecting additional options, principals and supervisors should try to accommodate teacher preferences but should retain final responsibility for deciding the appropriateness of a selected option and indeed should reserve the right to veto the teacher's choice.

Differentiated Supervision and the Contingency View

A *contingency view of supervision* is based on the premise that teachers are different and that matching supervisory options to these differences is important. In recent years developmental theorists such as Glickman (1985) and Costa (1982) have made considerable progress in suggesting how this matching might be done. These experts examine such dimensions as levels of professional maturity and cognitive complexity and suggest that as levels vary among teachers, so should supervisory approaches and styles. Another group of theorists, such as Dunn and Dunn (1979) and Kolb, Rubin, and McIntyre (1984), have been interested in the concept of learning styles and how, as these styles vary, opportunities for learning, problem solving, and personal growth should also vary. Accounting for motives of teachers provides still a third dimension to the matching of individual teachers with supervisory options. Social motives theories such as McClelland's (1953) find that as such important work motives as the need for achievement, power, and affiliation vary among workers, the work conditions and setting they find motivating vary as well. Matching supervisory options to individual needs, therefore, has great potential for increasing the motivation and commitment of teachers at work. The following sections explore these important individual dimensions and suggest compatible supervisory options. Readers should not be under the illusion that tight and concise matching is possible. It isn't. But more informed matching decisions can be made by considering the possibilities discussed.

Cognitive Complexity Levels of Teachers

Important to developmental theorists is the concept of *cognitive complexity*. These theorists are concerned with levels of cognitive growth for teachers as embodied in the cognitive complexity they exhibit in their teaching practice. Lower levels of growth are characterized by simple and concrete thinking and practice, whereas higher levels of growth are characterized by more complex and abstract thinking and practice. An important finding from the research on teaching is that teachers with higher levels of cognitive complexity provide a greater range of teaching environments to students and that their practice is characterized by a wider variety of teaching strategies and methods (Hunt and Bruce, 1976). Further, students of teachers with higher levels of cognitive complexity tend to achieve more than students of teachers with lower levels (Harvey, 1966).

Cognitive complexity is concerned with both the *structure and content* of a teacher's thoughts, with particular emphasis on the structure (Harvey, 1966). Two teachers may share the same beliefs about the value of informal teaching but may differ markedly in the complexity with which they view these beliefs. The content of these beliefs is similar, but the structure is different. The first teacher views informal teaching as universally applicable rather than as one of many strategies. The second teacher, on the other hand, views informal teaching as a strategy more appropriate for some teaching and learning settings but less appropriate for others. Though both teachers share common beliefs about informal teaching, they differ in the structure with which these beliefs are held. The second teacher's thinking is characterized by higher levels of cognitive complexity than is the first's. Teachers with higher levels of cognitive complexity are able to give attention to a number of different concepts relating to a particular issue and to see interconnections among these concepts. They are able to be more reflective in their practice, to understand better the subtleties of teaching, and to make more complex decisions about teaching.

Supervisory strategies that account for levels of cognitive complexity actually enhance this complexity. As Sprinthall and Theis-Sprinthall (1982) point out, cognitive complexity increases as teachers are exposed to more stimulating teaching environments. Examples would be teachers who have greater opportunities to interact with their supervisors and other teachers about teaching, have greater opportunities for obtaining feedback about their teaching and thus for reflecting on their practice, have greater opportunities for experimenting in a supportive environment, and have greater opportunities for assuming more responsibility for the outcomes of their teaching. The differentiated system of supervision that provides informal supervision combined with other options can provide these benefits. When teachers are provided with an intellectually stimulating, challenging, and supportive supervisory environment, levels of cognitive complexity increase, with subsequent improvements in teaching and learning (Harvey, 1966).

Supervisory Styles and Cognitive Complexity

Within any supervisory option, suprvisors may choose to provide leadership and help in a number of different ways. These behavioral choices represent styles of supervision. The developmental theorist Glickman (1985) refers to three major supervisory styles as directive, collaborative, and nondirective.

Styles are different from options in that different styles can be used when working with different teachers even though all the teachers may be involved in supervision using the same option. For example, when working with three different teachers within individualized supervision, it might make sense to use a directive approach with one, a collaborative with the second, and a nondirective approach with the third. The directive approach would emphasize structure and more frequent interaction with the teacher; the collaborative would emphasize shared responsibility, joint decision making, and collegiality; and the nondirective would emphasize facilitating the teacher's plans and efforts and providing necessary support.

The matching of teacher concerns, levels of responsibility, maturity, cognitive complexity, supervisory options, and supervisory styles is illustrated in Figure 14-1. This figure suggests an alignment between concerns of teachers and levels of responsibility and maturity and levels of cognitive complexity. Teachers primarily concerned with the problems, needs, and learning characteristics of students; who are autonomous with respect to accepting responsibility; and who are growing in levels of maturity are likely to display moderate or medium levels of cognitive complexity. Cognitive complexity is, therefore, an important construct. The intersection line brings together these dimensions of teacher development and indicates the recommended supervisory style and supervisory option.

Teachers located at or near point 1 on the intersection line would probably benefit best from directive supervision regardless of the supervisory option being used. Informal supervision characterized by frequent and direct contact with the supervisor is recommended as the most suitable option. Collegial and individual supervision would be appropriate as supplements. Should collegial be chosen (for example, teaming the teacher with another teacher who might be located at point 3 on the intersection line), the supervisor will need to be involved to ensure that this teacher is getting the direction and help most needed.

The collaborative supervisory style would be most appropriate for teachers at intersection point 2. In this case both teacher and supervisor tackle problems together, plan activities and events, and make decisions cooperatively. Individual professional development is highly recommended as an option.

Teachers with more professional concerns that bring together students with broader issues affecting quality schooling and who reflect higher levels of cognitive complexity in their practice will be found at or near point 3 on the intersection line. These mature professionals are more willing and able to assume full responsibility for their own self-evaluation and improvement. When this is the case, supervision is more appropriately nondirective. Cooperative professional development is ideally suited to teachers at point 3. Here, groups of teachers work together as mature colleagues. Individual professional development may be selected by some teachers who might prefer to work alone. Informal supervision would remain an important part of a comprehensive supervisory system in the school and thus should be used as well with teachers at or near point 3. For these highly motivated and competent teachers the purpose of informal supervision is one of providing needed recognition and support.

Peaks and dips appear periodically on the intersection line of Figure 14-1. Peaks represent occasions when teachers might require more intense and prolonged help

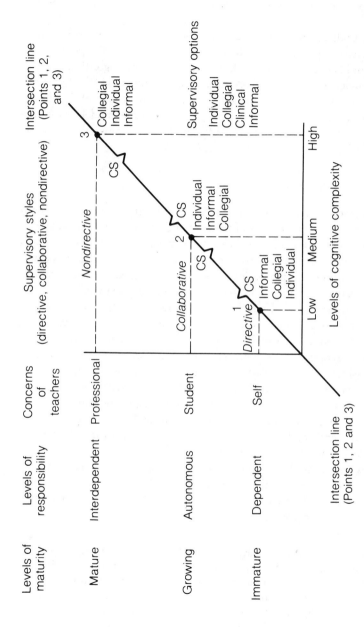

FIGURE 14-1 Matching Teacher Variables and Supervisory Styles

in the classroom, perhaps because they face a special problem or challenge. Dips represent trouble spots that might be identified by either the teacher or the supervisor. On these occasions clinical supervision can be an effective and appropriate option.

All of this sounds complicated, and it is. Whenever we try to accommodate individual differences in people and settings we have to deal with diverse strategies and tactics. Figure 14-1 can be helpful if it is viewed not as an alogorithm or script but merely as a model, a metaphorical one at that, which portrays ideas that might be helpful in sorting out what to do, when. Ultimately the process of deciding is one of trial and error much as physicians practice. In medicine, models suggesting treatments are tried but quickly abandoned for others as the physician monitors progress and gets feedback that something isn't working.

Learning Styles of Teachers

Two additional situational characteristics that should be considered in a contingency view of supervision are learning styles of teachers and the particular motivational needs that they bring to work. Teachers, like students, are unique in their learning styles and in the ways in which they solve problems. A reflective supervisory program would take note of these differences and seek to accommodate them in assigning teachers to supervisory options and in providing appropriate supervisory styles within options. David A. Kolb, Irwin M. Rubin, and James M. McIntyre (1984) provide a model of learning that conceives of adult learning and problem solving as one process. The model is intended to increase understanding of how adults generate from their experience the concepts, rules, and principles that guide their behavior in new situations and how they modify these concepts to improve their effectiveness in learning at work. Within the model, learning and problem solving are viewed as a four-stage cycle beginning with concrete experiences and progressing in turn through observation and reflection, the formulation of concepts and generalizations, to experimenting with what is learned in a new setting. This model represents an ideal conception of learning.

Kolb and his colleagues identify four different learning modes, each corresponding to one of the stages of this learning cycle: concrete experience (CE), reflective observation (RO), abstract conceptualization (AC), and active experimentation (AE). They believe that learners

> must be able to involve themselves fully, openly and without bias in new experiences (CE); they must be able to reflect on and observe these experiences from many perspectives (RO); they must be able to create conceptions that integrate their observations into logically sound theories (AC); and they must be able to use these theories to make decisions and solve problems (AE). (Kolb, Rubin, and McIntyre, 1984:32)

People give different weights to each of these learning styles. Some teachers feel more comfortable with and are more confident with some of the stages of the cycle than with others. Simply put, some teachers learn best when dealing concretely with something and may have difficulty responding to this same thing when presented abstractly. Others are confused by starting with concrete matters, preferring instead to read about something—to become cognitively oriented before experiencing it firsthand. Others might prefer to observe new learning possibilities in action first and then to reflect on what is observed before developing a conceptual map or having concrete experience. Still other teachers are quick to jump in and experiment with new ideas and practices, using a process of muddling through as they then move to more reflective, abstract, or concrete understandings. What is clear is that learning takes place best when all of the four learning modes are tended to. What is not clear is the order in which different individuals progress through the learning cycle. Some learn best starting with a concrete experience, others learn best starting with a more abstract approach, and so on. Typically one's actual learning style represents a blending of modes. For practical purposes it is more useful to think of a person as being oriented toward a particular learning mode than as being typed or labeled more rigidly. Patterns are intended to reveal relative emphases on one or another learning mode and to suggest strengths and weaknesses.

Teacher Learning Styles and Supervisory Options

Learning styles can be useful in helping to decide which particular supervisory option is most suitable for a given teacher. But the real value is less in deciding the option itself and more in suggesting ways in which supervisors and others can work most effectively with teachers within options. Following are some recommendations for matching supervisory option with teacher learning style. They are based on our interpretation of the literature and on our clinical experience as supervisors.

Collegial supervision is the recommended choice for teachers oriented toward concrete experience for it gives them opportunities to interact with other teachers about their work. Concrete-experience teachers are less interested in "bookish" interpretations of practice and more interested in knowing about and experiencing "what works" in the classroom next door. They often like the opportunity to try out a new idea or teaching practice, much as does an apprentice by working side by side with another teacher. Sometimes their concern for what is immediate prevents them from "seeing the forest because of the trees." Sometimes they adopt practices by mimicking them and thus do not understand them fully. As a result they may have difficulty in extending their practice, in applying newly learned practices to new situations, and in modifying practices as situations change.

Concrete-experience teachers typically like to interact with each other and are not likely to prefer options that require them to work alone. Thus they are not likely to be comfortable with individual professional development. Should this be the choice anyway, concrete-experience teachers will need a fair amount of close supervision and a reasonable amount of directiveness. In collegial supervision settings it makes sense to team concrete-experience teachers with those who have strengths in abstract conceptualization or reflective observation. Both types of teachers will profit by this combination.

High-reflective-observation teachers are likely to respond favorably to supervisory situations that allow them to be self-directed and to work collegially with other teachers. In each case, however, the teacher is likely to be passive, preferring to observe and make sense of what is going on rather than taking a more active role. If assigned to individual supervision and left alone, the reflective observer will often not make much progress. If this must be the choice it might be a good idea for supervisors to insist on the development of an explicit contract detailing the action outcomes of supervisions. Targets and goals should be action-oriented and should specify the teaching behaviors or classroom changes being sought. Care should be taken to ensure that targets have been met and the supervisory contract has been fulfilled.

A better choice for the reflective observer would be assignment to collegial teams, but care should be taken to provide that other team members are reasonably action-oriented and can provide the teacher with the kinds of practical assistance that will be needed to get on with the work of self-improvement. In exchange the reflective observing teacher can provide others with the kind of reflection that will help them to view their teaching with greater depth and meaning.

Abstract-conceptualization-oriented teachers resemble reflective-observation teachers in many ways but are more action-oriented and better able to focus on problems of practice and the theoretical ideas associated with these problems. They like reading about theoretical ideas, issues of practice, and reports of research regarding teaching and learning and discussing these issues and ideas in depth. They like to "see the data" and are frequently good at making sense of these data. Sometimes in their enthusiasm for abstract concerns they have less energy available for getting on with the day-to-day implementation of ideas. They are good planners, however, and when assigned to individual supervision will often prepare elaborate and reasoned sets of target-setting documents. This supervisory option works well for them if time is taken to ensure that action deadlines are set and that teachers follow these deadlines with evidence of practical accomplishments of their objectives and targets.

Teachers oriented toward abstract conceptualization often profit from collegial supervision and can contribute to it. But sometimes they can be distracting to group efforts because of their tendency to emphasize theoretical issues. To abstract conceptualizers the theoretical is a delight in its own right and well worth discussing regardless of implications for practice. In using the collegial option, therefore, care should be taken to form a team that includes more action-oriented teachers to provide the necessary balance.

Individual self-directed supervision is the most likely choice for teachers oriented toward active experimenting. These teachers are doers and as such are interested in getting on with their work. They like to set objectives and enjoy focusing on tasks. They are willing to take risks and are not afraid to modify their practice. Individual supervision provides these teachers with an opportunity to grow and develop at their own rates. They need help, however, in sticking with a course of action, in tempering their experiments, and in reflecting on their practice to ensure that it is reasonably stable and sensible. Active experimenters tend not to prefer collegial supervision and if assigned to this option can often be a hindrance to other teachers. Other teachers assigned to the same option are likely to view the active experimenter as being a maverick. As with teachers oriented toward each of the other three learning styles, an appropriate supervisory strategy is one that leads with the teacher's strengths and provides the necessary help, and sometimes discipline, to ensure that the less favored learning modes are tended to as well. If Kolb, Rubin, and McIntyre (1984) are right, sustained learning will not take place unless all four dimensions of the learning cycle are experienced.

Accounting for Motives of Teachers

Differences in reactions of teachers to the same supervisory option or style are in part natural reflections of the motives they bring to their work. Motivational theories are often grouped into two major categories—active and internal. Active theories assume that teachers bring to their work certain needs that are translated into goals and desires. According to active theories, teachers are motivated to work in exchange for achieving desired goals. Internal theories, by contrast, assume that teachers are already motivated to work and that this motivation is related more to complex personality characteristics than to desired goals. According to internal theorists, carrot and stick approaches to motivation are likely to be less effective than understanding underlying motives and creating conditions allowing these motives to be expressed. Thus, motives and aroused motivation are considered to be different. Motives are construed as underlying personality characteristics. They resemble energy valves that are related to motivation. When the valves are closed, a teacher's energy remains in a state of potential and behavior is not motivated. Aroused motivation results from opening the motive valve and is reflected in a release of energy in the form of motivated behavior. Key motives differ for different individuals. When teachers find themselves in work settings that correspond to their underlying motives, the motive valve is opened and the potential for motivation is greatly enhanced.

Three motives have been identified as having particular importance to the world of teachers at work: achievement, power influence, and affiliation. David C. McClelland (1961) found that the three motives are present in all people but not to the same degree. Some teachers are influenced greatly by the need for affiliation, only moderately by the need for power influence, and only modestly by the need for achievement. Other teachers might be very high on the need for achievement and comparatively low on the needs for affiliation and power and influence. The first group of teachers are likely to think more about social interaction, friendships, and human relationships at work and in controlling others at work than in job objectives and how well they can accomplish various teaching tasks. In contrast, the second group would probably be much more concerned with work issues and progress in achieving objectives than in interacting with and controlling others.

The achievement motive is associated with teachers wanting to take personal responsibility for their own success or failure, liking working situations where goals are clear and reasonably obtainable though challenging, and preferring frequent and concrete feedback allowing them to gauge their success and failure rates in a continuous fashion. High-achievement-motivated teachers are task-oriented, prefer short-range specific targets to more ambiguous and long-range targets, like to be on top of things, and seek personal responsibility for their actions. They find it difficult to delegate responsibility and to share authority with others. It is often difficult for them to emphasize human relationships and social interaction behaviors for their own sake. High-need-for-achievement teachers are likely to be committed to building achievement-oriented classrooms with visible and detailed standards. They seek and accept responsibility for their own work behaviors and growth and gladly accept moderate risks in an effort to achieve personal success.

Supervisory options that encourage individual initiative, target-setting, and charting of accomplishments are favored by high-achievement-oriented teachers. Self-directed supervision, for example, is ideally suited to them, but they are likely to respond less favorably to collegial supervision. They respond well to informal supervision if the feedback they desire is provided. Continuing with the valve metaphor, when the supervisory situation is properly matched, the achievement-motive valve is opened and motivation results.

The affiliation motive is associated with people who have a high concern for warm and friendly relationships and for social interaction. Teachers for whom this need is important enjoy working with other teachers in group settings and find teaching and other assignments that require them to work alone, learn alone, or problem solve alone to be less satisfactory. They depend heavily on other teachers for much of their work satisfaction and enjoy interacting with others about work. Affiliation-oriented teachers suffer more from isolation and experience more loneliness than do their achievement and power-influence counterparts. They need and seek opportunities to interact with other adults. Should they find this opportunity within the supervisory situation, their affiliation-motive valve is opened and they respond with motivated behavior.

Individual self-directed supervision and other supervisory options that leave them to their own devices are not likely to be viewed favorably by high-affiliation teachers. On the other hand, collegial supervision elicits a very positive response. Affiliation teachers can feel uncomfortable when involved in informal supervision unless the supervisor makes a point of providing *supportive* feedback after every classroom visit.

High-need-for-power-and-influence teachers are interested in influencing other people. They like group contacts and social interaction supervisory settings but view these less as opportunities for satisfying social interaction needs and more as opportunities that will enable them to exercise leadership. When provided with supervisory situations of this type, the power-influence-motive valve is opened and motivative behavior results.

High-power-influence teachers like to assume supervisory roles and will respond very positively to collegial supervision. Since they like to be in charge and enjoy assuming leadership roles they often resent competition in these areas from other teachers and from supervisors. An important strategy is to harness the motivational potential of high-power-influence teachers by delegating responsibility to them and in other ways sharing leadership roles and functions.

During the early stages of social motives research it was thought that the achievement motive was associated with increased performance at work and successful accomplishment of goals and that the other two motives actually interfered with the accomplishment of work. More recent reserch, however, suggests that none of the three emerges as being superior. Teachers with high needs for affiliation and teachers with high needs for power and influence can be every bit as productive and effective as teachers with high needs for achievement. Key to motivation is not the most pressing motive of a particular teacher but whether a person's work circumstances allow for expression of the motive—the opening of the motive-energy valve, so to speak.

Flexibility in Practice

Throughout this discussion of contingency views, supervisory options and styles have been characterized as models and ideal types with fairly fixed features that clearly differentiate one from another. Let's take the case of Bill, a high-need-for-achievement teacher with a learning style emphasizing abstract conceptualization. Bill likes to set targets, plan events in stages, and keep track of his progress. He derives a great deal of satisfaction from his own accomplishments and in this sense makes a game of learning. Individual self-directed supervision is a good choice for Bill.

As the principal thinks about how to work with Bill and to be helpful to him, certain issues come to mind. Bill's targets are typically abstract. He tackles such issues as: "How can I learn more about individual differences of the students I teach?" The principal would like Bill to focus more on developing actual teaching strategies and on experimenting with various classroom organizational patterns that emphasize individual differences in practice. The principal decides to keep close tabs on Bill, who will not mind close supervision if its main purpose is to provide him with feedback as to how well he is doing and with recognition for his success. These feedback sessions will also be used to emphasize other issues that the principal thinks are important—translating abstract ideas into concrete practices. The principal urges Bill to visit the classroom of another teacher working on a similar problem and, after this observation, discusses with Bill what has been observed. This develops links between Bill's theories and abstract understandings of individual differences and what has been observed in practice. Together they develop a plan for reorganizing the structure of the classroom for language arts teaching that illustrates some of the ideas Bill is working on with respect to individual differences. Throughout, the principal is sensitive to Bill's need for achievement and for feedback about his work and uses this need as a means to build bridges between abstract conceptualization and the other learning modes of reflective observation, concrete experience, and active experimentation.

Betty, on the other hand, is a high-need-for-affiliation teacher with a concrete-experience learning style. Working with Betty within individual self-directed supervision is possible but will require a different strategy by the principal. To begin with, Betty will need much more contact with the principal than Bill did. High-affiliation teachers seek and require social interaction. The issue for the principal in this case is how to give Betty a sound theoretical understanding of her practice that will enable her to teach with more meaning and to increase her practice reper-toire. Individual supervision can work for Betty if the principal is willing to take the neccessary time. In this case, however, collegial supervision might well be a better choice. Allowing Betty to work with other teachers not only provides her with the necessary interaction but also relieves the time demands of the principal as teachers assume supervisory responsibility. Within collegial supervision the prin-cipal's role will change from direct supervisor to general supervisor as she main-tains contact with the group to ensure that the process initially complements Betty's learning style and subsequently extends it.

Helping Teachers to Achieve Goals

Key to the contingency view and at the heart of reflective practice within the prin-cipalship is a very simple but deceptive axiom. Teachers have work goals that are important to them. Given the opportunity, they will work very hard at achieving these goals. This chapter has suggested that the nature of these goals is influenced by growth stages, cognitive complexity levels, learning styles, and motives that teachers bring to the school. Supervisory options and styles should respond to these differences among teachers, for such responsiveness makes it easier for work goals to be realized. In this sense, supervision is little more than a system of help for teachers as they achieve goals that they consider important. Principals are needed to provide help as this process unfolds.

Robert J. House (1971) has proposed a "path-goal" theory of leadership that summarizes much of our discussion and provides a handle on key aspects of effec-tive helping. He believes that leaders are responsible for "increasing the number and kinds of personal payoffs to the subordinates for the work-goal attainment and making paths to these payoffs easiest to travel by clarifying the paths, reduc-ing roadblocks and pitfalls, and increasing the opportunities for personal satisfac-tion en route" (323).

Translated to teacher supervision, principals assume responsibility for "clarify-ing and clearing the path" toward goals that teachers consider important. Clarify-ing the path requires that goals be set and reasonably defined and understood. Ambiguous and unstructured situations and unclear expectations can be a source of frustration and dissatisfaction for teachers. Thus it becomes important to pro-vide the necessary task emphasis to help clarify goals. Clearing the path requires that principals provide the necessary assistance, education, support, and reinforce-ment to help achieve goals. Key to a path-goal approach is understanding that the richer sources of satisfaction for teachers come not from an emphasis on human relationships and social interaction separate from the accomplishment of work but from having accomplished worthwhile and challenging tasks within a pleasant atmosphere.

Providing a system of differentiated supervision is one way in which principals can provide the necessary paths that enable teachers to accomplish work goals they consider to be important.

References

Cogan, Morris. 1973. *Clinical Supervision.* Boston: Houghton Mifflin.

Costa, Art L. 1982. *Supervision for Intelligent Teaching: A Course Syllabus.* Orangevale, CA: Search Models Unlimited.

Deal, Terence E., and Alan A. Kennedy. 1982. *Corporate Culture.* Reading, MA: Addison-Wesley.

Dunn, Rita S., and K. J. Dunn. 1979. "Learning Styles Teaching Styles: Should They . . . Can They . . . Be Matched?" *Educational Leadership* 36(4).

Garman, Noreen. 1982. "The Clinical Approach to Supervision," in Thomas J. Sergiovanni, Ed., *Supervision of Teaching,* 35–52. Alexandria, VA: Association for Supervision and Curriculum Development.

Glatthorn, Allan A. 1984. *Differentiated Supervision.* Alexandria, VA: Association for Supervision and Curriculum Development.

Glickman, Carl D. 1981. *Developmental Supervision.* Alexandria, VA: Association for Supervision and Curriculum Development.

Glickman, Carl D. 1985. *Supervision and Instruction: A Developmental Approach.* Boston: Allyn and Bacon.

Goldhammer, Robert. 1969. *Clinical Supervision: Special Methods for the Supervision of Teachers.* New York: Holt, Rinehart and Winston.

Goldhammer, Robert, Robert H. Anderson, and Robert A. Krajewski. 1980. *Clinical Supervision: Special Methods for the Supervision of Teaching,* 2d ed. New York: Holt, Rinehart and Winston.

Harvey, O. J. 1966. "System Structure, Flexibility and Creativity," in O. J. Harvey, Ed., *Experience, Structure, and Adaptability,* 39–65. New York: Springer.

House, Robert J. 1971. "A Path Goal Theory of Leadership Effectiveness," *Administrative Science Quarterly* 16(3), 321–338.

Hunt, David E. 1966. "A Conceptual Systems Change Model and Its Application to Education," in O. J. Harvey, Ed., *Experience, Structure, and Adaptability,* 277–302. New York: Springer.

Hunt, David E., and Bruce R. Joyce. 1967. "Teacher Trainee Personality and Initial Teaching Style," *American Educational Research Journal* 4(3), 253–255.

Kolb, David A., Irwin M. Rubin, and James M. McIntyre. 1984. *Organizational Psychology: An Experiential Approach to Organizational Behavior.* Englewood Cliffs, NJ: Prentice-Hall.

McClelland, David C. 1961. *The Achieving Society.* Princeton, NJ: Van Nostrand.

McClelland, David C., J. W. Atkinson, R. A. Clark, and E. L. Lowell. 1953. *The Achievement Motive.* New York: Appleton-Century-Croft.

Peters, Thomas J., and Robert H. Waterman. 1983. *In Search of Excellence.* New York: Harper & Row.

Peters, Tom, and Nancy Austin. 1985. *A Passion for Excellence.* New York: Random House.

Sprinthall, N. A., and L. Thies-Sprinthall. 1982. "Career Development of Teachers: A Cognitive Perspective," in H. Mitzel, Ed., *Encyclopedia of Educational Research,* 5th ed. New York: Free Press.

THE MORAL DIMENSION

CHAPTER 15

Administering as a Moral Craft

In this book a number of conceptions of the principal have been discussed: Strategic problem solver, cultural leader, barterer, and initiator are examples. It's fair to ask whether these are the roles and images of leadership that one should follow in order to be an effective principal. The answer is yes—well, no—actually maybe. Similarly, what about the motivational concepts and ideas presented in Chapter 11, the new principles of management and leadership presented in Chapter 3, the characteristics of successful schools, the forces of leadership, strategies for bringing about change, and the dimensions of school culture discussed in other chapters? Will these ideas, if routinely applied, help one to be an effective principal? The answer is the same. Yes—well, no—actually maybe. Unfortunately there is no guarantee that the concepts presented in this book will fit all readers or the contexts and problems they face in the same way. Leadership is a personal thing. It comprises three important dimensions—one's heart, head, and hand.

The Heart, Head, and Hand of Leadership

The *heart* of leadership has to do with what a person believes, values, dreams about, and is committed to—that person's *personal vision*, to use a popular term. To be sure, sharing personal conceptions of what is a good school will reveal many common qualities, but what often makes them personal statements is that they will differ as well. The *head* of leadership has to do with the theories of practice each of us has developed over time and our ability to reflect on the situations we face in light of these theories. This process of reflection combined with our personal vision becomes the basis for our strategies and actions. And finally, the *hand* of leadership has to do with the actions we take, the decisions we make, the leadership and management behaviors we use as our strategies become institutionalized in the form of school programs, policies, and procedures. As with heart and head, how we choose to manage and lead are personal reflections not only of our vision and practical theories but of our personalities and our responses to the unique situations we face as well. In this idiosyncratic world one-best-way approaches and cookie cutter strategies do not work very well. Instead, diversity will likely be the norm as principals practice. Each principal must find her or his way, develop her or his approach if the heart, head, and hand of leadership are to come together in the form of successful principalship practice.

Does that mean that the concepts presented in this book are not true? If they are not truths to be emulated and imitated, what are they? They comprise a different kind of truth. They represent a concept boutique on one hand and a metaphor repository on another. The idea is to visit the boutique trying on one idea after another seeking a fit here or there and to visit the repository seeking to create new understandings of situations one faces and new alternatives to one's practice. As boutique and repository the role of knowledge about schooling changes from being something that principals apply uniformly to being something useful that informs the decisions they make as they practice. This is the nature of reflective practice.

The Moral Imperative

Though many may prefer the work of administration to be some sort of an applied science that is directly connected to a firm knowledge base of theory and research, the reality we face is that it is much more craftlike. The message from this reality is equally clear. Successful practice requires the development of craft know-how. Craft know-how according to Blumberg (1989) includes the following:

- Being able to develop and refine "a nose for things."
- Having a sense of what constitutes an acceptable result in any particular problematic situation.
- Understanding the nature of the "materials" with which one is working. This includes oneself as a "material" that needs to be understood, as well as others. It also includes understanding the way other parts of the environment may affect the materials and the acceptableness of the solution at a particular point in time.
- Knowing administrative techniques and having the skill to employ them in the most efficacious way possible.
- Knowing what to do and when to do it. This involves not only pragmatic decisions—what behavior or procedure is called for at a particular time—but also implies issues of right and wrong. Much as Tom's (1984) description of teaching is that of a "moral" craft, so too is the practice of administration one in which there are moral dimensions to every action taken, with the possible exception of those that are simply mundane. This is not to suggest that administrators are aware of these moral dimensions at all times; it is simply to suggest that they are present.
- Having a sense of "process," that is, being able to diagnose and interpret the meaning of what is occurring as people interact in any problematic situation. (47)

But administering schools, as Blumberg suggests, is no ordinary craft. The bringing together of head, heart, and hand in practice, the unique nature of the school's mission, and the typically loosely structured, nonlinear, and messy context of schooling combine to make administering a *moral* craft, a fate shared with teaching (Tom,

1984) and supervision (Sergiovanni and Starratt, 1988). The reasons for this moral imperative are as follows.

1. The job of the principal is to transform the school from being an organization of technical functions in pursuit of objective outcomes into an *institution*. Organizations are little more than technical instruments for achieving objectives. As instruments they celebrate the value of effectiveness and efficiency by being more concerned with "doing things right" than with "doing right things." Institutions, on the other hand, are effective and efficient and more. They are responsive, adaptive enterprises that exist not only to get a particular job done but as entities in and of themselves. As Selznick (1957) points out, organizations become institutions when they transcend the technical requirements needed for the task at hand. In his words, "Institutionalization is a *process*. It is something that happens to an organization over time, reflecting the organization's own distinctive history, the people who have been in it, the groups it embodies and the vested interests they have created, and the way it has adopted to its environment. . . ." (Selznick, 1984:16). He continues:

> Organizations become institutions as they are *infused with value*, that is, prized not as tools alone but as sources of direct personal gratification and vehicles of group integrity. This infusion produces a distinct identity for the organization. Where institutionalization is well advanced, distinctive outlooks, habits, and other commitments are unified, coloring all aspects of organizational life and lending it a *social integration* that goes well beyond formal coordination and command. (Selznick, 1984:40)

Selznick's conception of institution is similar to the more familiar conception of school as *learning community*. To become either, the school must move beyond concerns for goals and roles to the task of building purposes into its structure and embodying these purposes in everything that it does with the effect of transforming school members from neutral participants to committed followers. The embodiment of purpose and the development of followership are inescapably moral.

2. The job of the school is to transform its students not only by providing them with knowledge and skills but by building *character* and instilling *virtue*. As Cuban (1988) points out, both technical and moral images are present in teaching and administering. "The technical image contains values that prize accumulated knowledge, efficiency, orderliness, productivity, and social usefulness; the moral image, while not disregarding such values, prizes values directed at molding character, shaping attitudes, and producing a virtuous, thoughtful person" (xvii). Technical and moral images of administration cannot be separated in practice. Every technical decision has moral implications. Emphasizing orderliness, for example, might serve as a lesson in diligence for students and might be a reminder to teachers that professional goals cannot be pursued to the extent that bureaucratic values are compromised.

3. Whether concern is for virtue or efficiency, some *standard* has to be adopted.

What is efficient in this circumstance? How will virtue be determined? Determining criteria for effective teaching, deciding on what is a good discipline policy, or coming to grips with promotion criteria standards, for example, all require value judgments. Answers to questions of how and what cannot be resolved objectively as if they were factual assertions, but must be treated as normative assertions. Normative assertions are true only because we decide that they are. As pointed out in Chapter 9, "we must decide what ought to be the case. We cannot *discover* what ought to be the case by investigating what is the case" (Taylor, 1961:248). Normative assertions are moral statements.

4. Despite commitments to empowerment and shared decision making, relationships between principals and others are inherently unequal. Though often downplayed, and whether they want it or not, principals typically have more *power* than teachers, students, parents, and others. This power is in part derived legally from their hierarchical position, but for the most part it is obtained de facto by virtue of the greater access to information and people that their position affords them. They are not chained to a tight schedule. They do a lot of walking around. They are the ones who get the phone calls, who are out in the streets, who visit the central office, who have access to the files, and so on. As a result they function more frequently in the roles of figurehead and liaison with outside agencies. They have greater access to information than do other people in the school. This allows them to decide what information will be shared with others, what information will be withheld, and frequently what information will be forgotten. Often teachers and others in the school rely on the principal to serve as the "coordinating mechanism" that links together what they are doing with what others are doing. In teaching, where much of the work is invisible, the coordinating function is a powerful one. Further, much of the information that principals accumulate is confidential. When teachers have problems they frequently confide in the principal. Information is a source of power, and the accumulation of power has moral consequences.

Whenever there is an unequal distribution of power between two people the relationship becomes a moral one. Whether intended or not, leadership involves an offer to control. The follower accepts this offer on the assumption that control will not be exploited. In this sense, leadership is not a right but a responsibility. Morally speaking, its purpose is not to enhance the leader's position or make it easier for the leader to get what she or he wants but to benefit the school. The test of moral leadership under these conditions is whether the competence, well-being, and independence of the follower are enhanced as a result of accepting control and whether the school benefits. Tom (1980) makes a similar argument in pointing out that "the teacher-student relationship is inherently moral because of its inequality" (317).

5. The context for administration is surprisingly loose, chaotic, and ambiguous. Thus, despite demands and constraints that circumscribe the principal's world, in actuality, *discretion* is built into the job, and this discretion has moral implication.

For example, frequently how things look is different than how things work. In their research on the reality of managing schools, Morris and colleagues (1984) discovered numerous instances in which principals and schools were able to develop implicit policies and pursue courses of action that only remotely resembled officially sanctioned policies and actions. They noted that not only maintaining student enrollment levels but increasing them was often viewed as a managerial necessity by principals. However, they were not motivated for official "educational" or "societal" reasons but to protect or enhance the resource allocation base of their schools. Staffing patterns and budget allocations were often linked to a principal's standing among peers and were related as well to morale and productivity levels among teachers. Further, principals of larger schools had more clout with the central office. Simply put, more staff and bigger budgets were viewed as being better. Schools losing resources, on the other hand, "usually suffer a decline in purposefulness, security, and confidence that goes beyond the loss of operating funds" (128).

As a result, principals tended to view monitoring, protecting, and increasing school enrollments and attendance as one of their key, albeit implicit, tasks. This led them to engage in courses of action that were at variance with the officially sanctioned definition of their tasks and roles. There was, for example, a concerted effort to change existing programs and revise the existing curriculum so they were more attractive to students thus better able to hold their enrollment. One of the principals reported, "We may have to cut physics, for instance, and add environmental science. It's in. . . . I've got to get my faculty to see that they have to reshape the traditional curriculum of the school. Their jobs are at stake" (Morris et al., 1984:128–129). Another principal in their study worked to change his school's kindergarten program so that it was more structured and "rigorous," not for educational reasons or philosophical commitments but so that the school would be better able to compete with the neighborhood Catholic school.

Despite clear guidelines governing attendance procedures (fixed attendance boundaries and age requirements, for example), principals became flexible by bending the rules for student admissions and taking liberties with reporting enrollment information to the central office. In the words of one principal, "In general, I'm not picky about where the students in the school live," noting further that if a youngster subsequently became a behavioral problem or was suspected of being a behavioral problem she always checked the home address (Morris et al., 1984:30). Some principals were inclined to look the other way even when they knew that students came from other school districts if they thought the students were "extremely bright." Some principals used leniency in enforcing attendance boundaries as the lever to extract better behavior and more achievement from students. Principals stressed that they were doing the parents and students a favor and expected good behavior in return. Not all students were treated equally. While bright students were encouraged to attend, "troublemakers" were not. In the words of one principal, "Let him go, that guy's been nothing but trouble for us" (Morris et al., 1984:131).

Though discretion can provide principals with a license for abuse, it is also a necessary prerequisite for leadership. "From choice comes autonomy. Autonomy is the necessary condition for leadership to arise. Without choice, there is no autonomy. Without autonomy, there is no leadership" (Cuban, 1988:xxii). Discretion, therefore, is necessary if principals are to function effectively. But how principals handle discretion raises moral issues and has moral consequences for the school.

Normative Rationality

Key to understanding the moral dimension in leadership is understanding the difference between *normative rationality* (rationality based on what we believe and what we consider to be good) and *technical rationality* (rationality based on what is effective and efficient). Happily the two are not mutually exclusive. Principals want what is good and what is effective for their schools. But when the two are in conflict, the moral choice is to prize the former over the latter. Starratt makes the point poignantly as follows: "'Organizational effectiveness' employs technical rationality, functional rationality, linear logic. Efficiency is the highest value, not loyalty, harmony, honor, beauty, truth. One can run an efficient extermination camp or an efficient monastery. The principles of efficiency are basically the same in either context" (Sergiovanni and Starratt, 1988:218).

Normative rationality provides the basis for moral leadership. Instead of just relying on bureaucratic authority to force a person to do something or a psychological authority to manipulate a person into doing something, the leader—principal or teacher as the case may be—provides reasons for selecting one alternative over another. The reasons are open to discussion and evaluation by everyone. To pass the test of normative rationality the reasons must embody the purposes and values that the group shares—the sacred covenant that bonds everyone in the school together as members of a learning community.

One might properly ask, What is the place of scientific authority in the form of expertness established by educational research in getting a person to do something? Isn't it enough that research says we ought to do this or that? Scientifically speaking, teaching, management, and leadership are underdeveloped fields. As a result, research findings are often so general as to comprise common understandings widely known to the general public (for example, a positive school climate provides a better setting for learning than a negative one; students who spend more time learning learn more; relating school content to personal experiences helps students understand better; teachers are more likely to accept a decision they help shape and make) or so idiosyncratic (for example, discovering that making Billy a blackboard monitor has helped his behavior in class; or noting that teacher Barbara does not respond well to one-on-one supervision but seems to get a lot out of collegial supervision) that they are difficult to apply beyond the setting from which they come.

Nonetheless, research and reflecting on personal experience can often provide us with patterns of characteristics to which many students or teachers are likely to respond in the same way. These insights can help, and this form of knowledge is often invaluable to principals. But this knowledge cannot represent a source of authority for action that replaces moral authority. As Smith and Blase (1987) explain,

> A leader in moral terms is one who fully realizes the . . . serious limitations on our ability to make accurate predictions and master the instructional process. Moreover, such a leader must encourage others to fully realize these limitations. Based on this awareness, a moral leader refuses to allow discussions of major pedagogical issues to be dominated by what the research supposedly demonstrates. . . . To do so would be to perpetuate the fiction that we have the kind of knowledge that we do not in fact possess. Rather, disagreements over how and what to teach must be played out in terms of reasoned discourse. The generalizations of educational inquiry can of course be part of these reasons, but they are not epistemologically privileged—they must share the stage with personal experience, a recounting of the experience of others, with philosophical and sociological considerations, and so on. (39)

Key is the phrase "epistemologically privileged." It is not that research findings are unimportant but that they are *no more important than other sources of authority.* One "so on" that might be added to Smith and Blase's list is conceptions of what is valued by the school that define it as a unique learning community.

Normative rationality influences the practice of leadership in schools in two ways. Principals bring to their job normative baggage in the form of biases and prejudices, ways of thinking, personality quirks, notions of what works and what doesn't, and other factors that function as personal theories of practice governing what they are likely to do and not do, and school cultures are defined by a similar set of biases that represent the center of shared values and commitments that define the school as an institution. Both are sources of norms that function as standards and guidelines for what goes on in the school. As a school's culture is strengthened and its center of values becomes more public and pervasive, normative rationality becomes more legitimate. Everyone knows what the school stands for and why and can articulate these purposes and use them as guidelines for action. This in-building of purpose "involves transforming [persons] in groups from neutral, technical units into participants who have a peculiar stamp, sensitivity, and commitment" (Selznick, 1984:150).

Followership Is the Goal

The importance of purposing to leadership changes how it is understood and practiced. With purposing in place in a school, one cannot become a leader without first becoming a follower. The concept of followership was discussed in Chapter 5. It was pointed out that what it means to be a follower and what it means to be a subordinate are very different. Subordinates respond to bureaucratic authority and sometimes to psychological authority. Followers, by contrast, respond to ideas. You can't be a follower unless you have something to follow. Further, as

Zaleznik (1989) suggests, subordinates may cooperate with the management system but are rarely committed to it. By contrast, one of the hallmarks of being a follower is commitment. As Kelly (1988) points out, followers "are committed to the organization and to a purpose, principle, or person outside themselves. . . . [And as a result] [t]hey build their competence and focus their efforts for maximum impact" (144). Followers, by definition, are never constrained by minimums but are carried by their commitment to performance that typically exceeds expectations. Subordinates, by contrast, do what they are supposed to; they tend not to do more.

When subordinateness is transcended by followership, a different kind of hierarchy emerges in the school. Principals, teachers, students, parents, and others find themselves equally "subordinate" to a set of ideas and shared conceptions to which they are committed. As a result, teachers respond and comply not because of the principal's directives but out of a sense of obligation and commitment to these shared values. That's what it means to be a follower.

The principal's job is to provide the kind of purposing to the school that helps followership to emerge. She or he then provides the conditions and support that allow people to function in ways that are consistent with agreed-upon values. At the same time the principal has a special responsibility to continually highlight the values, to protect them, and to see that they are enforced. The true test of leadership under these conditions is the principal's ability to get others in the school to share in the responsibility for guarding these values. This litany of roles was discussed in the text as leadership by purposing, empowerment and enablement, outrage, and finally kindling outrage in others.

One of the persistent problems of administration is obtaining compliance, and this problem is at the heart of the principal's role. Invariably, compliance occurs in response to some sort of authority, but not all sources of authority are equally powerful or palatable. In this book, four sources of authority have been described: bureaucratic, psychological, professional, and moral. All four have a role to play if schools are to function effectively. But the four compete with each other. When principals use bureaucratic authority, they rely on rules, mandates, and regulations in efforts to direct thought and action. When principals use psychological authority, they rely on their own interpersonal style, cleverness, guile, political know-how, and other forms of managerial and psychological skill in order to direct thought and action. When principals rely on professional authority, they appeal to expertness, expecting everyone to be subordinate to a form of technical rationality that is presumably validated by craft notions of what constitutes best educational practice or scientific findings from educational research. When principals rely on moral authority, they bring to the forefront a form of normative rationality as discussed above that places everyone subordinate to a set of ideas, ideals, and shared values and asks them to respond morally by doing their duty, meeting their obligations, and accepting their responsibilities. All are important. But the art of administration is balancing the four competing sources of authority in such a way that moral and professional authority flourish without neglecting bureaucratic and psychological.

The Challenge of Leadership

In the principalship the challenge of leadership is to make peace with two competing imperatives, the managerial and the moral. The two imperatives are unavoidable and the neglect of either creates problems. Schools must be run effectively and efficiently if they are to survive. Policies must be in place. Budgets must be set. Teachers must be assigned. Classes must be scheduled. Reports must be completed. Standardized tests must be given. Supplies must be purchased. The school must be kept clean. Students must be protected from violence. Classrooms must be orderly. These are essential tasks that guarantee the survival of the school as an organization. But for the school to transform itself into an institution, a learning community must emerge. Institutionalization is the moral imperative that principals face.

Discussions of the moral imperative in administration; proposing such leadership values as purposing, empowerment, outrage, and kindling outrage in others; and arguing for the kind of balance among bureaucratic, psychological, professional, and moral sources of authority in schools that noticeably tilts toward professional and moral challenge the "professional manager" conception of the principalship by placing concerns for substance firmly over concerns for process.

On the upside, the development of school administration as a form of management technology brought with it much needed attention to the development of better management know-how and of organizational skills badly needed to deal with an educational system that continues to grow in technical, legal, and bureaucratic complexity. On the downside, professionalism has too often resulted in principals thinking of themselves less as statespersons, educators, and philosophers and more as organizational experts who have become absorbed in what Abraham Zaleznik (1989) refers to as the *managerial mystique*. "As it evolved in practice, the mystique required managers to dedicate themselves to process, structures, roles, and indirect forms of communication and to ignore ideas, people, emotions, and direct talk. It deflected attention from the realities [of education] while it reassured and rewarded those who believed in the mystique" (2). The managerial mystique holds so strongly to the belief that "the right methods" will produce good results that the methods themselves too often become surrogates for results, and to the belief that management and bureaucratic controls will overcome human shortcomings and enhance human productivity that controls become ends in themselves. School improvement plans, for example, become substitutes for school improvements; scores on teacher appraisal forms become substitutes for good teaching; accumulating credits earned in courses and required inservice workshops become substitutes for changes in school practice; discipline plans become substitutes for student control; leadership styles become substitutes for purpose and substance; congeniality becomes a substitute for collegiality; cooperation becomes a substitute for commitment; and compliance becomes a substitute for results.

Zaleznik (1989) maintains that the managerial mystique is the antithesis of leadership. The epitome of the managerial mystique is the belief that anyone who can manage one kind of enterprise can also manage any other kind. It is the generic management techniques and generic interpersonal skills that count rather than issues of purpose and substance. Without purpose and substance, Zaleznik argues, there can be no leadership. "Leadership is based on a compact that binds those who lead and those who follow into the same moral, intellectual and emotional commitment" (15).

Building the Character of Your School

One of the major themes of this book is the importance of the school's culture. For better or for worse, culture influences much of what is thought, said, and done in a school. Character is a concept similar to culture but much less neutral. A school's character is known by how the school is viewed by members and outsiders in ethical and moral terms. Building and enhancing the school's character is the key to establishing its credibility among students, teachers, parents, and administrators and externally in the broader community. Wilkins (1989) notes that the components of an organization's character are its common understandings of *purpose* and identity that provide a sense of "who we are"; faith of members in the fairness of the leadership and in the ability of the organization to meet its commitments and to get the job done; and the distinctive cultural attributes that define the tacit customs, networks of individuals, and accepted ways of working together and of working with others outside of the organization. How reliable are the actions of the school? How firm is the school in its convictions? How just is its disposition? Wilkins points out that purpose, faith, and cultural attributes "add up to the collective organizational competence" (1989:27). To him, faith is a particularly important component of an organization's character, and loss of faith in either the organization or its leadership results in loss of character. Building faith restores character. Enhancing faith increases character. Without faith and character the organization and its members are not able to move beyond the ordinary to extraordinary performance. With faith such a transformation is possible. No matter how relentlessly principals pursue their managerial imperative, reliability in action, firmness in conviction, and just disposition are the consequences of the moral imperative. Without tending to the moral imperative there can be no organizational character, and without character a school can be neither good or effective.

A Commitment to Democratic Values

The inescapable moral nature of administrative work and in particular seeking to establish moral authority embodied in the form of purposing and shared values and expressed as "cultural leadership" raises important questions of manipulation and control. Cultural leadership can provide principals with levers to manipulate others that are more powerful than the levers associated with bureaucratic and psychological authority. Lakomski (1985) raises the question squarely:

> To put the objection more strongly, it may be argued that if all cultural analysis does is to help those in power, such as principals and teachers, to oppress some students more effectively by learning about their views, opinions, and 'student cultures', then this method is just another and more sophisticated way to prevent students (and other oppressed groups) from democratic participation in educational affairs. (15).

Her comments apply as well to teachers and others. Further, cultural leadership can become a powerful weapon for masking the many problems of diversity, justice, and equality that confront schools. There is nothing inherently democratic about cultural leadership, and, indeed, depending upon its substance this kind of leadership can compromise democratic values. Consensus building and commitment to shared values can often be little more than devices for maintaining an unsatisfactory status quo and for discouraging dissent. Finally, not all covenants are equal. The values that define the "center" of different school communities are not interchangeable.

Cultural leadership can be understood and practiced as a technology available to achieve any goal and to embody any vision or as a means to celebrate a particular set of basic values that emerge from the American democratic tradition. It makes a difference, for example, whether the basic values that define a school community revolve around themes of efficiency, effectiveness, and excellence or whether these are considered to be mere means values in service to such ends values as justice, diversity, equality, and goodness. In the spirit of the latter point of view, Clark and Meloy (1984) propose the Declaration of Independence as a metaphor for managing schools to replace bureaucratic. This metaphor guarantees to all persons that school management decisions will support such values as equality, life, liberty, and the pursuit of happiness based on the consent of the governed.

Discussion of democracy in schools typically wins nods from readers. But as Quantz, Cambron-McCabe, and Dantley (1990) point out, democracy is not always understood as both process and substance.

> There is often a confusion of democracy with pure process — the belief that as long as there is some form of participatory decision-making that democracy has been achieved. We argue, however, that democracy implies both a process and a goal, that the two, while often contradictory, cannot be separated. We believe that democratic processes cannot justify undemocratic ends. For example, we cannot justify racial and gender inequity on the basis that the majority voted for it. While this dual-reference test for democracy is not simple or clean, while it often requires us to choose between two incompatible choices, both in the name of democracy, we can conceive of no other way to approach it. In other words, even though an appeal to democratic authority cannot provide a clear and unequivocable blueprint for action in every particular instance, it can provide a general and viable direction for intelligent and moral decision-making by school administrators.

One of the challenges of moral leadership in schools is to engage oneself and others in the process of decision making without thought to self-interest. Can we discuss and decide our grading policies, discipline procedures, student grouping practices, supervisory strategies, and so on without regard to whether we will be winners or losers? Sending youngsters routinely to the principal's office for discipline, for example, or favoring homogeneous grouping of students may be in the interest of teachers but not students. Requiring all teachers to teach the same way may make it easier for the principal to hold teachers accountable but not for teachers who want to teach in ways that make sense to them. Discouraging parental involvement in school governance makes for fewer headaches for school people but disenfranchises the parents. What is just under these circumstances? John Rawls (1971) has suggested that decisions such as these should be made by people choosing in a hypothetical position of fairness under what he called "a veil of ignorance." The idea is to pretend that we don't know anything about ourselves—our sex, our race, our position in the school, our talents, and so on. We don't know, in other words, whether we are black or white, principal or teacher, student or custodian, parent or teacher aide. Our identities are only revealed when the veil of ignorance is lifted. Rawls maintains that in this way we are likely to fashion our principles and make decisions regardless of who we turn out to be. With bias diminished, chances are that the principles would be fairer and the decisions more just.

A Personal Note

How committed are you to becoming a successful school principal? Generally speaking, commitment to present job provides a good idea of one's overall commitment to work. For an indication of your present job commitment, respond on the Job Commitment Scale appearing as Exhibit 15-1. This scale contains 16 items about how people feel about their jobs. Indicate the extent to which you agree or disagree with each item. As you count your score, reverse-score items 6, 8, and 16. Your score will range from a low of 16 to a high of 64, with 64 representing the highest level of commitment. Keep in mind that there is always the chance that a person's commitment to work may be high but that her or his present job presents such unusual difficulties that low commitment and a low score result.

Anyone aspiring to the principalship had better have a strong commitment to work. This assertion should perhaps be modified as follows: Anyone who is aspiring to be a *successful* principal had better have a strong commitment to work. Success has its price. Consider, for example, the following statement:

> A passion for excellence means thinking big and starting small: excellence happens when high purpose and intense pragmatism meet. This is almost but not quite, the whole truth. We believe a passion for excellence also carries a price, and we state it simply: the adventure of excellence is not for the faint of heart.
>
> Adventure? You bet. It's not just a job. It's a personal commitment. Whether we're looking at a billion dollar corporation or a three-person accounting department, we see that excellence is achieved by people who muster up the nerve (and the passion) to step out—in spite of doubt, or fear, or job description (to maintain face-to-face contact with other people, namely customers and colleagues). They

EXHIBIT 15-1 Job Commitment Index

Responses: 4—Strongly Agree, 3—Agree, 2—Disagree, 1—Strongly Disagree

	1	2	3	4
1. Most of the important things that happen to me involve my work.	—	—	—	—
2. I spend a great deal of time on matters related to my job, both during and after hours.	—	—	—	—
3. I feel badly if I don't perform well on my job.	—	—	—	—
4. I think about my job even when I'm not working.	—	—	—	—
5. I would probably keep working even if I didn't have to.	—	—	—	—
6. I have a perspective on my job that does not let it interfere with other aspects of my life.	—	—	—	—
7. Performing well on my job is extremely important to me.	—	—	—	—
8. Most things in my life are more important to me than my job.	—	—	—	—
9. I avoid taking on extra duties and responsibilities in my work.	—	—	—	—
10. I enjoy my work more than anything else I do.	—	—	—	—
11. I stay overtime to finish a job even if I don't have to.	—	—	—	—
12. Sometimes I lie awake thinking about the next day's work.	—	—	—	—
13. I am able to use abilities I value in doing my job.	—	—	—	—
14. I feel depressed when my job does not go well.	—	—	—	—
15. I feel good when I perform my job well.	—	—	—	—
16. I would not work at my job if I didn't have to.	—	—	—	—

The Job Commitment Index is generally adapted from the Occupational Commitment Scale developed by Becky Heath Ladewig and Priscilla N. White, The Department of Human Development and Family Life, University of Alabama, University, AL.

won't retreat behind office doors, committees, memos or layers of staff, knowing this is the fair bargain they make for extraordinary results. They may step out for love, because of a burning desire to be the best, to make a difference, or perhaps, as a colleague recently explained, "because the thought of being average scares the hell out of me." (Peters and Austin, 1984:414)

In his studies of high-performing leaders, Peter Vaill (1984) found that "(1) Leaders of high-performing systems put in extraordinary amounts of *time*; (2) Leaders of high-performing systems have very strong *feelings* about the attachment of the system's purposes; and (3) Leaders of high-performing systems *focus* on key issues and variables" (94). Vaill notes that "there are of course many nuances, subtleties, and local specialists connected with the leadership of many high-performing systems, but over and over again, Time, Feeling, and Focus appear no matter what else appears" (94). The three go hand in hand. Vaill states, for example, that administrators who put in large amounts of time without feeling or focus are exhibiting "workaholism." Time and feeling without focus, on the other hand, often lead to dissipated energy and disappointment. Finally, time and focus without feeling seem to lack the necessary passion and excitement for providing symbolic and cultural leadership. Successful leaders—principals among them—are not afraid of hard work. By putting in large amounts of time, they demonstrate that they are not afraid of hard work; but they don't dissipate this time by taking on everything. Instead, they concentrate their efforts on those characteristics and values that are clearly more important to the success of their organization than are others. Further, unlike cold, calculated, objective, and uninvolved managers, they bring to their enterprises a certain passion that affects others deeply.

As a result of his extensive studies of the principalship and school leadership, William Greenfield (1985) concludes that principals need to be more passionate about their work, clearer about what they seek to accomplish, and more aggressive in searching for understandings that lead to improved schooling. Greenfield speaks of passion as "believing in the worth of what one seeks to accomplish and exhibiting in one's daily action a commitment to the realization of those goals and purposes" (17). He maintains that clarity about goals and outcomes should be accompanied by a commitment to flexibility regarding processes, procedures, and other means to attain ends.

And, finally, anyone who is aspiring to be a good principal needs to have some sense of what she or he values, something to be committed to, a compass to help navigate the way—a personal vision. As Roland Barth (1990) points out,

> Observers in schools have concluded that the lives of teachers, principals, and students are characterized by brevity, fragmentation, and variety. During an average day, for instance, a teacher or principal engages in several hundred interactions. So do many parents. A personal vision provides a framework with which to respond and to make use of the many prescriptions and conceptions of others. But more important, these ideas centered around schools as communities of learners and leaders have provided me with a road map which has enabled me to respond to the hundreds of daily situations in schools . . . in a less random and more thoughtful way. Without a vision, I think our behavior becomes reflexive, inconsistent, and shortsighted as we seek the action that will most quickly put out the fire so we can get on with putting out the next one. In five years, if we're lucky, our school might be fire free—but it won't have changed much. Anxiety will remain high, humor low, and leadership muddled. Or as one teacher put it in a powerful piece of writing, "Without a clear sense of purpose we get lost, and our activities in school become but empty vessels of our discontent." Seafaring folk put it differently: "For the sailor without a destination, there is no favorable wind." (211)

One of the great secrets of leadership is that before one can command the respect and followership of others, she or he must demonstrate devotion to the organization's purposes and commitment to those in the organization who work day by day on the ordinary tasks that are necessary for those purposes to be realized. As Greenleaf (1977) points out, people "will freely respond only to individuals who are chosen as leaders because they are proven and trusted as servants" (10). This perspective has come to be known as *servant leadership* (Greenleaf, 1977), with its basic tenets found in the biblical verse: "Ye know that the rulers of the Gentiles lorded over them, and that their great ones exercised authority over them. Not so shall it be among you: but whosoever would become great among you shall be your minister and whosoever would be first among you shall be your servant" (Matthew 20:25).

Servant leadership describes well what it means to be a principal. As pointed out in Chapter 6, principals are responsible for "ministering" to the needs of the schools they serve. The needs are defined by the shared values and purposes of the school's covenant. They minister by furnishing help and being of service to parents, teachers, and students. They minister by providing leadership in a way that encourages others to be leaders in their own right. They minister by highlighting and protecting the values of the school. The principal as minister is one who is devoted to a cause, mission, or set of ideas and accepts the duty and obligation to serve this cause. Ultimately her or his success is known by the quality of the followership that emerges. Quality of followership is a barometer that indicates the extent to which moral authority has replaced bureaucratic and psychological. When moral authority drives leadership practice, the principal is at the same time a leader of leaders, follower of ideas, minister of values, and servant to the followership.

References

Barth, Roland S. 1990. *Improving Schools from Within*. San Francisco: Jossey-Bass.

Blumberg, Arthur. 1989. *School Administration as a Craft*. Boston: Allyn and Bacon.

Clark, David L., and Judith M. Meloy. 1984. "Renouncing Bureaucracy: A Democratic Structure for Leadership in Schools," in T. J. Sergiovanni and J. H. Moore, Eds., *Schooling for Tomorrow Directing Reforms to Issues that Count*. Boston: Allyn and Bacon.

Cuban, Larry. 1988. *The Managerial Imperative and the Practice of Leadership in Schools*. Albany, NY: State University of New York Press.

Greenfield, William D. 1985. "Instructional Leadership: Muddles, Puzzles, and Promises." Athens, GA: The Doyne M. Smith Lecture, University of Georgia, June 29.

Greenleaf, Robert K. 1979. *Teacher as Servant*. New York: Paulist Press.

Lakomski, Gabriele. 1985. "The Cultural Perspective in Educational Administration," in R. J. S. Macpherson and Helen M. Sungaila, Eds., *Ways and Means of Research in Educational Administration*. Armidale, New South Wales: University of New England.

Morris, Van Cleave, Robert L. Crowson, Cynthia Porter-Gehrie, and Emanual Hurwitz, Jr. 1984. *Principals in Action*. Columbus, OH: Merrill.

Peters, Tom, and Nancy Austin. 1985. *A Passion for Excellence*. New York: Random House.

Quantz, Richard A., Nelda Cambron-McCabe, and Michael Dantly. 1990. "Preparing School Administrators for Democratic Authority: A Critical Approach to Graduate Education," *The Urban Review*.

Rawls, John. 1971. *A Theory of Justice*. Cambridge, MA: Harvard University Press.

Selznick, Philip. 1957. *Leadership in Administration A Sociological Interpretation*. New York: Harper & Row. California Paperback Edition 1984. Berkeley, CA: University of California Press.

Sergiovanni, Thomas J. 1990. *Value-Added Leadership*. San Diego, CA: Harcourt Brace Jovanovich.

Sergiovanni, Thomas J., and Robert J. Starratt. 1988. *Supervision: Human Perspectives*. New York: McGraw-Hill.

Smith, John K., and Joseph Blase. 1987. "Educational Leadership as a Moral Concept." Washington, DC: American Educational Research Association.

Taylor, Paul W. 1961. *Normative Discourse*. Englewood Cliffs, NJ: Prentice-Hall.

Tom, Alan. 1980. "Teaching as a Moral Craft: A Metaphor for Teaching and Teacher Education," *Curriculum Inquiry* 10(3).

Tom, Alan. 1984. *Teaching as a Moral Craft*. New York: Longman.

Vaill, Peter B. 1984. "The Purposing of High-Performing Systems," in Thomas J. Sergiovanni and John E. Corbally, Eds., *Leadership and Organizational Culture*. Urbana-Champaign, IL: University of Illinois Press.

Wilkens, Alan L. 1989. *Developing Corporate Character*. San Francisco: Jossey-Bass.

Zaleznik, Abraham. 1989. *The Managerial Mystique Restoring Leadership in Business*. New York: Harper & Row.

Index